SIR JOSHUA REYN

THE ACQUISITION OF GENIUS

To Eric Stevens
Best wishes –
Sam Smiles

SIR JOSHUA REYNOLDS

THE ACQUISITION OF GENIUS

Donato Esposito
Jenny Graham
Cristina S. Martinez
Martin Postle
Richard Stephens

Edited by
Sam Smiles

Sansom & Company
with
The University of Plymouth
and
Plymouth City Museum and Art Gallery

First published in 2009 by Sansom & Company Ltd,
81G Pembroke Road, Bristol BS8 3EA

www.sansomandcompany.co.uk
info@sansomandcompany.co.uk

The publishers and authors wish to acknowledge the financial support of The Paul Mellon Centre for Studies in British Art

ISBN 978-1-906593-40-7
British Library cataloguing-in-publication data:
A catalogue record for this book is available from the British Library.

Design and typesetting by E&P Design, Bath
Printed by HSW Print, Tonypandy

CONTENTS

Foreword 7
Acknowledgements 8
Abbreviations 9
Introduction (SAM SMILES) 11

SIR JOSHUA REYNOLDS
PAINTER

City and country (RICHARD STEPHENS) 17
West Country portraits 28
The road to the Royal Academy (MARTIN POSTLE) 75
Capturing celebrity 88
Self-portraits (CRISTINA S. MARTINEZ) 97

SIR JOSHUA REYNOLDS
COLLECTOR

'Care, taste and judgement': Reynolds's collection of works on paper (DONATO ESPOSITO) 102
Prints and drawings acquired by Reynolds 109

SIR JOSHUA REYNOLDS
LEGACY

Posthumous fortunes (JENNY GRAHAM) 161
Artistic responses and Reynoldsiana 168

APPENDIX

Other exhibits 174
Endnotes 183
Collections 200

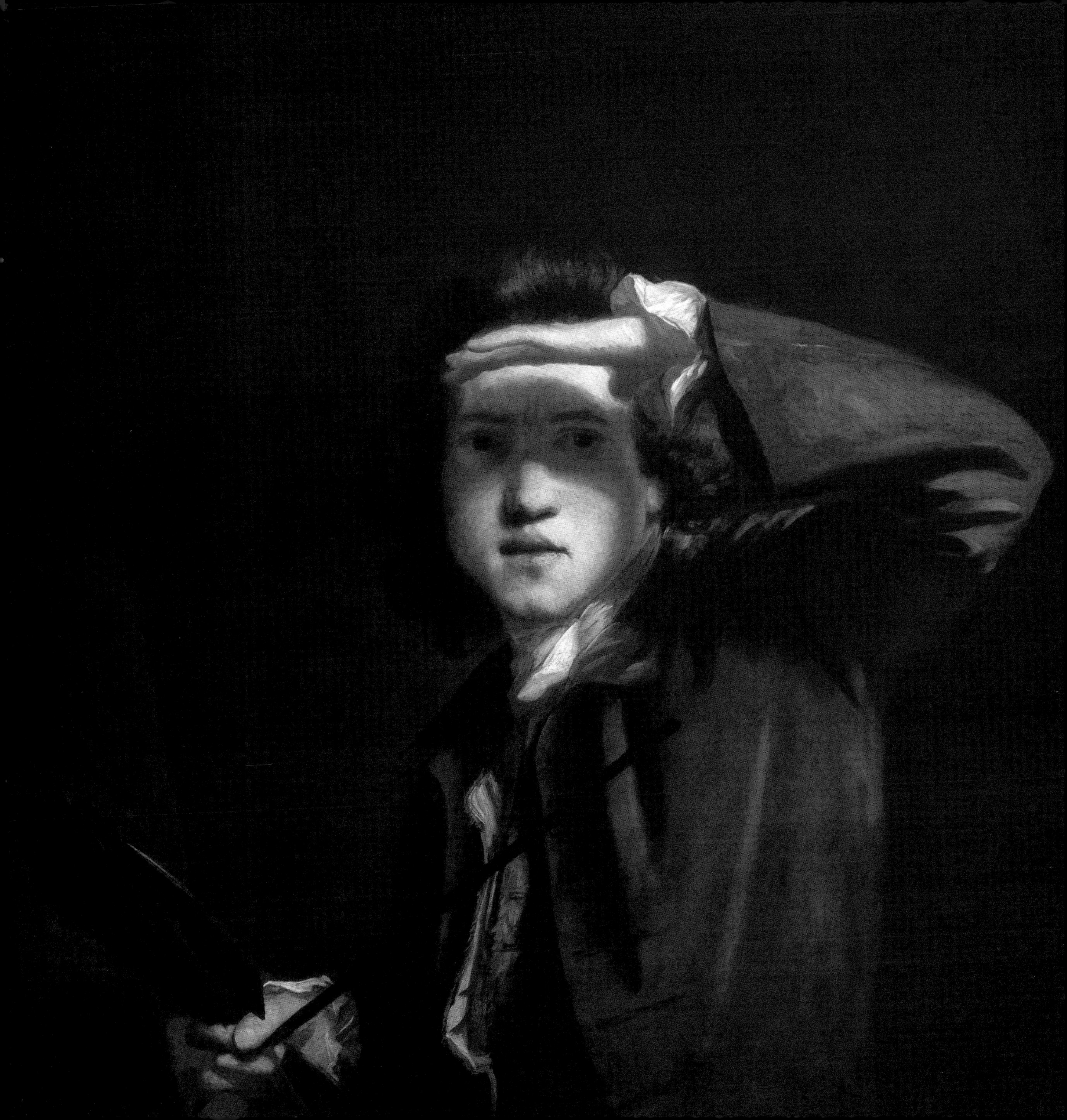

FOREWORD

TWO YEARS AGO PLYMOUTH CITY Museum and Art Gallery acquired an important collection of portraits by Sir Joshua Reynolds from the Earl of St Germans under the Acceptance in Lieu Scheme. This sparked the beginnings of a discussion between the Museum and the University of Plymouth's Art History department around the significance of Reynolds to Plymouth and the Southwest. Today this has culminated with a publication and an exhibition at Plymouth City Museum & Art Gallery, *Sir Joshua Reynolds: The Acquisition of Genius* (21 November 2009 to 20 February 2010).

Born in Plympton on the outskirts of Plymouth in 1723, Sir Joshua Reynolds has many connections with Plymouth and the City Museum. He was an acquaintance of Charles Rogers, an eminent collector of the eighteenth century, whose collection of prints, drawings and library was bequeathed to Plymouth in 1863 by William Cotton MA FSA (1794–1863) and is now housed in Plymouth City Museum & Art Gallery. Indeed the collection includes a number of family portraits by Reynolds and a collection of memorabilia relating to the artist.

It has been over seventeen years since Plymouth City Museum and Art Gallery undertook a serious examination of Reynolds. Thanks to the Paul Mellon Centre and the University of Plymouth, this has been addressed with this publication that presents an overview of Reynolds's career, particularly his works for patrons in Devon and Cornwall, and his collection of old master prints and drawings. Thanks also to the Heritage Lottery Fund and the Friends of Plymouth City Museum & Art Gallery we have been able to present the accompanying exhibition that contains much of the key interpretation alongside the works themselves.

Finally, I should like to extend my thanks to the many institutions and private collectors who have kindly agreed their works of art being lent for the exhibition and inclusion in this publication.

Nicola Moyle
City Curator, Museums and Heritage

City of Plymouth

RENAISSANCE SOUTH WEST museums for changing lives

heritage lottery fund LOTTERY FUNDED

PLYMOUTH CITY MUSEUM AND ART GALLERY

THE UNIVERSITY OF PLYMOUTH

PM

ACKNOWLEDGEMENTS

The authors would like to thank Plymouth City Museum and Art Gallery, whose enthusiasm for the project sustained it throughout its planning and their hard work and perseverance in bringing the project to fruition: Nicola Moyle, City Curator, Museums and Heritage; Maureen Attrill, Keeper of Art; Erana Blandford, former Digital Assistant; Jo Clarke, Marketing & Audience Development Officer; Helen Fothergill, Acting Collections Manager; Adam Milford, Education Assistant; Emma Philip, Assistant Exhibitions Officer; Judith Robinson, Exhibitions Officer; Dave Tetley, Design Assistant; Catherine Wallace, Reynolds Coordinator; Neil Wressel, Senior Conservation Officer; Jonathan Wilson, former Collections Manager. We would particularly like to express our thanks to Melanie Blake, who undertook the initial research on Reynolds's Cornish patrons. We owe a special debt of gratitude to Brian Allen, Director of the Paul Mellon Centre for Studies in British Art, in recognition of the Paul Mellon Centre's generous support for the research that underpins the exhibition and for granting additional funds for the production of the catalogue. We are indebted to our publisher, John Sansom, for all his help and assistance in seeing the catalogue through the press and to Ian Parfitt for the care and attention he lavished on its design.

The staff of the following institutions provided invaluable research help: Bedfordshire and Luton Archives and Records Service; the Bodleian Library, Oxford; the British Library; Devon Record Office, Exeter; Lewis Walpole Library, Farmington CT; Plymouth and West Devon Record Office; West Yorkshire Archives Service; West Country Studies Library, Exeter. The exhibition could not have been achieved without the agreement of a number of public and private collections to lend their works and we would like to thank them all for their understanding and assistance.

We also received valuable help and encouragement from: Maggie Allen, Stephen Astley, Patrick and Liz Aubrey-Fletcher, Richard Aylmer, Diederik Bakhuÿs, Peter Basham, Holm Bevers, Rhea Blok, Jonathan Bober, Pat Boulware, Viscount Boringdon, Paul Brady, David Bridgwater, Hannah Brocklehurst, Xanthe Brooke, Julian Brooks, Stephanie Buck, Alisa Bunbury, Michael Bury, Hugo Chapman, John Collins, Dominique Cordellier, Colette Crossman, Laura Down, Diana Dethloff, Samuel Ducroz, Anne Dulau, Jessica Fletcher, Nicholas Flicher, Peter Fuhring, Elizabeth Gallagher, Jim Ganz, Nicole Garnier, Zsuzsa Gonda, Elena Greer, Peter Greenhalgh, Antony Griffiths, Gabrielle Gunther, Marit Gruijs, Camilla Hampshire, Emily Hankle, Avril Harding, Craig Hartley, Rachel Hewitt, Stephen Hobbs, Martin Hopkinson, Valerie Hunter, Sally Huxtable, Paul Joannides, Alastair Laing, Laura Latman, Charlotte Lepetoukha, Laurence Lhinares, Elenor Ling, Elizabeth Lloyd, Catherine Loisel, Margareta Nisser-Dalman, Connie McPhee, Christopher Mendez, Lucinda Middleton, Mr & Mrs A Mildmay-White, Sandy Nairne, Martin Olin, Lucy Peltz, Stephen Pettet-Smith, Mark Pomeroy, Matthew Potter, Stephanie Pratt, Roger Quarm, Maisoon Rehani, Jennifer Ramkalawon, Angela Roche, Michael Rosenthal, Douglas Schoenherr, Anna Schulz, Jennifer Scott, David Scrase, Joanna Selbourne, Penny Sexton, Emma Shepley, Kim Sloan, Madeleine Pinault Sørensen, Bent Sørensen, Carel van Tuyll van Serooskerken, Inga Stevens, Lord and Lady St Germans, Kerrianne Stone, Jesper Svenningsen, Cécile Tainturier, Naoko Takahatake, Sarah Thomas, Lawrie Thorne, Simon Turner, Susan Walker, Aidan West-Lewis, Annette Wickham, Kirsty Woomble and Catherine Zinser.

ABBREVIATIONS

Abbreviations used in catalogue essays and entries

Acc Bk 1770–78	Plymouth and West Devon Record Office, Acc 3102 Box 3, John Parker's Account book 1770 to 1778
Acc Bk 1770–88	Plymouth and West Devon Record Office, Acc 3102 Box 3, John Parker's Account book 1778 to 1788
Adams and Lewis	C K Adams and W S Lewis 'The Portraits of Horace Walpole', *Walpole Society*, vol.xlii, 1968–70, p.1–34
Ambrose	G Ambrose, *Catalogue of the Collection of Pictures belonging to the Marquess of Lansdowne, KG*, London and Bowood, 1897
Archibald	A Archibald, *Catalogue of Portraits in Oil*, London: National Maritime Museum, 1961
Beechey	William Beechey, 'Memoir' in *The Literary Works of Sir Joshua Reynolds*, London, 1835
BL	British Library
BLARS	Bedfordshire and Luton Archives & Record Service
Britton & Brayley	John Britton and Edward Wedlake Brayley [and others], *The Beauties of England and Wales*, London, 18 vols, 1801–15
Broun 1987	Francis J P Broun, *Sir Joshua Reynolds' Collection of Paintings*, Princeton 1987 (unpublished PhD thesis)
Busch	W Busch, 'Hogarths und Reynolds' Porträts des Schauspielers Garrick,' Zeitschrift für Kunstgeschichte, xlvii, 1984, pp.82–99
Cotton 1856	William Cotton, *Sir Joshua Reynolds and his works*, London, 1856
Cotton 1859	William Cotton, *Some Account of the Ancient Borough Town of Plympton St Maurice*, Plympton, 1859
DNB	C Matthew, B Harrison and L Goldman (eds), *Dictionary of National Biography*, Oxford 2004
Duleep Singh	Duleep Singh, Portraits in Norfolk Houses, 1928
Edwards	Edward Edwards, Anecdotes of Painters, London, 1808
Farington 1819	Joseph Farington, *Memoirs of the Life of Sir Joshua Reynolds*, London, 1819
Graves & Cronin	A Graves and W Cronin, *A History of the Works of Sir Joshua Reynolds*, 4 vols, London 1899–1901
Hoare	Archive of Hoare's Bank, London, Records of John Parker I and II
Johnson 1998	Ceri Johnson and Alastair Laing, *Saltram* (National Trust Guide), London 1998
Kerslake	J Kerslake, *Early Georgian Portraits*, London: National Portrait Gallery, 1977
Leslie and Taylor	C R Leslie and Tom Taylor, *Life and times of Sir Joshua Reynolds: with notices of some of his contemporaries*, London, 1865
Letters	John Ingamells and John Edgcumbe (eds), *The Letters of Sir Joshua Reynolds*, Yale, 2000
Literary Career	Frederick Whiley Hilles, *The Literary Career of Sir Joshua Reynolds*, Cambridge 1936
Neatby 1977	Nigel Neatby (ed.), *The Saltram Collection*, London, 1977
Malone	*The Works of Sir Joshua Reynolds…* to which is prefixed an account of the life and writings of the author by Edmund Malone, 2 vols, London, 1798 (second edition)
Mannings 2000	David Mannings, *Sir Joshua Reynolds: A Complete Catalogue of his Paintings*, Yale 2000
Millar	Oliver Millar, *The later Georgian pictures in the collection of Her Majesty the Queen*, 2 vols, London 1969
Neatby 1977	Nigel Neatby (ed.), *The Saltram Collection*, London, 1977
Northcote 1819	James Northcote, *The Life of Sir Joshua Reynolds*, 1819
O'Malley	L O'Malley and C H Collins-Baker, 'Reynolds' first portrait of Keppel', *Walpole Society*, vol.I, 1912
Panofsky	Erwin Panofsky, *Hercules am Scheidewege*, Leipzig-Berlin, 1930
Penny 1986	Nicholas Penny (ed.), *Reynolds*, London 1986
Postle	Martin Postle, *Sir Joshua Reynolds: The Subject Pictures*, Cambridge, 1995
Postle 2005	Martin Postle, *Joshua Reynolds: The Creation of Celebrity*, Tate, 2005

PWDRO	Plymouth and West Devon Record Office
RA	Royal Academy, London
Saltram 1819	*Catalogue of the Pictures, Casts and Busts, belonging to the Earl of Morley at Saltram*, Plymouth, 1819
Saltram 1844	*Catalogue of the Pictures, Casts and Busts, belonging to the Earl of Morley at Saltram*, Plymouth, 1844
Steegman	J Steegman, 'Portraits of Reynolds', *Burlington Magazine*, lxxx, February 1942, pp.33–35
Waagen	G Waagen, *Treasures of Art in Great Britain*, London, 1854
Waterhouse 1941	Ellis K Waterhouse, *Reynolds*, London, 1941
Waterhouse 1973	Ellis K Waterhouse, Reynolds, (revised edition), London, 1973
Waterhouse 1985	Ellis K Waterhouse, 'Reynolds, Angelica Kauffmann and Lord Boringdon', *Apollo*, vol.cxxii, no.284 (October 1985), pp.270–74
Wendorf 1998	Richard Wendorf, *Sir Joshua Reynolds the Painter in Society*, Harvard, 1996
White	Christopher White, *Rembrandt in Eighteenth-century England*, Yale Center for British Art, New Haven, CT, 1983
Whitman	A Whitman, *Samuel William Reynolds*, London, 1903
Wind	Edgar Wind, *Hume and the Heroic Portrait*, London, 1986
WYAS	West Yorkshire Archive Service, Leeds
Yung	K K Yung, *Complete Illustrated Catalogue, 1856–1979*, London: National Portrait Gallery, 1981

INTRODUCTION

SIR JOSHUA REYNOLDS'S ACTIVITIES AS a portrait painter, as an art theorist and as the first President of the Royal Academy helped establish the fine arts in England on a secure basis and his achievement has remained central to any understanding of the development of British art. The purpose of this book is to present an overview of Reynolds's career and especially to highlight two areas that have not been afforded close examination to date: his work for patrons in Devon and Cornwall and his collection of Old Master prints and drawings. Research into both of these aspects makes a valuable contribution to our knowledge of Reynolds's activities and they are of intrinsic interest for that reason. But they also bear on the artist's ideas about the importance of proper artistic training, of eye, hand and mind, and of professional diligence as the foundations for an English school of painting.

To a modern ear 'the acquisition of genius' – the subtitle of the book and accompanying exhibition – sounds paradoxical, for genius speaks to us of innate ability, beyond instruction or improvement. Indeed, Reynolds's detractors found his insistence on this point hard to stomach. William Blake's caustic comments, written in the margins of his copy of Reynolds's *Discourses*, epitomise that discomfort: 'The Man who says that Genius is not Born, but Taught – Is a Knave.'[1] But Reynolds insisted that genius on its own was insufficient to make an artist; the art he advocated combined natural talent with training and constant observation. As he noted in a memorandum about the place of genius in the arts, 'I agree therefore with all those who say that labor is in vain without this Genius this feeling or this good sense but I differ in supposing this is not to be acquired.'[2] It is not surprising, therefore, that Reynolds headed one of his working drafts 'Genius taught',[3] on which he focused his sixth Discourse, delivered at the Royal Academy in 1774. What particularly exercised him was the popular idea that the artist of genius needed no rules, whereas for Reynolds genius was better understood instead as a creative power that was systematically deployed by great artists and was thus intellectually comprehensible: 'even works of Genius… as they must have their cause, must likewise have their rules.'[4] If works of genius could be subjected to rational analysis it followed that genius was not at odds with training but could be supported by it. This would ensure that artists were neither seduced nor overawed by the workings of genius. As Reynolds declared:

> *The purport of this discourse, and, indeed, of most of my other discourses, is, to caution you against that false opinion, but too prevalent among artists, of the imaginary power of native genius, and its sufficiency in great works. That opinion, according to the temper of mind it meets with, almost always produces, either a vain confidence, or a sluggish despair, both equally fatal to all proficiency.*[5]

Throughout the fifteen Discourses he delivered at the Royal Academy Reynolds frequently returned to the idea that an artist's creative potential cannot be fulfilled unless it is channelled effectively; genius can flourish properly only when the artist's craft is thoroughly understood.

However, Reynolds's understanding of the artist's craft embraced much more than technical excellence: the professional artist should also be able to draw on the resources of a well-stocked mind. For Reynolds, it was 'indisputably evident that a great part of every man's life must be employed in collecting materials for the exercise of genius.'[6] If the artist was not to exhaust his imaginative capabilities the mind's intellectual and creative resources needed to be enhanced, primarily by studying the Old Masters and observing natural appearances. And he emphatically rebutted those who claimed that such knowledge would inhibit their creativity: '...there is no danger of the mind's being over-burthened with knowledge, or the genius extinguished by any addition of images; on the contrary, these acquisitions may as well, perhaps better, be compared... to the supply of living embers which will contribute to strengthen the spark, that without the association of more fuel would have died away.'[7] Genius must therefore be directed and cultivated if it is to animate the arts and it is the responsible artist's duty to work towards that goal. This is why Reynolds claimed that genius on its own was not enough, leading only to 'vain confidence' if it was not combined with proper study and hard work. As he noted in 1769, 'excellence is never granted to man, but as the reward of labour'[8] and his own career can be examined with this in mind.

In reviewing the portraits he painted in the West Country in the later 1740s, after he had finished his studies with his master, Thomas Hudson, in London, we are witnessing Reynolds working assiduously, becoming a professional artist. The paintings he produced for patrons living in and around Plymouth demonstrate how successfully the young Reynolds challenged the complacency of mundane face-painting, using a variety of means to avoid unimaginative stock poses and beginning to develop a highly distinctive style of portraiture. Working in Devon, however, was extremely limiting for an ambitious artist; there were very few good collections of pictures in the county and too small an intellectual community to foster a serious and sustained engagement with the visual arts. Indeed, Reynolds would later describe Plymouth as having 'the fewest admirers of pictures and prints... of any town of its size that he knew of.'[9] The prospect of foreign travel was therefore very welcome and his two years in Italy (1750–52) provided Reynolds with a priceless opportunity to deepen his artistic knowledge; in Rome, Naples, Florence, Bologna and Venice he studied important examples of Italian painting. The extensive collection of Old Master paintings, prints and drawings which he acquired throughout his career, was, similarly, not merely the indulgence of a connoisseur but also a valuable resource that could impart useful lessons. As he exhorted the students of the Royal Academy:

> *Study therefore the works of the great masters, for ever. Study as nearly as you can, in the order, in the manner, and on the principles, on which they studied. Study nature attentively, but always with those masters in your company; consider them as models which you are to imitate, and at the same time as rivals with whom you are to contend.*[10]

Reynolds returned to England from Italy in 1752. The following year he established himself in London and over the next decade, in his thirties, he built the reputation that sustained his career. He maintained his connections with important West Country patrons and developed an extensive portrait practice among the social elite of England, he was friends with many of the most creative personalities of the day and he was a figure to be reckoned with among his fellow artists. This professional prominence saw him elected President of the newly established Royal Academy in 1768. On the evidence of his pronouncements in the Discourses, Reynolds would have understood his pre-eminence in the London art world as the reward not merely of his creative talent, but of his diligence and application in his profession. He was knighted in 1769, the University of Oxford conferred on him the title of Doctor of Civil Law in 1773, the same year he was made Mayor of Plympton, and in 1784 he was appointed Painter in Ordinary to King George III.

As President of the Royal Academy, Reynolds was in a good position to argue for the intellectual and cultural worth of the fine arts. The Discourses, although ostensibly addressed to the students of the Royal Academy, were designed to make a contribution to contemporary discussions on aesthetics, the history of art and the cultivation of taste. Reynolds's characterisation of the artist as a professional, combining intellectual understanding with facility of hand, his insistence that genius can be taught, may be understood as necessary strategies within a wider campaign to raise the standing of the artist in Georgian England. Throughout his writings he is at pains to present painting as a liberal profession, combining intellectual powers with creative imagination, and thus quite distinct from what its detractors would call merely a mechanical trade, reliant solely on technical skills and the servile imitation of reality. In essence, what Reynolds proposes is that artists have the ability to conceive a subject imaginatively and can convey its essential quality or significance by employing a generalised treatment of visual appearance, beyond any concern with minute details. This ability is 'an instance of that superiority with which mind predominates over matter, by contracting into one whole what nature has made multifarious.'[11]

With respect to portraiture, although Reynolds acknowledged that 'likeness... is what is most generally required by such as sit to the painter,' ideally the artist would avoid exact resemblance and aim instead to 'ennoble the character of a countenance... at the expense of the likeness.'[12] The portrait painter, Reynolds believed, should aim at a general effect rather than 'the exact expression of the peculiarities, or minute discrimination of the parts.' The sitter's features should naturally be 'planted in their proper places, which so much contributes to giving the effect and true impression of the whole,' but any peculiarities of countenance 'may be reduced to classes and general descriptions; and there are therefore large ideas to be found even in this contracted subject.'[13] His study of Old Master portraits had shown him that their merits as paintings and as studies of general character were independent of their fidelity as likenesses. Portraiture was therefore implicitly included in his declaration that only works 'built upon general nature, live for ever.'[14]

As part of this assertion of the dignity of his profession, and notwithstanding the fact that he enjoyed a good living from his portrait practice, Reynolds drew a sharp distinction between cultural value and economic value. His pupil James Northcote transcribed one of Reynolds's notes recording his rebuttal of a remark made by the economic theorist Josiah Tucker, the Dean of Gloucester, that 'a pin-maker was a more useful member of society than Raffaelle.' Reynolds vigorously opposed such thinking, pointing out that the arts and sciences contributed to civilization by providing 'the rational enjoyment of life... opening scenes of intellectual pleasure and instruction by means of the senses.'[15] The arts and sciences would thus improve society, which Reynolds understood as a community of rational beings bound together in a common purpose. By comparison, Tucker's high estimation of commerce was, for Reynolds, the product of 'a very narrow mind' which elevated mercantile self-interest over the commonweal.[16] As he noted in his ninth Discourse, delivered in 1780:

> *The estimation in which we stand in respect to our neighbours, will be in proportion to the degree in which we excel or are inferior to them in the acquisition of intellectual excellence, of which Trade and its consequential riches must be acknowledged to give the means; but a people whose whole attention is absorbed in those means, and who forget the end, can aspire but little above the rank of a barbarous nation.*[17]

The intellectual excellence that Reynolds recommends is something to which artists can contribute and one of the principal aims of the Discourses is to show how this can be achieved.

Assessing the value of artistic creativity in contemporary society is, of course, not just an eighteenth-century concern. The terms of the debate change, and the structure and funding of today's art world are very different from anything Reynolds can have imagined, but the fundamental issue remains the same: what is the purpose of creative and intellectual activity and how can its contribution to society be fostered? The temptation is always to subordinate creative work to the pressing needs of trade and industry. Reynolds, however, was adamant that economic priorities alone cannot sustain a healthy society. Genius, whether innate or acquired, makes a contribution beyond the reach of a commercial reckoning.

SIR JOSHUA REYNOLDS PAINTER

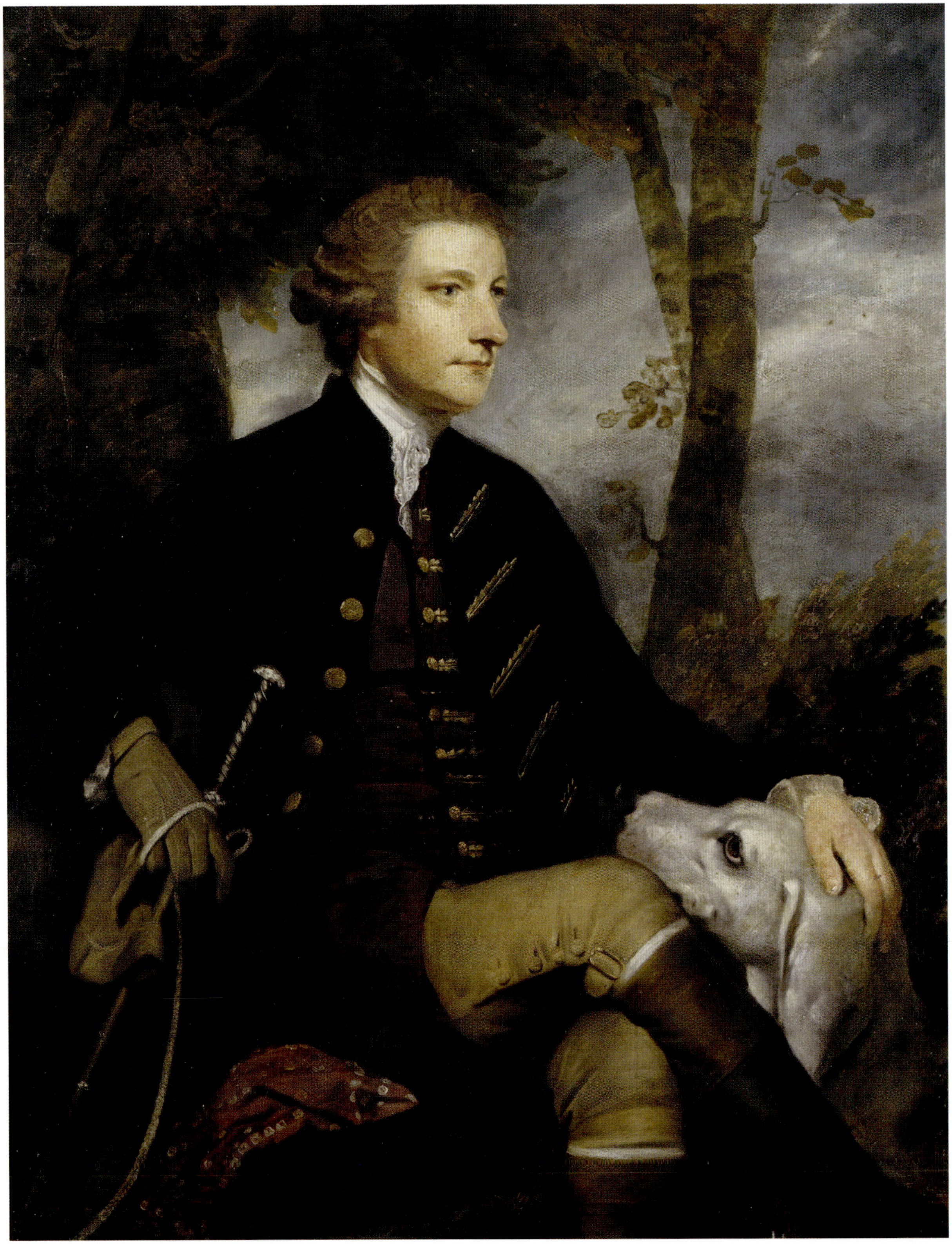

FIG. 1

Sir Thomas Acland
(1776–77)
oil on canvas,
125 x 99 cm
Killerton

CITY AND COUNTRY

JOSHUA REYNOLDS WAS BORN IN THE small west Devon town of Plympton on 16 July 1723, the seventh child of Reverend Samuel Reynolds, the local schoolmaster, and his wife Theophila. Joshua attended his father's school where, by the artist's own account, he was 'instructed in the classicks; but at an early age his inclination for that art of which he afterwards became so illustrious a professor, began to display itself; and his early attempts at delineation were encouraged by his father, who was himself fond of drawings, and had a small collection of anatomical and other prints.'[1] The schoolmaster's first inclination was to bring up his son to be an apothecary, and the teenage Joshua 'spent a great deal of time and pains with that view.'[2] Joshua's future was a matter of debate within Samuel Reynolds's circle, including James Bulteel of Flete (1676–1756) and two lawyer friends, John Cranch (1710–c.1772) of Plympton and Charles Cutcliffe (1683–1745) of Bideford.[3] By 1740, Reynolds's interest in art was such that his father could write of his 'very great genius for drawing, and lately, on his own head, [he] has begun even painting.'[4] Joshua's promise had already persuaded one West Country-based artist to offer to train him free of charge, waiving the usual apprenticeship fee. Under John Warwell (d.1767), Reynolds might have become a house painter offering the same miscellaneous services that Warwell advertised: 'history pieces; heraldry; alter pieces; coaches, landscapes, window blinds, sea pieces; chimney blinds, flowers; skreens, fruit; gilding. Pictures copied, cleansed, or mended. Rooms painted in Oil or Water, in a new Taste. Deceptive Temples, Triumphal Arches, Obelisks, Statues, &c. for Groves or Gardens.'[5] But already showing his ambition and calculation, young Reynolds had answered that 'he would rather be an apothecary than an *ordinary* painter; but if he could be bound to an eminent master, he should choose the latter.'[6] The family instead approached a leading portrait painter, the Exeter-born Thomas Hudson (1701–79), who was based in London but had an active West Country practice; he was just then working on a large series of portraits of the Barnstaple Corporation. Reynolds went to meet Hudson, who agreed to take him on as an apprentice for four years, and in October 1740 the seventeen-year-old Reynolds arrived in London to begin his training.[7]

Reynolds's father maintained his profile at home. Craunch and Warwell continued to take an interest; the Plymouth physician Dr John Huxham (1692–1768) praised Reynolds's drawing of Laocoon, 'that he who drew that would be the first hand in England'; a Plymouth painter called Tucker also 'admired them exceedingly.'[8] So when a disagreement with Hudson interrupted Reynolds's apprenticeship in the summer of 1743 and caused him to return home to his father, Reynolds was by no means unknown around Plymouth. His fairly brief period under Hudson equipped him to set up as a portrait painter and he quickly attracted customers among the West Country bourgeoisie. Dividing his time now between Devon and the metropolis, Reynolds was starting to develop his circle of patronage and the social skills which were to be such a critical part of his later success. No doubt Reynolds also inherited some of Hudson's West Country business, now that his master was well-established in the capital, and it is clear from Samuel Reynolds's correspondence that Hudson continued to mentor Reynolds informally.

Reynolds's earliest surviving portraits provide a unique window onto mid-eighteenth-century Plymouth. The area's professional class formed the bulk of his first clientele. Some, like Charles Cutcliffe, must have been his father's friends. Several were involved in local politics: the town clerk Walter Kendall of Pelyn, Cornwall, and his family; Elizabeth, Mrs John Kerley whose husband was Recorder of Plymouth 1749–50; the Plympton Corporation itself employed Reynolds in 1748.[9] Other middle-class sitters included Henry Mervyn of Dock, and his wife; surgeon Thomas Woollcombe; Reginald Pole of Dock; Rev John Hockin, vicar of Okehampton; Grace Goddard, whose father William was curate of Plympton; and members of Reynolds's own family.[10] After his father's death at the end of 1745, Reynolds's studio was in Dock, which adjoined the navy base, and several mariners were among his early clients: Lieutenant Robert Haswell; Captain John Roberts; sub-Engineer Kane William Horneck; Lieutenant Thomas Brodrick; Elizabeth, daughter of Captain Limeburner; the dockyard chaplain Rev William Beele; and others, unidentified.[11] Reynolds began also to attract the region's landowning and political dynasties: Richard Eliot of Port Eliot; Sir William Morice, 3rd Bt of Werrington; William Trevanion of Caerhayes; and, above all, Richard Edgcumbe, 1st Lord Edgcumbe of Mount Edgcumbe, who was to be instrumental in forwarding Reynolds's career in the decade following the death of Samuel Reynolds in 1745.[12] Some of Reynolds's earliest London clients can also be identified: aristocrats Richard, 2nd Earl of Rosse and Clotworthy Skeffington; and the children of the Quaker Martha Neate, 'a beautiful Lady, with a handsome Fortune' who twice married City of London entrepreneurs.[13]

For a time in the 1740s Reynolds worked at Dock in partnership with another painter, probably the Chudleigh-born pupil of Hudson Thomas Rennell (1716–88), who lived in Plymouth for 'many years, and drew several pictures, which were much admired in that neighbourhood' including a portrait of Dr Huxham (Royal Society).[14] The similarities between early Reynolds and Rennell are intriguing. According to its eighteenth-century owner, the Exeter musician William Jackson (1730–1803) who knew both artists, in Rennell's self-portrait 'the Face is half-shadowed'; Reynolds's own portrait from this Plymouth phase (CAT. 32, p. 96), deploys the same effect. Jackson observed that Rennell's pictures 'are called the early works' of Reynolds. Rennell's irreverent portrait of Miss Irons, in which he painted a print of Dr Huxham over the sitter's face, chimes with Northcote's anecdote about Reynolds and his partner having produced a portrait with two hats, one on the sitter's head and another under his arm.[15] Rennell had gained a reputation for idleness and 'an *apparent* Contempt of the World; which was returned in *reality*, four-fold; in consequence he lived unnoticed and in bitter Poverty.' Perhaps, then, Reynolds was thinking of Rennell when he told Edmund Malone many years later that he 'became very careless about his profession, and lived for near three years at Plymouth in a great deal of dissipation with but indifferent company, at least such company as from whom no improvement could be gained.'[16] However Reynolds 'saw the error in time, and sat down seriously to his art' so that 'he always considered the disagreement with Mr. Hudson as a very fortunate circumstance, since by this means he was led to deviate from the tameness and insipidity of his master, and to form a manner of his own.'

In May 1749, the conclusion of the War of the Austrian Succession gave Reynolds the opportunity to travel to Italy,[17] a vital training ground for young painters; as a 1747 book of careers advice put it, 'the good Face-Painter must have the Name of having travelled to Rome.'[18] There Reynolds studied the classical past and the great Italian painters of the sixteenth and seventeenth centuries who were to remain an inspiration throughout his career. Reynolds returned to England in October 1752 and launched himself in London with a majestic portrait of Augustus Keppel (1725–86), the navy captain with whom he had sailed to Italy (FIG. 12, p. 73). With this painting, among others, Reynolds 'was not only universally acknowledged to be at the head of his profession, but to be the greatest painter that England had seen since Vandyck.'[19] By the mid-1750s Reynolds was well established as London's most fashionable portrait painter, a status he maintained until his death on 23 February 1792 at his grand house in Leicester Square. As well as being a hugely successful painter, Reynolds's social life came to represent the Enlightenment ideal of the city as a progressive melting pot of intellectual debate, his famous house 'a common centre of union for the great, the accomplished, the learned and the ingenious' in Boswell's words.[20] Reynolds also achieved distinction as the founding President of the Royal Academy, for which he was knighted in 1769 and where he delivered his influential Discourses. As the gentlemanly figurehead of English painting, Reynolds was credited with elevating the status of artists in society at large. Contemporaries celebrated Reynolds as much for his accomplishments outside the studio – as an author and high-society figure – as for his talent within it.

Reynolds's early years in Plymouth laid the ground for his later success and fame in London. In Plymouth Reynolds gained the patronage of Lord Edgcumbe; he made decisive progress towards a new and distinctive style of portraiture; and he discovered the personal drive, his tireless pursuit of excellence, which was to fuel his long and busy London career lasting from the early 1750s to the late 1780s. In London Reynolds maintained links with the West Country, which he visited in 1762, 1770, 1773, 1780 and 1783. He enjoyed friendships with regional grandees, such as John Parker of Saltram, George Edgcumbe and Edward Eliot. Occasionally he attended London's Devonshire Club, a social gathering of the visiting gentry, and over the years members of many West Country families passed through Reynolds's studio: Fortescue of Castle Hill and Buckland Filleigh; Courtenay of Powderham; Lisburne of Mamhead; Palk of Haldon; Drake/Heathfield of Nutwell; Bampfylde; Acland of Killerton; Parker of Saltram; St Aubyn of Clowance; Molesworth of Pencarrow; Bastard of Kitley.[21] Reynolds also occasionally painted friends from childhood, like Rev Zachariah Mudge and John Craunch.[22] Yet when setting up in London after returning from Italy, Reynolds had moved from the regional to the national, and even international, stage. Thereafter he made as many visits to continental Europe as to the West Country. When he did visit Plymouth, it was as a celebrity; he attracted crowds as he walked, and was a guest in the region's grandest mansions. From the 1750s onwards, Devon and Cornwall clients sat to Reynolds not because of their shared regional connection but because Reynolds had become England's pre-eminent cosmopolitan cultural figure.

OUR UNDERSTANDING OF THESE TWO different settings for Reynolds's portrait practice – London and the West Country – has been shaped by the eighteenth century's contrasting ideals of the city and the country. Debates about personal morality, government, nationalism, commerce, fashion, gender and culture were framed as arguments between these two opposites. Cities were either progressive hubs of government, commerce, science and cosmopolitanism; or markets of corruption, greed and aristocratic effeminacy. Country life was either parochial, backward and ignorant, or honest, independent, unaffected, manly and virtuous.[23] As Dror Wahrman has noted, city and country represented 'the fundamental socio-cultural divide which characterised eighteenth-century society' as it grappled with an emergent middle class.[24] On the one hand, a 'national society' of aristocratic consumerism was centred on London; the seasonal tide of genteel visitors to the capital transmitted its ideas, luxury goods and services throughout the nation.[25] On the other, an alternative provincial culture reinforced regional identities, expressing hostility to central government, praise of ancient constitutional rights, and the importance of local militias for national defence. Wilkes and American independence were two issues where people divided on these tribal grounds, whether they lived in London or the provinces, town or countryside.[26] The city and country, then, were less real places than ways of seeing the world that transcended geography.

Hogarth's acerbic critiques of fashionable London life articulated the unpolished but honest voice of the painter's country ancestors: London born and bred, Hogarth was not schooled by the illustrious painters of his age, but 'was the pupil – the disciple, – the worshipper of Nature! ...his grandfather was an honest yeoman, the inhabitent of a small tenement.'[27] By contrast Reynolds, raised in a small town 200 miles from London, came to personify elite urban culture.

As the capital of art, trade and politics, London attracted talented youths like Reynolds who naturally made their way there to compete in the nation's biggest marketplace. The corollary – the mediocrity of provincial society – was rejected by genteel provincials with growing conviction and vehemence but it was nevertheless a truism of eighteenth-century metropolitan opinion that Reynolds himself reflected. As his friend Edmund Malone commented, Reynolds's 'profession did not permit him often to make excursions from town. In the summer, however, he at different periods visited the seats of the Duke of Marlborough, Lord Boringdon, Lord Eliot, Lord Ossory, Lord Palmerston, Mr. Burke, and other friends; and occasionally spent a few days at his villa on Richmond Hill; but he had very little relish for a country life, and was always glad to return to London, to which he was not less attached than Dr. Johnson; with him, justly considering that metropolis as the head-quarters of intellectual society.' On Reynolds's rare adult visits to Plympton, he showed a concern to revisit his childhood haunts, and a childhood which was irrecoverable not only because he had grown up, but in the sense that his adult life of cosmopolitan celebrity was so far removed from the culture of his early family life. In 1770 Reynolds was a house-guest at Saltram and spent much of his time in the aristocratic country pursuits of hunting and shooting. Even when visiting old friends and relatives in Devon, Reynolds took pains to limit his exposure to the realities of middling provincial living by staying in the grandest mansions available, each one a mini-township of metropolitan culture and sociability. On his way back to London in 1770 he had supper with his brother, a respectable Exeter ironmonger, but slept at Whiteway, the Parker family seat near Chudleigh.

Reynolds also told Malone that returning to Devon to become a respectable provincial painter after leaving Hudson in 1743 had been 'so much time thrown away (so far as it related to a knowledge of the world and of mankind,) of which he ever afterwards lamented the loss. However, after some little dissipation, he sat down seriously to the study and practice of his art; and he always considered the disagreement which induced him to leave Mr. Hudson as a very fortunate circumstance, since by this means he was led to deviate from the tameness and insipidity of his master, and to form a manner of his own.'[28] So Reynolds took the disdainful 'city' view of provincial England as lacking refinement and culture, but at the same time he took the 'country' view of it, as a place of study, reflection and independence, where individuality could develop away from the city's fads and short-termism. Joseph Farington, the London artist whose biography of Reynolds appeared in 1819, did not dispute the implications of Malone's statement, that provincial society knew little of the wider world. But he did conclude that Malone must have misunderstood Reynolds. For surely, he argued, the little knowledge that Devon had offered him hitherto had been 'sufficient for all useful purposes, especially as he must have associated with the best society that country afforded.'[29] All of Reynolds's early biographers shared these 'city' assumptions about the limitations of provincial life, emphasising instead the quiet virtues of the country which they idealised in the person of Samuel Reynolds, a man 'eminent for his learning and moral character, to which he united such innocence of heart and simplicity of manners, that he has often been mentioned as another parson Adams.'[30] Anecdotes about the elder Reynolds, such as when he is said to have left the house having forgotten to put on his shoes, emphasise his absent-mindedness and even indolence.

The city and country paradigm opposed the rural and urban at the expense of recognising their interdependency and connection, and these characterisations of Samuel Reynolds overplay his naivety and seclusion. Reynolds's father had the tenacity to place his son in a highly insecure profession; the network to secure his apprenticeship with a leading painter in London; and the credit to fund the extremely expensive training. One, perhaps two, of Joshua's uncles lived in London, with whom Joshua could lodge, and family friends like Cranch owned land there.[31] On top of free housing, Samuel Reynolds's salary placed him among the area's prospering farmers, professionals and clerics.[32] Samuel Reynolds demonstrated a wide-ranging academic curiosity, read political tracts and had friends and contacts in the professional class with whom to debate. Many of the era's key texts were on the shelves in the Plympton schoolhouse, for his son to absorb. These included, famously, essays on connoisseurship by Jonathan Richardson which promoted polite urban culture.

Although the progress of Reynolds's earliest career in Devon cannot be reconstructed in any detail, the broadening of his horizons was no doubt accelerated by Samuel Reynolds's death at the end of 1745. Reynolds could no longer rely on the guidance of his bookish and reflective father, but a new and powerful mentor was emerging in the worldly Lord Edgcumbe, the recently ennobled Lord Lieutenant of Cornwall. Aged 22, Reynolds was now the head of his own household in Dock, and responsible for two unmarried sisters. At the height of his fame Reynolds made public demonstrations of affection towards Plympton but, as Malone's comments indicate, success on the national stage required him to disown much of what middling provincial society stood for; to distance himself from his father's regional network of house-painters, clerics and apothecaries, and instead embrace the elite national society of politics, patronage and power represented by Edgcumbe. Samuel Reynolds anticipated this. Joshua's apprenticeship to Hudson, wrote the schoolmaster, was a training more appropriate to the younger son of a landowning courtier like the Plympton MP, George Treby, than his own mere seventh child.[33] The Hudson connection was changing the way people treated the elder Reynolds: 'As if a piece of good fortune had already actually befallen my family, it seems to me I see the good effects of it already in some persons' behaviour.'[34]

We now understand the eighteenth-century myth of the quiet countryside as an urban response to the huge growth in cities; a vision of dependability and consistency amid the change and uncertainties of London's new economy and social order. But these changes were not contained within London; rural England was not insulated and the divisions of city and country were evident across Devon. The ideological dividing line – of middling regional and elite national society, Samuel Reynolds and Lord Edgcumbe – is evident also in the relationship between Plymouth and Dock, the new satellite town of the great naval dockyard. For a small community 200 miles from London, Dock had surprisingly direct links with the capital city, which made it an auspicious base for Reynolds's training in aristocratic clientele.[35] The Plymouth dockyard and its dependency of Dock are best understood as the western limb of the metropolitan body politic. The naval dockyard, the great engine room of England's military power and a major centre of government employment, received a steady traffic of visiting political grandees. News about great European events were received in Plymouth Dock even before reaching the capital, and navy reports from the town were often in the London newspapers, regularly piercing the consciousness of the metropolitan elite. The town of Dock, owned by Sir William Morice, was populated by London-educated government employees, professionals such as navy agent Reginald Pole and barrister John Buller, who earned a salary of £500 as Secretary to the Chancellor of the Exchequer, and another £350 as Comptroller of the Mint; its inhabitants relied entirely, directly or indirectly, on government patronage.[36] Like few other places, Dock was a model of Wapolian society.

Reynolds moved to Dock when the town's population was ballooning, fuelled by the government's investment in the naval base. Dock parish church was rebuilt in 1750 to accommodate new parishioners; 'within the last 70 Years', commented a 1792 guide-book, 'the Inhabitants have increased to five Times their Number.' Whereas most towns based their status claims on their long history, Dock 'has no Pretences whatever to Antiquity… it has sprung up almost instantaneously.'[37] Its streets were, literally, paved with marble; one visitor of 1788 was surprised 'with a very large display of spacious streets, intersecting each other at right angles, very different from the place we had just left.'[38] All of this was in marked contrast to Dock's neighbour, the ancient town of Plymouth where 'the streets in general are narrow, and not so clean as those of Dock… Plymouth has not extended within a Century past.'[39] Boswell's anecdotes of Samuel Johnson's 1762 visit to Plymouth with Reynolds includes a fascinating expression of the cultural divide between the two towns, as experienced by their inhabitants. Johnson perceived 'that this new and rising town could not but excite the envy and jealousy of the old… he therefore set himself resolutely on the side of the old town, the *established* town, in which his lot was cast, considering it as a kind of duty to *stand by* it. He accordingly entered warmly into its interests, and upon every occasion talked of the *dockers*, as the inhabitants of the new town were called, as upstarts and aliens.'[40] Alluding to Dock's bid to divert Plymouth's water supply, 'Johnson, affecting to entertain the passions of the place, was violent in opposition; and, half-laughing at himself for his pretended zeal where he had no concern, exclaimed, 'No, no! I am against the *dockers*; I am a Plymouth-man. Rogues! let them die of thirst. They shall not have a drop!'[41]

DOCK'S RIVALRY WITH PLYMOUTH represents more than parochial rivalries or a struggle for water resources; it stands for wider political and cultural divisions of city and country that were felt across West Country towns. Though much larger than Dock, and superficially the region's most important city, Exeter was of no strategic importance to the government, and under George III became a centre of nationalist Country ideology deeply critical both of the London ministry and, more broadly, of London cosmopolitanism. This Country counter-culture helps to explain why there were so few connoisseurs among Devon landowners. As a West Countryman put it in 1779: 'very few of Sir Joshua Reynolds's pictures ever found their way into Devonshire.'[42] Of Reynolds's identifiable oeuvre, perhaps 5% have a West Country association.

One of the few significant Devon art collectors, and one of Reynolds's closest friends, was John Parker of Saltram (d.1788), responses to whose artistic patronage exemplify Country attitudes to cosmopolitan culture. As an MP for the county of Devon, he represented not the private interests of a single powerful family, as was the characteristic of the Cornish rotten boroughs, but one of the largest freeholding electorates in England, comprised of the county's middling gentry; unlike the typical borough MP who sought lucrative government 'places', county MPs accepted no jobs and considered themselves to be in nobody's pocket. In some ways Parker was the archetypal independent country gentleman. It was said that he feared an invitation to Reynolds's Literary Club in case he could not keep pace with its wits and intellects; and, on his wife's visit to London in 1769, he expressed 'doubts whether it was safe to carry Therese to that wicked place.'[43] This was an age when guidebooks to London were published specifically to help provincial gentry navigate the city with the minimum exposure to its debauchery.[44] Parker loved to hunt and race horses; like his close friend and fellow 'knight of the shire' Sir Thomas Acland, Reynolds's portrait (FIG. 1, p. 16) shows him in hunting gear, rather than in a setting that emphasised his learning, sociability, power or fashion. The country gentleman's claim to status and a voice in public life was his relationship to the land, rather than his manners or taste. Parker's bride Therese Robinson, on the other hand, was the cosmopolitan god-daughter of the Empress of Austria, whose status and wealth derived from her family's government appointments. Therese hated the endless visits of county gentry to Saltram, with their talk of shooting and fishing. She told her brother in 1772: 'we expect a good deal of Company this week Sr Thos Acland. Sir J: Chichester & half the County, you may guess how agreable [sic] it will be, how far I shall think so, I may as well keep to myself.'[45] Even London was sometimes no better: 'The worst of Spring in London,' she wrote in 1773, 'is that the whole County of Devonshire come up to town.'[46] The Robinsons were endlessly rude about their country cousins, the Bastards of Kitley. Like the Edgcumbes, the Robinsons were Whig lieutenants. Therese's father was a close friend and confidant of Walpole's successor Thomas Pelham, the Duke of Newcastle; her brother was a loyal supporter of the

Newcastle and Rockingham administrations.

With guidance from Reynolds, in the early 1770s Parker's wife created a grand suite of rooms at Saltram designed by Robert Adam (FIG. 9, p. 60). Adam's great saloon represented a sharp intrusion of London tastes and courtly manners into county society. When visiting the estate in 1793, John Swete (1752–1821) of Oxton House, near Dawlish, caught both the room's undeniable impressiveness and its incongruity: 'that handsome room – which for its size, elegance and expensiveness of its furniture is not surpass'd by many in the kingdom: I was struck with its magnificence, but at the same time I could not but observe how ill it accorded with the remainder of the apartments.'[47] Richard Polwhele (1760–1838) alleged the saloon's cost was £10,000; the actual figure was probably a fraction of that, but the estimates indicates how the room attracted superlatives.[48] The Parkers set out to raise the reputation of their house and attract London visitors, a project crowned in 1789, not long after John Parker's death, by the brief residence at Saltram of the convalescing George III. Yet county society – whose visits Therese Parker found so tiresome, and who felt keenly their exclusion from Saltram's fashionable parties – delighted in a story that the King never set foot in the Saloon, believing it too grand for him. As Swete reported: 'The King, Queen, and three eldest Princesses… Took up their residence at Saltram – free and unrestrained, they delighted in the beauty of the spot and in the comfortable snugness and privacy of a Country Gentleman's House and as the Story went, never during their stay occupied the very fine Saloon.' Stripped of the ceremony and court etiquette, in other words, 'Farmer' George shared the down-to-earth freedoms and family values of his middling subjects. Like the great saloon itself, the cosmopolitan airs and graces of the Parkers and their luxurious London friends 'ill accorded' with the prevailing Devonshire sense of plain English living.

Many patriotic Country Englishmen regretted, like Swete, the influence of continental Europe on provincial society. A tract by the Rev John Trusler (1735–1820), widely circulated in the last quarter of the century, described how 'the luxuries and effeminacies of the age have softened down the hardy roughness of former times; and the country, like the capital, is one scene of dissipation.' With the improved road network, 'the infection of the first class soon spread among the second, and what they formerly censured, they presently approved… The several cities and large towns of this island catch the manners of the metropolis… Scarce a town now, of any magnitude, but has its Theatre Royal, its concerts, its balls, and its card-parties… The honest frankness of the country gentleman is obliterated by the equivocal politeness of the courtier, and the open sincerity of the good neighbour lost in the artifice and deceit of the man of fashion.' By contrast, 'the country *squire* lives upon his estate, spends his patrimony among his tenants and his neighbours… while the fine gentleman visits his domain, perhaps, but once in the summer, stays there as little as he can help, disdains any familiarity with his neighbours… In short, an effeminate life emasculates the fine gentleman, and renders him unfit for any thing but sipping of tea, and dealing the cards; whilst the robust and manly exercises of the *squire*… enable him, when called upon in the public cause, to be of *real* service to his country.'[49]

The same deep antipathy felt by middling provincial England for London's cosmopolitanism is evident in a 1792 commentary on Thomas Hudson's success among 'the country gentlemen [who] were faithful to their compatriot, and were contented with his honest similitudes', in contrast with his foreign rivals Vanloo and Liotard who 'diverted the torrent of fashion' for a few years.[50] When the independent country gentleman George Lipscomb visited Port Eliot around 1799, what impressed him most was not the collection of Reynolds portraits but a gallery of pre-Reformation religious paintings. Standing in front of Reynolds's *The Eliot Family*, he commended its excellent state of preservation: 'It is particularly remarkable, that, while so many fine performances of that great master are fading almost visibly before us, this still retains it's colours in all their pristine beauty. How greatly it is to be regretted, that Sir Joshua ever went abroad to learn the art of spoiling his own paintings. I believe very few have been executed by him, since that period, which retain their colouring.'[51] Much of the criticism of Reynolds's project to shape the Royal Academy on a continental model, and with foreign artists, drew from the same nationalist intellectual tradition. Reynolds's vision of an English school of history painting failed; instead rural landscapes came to embody the national identity.[52]

Provincial middling politeness was 'pragmatically rooted in a code of morality which was suspicious of extravagance, idleness and irreligion.'[53] Genteel provincials preferred morally improving plays to farce or pantomime; bowls or music to dice games; card games were permitted for their sociability only. Reynolds's secular cosmopolitan lifestyle transgressed his own family's values for, although rarely far from the fashionable west end of London, Reynolds did retain a link with West Country manners and morals through his sister Frances, who lived in London as his housekeeper from Reynolds's return from the 1750s until the late 1770s. Although Reynolds was very industrious, and plain in his manners and habits by metropolitan standards of excess, he nevertheless drank alcohol, gambled, visited brothels and painted the notable courtesans of his era; gossip about his affairs even reached the newspapers. According to James Northcote in 1772, Reynolds 'never goes to church'[54] and Mrs Thrale scored him zero when she gave her friends marks out of twenty for religion and morality (Frances Reynolds gained the top mark for 'worth of heart').[55] Frances 'frequently reminded Him that He was a clergyman's Son & that it was very improper for Him to set the example of painting on a Sunday', an issue that contributed to Reynolds's resentful ejection of her in the late 1770s, to be replaced by their more amenable niece, Mary.[56] Samuel Johnson's close friendship with Frances Reynolds was based on their shared morality, forced onto a constant state of alert by the secular character of London life; Johnson's deathbed wish was that Reynolds should go to church, read the bible daily and cease Sunday painting. Reynolds's instinctive lack of religious piety shows in his misjudged 1773 project to exploit St Paul's Cathedral as an advertising medium for contemporary history painting: of the six artists he selected to donate works for display in the church, at most one was a practising Anglican, and two were Catholics. Reynolds's devout sister Elizabeth considered him 'the greatest villain upon the earth,'[57] writing that: 'thy soul is a shocking spectacle of poverty… it may be, thy soul is past all recovery. If so, I shall never see thee more.'[58] These were accusations grounded in evangelical ideas about the city as the sinful creation of man. In the mid-1770s Elizabeth had refused to let her son lodge with Reynolds because of the London corruption it would expose him to. For Frances, her brother's tireless work schedule was just one symptom of man's fruitless search for glory in the near term, to the neglect of his eternal fate.[59]

THE MAJOR POLITICAL CRISES OF THE 1760s and 1770s – Wilkes's ejection, American independence, the county association movement – saw middling provincials emerge as a reformist political force in what they characterised as a defence of the inherited rights of freeborn Englishmen against the absolutist infringements of the corrupt London ministry. Through his presidency of the King's new Academy, Reynolds was already publicly associated with the unpopular government. Two incidents in Reynolds's life at this time show that Reynolds had come to be identified with London's reactionary political class, even by close friends and in private.

In 1770 Oliver Goldsmith published one of the period's most eloquent and controversial expositions of oppositional Country ideology, *The Deserted Village*, which he dedicated to Reynolds. The poem was a complaint about the damaging social effects of the commerce and consumerism which had been nurtured by Walpole and the Whig oligarchy, and drew from the same intellectual tradition as Trusler's polemic, quoted earlier. The vigour of the state itself was now under threat:[60]

Princes and lords may flourish, or may fade;
A breath can make them, as a breath has made:
But a bold peasantry, their country's pride,
When once destroyed, can never be supplied.

A time there was, ere England's griefs began,
When every rood of ground maintained its man;

For him light labour spread her wholesome store,
Just gave what life required but gave no more;
His best companions, innocence and health;
And his best riches, ignorance of wealth.

But times are altered; trade's unfeeling train
Usurp the land and dispossess the swain;

Goldsmith, the son of a country parson, emphasised that the poem's dedication was a declaration of his brotherly love for Reynolds. So it is especially notable that he personified the public-mindedness and traditional social structures, which were being undermined, in the occupations of their respective fathers, who were:

...to all the country dear,
And passing rich with forty pounds a-year;
Remote from towns he ran his godly race,
Nor e'er had changed, nor wish'd to change his place;
Unskilful he to fawn, or to seek for power,
By doctrines fashioned to the varying hour;

Forced off the land, the village dweller flees to the city:

...What waits him there?
To see profusion that he must not share;
To see then thousand baneful arts combined
To pamper luxury, and thin mankind;
To see each joy the sons of pleasure know,
Extorted from his fellow-creatures woe.
...Tumultuous grandeur crowds the blazing square,
The rattling chariots clash, the torches glare:
Sure scenes like these no troubles e'er annoy!
Sure these denote one universal joy!

Goldsmith and Reynolds stood at opposite ends of the argument about the impact on society of commerce and 'luxury'. In his dedicatory letter to Reynolds, Goldsmith decried the 'increase of our luxuries... For twenty or thirty years past, it has been the fashion to consider luxury as one of the greatest national advantages; and all the wisdom of antiquity in that particular, as erroneous.' Having grown rich by 'pampering luxury', living in 'the blazing square' and travelling in a 'rattling chariot', Reynolds is implicitly one of the poet's targets. In his opening remarks to the Royal Academy in 1769, Reynolds had praised 'a great, a learned, a polite, and a commercial nation', anticipating that the 'superfluity of wealth among the people' would stimulate an English school of morally-impoving history painting.[61] Reynolds could not easily acknowledge the long-established cyclical model of history, which underpinned *The Deserted Village*, under which luxury was the inevitable precursor of a nation's moral decline.

Goldsmith's was a lone voice within his cosmopolitan circle and, in his dedicatory letter to Reynolds, he acknowledged the gulf between himself and his friend on the issues: 'I know you will object (and indeed several of our best and wisest friends concur in the opinion) that the depopulation it deplores is no where to be seen, and the disorders it laments are only to be found in the poet's own imagination. To this I can scarce make any other answer, than that I sincerely believe what I have written... In regretting the depopulation of the country, I inveigh against the encrease of our luxuries; and here also I expect the shout of modern politicians against me... Still, however, I must remain a professed ancient on that head, and continue to think those luxuries prejudicial to states by which so many vices are introduced, and so many kingdoms have been undone.'[62] Reynolds invited Goldsmith to accompany him to Devon in August 1770, perhaps to convert his friend to his own point of view by exposing him to the deferential society controlled by Reynolds's landowning friends.

Reformist middle-class attitudes to the London political machine at this time, such as Goldsmith's poem articulates, are brilliantly encapsulated in the much misunderstood comments of the Plymouth watchmaker, Samuel Northcote, on hearing with 'much surprise' in 1772 that Reynolds was to become a Plympton alderman: 'I gave not the least credit to the information, looking upon the foul transactions of a dirty borough as things quite foreign to Sir Joshua Reynolds's pursuits. Indeed, the only way I can account for this is by supposing that Sir Joshua's mind has been so much engaged in the pursuits of knowledge in the art that he has not looked abroad to observe the villainy and corruption in those affairs. But, on the contrary, he perhaps retains somewhat of the ideas he had of a Plympton alderman when he was a boy looking up at them all as persons of dignity. How much will he be surprised when he finds into what a nasty jakes he has put his hands!... And if ever the devil should take it into his head to stand forth himself as a candidate for the borough... Lord E[dgcumbe] and all his clan must vote accordingly.'[63] While charitably excusing Reynolds's acquiescence in the rotten borough system, Samuel Northcote merely reflects the reformist critique of the provincial middle class in the 1770s, that the constitutional system was at breaking point, 'sinking under the debasing influence of our Government, ...defaced by the wear of passing ages, and almost lost under the immense accumulation of abuses.'[64] What for reformers was the wear of passing ages, though, was for Reynolds the authority of custom that legitimised the power of his patrician clients and friends, such as Lord Edgcumbe to whose influence Reynolds owed his seat on the Plympton corporation.[65] To men like Samuel Northcote, grandees like Edgcumbe were a corrupting influence on the system of parliamentary representation and a financial burden on the state. As one newspaper tersely reported in 1795: 'By the death of the late Earl of Mount Edgcumbe, a pension of £3,500 per annum, is saved to the public.'[66]

SAMUEL NORTHCOTE'S SUGGESTION, that Reynolds never shook off his childhood respect for his hometown's 'dirty' and 'corrupt' elders, was perceptive. The artist had to correct himself when confiding to George III that being named a Plymouth alderman was the greatest honour of his life – it was, he quickly added, second only to the knighthood that the monarch himself had conferred. But if Northcote was right, by the same token Reynolds never ceased looking at London with the faith of a small country boy steeped in the big city literature of Addison, Steele and Richardson.

This essay has suggested that Reynolds's career took him far from his Plympton origins, not only geographically but ideologically. Yet Reynolds was not identified exclusively with Whiggish aristocratic culture. His public celebration of his Plympton origins exposed him to criticism from within the aristocratic establishment. A fellow house guest at Saltram observed of Reynolds, during his 1770 visit: 'Sr Joshua... is bigotted to the place of his nativity, which many a man in his circumstances would choose to forget.'[67] Gossip about Reynolds, designed to undermine the intellectual credentials of his *Discourses*, centred on the modesty of his country education, a judgement endorsed by Farington who agreed that 'in his youth he was illiterate'.[68] For many among Reynolds's metropolitan contemporaries, coming from a small rural community *meant* being illiterate. Reynolds's origins were obvious to anyone, whether they found this problematic or not. Many were, like Mrs Thrale, matter of fact in their acceptance, who believed Reynolds to be like 'many low People oddly come to Fortune'.[69] Others, like the patrician John West, plainly found it offensive: 'I think, in my life, I never saw so vulgar & so familiar a forward fellow.'[70]

In the decades after Reynolds's death, politics and society were being reshaped in the image of the new urban middle classes. The regional power bases of many of Reynolds's aristocratic clients began to wane after the abolition of rotten boroughs in 1832; society's leaders were now less concerned to demonstrate the gentlemanly politeness and ease of manners that had been Reynolds's hallmark than manly simplicity, moral rectitude and public good works. It is a measure of how far sober Country values had triumphed over City politeness by about 1820 that even the artist's adulatory early biographers could not refrain from condemning him for the time he had squandered, in Rome seventy years or so earlier, by painting caricatures of grand tourists in Italy. Such images seemed like a degenerate aristocratic private joke, out of step with the moral seriousness with which Reynolds ought to have approached his studies in Italy.

If the middle classes rose at the expense of deference, they also raised interest in Reynolds's Plympton background, to which so many among the middle classes could relate. For the following generations of artists, Reynolds's country origins became not something to hide away, but a vital part of the success story they wished to emulate. These were, in the main, provincial men from much the same station in society, keen to follow Reynolds's example by breaking into the metropolitan market and gaining respect from the highest levels of society. Several painters even made Reynolds pilgrimages, visiting his Plympton school room and knocking on the doors of elderly residents to glimpse rare early works, in awe at the humble beginnings of the greatest exponent of their profession.[71] Reynolds's story appeared as a 'rags to riches' narrative in popular Victorian compilations of exemplary biography, showing the vast uneducated urban population that greatness was also within their reach. The town of Plympton itself claimed Reynolds as one of its own, notably through the work of William Cotton (1795–1863), a Plympton antiquary, who researched Reynolds's life and hoped to establish a museum of the artist's work in the town (it instead became the Cottonian Collection at Plymouth City Museum and Art Gallery). Gradually, Reynolds's name has become indelibly linked with Plympton.

CAT. I

Samuel Reynolds
(c. 1746)
oil on canvas,
76.1 x 63.1 cm
Plymouth City Museum and Art Gallery: Cottonian Collection

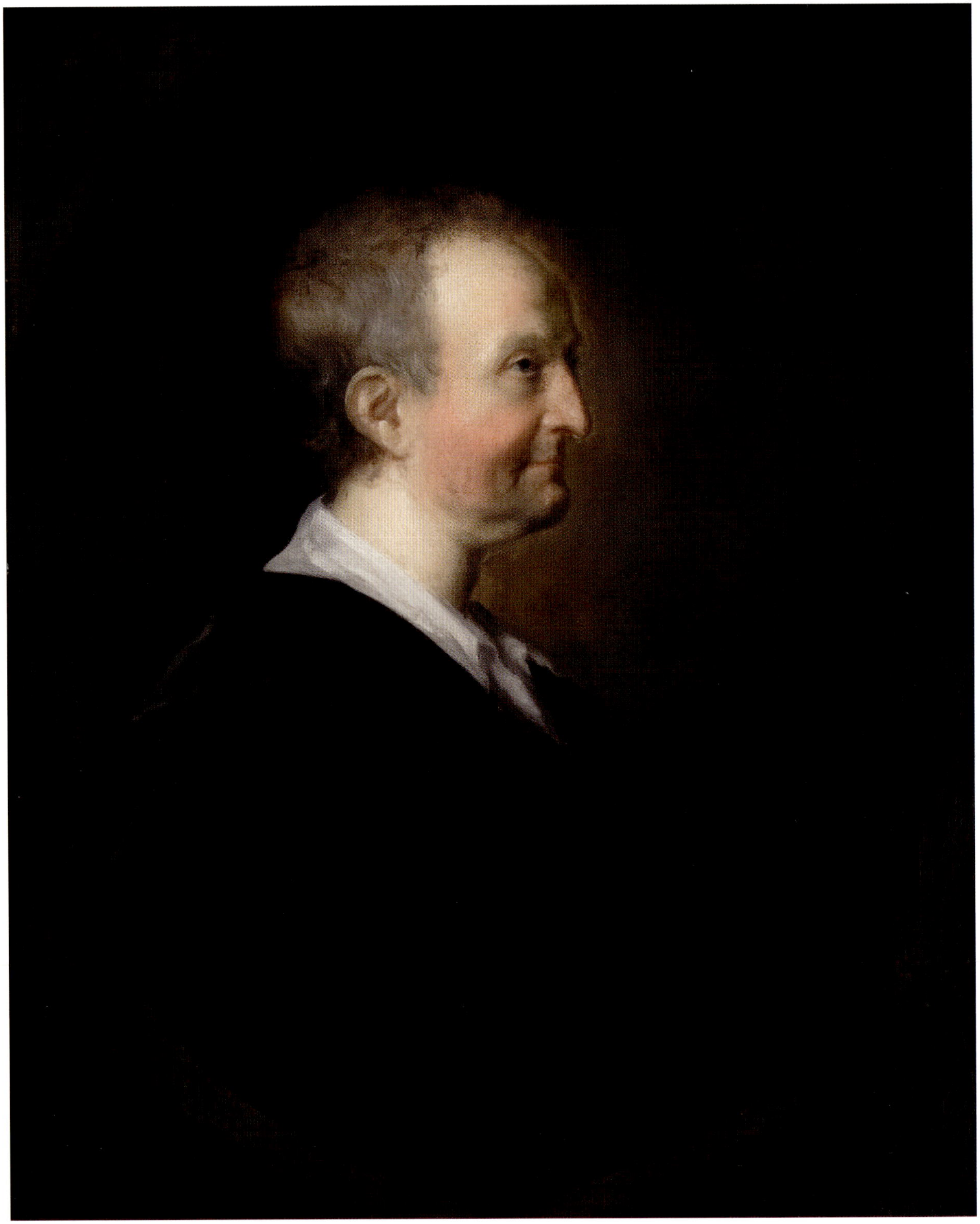

PROVENANCE: By descent; acquired by William Cotton, who bequeathed it in 1853 to the City of Plymouth.

EXHIBITION HISTORY: 1867, South Kensington, 'Second Special Exhibition of National Portraits', no.558; 1951 Plymouth, 'Paintings by Sir Joshua Reynolds', no.2; 1953, Plymouth, 'Cottonian Collection: Centenary Exhibition'; 1973, Plymouth, 'Sir Joshua Reynolds', no.8; 1986, Royal Academy, London, 'Reynolds', no.4.

LITERATURE: L Jewitt, *A Catalogue of the Pictures... in the Cottonian Collection,* Plymouth 1853, p.1; Graves and Cronin, vol.2, p.816; Waterhouse 1941, pp.6, 37; C. White and others, *Rembrandt in Eighteenth Century England*, New Haven 1983, pp.33–34.

WEST COUNTRY PORTRAITS

THE REYNOLDS FAMILY

REYNOLDS'S PORTRAITS OF HIS FATHER, Rev Samuel Reynolds (1681–1745), and younger sister Frances (1729–1807) were part of a group of family portraits painted around 1746 that also included Reynolds's other sisters Elizabeth, Mrs William Johnson (1719/21–92) and Mary, Mrs John Palmer (1716–94).[1] No portraits of Reynolds's mother or brother are known. It seems likely that Reynolds painted the portraits after the death of his father on Christmas Day 1745, after which the family moved out of the Plympton school house. Perhaps Reynolds used the portraits to advertise his services after he moved to Dock with Elizabeth and Frances.

In depicting Samuel Reynolds in profile, Reynolds followed the convention for portraying distinguished intellectual figures established by Arthur Pond, Jonathan Richardson and Sir Godfrey Kneller.[2] Frances Reynolds, too, was a writer and painter, and the close friend of Dr Johnson and Hannah More; her brother, though, was unwilling to acknowledge his sister's aspirations. She moved to London in 1753, to serve as Reynolds's housekeeper, but the two siblings had a very difficult relationship, based on their hugely different moral outlooks. Relations deteriorated so much that Reynolds ejected Frances from his house in the 1770s.[3]

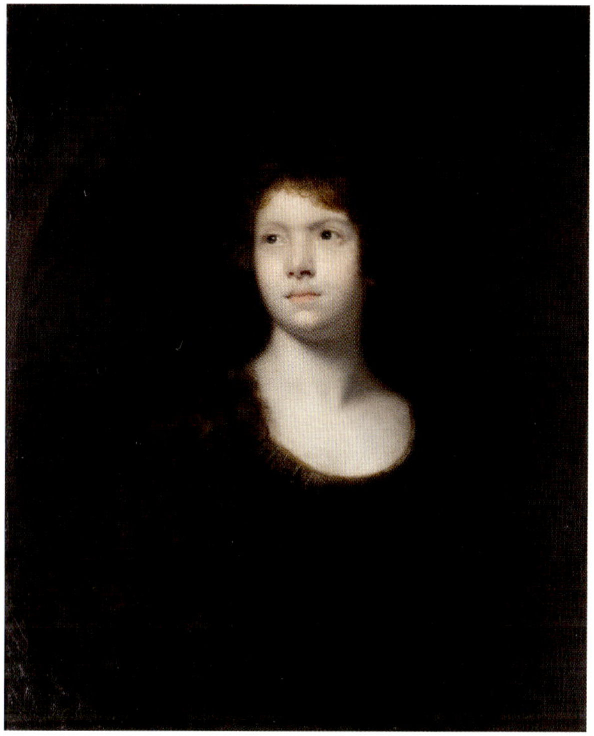

CAT. 2

Frances Reynolds
(c.1746)
oil on canvas, 76.9 x 63.7 cm
Plymouth City Museum and Art Gallery: Cottonian Collection

PROVENANCE: By descent; acquired by William Cotton, who bequeathed it in 1853 to the City of Plymouth.

EXHIBITION HISTORY: 1867, South Kensington, 'Second Special Exhibition of National Portraits', no.559; 1932, Exeter, 'Loan Collection of Works by Early Devon Painters'; 1949, Arts Council, 'Sir Joshua Reynolds. An Exhibition of Paintings', no.1; 1951, Plymouth, 'Paintings by Sir Joshua Reynolds', no.3; 1953, Plymouth, 'Cottonian Collection: Centenary Exhibition'; 1973, Plymouth, 'Sir Joshua Reynolds', no.9; 1986, Royal Academy, London, 'Reynolds', no.5.

LITERATURE: L Jewitt, *A Catalogue of the Pictures... in the Cottonian Collection*, Plymouth 1853, p.1; Graves and Cronin, vol.2, pp.817–18; Waterhouse 1941, pp.6, 37; D. Mannings, 'The sources and development of Reynolds's pre-Italian style', *Burlington Magazine*, cxvii (1975), p.216; Mannings 2000, vol.1, p.390, no.1515.

THE EDGCUMBE FAMILY

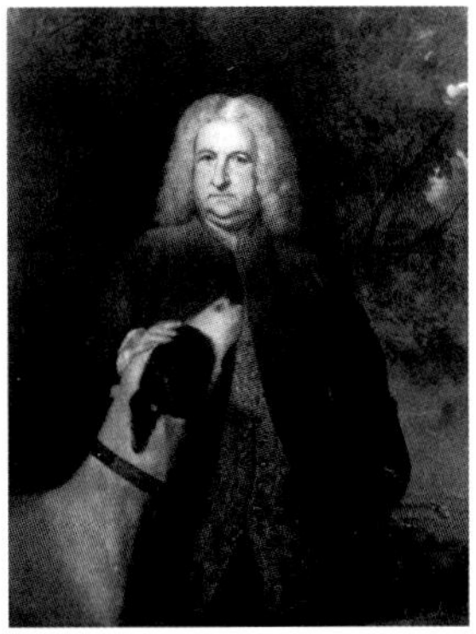

FIG. 2

Richard, 1st Baron Edgcumbe
(early 1750s)
oil on canvas,
127 x 101 cm
Destroyed 1941

RICHARD, 1ST BARON EDGCUMBE

Richard Edgcumbe (1680–1758), 1st Baron Edgcumbe, had a formative influence on the young Joshua Reynolds. Edgcumbe was a veteran political fixer and borough manager; as Sir Robert Walpole's 'most intimate friend', he personified the electoral corruption of the Whig Robinocracy.[1] No local grandee was better placed to nurture the young artist's career, especially from 1742 when Edgcumbe was made a peer and became Lord Lieutenant of Cornwall. Reynolds befriended both of Edgcumbe's sons, who typified contrasting models of aristocratic conduct: gambler Richard 'Dick' Edgcumbe (1716–61) became a by-word for moral degeneracy; sailor George Edgcumbe (1720–95) demonstrated public service and military leadership.

In an age before public exhibitions and newspaper reviews provided artists with an open marketplace, young painters like Reynolds would rely on the help of an aristocratic patron or protector to build up their reputation and introduce them to rich clients. Reynolds was fortunate indeed to have at his disposal the 'persuasion' and 'strong urgings' of Lord Edgcumbe and, in a letter he sent from Rome in 1750, the young artist described the positive impact of Edgcumbe's assistance (*Letters*, 6). Edgcumbe can be linked with almost every move in Reynolds's early career. Reynolds first came to the family's attention during his period in Plymouth after leaving Hudson.[2] Edgcumbe's employment of Reynolds attracted other local clients.[3] In 1749 he 'strongly recommended' Reynolds to Commodore Keppel, who took the artist to Italy.[4] Edgcumbe even advised the artist on his course of study: 'so widely spread was the fame of Battoni, that, before Reynolds left England, his patron, Lord Edgcumbe, strongly urged the expediency of placing himself under the tuition of so great a man'; Reynolds, however, rejected this advice.[5] On his return to England, Reynolds was briefly based in Plymouth again, but was 'strongly urged by his friend Lord Edgcumbe to return, as soon as possible, to the metropolis, as the only place where his fame could be established and his fortune advanced.'[6] In the capital, Lord Edgcumbe 'persuaded many of the first nobility to sit to him for their pictures,'[7] including the Dukes of Devonshire and Grafton, the Earl of Godolphin and Henry Fox, later Lord Holland.[8] Reynolds's portrait of Edgcumbe, which was destroyed in 1941, has been dated 'c.1740(?)' but it was described in 1785 as a work of the early 1750s.[9]

Mount Edgcumbe, the picturesque family seat overlooking Plymouth Sound, was hard-wired into the myth of England's maritime nationhood. According to the popular story, the estate had even been coveted by the Admiral of the Spanish Armada. Eighteenth-century visitors were routinely overwhelmed by the beauty of Mount Edgcumbe's dramatic situation, but the sixteenth-century house itself was not considered particularly distinguished. An 1803 guide described alterations undertaken by

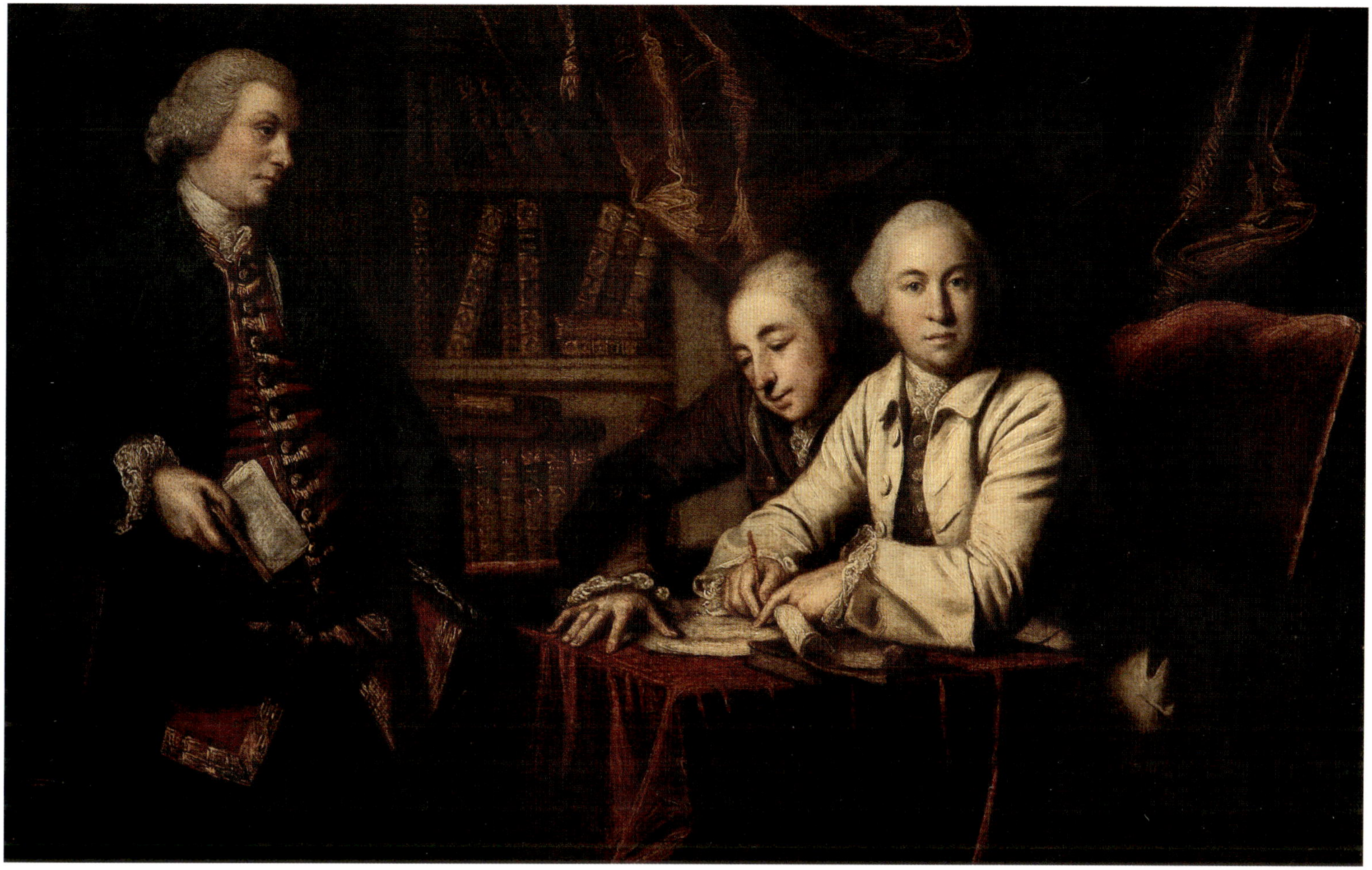

CAT. 3

A Conversation
also known as
The Out of Town Party
(1759–61)
oil on canvas, 53.3 x 82.5 cm
City Art Gallery, Bristol

PROVENANCE: Painted for Horace Walpole; Strawberry Hill sale,Robins, 18 May 1841, lot 43; Henry Labouchere, by 1843, and by descent to E A V Stanley, who sold it in 1920 to F N Schiller; bequeathed to Bristol City Art Gallery, 1946.

EXHIBITION HISTORY: 1843, British Institution, London, 'The Works of Sir Joshua Reynolds', no.40; 1868 South Kensington, London, 'Third and Continuing Exhibition of National Portraits', no.824; 1927, Burlington Fine Arts Club, London, no.71; 1946 Arts Council, Aberystwyth, 'Some Masterpieces from Welsh Houses', no.17; 1951 Plymouth, 'Paintings by Sir Joshua Reynolds', no.29; 1961, Birmingham, 'Exhibition of Works by Sir Joshua Reynolds', no.34; 1962 RA, no.163; 1968 Bregenz and Vienna, 'Angelica Kauffmann und ihre Zeitgenossen', no.393; 1973 Plymouth, 'Sir Joshua Reynolds', no.37; 1980 Orleans House, Twickenham, 'Horace Walpole and Strawberry Hill', no.18; 1985 Paris, 'Sir Joshua Reynolds', no.20; 1986 Royal Academy, London, 'Reynolds', no.41

LITERATURE: H Walpole, *A Description of the Villa of Mr Horace Walpole*, Twickenham 1784, p.3; Graves and Cronin, vol.1, p.276; Waterhouse 1941, p.45; F W Hilles, 'Horace Walpole and the Knight of the brush,' in W H Smith (ed.), *Horace Walpole*, Yale 1967, p.145; Bristol City Art Gallery, *Catalogue of Oil Paintings*, 1970, p.98; B Fothergill, *The Strawberry Hill Set*, London 1983, pp.74–82; Mannings 2000, vol.1, p.177, no.563.

CAT. 4

Richard Edgcumbe
(c.1748)
oil on canvas,
127 x 102 cm
Mount Edgcumbe
House Collection

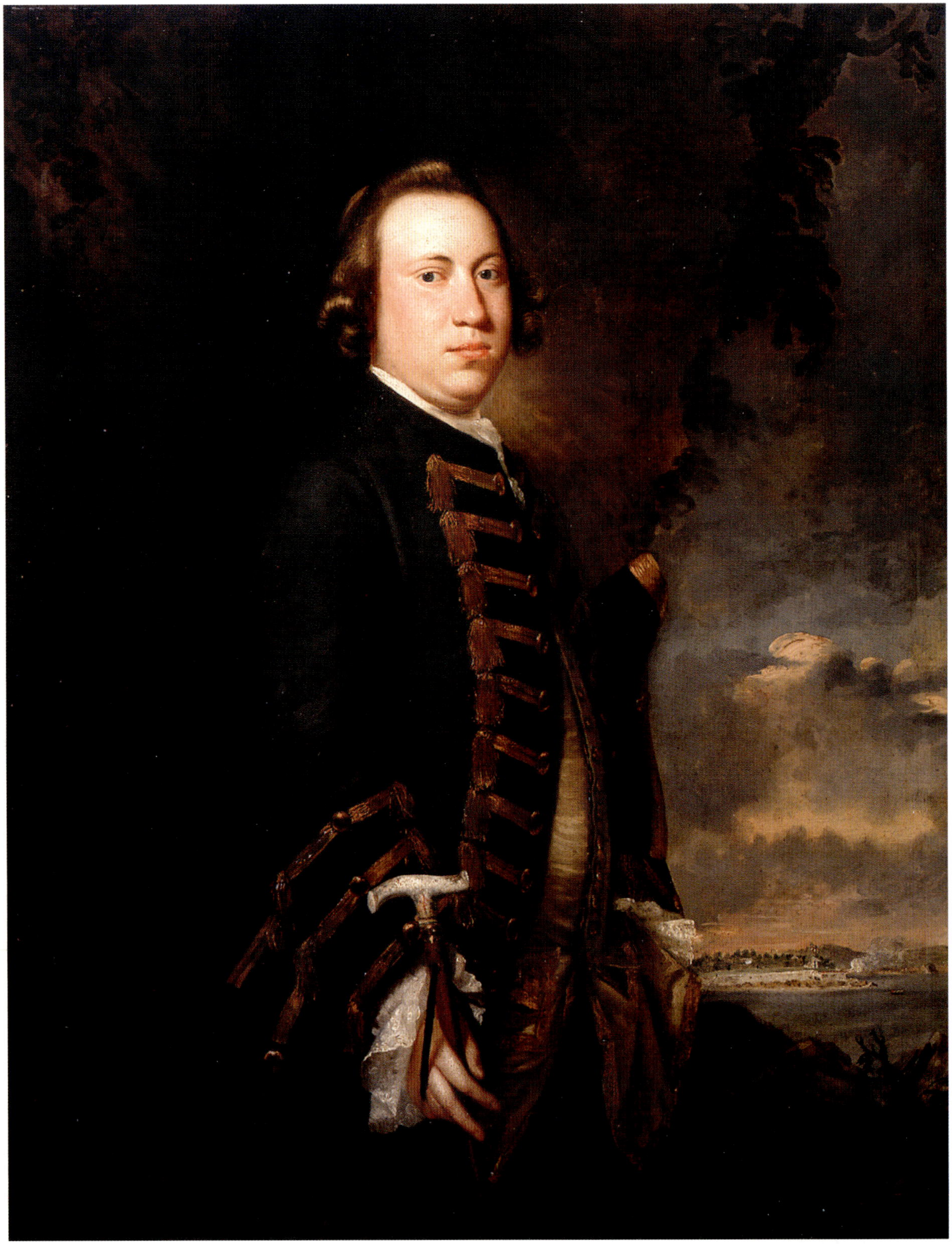

PROVENANCE: By descent until 1985, when acquired jointly by Plymouth City Council and Cornwall County Council.

EXHIBITION HISTORY: 1970, Plymouth, 'Art Treasures from West Country Collections', no.36; 1973, Plymouth, 'Sir Joshua Reynolds', no.18.

LITERATURE: Waterhouse 1941, pp.38, 119; Mannings vol.1, p.177, no.560.

Lord Edgcumbe: the house's towers 'were originally round; but about forty years ago were pulled down, and rebuilt in an octagon shape, and of a larger size. The Hall occupies the centre of the house, and rises to the height of the second story. This room was newly fitted up by Richard, the first Lord Edgcumbe, in the Grecian style of architecture, and is handsomely decorated.'[10] The house was gutted by fire in 1941, destroying among much else the busts of Julius Caesar, Caracalla and Cicero that Reynolds had procured for Lord Edgcumbe from his sculptor friend, Joseph Wilton (1722–1803) at the end of his time in Italy (*Letters* 9) and which stood in the hall. Reynolds's receipt for this work was also destroyed.[11] Beyond family portraits there were few paintings at Mount Edgcumbe.[12]

RICHARD, 2ND BARON EDGCUMBE

Lord Edgcumbe's elder son, Dick, was a gifted amateur painter and poet whose life was defined by an addiction to gambling. When one of Edgcumbe's poems was published posthumously in 1786, the editor commented that 'in him we have the most affecting example, how health, fame, ambition, every thing, are drawn into that most destructive of all whirlpools – gaming. No man was ever more calculated by nature to serve the public, and charm society – I shall leave the shades of this picture unfinished, as, perhaps, they were not wholly owing to his own indiscretion, but his F[ather]'s rigor.'[13]

Dick Edgcumbe was 'the particular and early friend of Mr. Reynolds'[14] but stories locating this in Reynolds's childhood are nineteenth-century fictions that reveal the Victorians' desire for evidence of the artist's earliest years befitting his later fame. The first generation of Reynolds's biographers state in unison that Reynolds became acquainted with the Edgcumbes not in childhood but during his 1740s residence in Plymouth, when Reynolds made the portrait of Dick shown here (CAT. 4). Not only was Dick Edgcumbe abroad for much of Reynolds's childhood, but the age gap and divergent life experiences argue against a boyish friendship: by the mid-1730s Edgcumbe was a dissolute young man already mired in gambling debts; Reynolds, the country parson's son, was barely a teenager. The story that Edgcumbe encouraged the 11-year-old Reynolds to paint Rev Thomas Smart (d.1735) in a boat house on Cremyll beach, having first made a sketch on his thumb while listening to Smart preach in Maker church, was recognised as 'very apocryphal' as early as 1857.[15] The painting has somehow gained acceptance as Reynolds's work, even though Smart died some five years before Samuel Reynolds wrote in March 1740 of his son's 'first performances' in oil, having as a 16-year-old only 'lately' begun to paint.[16]

Edgcumbe's artistic inclinations were evident at school, where he 'painted a set of scenes in oil, for a play acted by Boys at Eton School'; his schoolfriend Horace Walpole (1717–97) judged him 'the greatest genius for Drawing I ever knew.'[17] Edgcumbe left Eton in 1732 and gambling soon overtook him. Within a few years 'he had so completely ruined himself by play, that his father smuggled him on board of ship and sent him to Constantinople… under the care of Sir Everard Fawkener. On the passage he engaged the captain in play and they lost and won to each other during the voyage £22,000.'[18] In Turkey, Edgcumbe patronised the Swiss portrait artist Jean-Etienne Liotard (1702–89), whose hitherto unidentified sketch of Edgcumbe is in the Rijksmuseum.[19] Edgcumbe was back in England by January 1744, having spent seven years in Turkey; probably his father recalled him in late 1742, when Dick succeeded the newly ennobled Lord Edgcumbe as MP for Plympton Erle, the family's pocket borough.[20] In the later 1740s Lord Edgcumbe began to familiarise Dick with Cornish politics, but he was a reluctant trainee and felt an 'utter aversion… for every Branch of the Parliamenteering Trade.'[21] In debt through the 1740s and 1750s, he was forced to write wearily to friends, asking for employment: 'I find I am growing a middle-aged man, for I begin to feel symptoms of the passions of that state of life. But I hope you will not look upon it as a degree of ambition more than is laudable, to be desirous to keep pace with my equals, who if I don't start soon, will all distance me… Indeed, Sir, I am tired of absolute idleness and want some better food for my brain than what it now feeds upon.'[22]

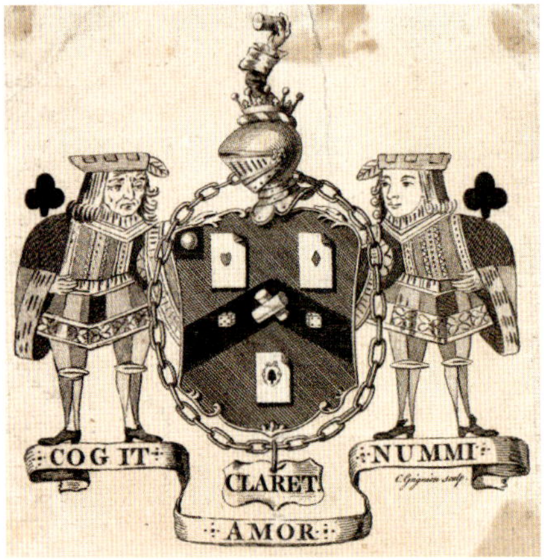

FIG. 3

Charles Grignion the Elder
(1716–1810)
after Richard Edgcumbe
A Coat of Arms
(c.1756)
engraving
Courtesy of the Lewis Walpole Library, Yale University

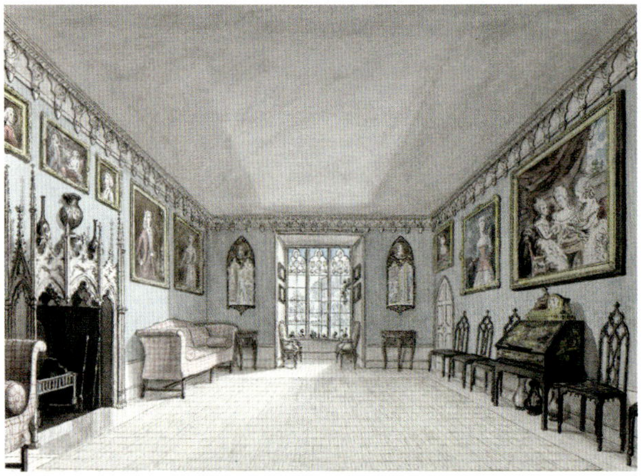

FIG. 4

John Carter
(1748–1817)
The Refectory at Strawberry Hill
(late 18th century)
watercolour
Courtesy of the Lewis Walpole Library, Yale University

It is little surprise, then, that when Reynolds painted Edgcumbe not long after he became the 2nd Baron, Dick sought the dignity of his peer's robes and the regalia of his job as Comptroller of the Household.[23] But in Reynolds's final portrait, painted 1759/1761, he appears in a more familiar and convivial guise, surrounded by gambling friends in the library at Strawberry Hill, the gothic villa of his old friend Horace Walpole who commissioned the picture (CAT. 3). Walpole hung the painting in the Refectory at Strawberry Hill (FIG. 4), as he described in 1774: 'Over the chimney, a conversation, by Reynolds, small life: Richard, second lord Edgcumbe, is drawing at a table in the library at Strawberry-hill; George James Williams is looking over him; George Augustus Selwyn stands on the other side, with a book in his hand.'[24] The painting commemorates the holidays that Walpole organised twice a year at Strawberry Hill for Edgcumbe and his two aristocratic friends, Williams (1719–1805) and Selwyn (1719–91). After Edgcumbe's death the parties continued but, as Walpole acknowledged, 'it was melancholy the missing poor Edgcumbe, who was constantly of the Christmas and Easter parties. Did you see the charming picture Reynolds painted for me of him, Selwyn and Williams? It is by far one of the best things he has executed.'[25] It was at such a gathering in 1756 that Edgcumbe designed a humorous coat of arms, as Walpole reported: 'Dick Edgcumbe, George Selwyn and Williams were with me; we composed a coat of arms for the two clubs at White's, which is actually engraving, from a very pretty painting of Edgcumbe, whom Mr Chute, as Strawberry-King-at-arms has appointed our chief Herald painter'[26](FIG. 3).

GEORGE, 1ST EARL MOUNT EDGCUMBE

Dick Edgcumbe had four children but, as he never married, the title passed to his younger brother George, his father's 'best beloved Son'.[27] George Edgcumbe was one of Reynolds's close friends; Mannings notes that his name appears in the pocket

CAT. 5

George Edgcumbe
(1748)
oil on canvas,
128 x 102.5 cm
National Maritime Museum, Greenwich

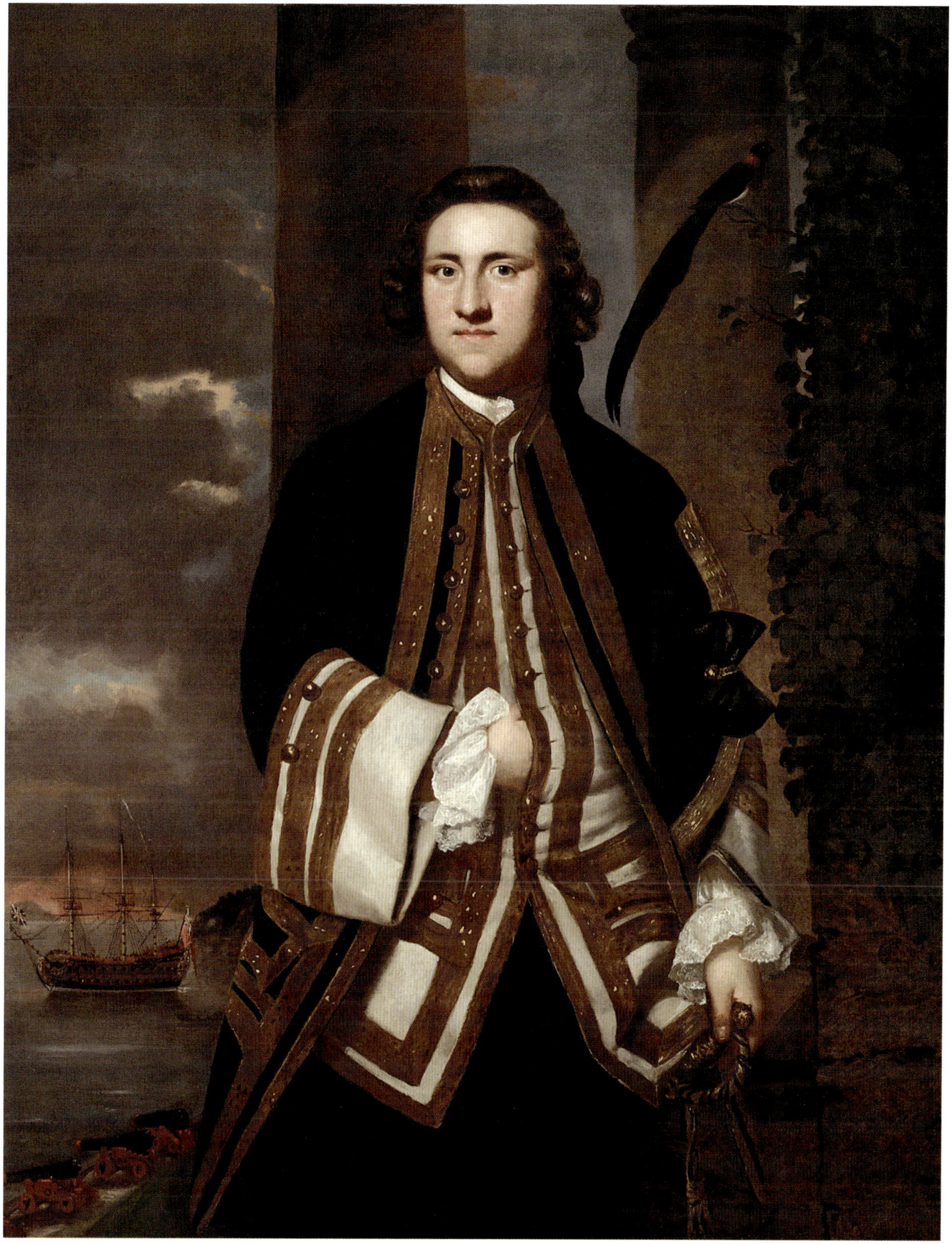

PROVENANCE: Painted for the Corporation of Plympton, on whose disenfranchisement in 1832 it was sold to Lord Mount Edgcumbe, who gave it to W Deeble Boger of Wolsdon; Christie's 30 May 1919, lot 116; C Wollett; Sotheby's 14 October 1953, lot 106 (bought in); Colnaghi, 1954, from whom bought by the National Maritime Museum.

EXHIBITION HISTORY: [?]1876 RA, no.10; 1961, Birmingham, 'Exhibition of Works by Sir Joshua Reynolds', no.6; 1973, Plymouth, 'Sir Joshua Reynolds', no.19.

LITERATURE: Cotton 1856, p.254; Graves and Cronin, vol.1, pp.277–78; E Archibald, *Preliminary Descriptive Catalogue of Portraits in Oil*, London, p.42; E K Waterhouse, 'Additions to the list of pre-Italian portraits by Reynolds,' *Minneapolis Institute of Arts Bulletin*, 1968, p.167; D Mannings, 'The Sources and Development of Reynolds's pre-Italian style,' *Burlington Magazine*, volc cxvii, 1975, p.220; Mannings 2000, vol.1, p.176, no.554.

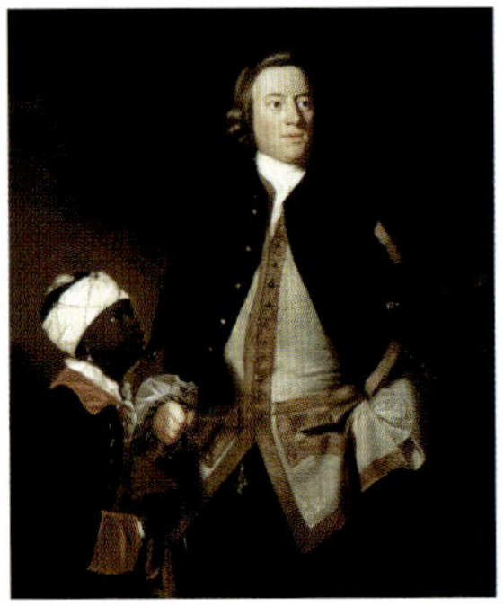

FIG. 5

Paul Henry Ourry
(1748)
oil on canvas,
127 x 102 cm
Saltram, The Morley Collection (accepted in lieu of tax by H.M. Treasury, and transferred to the National Trust in 1957) ©NTPL/Rob Matheson

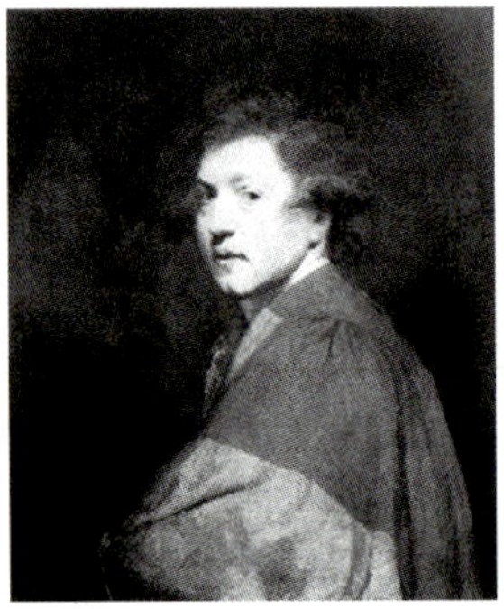

FIG. 6

Self-portrait
(1773)
oil on canvas,
76 x 63.5 cm
Private collection

books 'almost as often as John Parker's'.[28] Reynolds painted George Edgcumbe four times, twice circa 1748 and twice a decade later. Reynolds painted his wife Emma (1739–1807) in 1762 and their son Richard, 2nd Earl of Mount Edgcumbe (1764–1839) in 1773.[29]

Edgcumbe was away on naval service for much of the 1740s and 1750s so that, although a longstanding MP, he was not much engaged in politics until 1761, when he inherited Mount Edgcumbe, got married and was made Lord Lieutenant of Cornwall. He was commander-in-chief at Plymouth 1766–1770 and in 1773, and gained several lucrative government posts. While Edgcumbe's father had been employed by Walpole to manage many parliamentary boroughs, the Edgcumbe family itself controlled only one, Plympton Erle, which they shared with the Treby family of Plympton House. A portrait of George Edgcumbe (CAT. 5, p. 35) was commissioned by the Plympton Corporation, probably in 1748 when the Corporation also paid Reynolds four guineas for his portrait of Edgcumbe's first lieutenant Paul Ourry (1719–83) now at Saltram (FIG. 5); Ourry was to marry Treby's daughter the following year, and was later a Plympton MP. The two pictures, of an identical size, were displayed next to each other in the dining room next to the Plympton Guildhall.[30] Internal details of Reynolds's portrait of Edgcumbe help to clarify its date: Edgcumbe's uniform was introduced to the navy in 1748; in the background are the Mount Edgcumbe battery, restored in 1747;[31] as captain of the *Salisbury*, depicted in the painting, Edgcumbe captured a French East-Indiaman which he brought into Plymouth in March 1748; the exotic African paradise bird shown in the portrait may well be a reference to this triumph.[32] The bird, and the African servant who features in the portrait of Ourry, are vivid allusions to the vast imperial trading network that reached into ostensibly sleepy Plympton. On his visit to Devon in 1809, Joseph Farington saw the 'two half length portraits, one of them of Admiral Lord Edgcumbe, the other also of an Admiral [Ourry], both painted by Sir Joshua before He went to Italy, and both shewed that He had acquired a great deal of ability in his art at that early period of his life considering the low state in which it was at that period.'[33]

In 1772 George Edgcumbe had Reynolds elected an alderman of Plympton, which 'gave him more pleasure than any other honour which he had received during his life' according to James Northcote, his pupil at the time.[34] Reynolds was sworn Mayor of Plympton on 4 October 1773, and sent his self-portrait, apparently completed in a single day, which was displayed between his two portraits of Edgcumbe and Ourry (FIG. 6).[35] A letter to an existing alderman reveals Edgcumbe's peremptory relationship with the Corporation: 'Sir Joshua Reynolds, a native of Plympton and one who will do honour to our Bench (or any Society he is a member of), is the person I would take the liberty of proposing for the other vacancy, and it will give me great pleasure to find these two gentlemen meet your approbation as I am thoroughly persuaded they will meet with the approbation of the Borough in general.'[36] A letter from Reynolds, thanking Paul Ourry for his role in the election, survives in the Cottonian collection at Plymouth (*Letters* 32).

THE ELIOT FAMILY

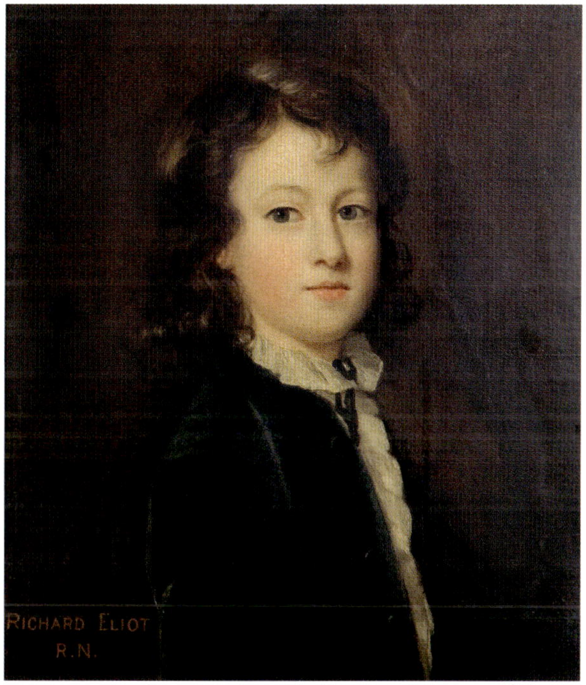

CAT. 6

Richard Eliot
(1743–44)
oil on canvas, 48.2 x 43 cm
The Trustees of the Port Eliot Estate

PROVENANCE: By descent.

EXHIBITION HISTORY: None.

LITERATURE: H R Bolton, *Manuscript Catalogue of the Pictures at Port Eliot*, 1859, no.43; Graves and Cronin, vol.1, p.286; Waterhouse 1941, p.37; Mannings 2000 vol.1, no.575.

REYNOLDS'S PORTRAITS OF THE ELIOTS, most of which remain in the family's ancestral home at Port Eliot, represent the largest group of his early Plymouth work now surviving. They began a lifelong association with the family, with whom Reynolds was 'ever upon the strictest terms of intimacy.'[1] Richard Eliot (1694–1748) of Port Eliot, was a borough patron and MP. Eliot was aligned to Frederick, Prince of Wales, by whom he was appointed Receiver-General of the Duchy of Cornwall, at £2,000 a year; even so, he died in debt. In 1726 he married Harriot Craggs (1709/14–69), the illegitimate daughter of the diplomat and politician James Craggs (1686–1721). After Richard Eliot's death, in 1749 his widow Harriot married John Hamilton (d.1755), an aristocratic navy captain and family friend, by whom she had two children. Harriot and Richard Eliot had three sons: politician Edward (1727–1804, 1st Lord Eliot from 1784); midshipman Richard (1733–46); and John (1741–69), governor of West Florida in 1769. Their daughters were Ann (1729–1810), who married navy captain Hugh Bonfoy (c.1720–62) in 1751; Harriot (1731–76); Elizabeth (1739–71), who married Charles Cocks, afterwards 1st Lord Somers, in 1759; and Catherine (b.1743).[2]

Reynolds was particularly friendly with the eldest son, Edward, with whom he socialised frequently in London. Edward Eliot was a member of the Literary Club and a pallbearer at Reynolds's funeral. Reynolds's pocket books record their meetings in 1764–65, 1772 and 1777, but this underplays the

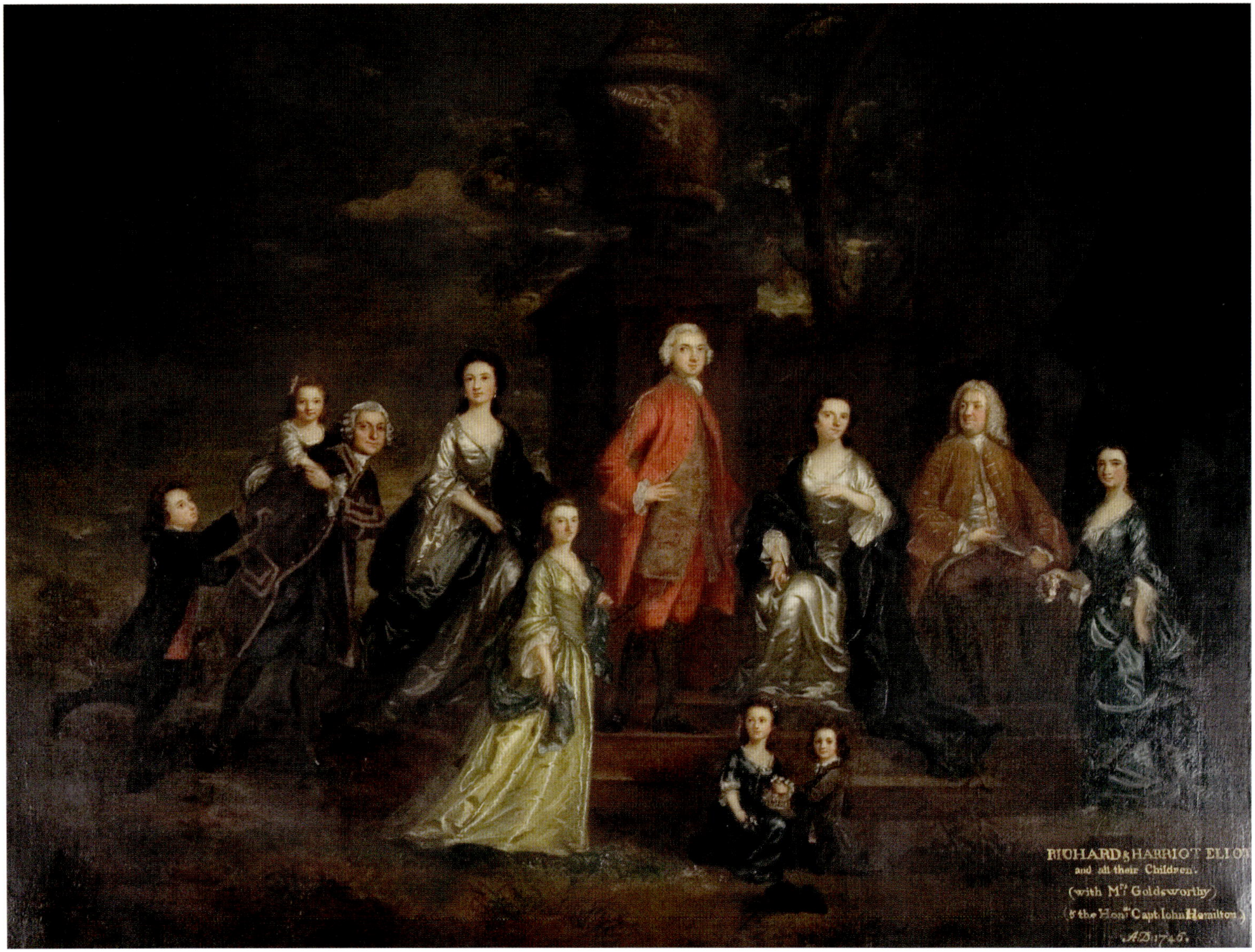

CAT. 7

The Eliot Family
(c.1746)
oil on canvas, 87 x 114 cm
Plymouth City Museum and Art Gallery: Port Eliot Collection

PROVENANCE: By descent; acquired by Plymouth Museum and Art Gallery in 2007.

EXHIBITION HISTORY: 1876 Royal Academy, London, 'Loan exhibition of Old Masters and deceased masters of the British School', no.3; 1985, Paris, 'Sir Joshua Reynolds', no.1; 1986, Royal Academy, London, 'Reynolds', no.2.

LITERATURE: ed Edmund Malone, *The Works of Sir Joshua Reynolds*, London 1798, vol.1, p.x; George Lipscomb, *A Journey into Cornwall*, London 1799, pp.287–8; Britton and Brayley, vol.2, p.382; H R Bolton, *Manuscript Catalogue of the Pictures at Port Eliot*, 1859, no.50; Leslie and Taylor, vol.1, p.29; Graves and Cronin, vol.1, pp.284–5; Waterhouse 1941, pp.37, 119; D. Mannings, 'The sources and development of Reynolds's pre-Italian style', *Burlington Magazine*, cvxii (1975), pp.221–2; Mannings 2000, vol.1, no.576.

extent of their acquaintance. In the early 1780s the two men had almost become relations when Reynolds's niece, Mary Palmer, was engaged to Eliot's son, Edward James Eliot (1758–97), whom Reynolds painted c.1778; Mary and her sister both made visits to Port Eliot in 1783[3] and Reynolds visited Port Eliot on his visits to Devon in 1773 and 1780, and perhaps also 1783.[4] He also considered visiting Cornwall in 1772 and 1784.[5] Reynolds was familiar with the paintings at Port Eliot, for he attributed one to Rembrandt and Quentin Massys.[6]

With four parliamentary seats in his gift, Edward Eliot looked forward to a prominent political career, and from 1746 to 1748 he travelled in Europe to prepare for public life, accompanying Philip Stanhope (d.1768), the Earl of Chesterfield's son to whom Chesterfield's famous series of letters was addressed. However, Eliot's political ambitions were disappointed and he was widely seen to have failed to live up to his early promise. His personal manner, which attracted much comment, was to blame: 'He is a Young man from whom there is nothing good that one may not expect... Yet with all this the Young man has a Lowness of spirits, and shyness about him which unless quickly removed, will prevent his making that figure in the world which he ought to make.'[7] When Eliot came to dinner with John Parker of Saltram in 1778, a guest reported that 'his spirits are as usual very unequal, but we had no reason to complain of them on that day.'[8]

The Eliots were among Reynolds's very first clients after his return from London to Plymouth in 1743, following his disagreement with Hudson. Reynolds's portrait of young Richard Eliot (CAT. 6) may well have been one of the twenty portraits that Reynolds had completed by 3 January 1744; these sitters included 'the greatest man of the place, the commissioner of the dockyard', Philip Vanbrugh (1682–1753).[9] Reynolds's earliest portrait of Edward Eliot is datable to 1744–45; others followed c.1747 and 1781–82.[10] Reynolds painted Eliot's sister Elizabeth c.1746–47, and her mother c.1748–49. Reynolds also painted close family friends: John Hamilton twice before Italy, c.1746 and c.1747, and once just after, c.1753; and Edward Eliot's best friend, William Trevanion (1727–67) of Caerhayes c.1748, whom Reynolds had clearly also befriended, for when Philip Stanhope reached Rome in 1750, his tutor wrote home to Eliot that: 'Reynold's the Painter is here, who has told me all the Local Cornubian news, & that Jack Trevanion has got a good place.'[11] Reynolds also painted Ann Eliot as Mrs Bonfoy, probably in 1754; his decision to have the portrait engraved – even though the sitter was not famous – is a mark of Reynolds's satisfaction with the picture.

Reynolds's work for the Eliots was not limited to portraiture, and it is two commissions outside the genre which reveal most about Reynolds in his early marketplace. A panorama of *Plymouth Sound*, dated 1748, shows that even at this relatively late date he knew nothing either of English artists working in the tradition of Gaspar Poussin, such as George Lambert, or of Canaletto and his followers. The existence of this early landscape commission indicates that the Plymouth market may have been too small to sustain a pure portrait specialist; no doubt Reynolds took what commissions came his way. For even though his clientele had grown to include many of the region's prominent landowning families, Reynolds had still been unable to accumulate enough savings by 1749 to finance his time in Italy himself. In Reynolds's most notable and ambitious early commission from the Eliots he was again working outside the genre of portraiture. *The Eliot Family* is a group of 11 figures comprising the whole family, plus John Hamilton and his friend, Philip Vanbrugh's daughter Philippia (1716–77), wife of Burrington Goldsworthy, British Consul in Leghorn. The patriarch Richard Eliot is seated on the right next to his wife. In the middle stands their eldest son Edward. His younger brother Richard runs in from the left, grabbing at the coat of John Hamilton, who stands next to Mrs Goldsworthy. Ann Eliot is in front of her, and Harriot is at the far right. As Hamilton's correspondence makes special reference to 'lovely little Kitty', Catherine is probably the child on his back.[12] John and Elizabeth are playing in the foreground.

The obvious model for Reynolds's composition is the famous Van Dyck group portrait of the Pembroke family at Wilton House, which Reynolds had surely seen during a stop at Salisbury on one of his journeys between Devon and London. Reynolds would also

CAT. 8

Harriot Craggs, Mrs Eliot
(c.1748)
oil on canvas,
124.5 x 99 cm
Plymouth City Museum and Art Gallery: Port Eliot Collection

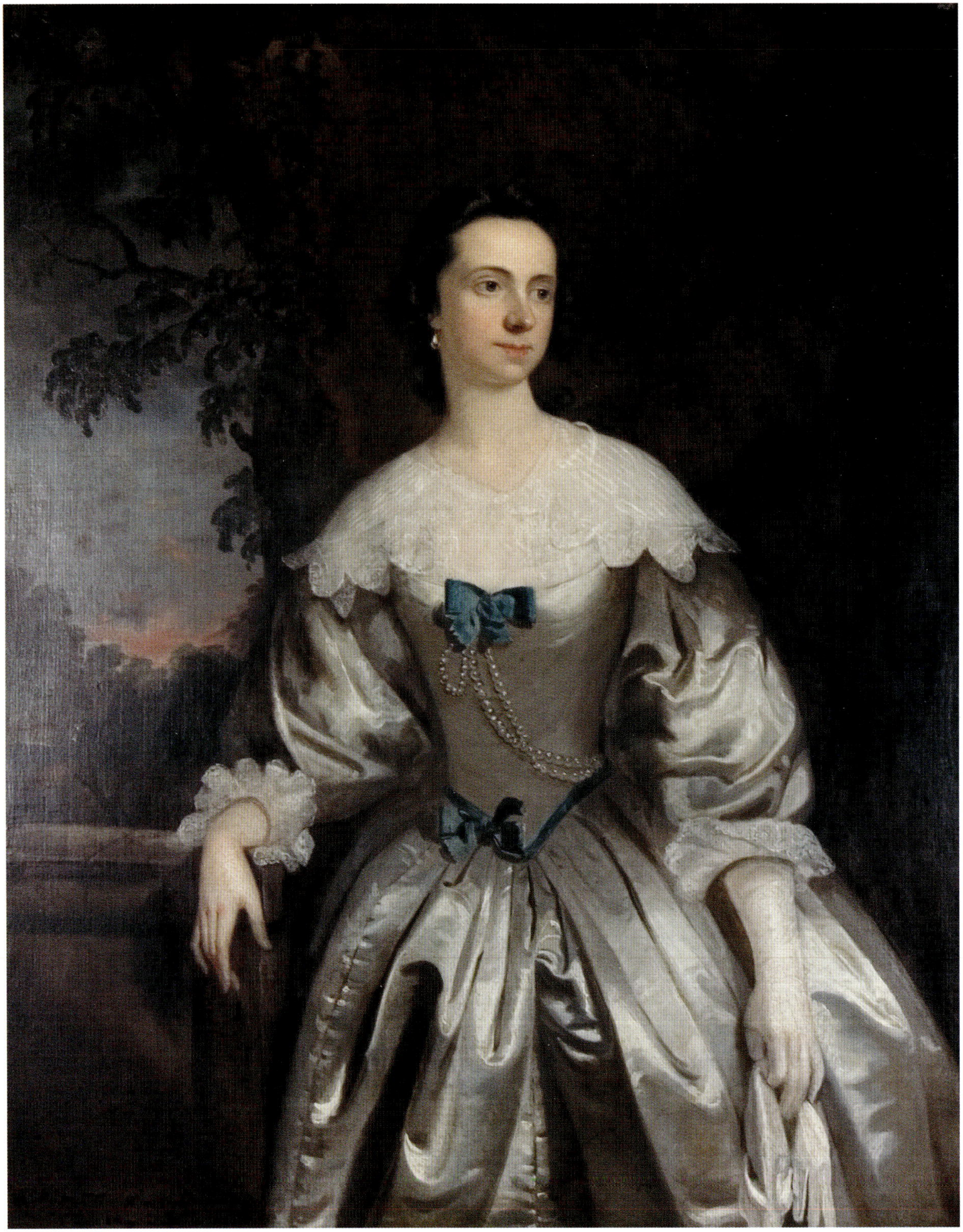

PROVENANCE: By descent; acquired by Plymouth Museum and Art Gallery in 2007.

EXHIBITION HISTORY: None.

LITERATURE: H R Bolton, *Manuscript Catalogue of the Pictures at Port Eliot*, 1859, no.21; Graves and Cronin, vol.1, p.285; Waterhouse 1941, p.39; Mannings 2000, vol.1, p.180, no.574.

CAT. 9

Ann Bonfoy
(1754)
oil on canvas,
124 x 100 cm
Plymouth City Museum
and Art Gallery:
Port Eliot Collection

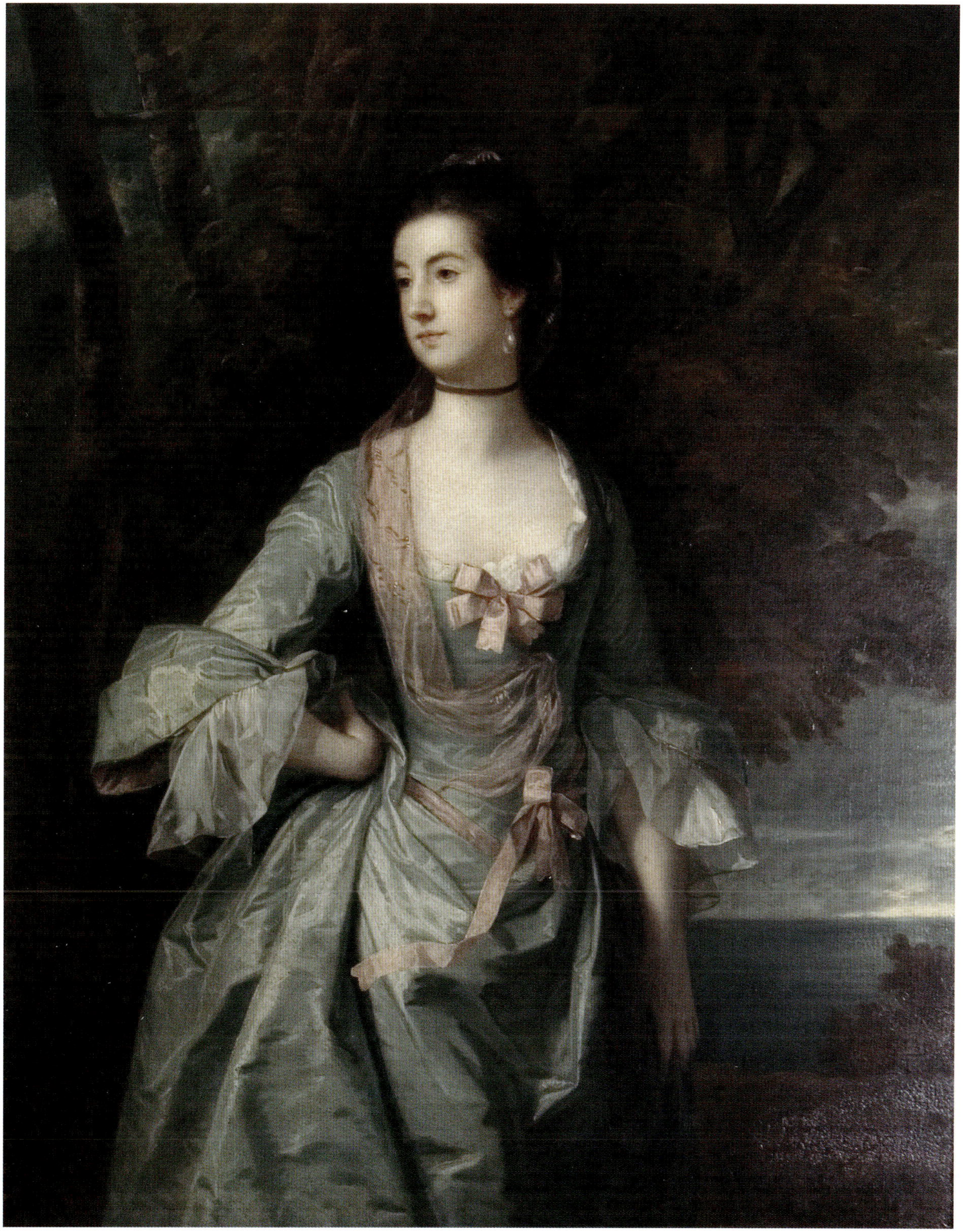

PROVENANCE: By descent; acquired by Plymouth Museum and Art Gallery in 2007.

EXHIBITION HISTORY: 1882, Royal Academy, London, 'Loan exhibition of Old Masters and deceased masters of the British School', no.269; 1913 Grosvenor Gallery, London, 'Woman and Child in Art', no.22; 1986, Royal Academy, London, 'Reynolds', no.23.

LITERATURE: H R Bolton, *Manuscript Catalogue of the Pictures at Port Eliot*, 1859, no.4; Leslie and Taylor, vol.1, p.128; Graves and Cronin, vol.1, pp.93-4; Waterhouse 1941, p.38; Waterhouse 1968, p.143; David Mannings, 'Reynolds, Hogarth and Van Dyck', *The Burlington Magazine*, vol.126 no.980 (November 1984), pp.686–90; Mannings 2000, vol.1, no.200.

ENGRAVED: James McArdell, 1755.

CAT. 10

Charles Cornwallis
(1761)
oil on canvas,
124 x 99 cm
Plymouth City Museum
and Art Gallery:
Port Eliot Collection

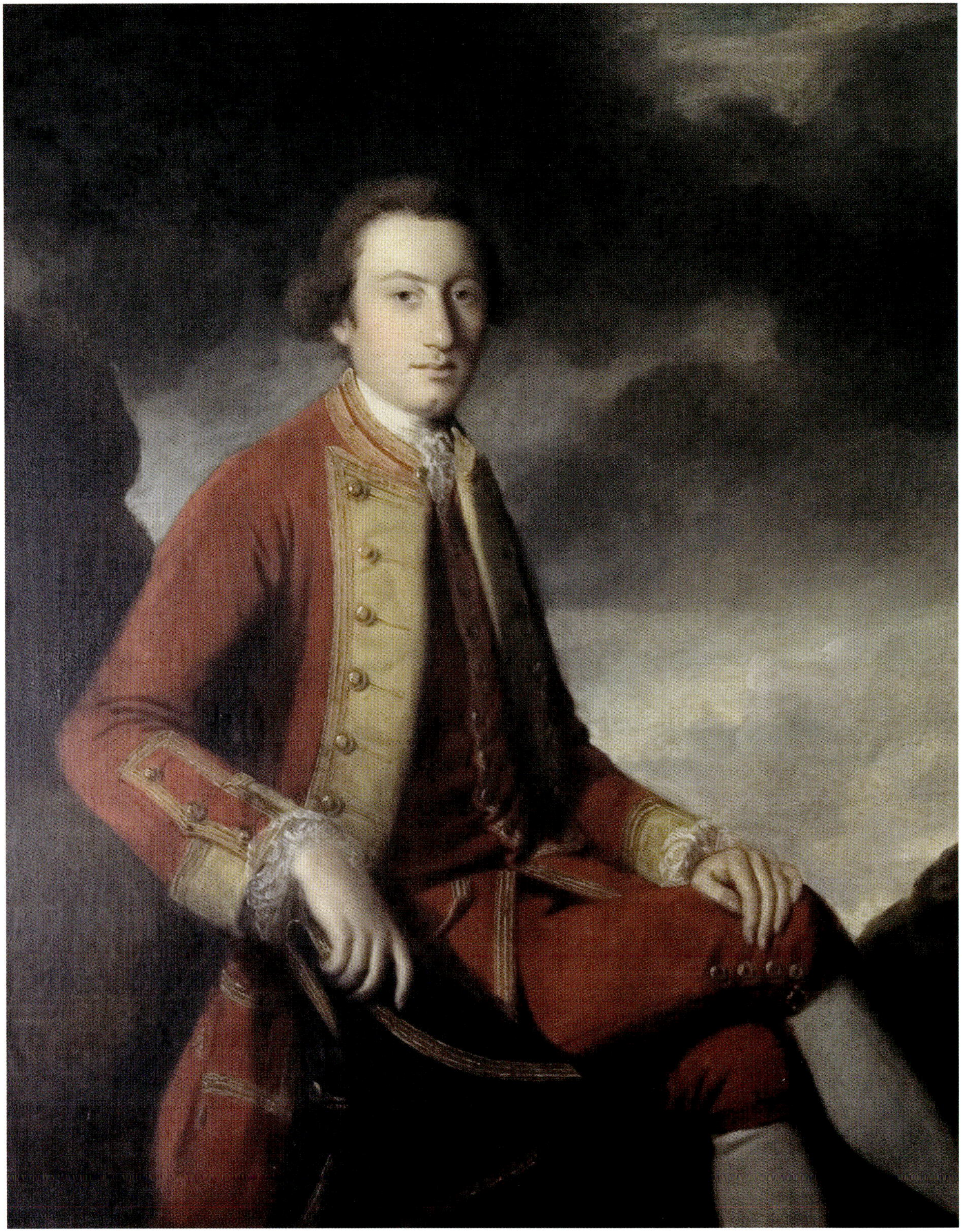

PROVENANCE: By descent.

EXHIBITION HISTORY: 1882 Royal Academy, no.174.

LITERATURE: Graves and Cronin, vol.1, p.114; Waterhouse 1941, p.49; Mannings 2000, vol.1, p.147, no.422.

CAT. 11

Hope Nursing Love
(c.1769)
oil on canvas,
127 x 102 cm

Plymouth City Museum
and Art Gallery:
Port Eliot Collection

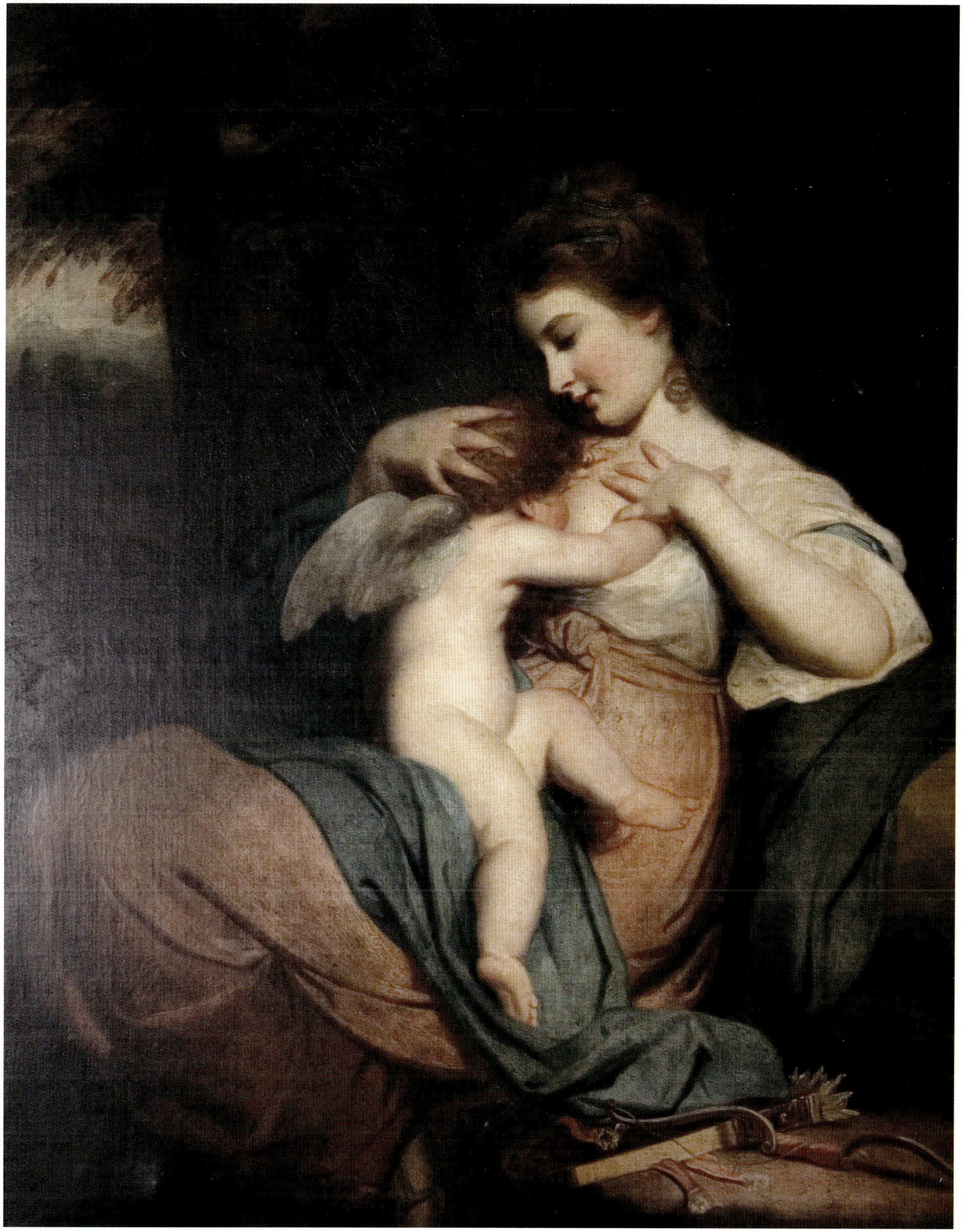

PROVENANCE: Sold Greenwood's, 16 April 1796, lot 64 to Henry Hope; his sale, 28 June 1816, lot 91 to Carew; R. Pole Carew's sale at Elgood and Ward, 1835.

EXHIBITION HISTORY: 1813, British Institution, London, 'Pictures by the late Sir Joshua Reynolds', no.138; 1876, Royal Academy, London, 'Loan exhibition of Old Masters and deceased masters of the British School', no.18; 1895, Grafton Galleries, London, 'Fair Children', no.124.

LITERATURE: Graves and Cronin, vol.2, pp.671–72; Waterhouse 1941, p.60; Mannings 2000, vol.1, p.344, no.1303.

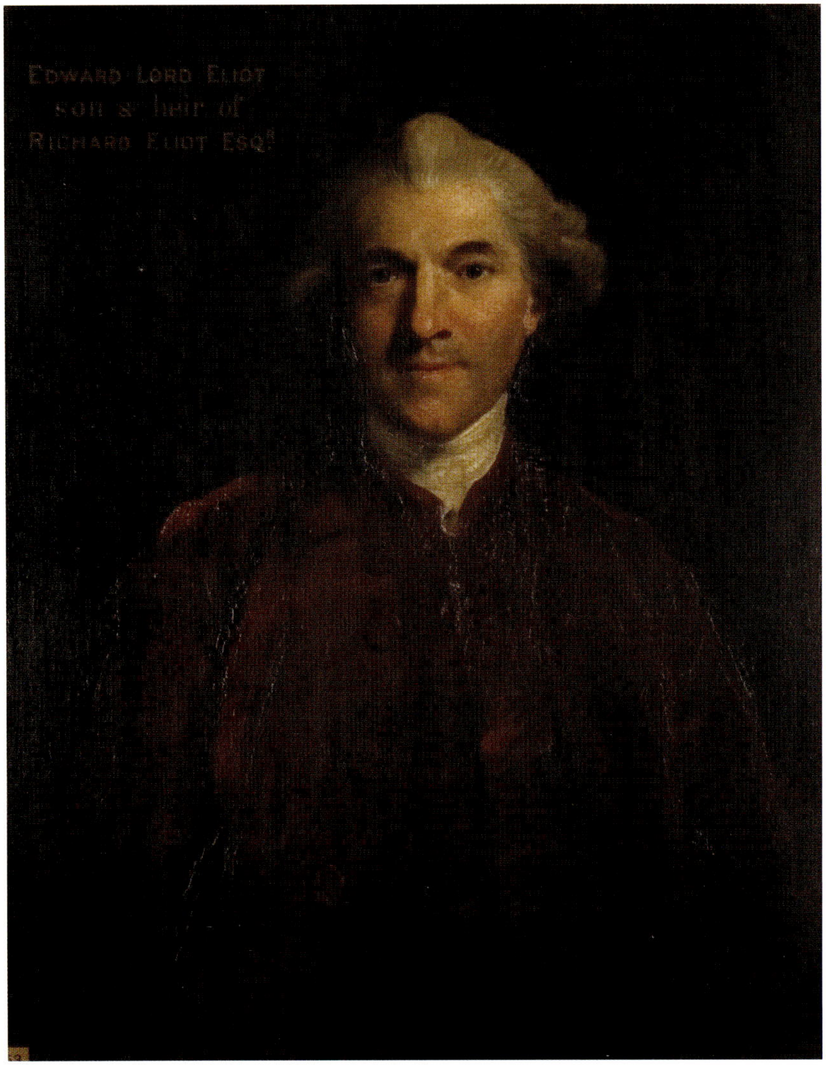

CAT. 12

Edward Eliot
(1781–82)
oil on canvas, 76 x 63 cm
Plymouth City Museum and Art Gallery: Port Eliot Collection

PROVENANCE: By descent; acquired by Plymouth Museum and Art Gallery in 2007.

EXHIBITION HISTORY: None.

LITERATURE: H R Bolton, *Manuscript Catalogue of the Pictures at Port Eliot*, 1859, no.100; Waterhouse 1941, p.73; Mannings 2000, p.179, no.571.

have been aware of a large family portrait of the Radcliffes of Warleigh, painted c.1742–43 by his own master, Thomas Hudson, which also derives from the Van Dyck; as Hudson's apprentice, Reynolds may even have been involved in its creation.[13] Yet from its small scale, and the inclusion of friends, it is evident that *The Eliot Family* was not conceived as a grand dynastic statement like these much larger antecedents, in which sitters were represented at full-scale. Rather, it was an informal conversation piece, in the tradition of William Hogarth (1697–1764), Bartholomew Dandridge (1691–c.1754), Joseph Francis Nollekens (1702–48) and others from the 1730s. The theme of companionability that is so characteristic of the conversation genre is prominent in Reynolds's picture. On an urn dominating the scene is the Latin word 'Amiticia', meaning friendship – highlighting the Eliot family's welcome of their two friends into the family circle. In particular, the Eliots had good reason to express solidarity with Mrs Goldsworthy, a recent arrival in Plymouth. In the late 1730s and early 1740s she was the victim of a smear campaign orchestrated by friends of Horace Mann, whose job as the British representative in Florence the Goldsworthys coveted. It was alleged that Mrs Goldsworthy, formerly a companion to the Duchess of Richmond, was the mistress of the Tuscan General Wachtendonck; Mann called her 'a horrid fool', and to Horace Walpole she was 'a pert, little unbred thing'.[14] In 1743 the scandal forced Mrs Goldsworthy to separate from her husband and move to Plymouth, to live with her father; she was reunited with Burrington Goldsworthy in 1747.

Traditionally *The Eliot Family* is dated 1746; if so, it must predate the start of Edward Eliot's European travels that July; Captain Hamilton was also absent from Cornwall from July or August.[15] But *The Eliot Family* is so loose and unassured, compared with Reynolds's other paintings from that year, that perhaps it is somewhat earlier. It seems to have more in common with portraits of Richard Eliot and Reginald Pole that date from the very outset of Reynolds's Plymouth career. *The Eliot Family* has been an object of curiosity since the eighteenth century. According to George Lipscomb, a visitor to Port Eliot in the 1790s, 'Lord Eliot assured me [it]

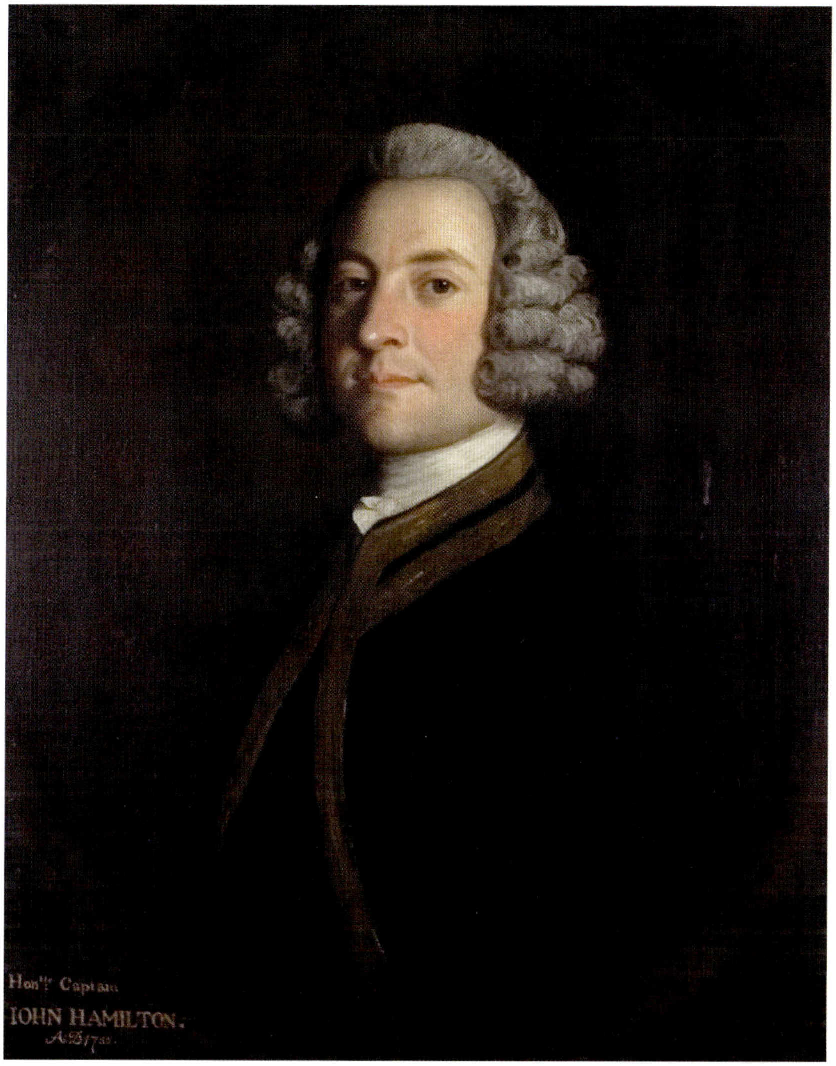

CAT. 13

John Hamilton
(c.1753)
oil on canvas, 76 x 63 cm
Plymouth City Museum and Art Gallery: Port Eliot Collection

PROVENANCE: By descent; acquired by Plymouth Museum and Art Gallery in 2007.
EXHIBITION HISTORY: None.
LITERATURE: H R Bolton, *Manuscript Catalogue of the Pictures at Port Eliot*, 1859, no.71; Graves and Cronin, vol.2, p.419; Waterhouse 1941, p.39; Mannings 2000, vol.1, p.238, no.820.

was the first groupe which that admired painter ever attempted.'[16] Reynolds's inexperience was evident to another early visitor, to whom 'the whole performance seems deficient in those great points which our artist afterwards so particularly excelled in, and strenuously recommended to others – grouping, composition, incident, and harmony.'[17] Yet perhaps the young artist was also credited for his ambition in attempting such a complex group. Lipscomb, certainly, was 'much pleased with an admirable groupe of eleven figures,'[18] and it seems that, before he had launched himself in London in 1753, Reynolds had become known in the region for his group portraiture. Early that year the Drake family agent had informed his master that Reynolds had just left Plymouth for the capital: 'it looks as if He wou'd Turn out a Vandike, at Least to Family Pieces.'[19]

In the nineteenth century three further Reynolds paintings came to Port Eliot: *Hope Nursing Love*; a portrait of Charles, 2nd Earl Cornwallis (1738-1805), painted 1761; and of his wife Jemima (d.1779) and their son, painted 1769 and 1778 (when the child was added). Cornwallis was appointed Governor-General of India and evidently took his wife's portrait with him, as he wrote to his brother in 1786, just before he embarked: 'I sent up a Picture, which you know is very dear to me, to Sir Joshua Reynolds to be cleaned & have the colours a little helped. May I beg of you to tell Thomas Finney[?] to call at Sir Joshua's, & inquire when it will be finished, & see it safely packed and sent down.'[20]

JAMES BULLER

JAMES BULLER (1717–65) WAS THE ELDEST son of John Francis Buller (d.1751) of Morval and Rebecca Trelawney. He succeeded Sir Coventry Carew as county MP for Cornwall, serving from 1748 until his death as a Tory country gentleman. After a brief marriage in 1739 to Elizabeth Gould (d.1742) he married Lady Jane Bathurst (c.1719–94) in 1744.

In 1746 James Buller commissioned a Dorset builder, Francis Cartwright (c.1695–1758), to build a house at his newly-purchased estate of King's Nympton, at South Molton, Devon, whose design was inspired by the celebrated Palladian villa, Marble Hill House in Middlesex.[1] The family archive records Buller's many purchases, in the 1750s and 60s, of furnishings and other household goods from leading suppliers: the furniture makers William Gomm & Son, Joshua Lewis and Thomas Chippendale; the clock maker Thomas Mudge; and the carpet maker Thomas Whitty of Axminster.[2] However, these were not necessarily luxurious purchases: Buller's 1757 invoice from Chippendale itemises a clothes press, nursing chair and repairs to a breakfast table.[3] James Buller sat to Thomas Hudson in 1741, whose receipt for 'twenty four Pounds & Sixteen Shillings in full for two Half Lengths, & two Gold Frames & Case' is dated 29 July.[4] In 1759 Buller employed Hudson again, purchasing 'One ¾ Picture of his Lady £12.12.0 / One Ditto Himself £12.12.0 / Two Burnished Gold Frames £7.7.0 / A Case to Ditto £0.8.0 / [sub-total] £32.19.0 / To cleaning & Mending Ptd Pictures £1.10.0 / Frames to ditto £3.3.0.'[5]

Buller and his wife sat to Reynolds in 1757. James Buller's portrait is exhibited here from Antony, but his wife's portrait was sold by the family in 1891.[6] The portrait of Buller's sister Rebecca, who married naval officer Charles Watson in 1741, also probably dates from 1757.[7] Reynolds's portraits of Buller's younger brother, John Buller (1721–1786) and his wife Mary St Aubyn (d.1767) date from about 1763.[8] James Buller's eldest son John married Anne Lemon, whom Reynolds painted in 1771.[9] The Buller archive also contains a note of an annuity of £100 that John Buller agreed to pay to Reynolds on 4 May 1772: 'agreed to pay Sr Joshua Reynolds 100 pr Annm for Lord Clare's Life from this Day.'[10]

Reynolds's pocket book records sittings for James Buller at 10am on 14 and 25 January, 9am on 27 January and 10am on 3 and 21 February.[11] Mrs Buller sat at midday on 26 January, 2pm on 27 January, midday on 3 February and 1pm on 10 February.[12] Reynolds also noted 'Jas Buller Esq / at King's Nympton / near Chulmleigh / Devon' and, opposite the weeks of 11 and 25 April, 'Write to Mr Buller'. No doubt this was about payment for the portraits, as he sent a letter to Buller dated 26 April: 'I receivd the honour of yours of April 22d with a Bill of thirty two Pounds for which I return you many thanks. my name is Joshua but I apprehend tis of no great importance the mistake… Received of Jas. Buller Esq the sum of thirty two Pounds for his & Mrs Buller's Pictures with Frames.'[13]

CAT. 14

James Buller
(1757)
oil on canvas,
76 x 63.5 cm

Trustees of the Carew Pole
Family Trusts, Antony House

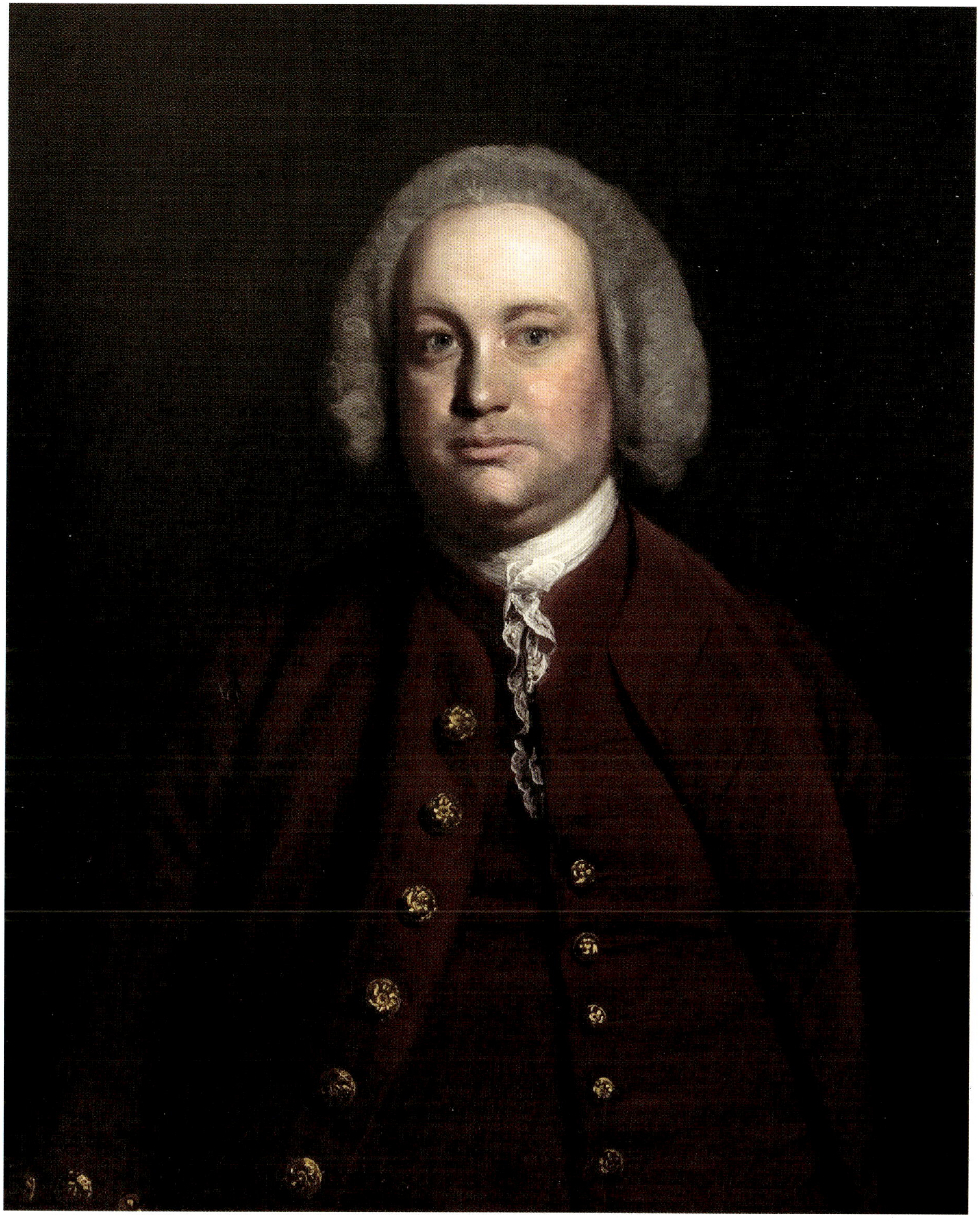

PROVENANCE: by descent

EXHIBITION HISTORY: 1961 Birmingham, 'Exhibition of Works by Sir Joshua Reynolds', no.23; 1973 Plymouth, 'Sir Joshua Reynolds', no.34.

LITERATURE: Graves and Cronin, vol.2, p.122; *Letters*, no.256; Mannings 2000, vol.1, no.271.

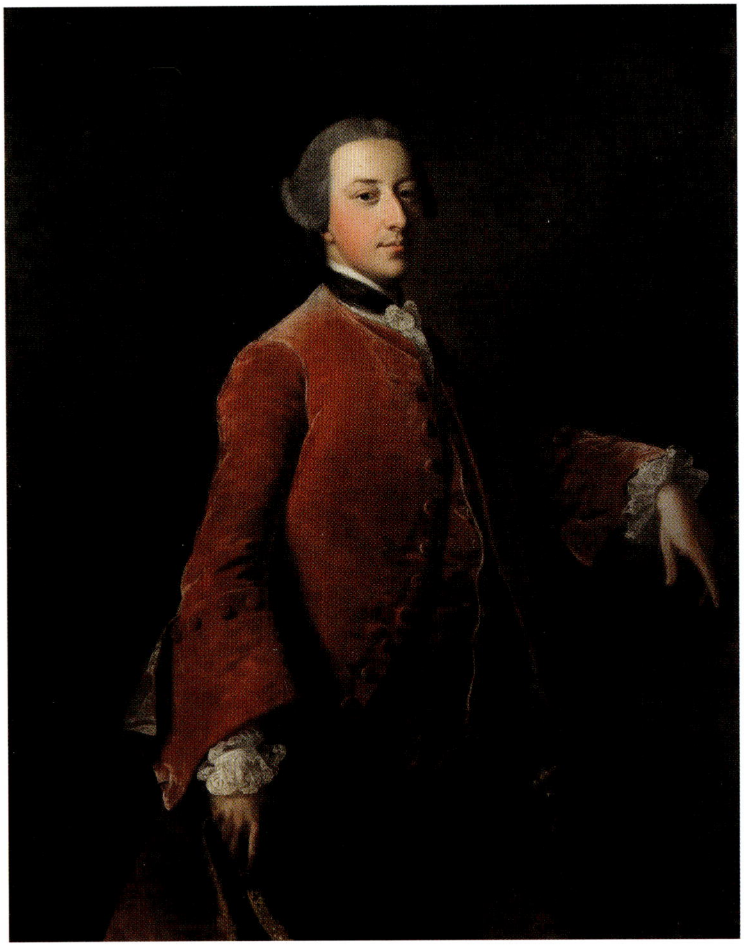

CAT. 15

William Molesworth

(1756)

oil on canvas, 128 x 102 cm

The Trustees of the Molesworth-St Aubyn Heritage Trust

PROVENANCE: By descent.

EXHIBITION HISTORY: 1951, Plymouth, 'Paintings by Sir Joshua Reynolds', no.10; 1973, Plymouth, 'Sir Joshua Reynolds', no.29.

LITERATURE: Graves and Cronin vol.2, p.651; Waterhouse 1941, p.40; Mannings 2000, vol.1, p.336, no.1265.

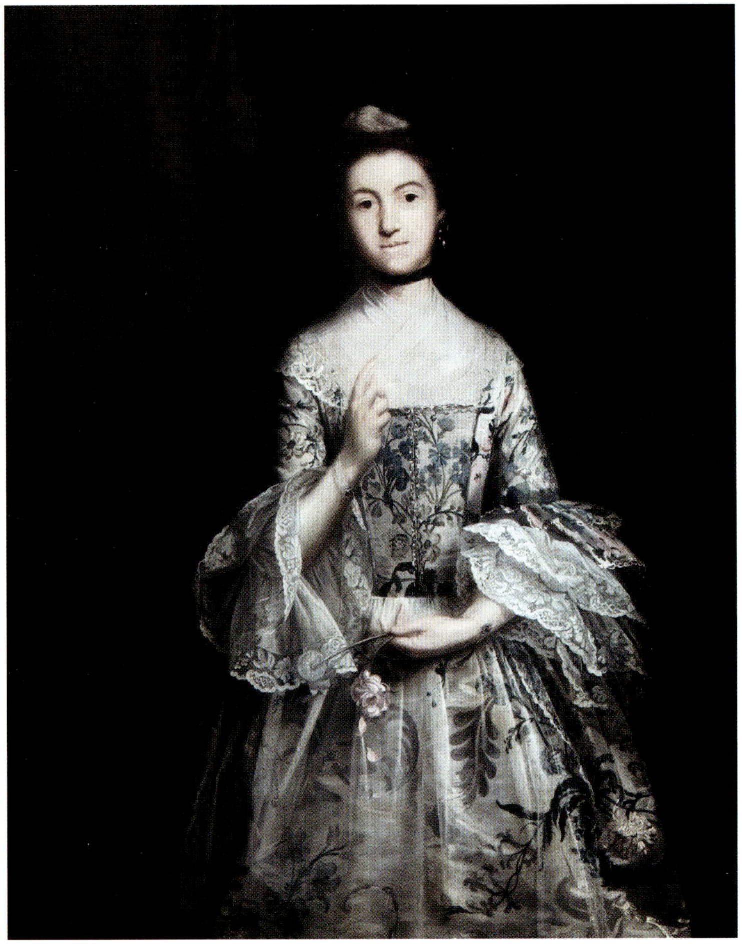

CAT. 16

Anne Molesworth

(1755)

oil on canvas, 128 x 102 cm

The Trustees of the Molesworth-St Aubyn Heritage Trust

PROVENANCE: By descent.

EXHIBITION HISTORY: 1937, 45 Park Lane, London, 'Sir Joshua Reynolds Loan Exhibition', no.41; 1947, Plymouth, 'Art Treasures in the West Country', no.28; 1951 Plymouth, 'Paintings by Sir Joshua Reynolds', no.9; 1970 Plymouth, no.39; 1973, Plymouth, 'Sir Joshua Reynolds', no.28.

LITERATURE: Leslie and Taylor, vol.1, p.145; Graves and Cronin vol.2, p.651; Waterhouse 1941, p.40; Waterhouse 1968, p.160; Mannings 2000, vol.1, no.1266.

THE MOLESWORTH FAMILY

SIR JOHN MOLESWORTH, 5TH BT (1729–75), was MP for Cornwall from 1765 and politically was an independent country gentleman. He rebuilt his house, Pencarrow, in the mid-1760s, perhaps using money from his second wife Barbara, daughter of Sir John Aubyn, 3rd Bt, of Clowance.[1] Their grandson succeeded to the St Aubyn estates and in 1839 changed the family's name to Molesworth-St Aubyn.

Pencarrow now holds six portraits by Reynolds.[2] Three are portraits of Sir John Molesworth painted in the 1750s and 1760s,[3] including a full-length portrait of 1762–63 showing Molesworth as colonel of the county militia, emphasising the landowner's traditional role of leadership within rural society.[4] Molesworth and his brother William (d.1762) married two sisters, Frances Smyth (d.1758) and Anne Smyth (d.1767); Reynolds's portrait of Sir John and of William and Anne (CAT. 15–17), commemorate their respective marriages in 1755 and 1756. Reynolds's portrait of William and Anne's daughter Frances, later Marchioness of Camden, is dated 1777.[5]

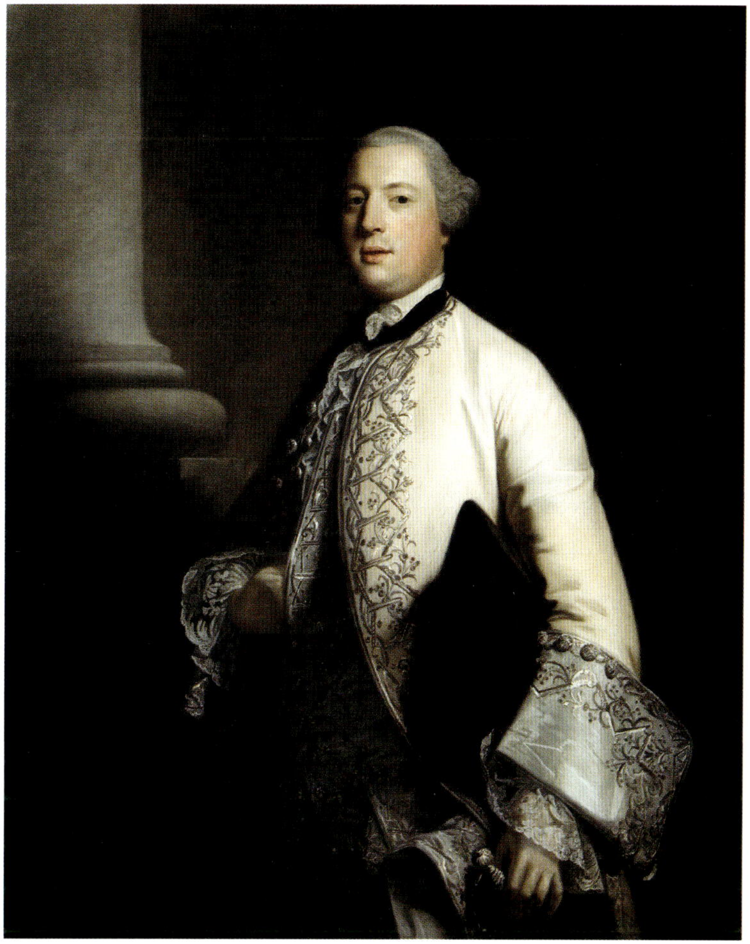

CAT. 17

Sir John Molesworth
(1755)
oil on canvas, 127 x 102 cm
The Trustees of the Molesworth-St Aubyn Heritage Trust

PROVENANCE: By descent.

EXHIBITION HISTORY: 1873 Royal Academy, London, 'Loan exhibition of Old Masters and deceased masters of the British School', no.119; 1951, Plymouth, 'Paintings by Sir Joshua Reynolds', no.8; 1973, Plymouth, 'Sir Joshua Reynolds', no.38.

LITERATURE: Graves and Cronin, vol.2, p.650; Waterhouse 1941, p.40; Mannings 2000, vol.1, no.1262.

CAT. 18

Reginald Pole
(c.1743–44)
oil on canvas,
76 x 63.5 cm

Trustees of the Carew Pole Family Trusts, Antony House, Cornwall

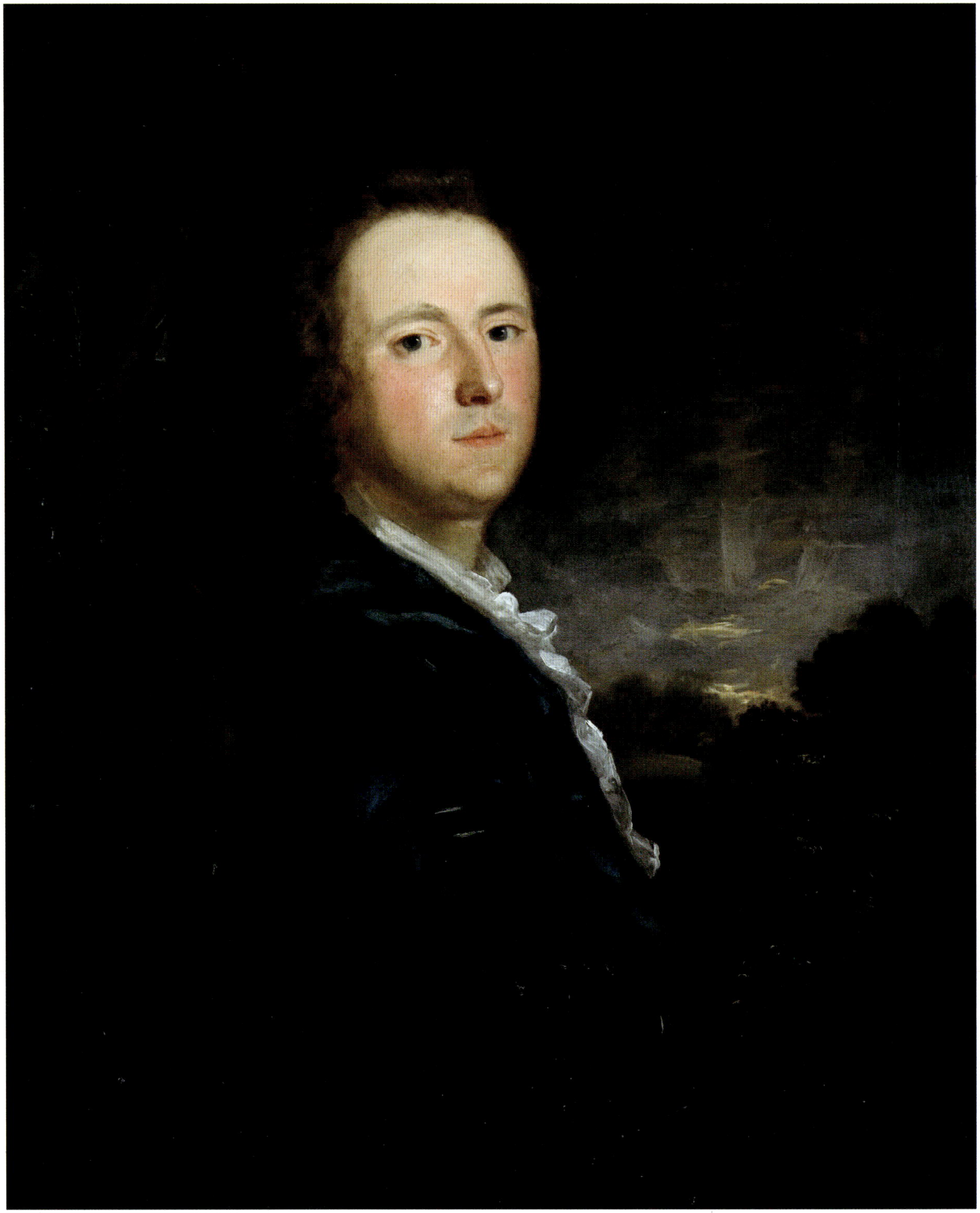

PROVENANCE: By descent.

EXHIBITION HISTORY: 1961, Birmingham, 'Exhibition of Works by Sir Joshua Reynolds', no.4a; 1973 Plymouth, 'Sir Joshua Reynolds', no.14.

LITERATURE: Waterhouse 1966–68, p.166; Mannings 2000, vol.1 no.1458.

THE POLE FAMILY

REGINALD POLE (1717–69) WAS THE son of Rev Carolus Pole (1686–1731), rector of St Breock in Cornwall, who was a younger son of Sir John Pole of Shute. Carolus died a genteel clergyman with few assets, but noted in his will that 'My brother Sir William Pole hath frequently declared and promised unto me that he intended and was fully resolved to settle all his lands and estate on my eldest son Reginald. I commit the guardianship of my said son unto my said brother.'[1]

Sir William, who died in 1741, raised Reginald Pole as a lawyer: he was 'of the Inner Temple' in 1743 and later had chambers in the Middle Temple.[2] Pole was close to the family of his mother, Sarah Rashleigh. He was living at the Rashleigh estate, Menibilly, in 1751, when he married Anne Buller, 'a most accomplished lady',[3] who died in 1758 at Stoke Damarel, where Reginald is recorded as a navy agent in the 1760s.[4]

In 1765 Pole became Recorder for the borough of Fowey, through the influence of the Rashleigh family; he succeeded his uncle, the London merchant Jonathan Rashleigh (1793–64),[5] whose son, the mineralogist and antiquary Philip Rashleigh (1729–1811), was Fowey MP from 1765. Philip Rashleigh was both Pole's cousin and brother-in-law, having married Jane Pole (b.1720).

Pole was connected to several other prominent West Country families: as well as his in-laws the Bullers of Morval, the Poles of Shute, and the Rashleighs; Humphrey Morice (1723–85) of Werrington was his cousin and executor. Pole was a friend of Reynolds's patron, Lord Edgcumbe, by the mid-1740s.[6] Furthermore, through his grandmother, Jane Carew, Reginald Pole's son inherited the Carew estate of Antony in 1771, and other estates in 1799 after the extinction of the Carew baronetcy; he became known as Reginald Pole-Carew (1753–1835). Pole bequeathed to him his 'family pictures [which] I desire and request may never be disposed of'; presumably these included the portrait by Reynolds exhibited here which, true to Pole's bequest, remains the property of his descendants at Antony.[7]

THE PARKER FAMILY

NO STATELY HOME IS MORE CLOSELY associated with Sir Joshua Reynolds than Saltram, the great Parker mansion west of Plympton. Samuel Reynolds and his friend John Cranch were the trusted acquaintances of George Parker (d.1743), the pious landowner from North Molton who bought the estate in 1712.[1] Parker's daughter-in-law, Lady Catherine Parker (1706–58), is said to have given the child Joshua his first pencil.[2] As an adult Reynolds became the very close friend of her son, John Parker [II] (c.1732–88), but their well-documented relationship has obscured Reynolds's much earlier dealings with the family. Over two generations, Saltram was transformed from an undistinguished Tudor mansion to one of Georgian England's grandest stately homes, an elevation paralleled in the Parker family's own social ascent, from country squires to fashionable metropolitan aristocrats. As their friend and adviser over five decades, Reynolds was a significant catalyst of the changing fortunes both of the Parkers themselves and of their magnificent house.

George Parker bought Saltram, but the first Parkers to live there appear to have been his son John [I] (1703–68) and Lady Catherine his wife, who was a daughter of John, 1st Earl Poulett, the Lord Lieutenant of Devon and a senior courtier under Queen Anne.[3] The couple's younger son, Montagu (1737–1813) was married in 1775 to Charity, daughter of the Plympton MP Paul Ourry, and settled at Whiteway, near Chudleigh. His elder brother John Parker [II] (c.1732–88) studied at Oxford, where he befriended Lord Shelburne, whose cousin Frances Hort c.1734–64) he married in 1764.[4] With Shelburne's help, in 1761 John Parker was elected MP for Bodmin, but he quickly resigned and sat instead as MP for Devon between 1762 and 1784, when he was created 1st Baron Boringdon. Parker's wife died shortly after their marriage, and in 1769 he was married again to the Empress of Austria's god-daughter, Therese Robinson (1744–75), a daughter of the Whig diplomat Thomas Robinson, 1st Baron Grantham (1695–1770) of Newby and Frances Worsley (1716–50) of Hovingham.[5] John and Therese Parker had one son, John [III] (1772–1840) and a daughter, Therese [II] (1775–1856).

In 1775 Parker was widowed for a second time, and thereafter Therese's sister Ann 'Nanny' Robinson (1742–after 1812) acted as a surrogate mother. Her brothers Frederick 'Fritz' Robinson (1746–92) and Thomas Robinson, 2nd Baron Grantham (1738–86) were also closely involved with life at Saltram and raising the two Parker children, although both lived in Spain for most of the 1770s. John Parker [III] became 2nd Baron Boringdon on his father's death in 1788 and was active in politics; he was created 1st Earl of Morley in 1815. His descendants retained Saltram until 1957, when the house and much of its contents became the property of the National Trust.

CAT. 19

John Parker
(?1770)
oil on canvas, 91.4 x 68.6 cm

Saltram, The Morley Collection (accepted in lieu of tax by H.M. Treasury, and transferred to the National Trust in 1957). ©NTPL/John Hammond

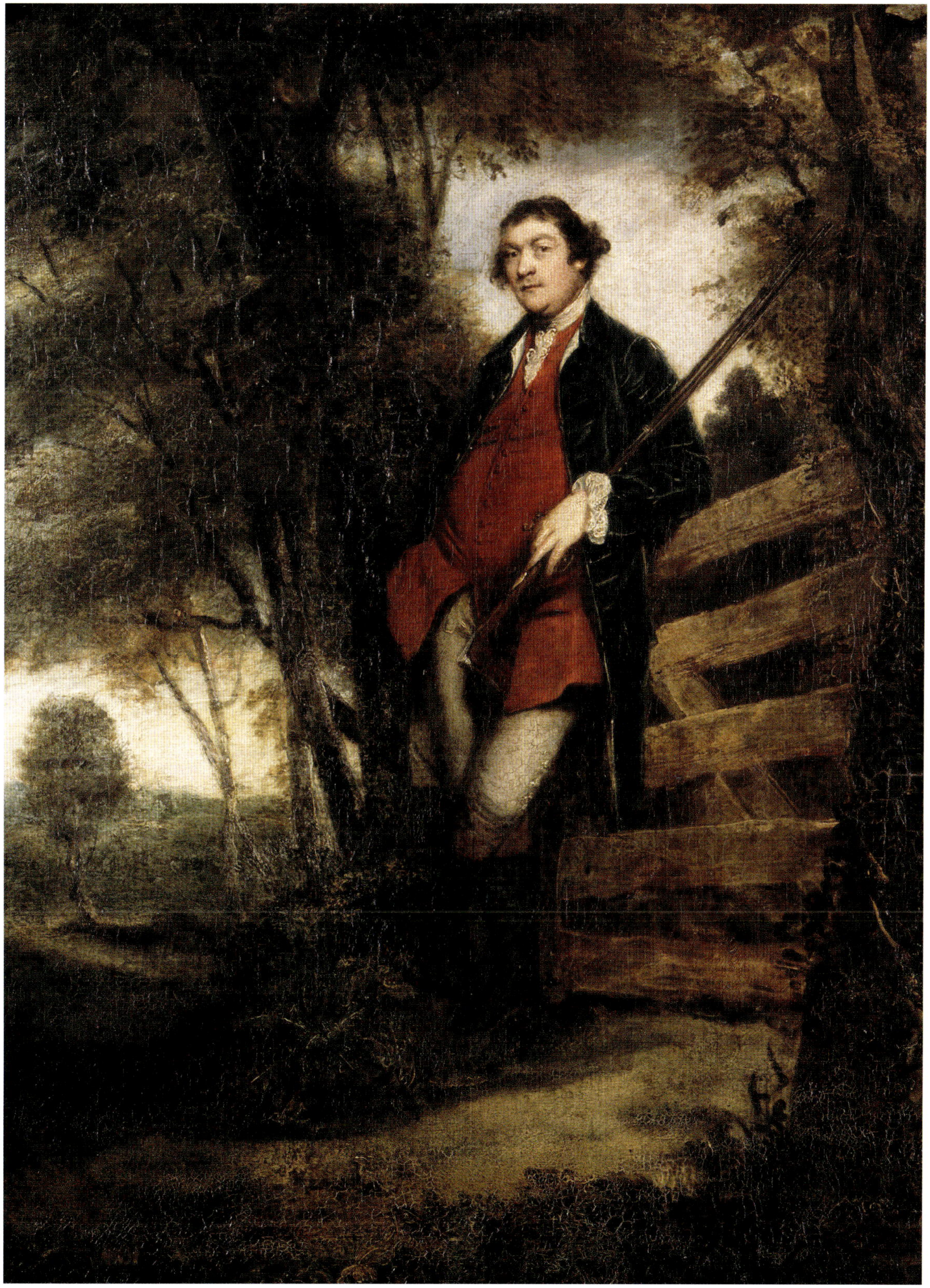

PROVENANCE: By descent to 4th Earl of Morley (1877–1951); acquired from his executors by the National Trust, 1957.

EXHIBITION HISTORY: 1813, British Institution, London, 'Pictures by the late Sir Joshua Reynolds', no.57; 1867, South Kensington, 'Second Special Exhibition of National Portraits', no.620; 1876, Royal Academy, London, 'Loan Exhibition of Old Masters and Deceased Masters of the British School', no.251; 1883, Grosvenor Gallery, London, 'Works of Sir Joshua Reynolds', no.16; 1932, Exeter, 'Loan Collection of Works by Early Devon Painters', no.235; 1937, 45 Park Lane, London, 'Sir Joshua Reynolds Loan Exhibition', no.48.

LITERATURE: Saltram 1819, p.28, no.124; Saltram 1844, p.19, no.79; Graves and Cronin, vol.2, pp.726–7; Waterhouse 1941, p.57; Neatby 1977, pp.24–5; Waterhouse 1985, p.274; Johnson 1998, pp.10, 45; Mannings 2000, vol.1, p.365, no.1394.

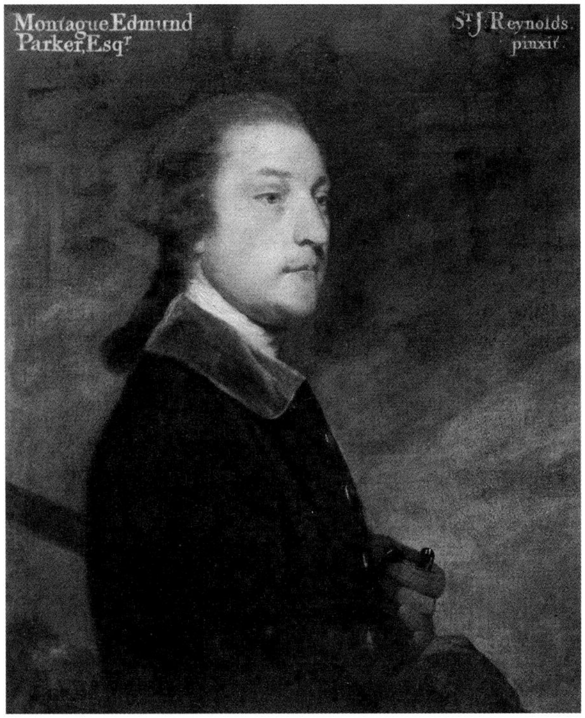

FIG. 7

Montagu Parker
(1768)
oil on canvas, 76 x 63.5 cm
Saltram, The Morley Collection (accepted in lieu of tax by H.M. Treasury, and transferred to the National Trust in 1957)

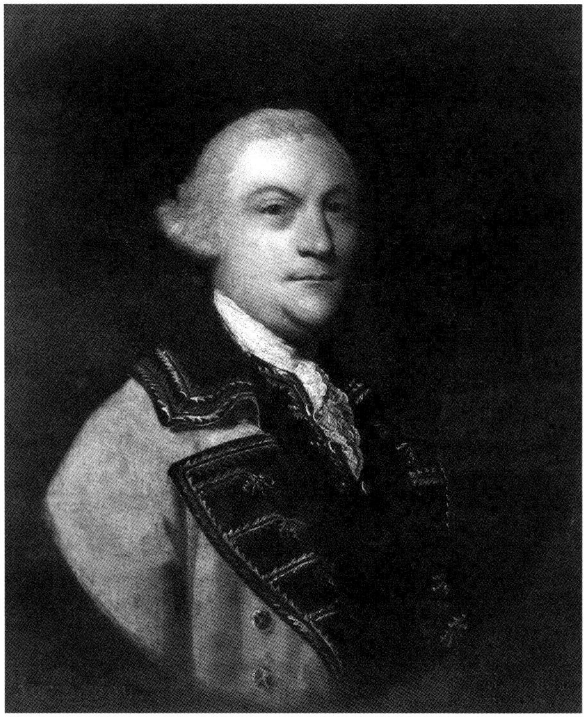

FIG. 8

John Parker
(1767)
oil on canvas, 76 x 63.5 cm
Saltram, The Morley Collection (accepted in lieu of tax by H.M. Treasury, and transferred to the National Trust in 1957)

JOHN AND LADY CATHERINE PARKER

If Lady Catherine Parker had given Reynolds art materials as a promising child, no doubt she had continued to follow his progress, and by the mid-1740s he was working at Saltram, where he painted Elizabeth Chudleigh, later Duchess of Kingston.[6] John Parker had inherited Saltram in 1743, just as Reynolds was establishing his portrait practice in Plymouth; over the ensuing decade the Tudor building was remodelled with a symmetrical Palladian exterior and many new rooms. The grounds, too, were transformed in the mid-century fashion. Lady Catherine Parker, rather than her husband, is credited with all this work. When King George III visited in 1789, he asked 'many questions abt. the building of the House, & Lady Catherine… her manner of getting the house built.'[7] The Parkers kept a London house in Conduit Street and Lady Catherine was familiar with eminent sculptors and painters there, including Hudson whose portrait of her is at Saltram.[8] As the daughter of a Lord Treasurer of England and the sister of a Lord of the Bedchamber and the Lord Lieutenant of Somerset, Lady Catherine had political connections.[9] From the small evidence that remains, these were centred around the court of Frederick, Prince of Wales (1707–51). Elizabeth Chudleigh was maid of honour to the Princess of Wales; Prince Edward, his favourite son, visited Saltram in 1759.[10] The Parkers must have known Frederick's informal art advisor, General Guise, whose portrait by Reynolds was at Saltram in 1785.[11]

There is little evidence of art collecting at Saltram at this period, and there are no portraits by Reynolds of either John or Lady Catherine Parker. Perhaps a payment of £210 from Parker to Richard Mead on 3 July 1746 relates to the acquisition of works of art from that eminent collector.[12] But the earliest detailed account of the collection, a 1819 tourist catalogue published by the family, states that 'a very considerable portion of the Collection, was purchased at Rome in 1750 or 1751' by Reynolds.[13] Other than a *Fruit Piece* by Michelangelo di Campidoglio (c.1610–70) this catalogue does not identify any of his acquisitions; no doubt several of the continental paintings of an uncertain attribution are among them.[14] Perhaps the 'Box from Dover' whose carriage John Parker paid for on 5 March 1753 contained items from the continent assembled by Reynolds, just as he had procured busts of classical figures for Mount Edgcumbe.[15] Reynolds's visit to Italy must have given Lady Catherine the chance to enlarge the collection, after war had starved the London art market of continental imports for almost a decade.[16] Although Ellis Waterhouse doubted that Reynolds could have helped the Parkers so early in his career, when he was 'very little qualified to advise on such matters,' the 1819 statement cannot be dismissed easily.[17] The catalogue was written with the knowledge of his grandson, John Parker [III]. It must have been based on the information screens displayed in Saltram's public rooms for the benefit of visitors, which were created in 1797 by Therese Parker [II], Nanny Robinson and Lady Elizabeth Moncke, and which were still in use in the 1820s.[18] Like John Parker [III], these authors had known Reynolds and Saltram for decades; Nanny had been living there since 1769. Waterhouse's question about Reynolds's suitability for the job, on the other hand, echoes the doubts raised during Reynolds's lifetime about his standards of connoisseurship.

Several Reynolds portraits once in the Parkers' collection date from the decade after his return from Italy in 1752, but when and how they came to Saltram is unclear; not one was commissioned by the family. The two paintings still at Saltram depict contemporaries of John Parker [II].[19] One is a portrait of his confidant Walter Radcliffe (1733–1803) of nearby Warleigh House, painted 'mainly' in 1757.[20] The other is here identified as a portrait of the Parkers' immediate neighbour, Thomas Harrison (d.1768) of Leigham Manor, just north of Saltram, which Mannings dated on stylistic grounds to 1763.[21] In both cases the paintings were commissioned by the sitters and were first recorded at Saltram in the 1819 catalogue.[22] Two other early portraits, no longer at Saltram, were painted for admirers of the women portrayed. *Kitty Fisher as Cleopatra* (c.1759), now at Kenwood, was at Saltram by 1813,[23] as was *Miss Fordyce* (1762), a portrait of Walter Radcliffe's girlfriend which is now at Waddesdon.[24]

The uncertainty about these portraits extends to the meetings with 'Mr Parker' that Reynolds noted in his pocket books up to 1768: did he mean the father or the son?[25] Reynolds presumably saw John Parker [I] when he visited Saltram with Samuel Johnson in 1762, but it is questionable whether the elder Parker continued to pay regular visits to London right up to his death in April 1768, and so long after the death of his inspirational wife. He wrote his will in 1762, in which the bequest of his stable was a prominent feature. A keen horseman like his sons, perhaps Parker [I] lived as a retired countryman in his final years. By contrast, 1762 was the year his son John Parker [II] became a young 'knight of the shire'; he was thereafter regularly in London on parliamentary business. Surely this is why 'Mr Parker' starts to appear in Reynolds's pocket books from the early 1760s onwards. Early in 1764 the younger Parker travelled to Italy, but his wife's death at Naples appears to have cut the trip short, and he arrived back in London on 7 November.[26] Mannings read Parker [II]'s absence from England in 1764 as evidence that Reynolds's meetings during that year must have been with the father; but in fact no meetings were scheduled during his son's time abroad, and Reynolds's 11 January 1765 note 'Pictures for Mr Parker' might well refer to continental purchases. Other such notes follow: 'Mr Parkers Picture' at the end of May 1765; 'Mr Parker's Copy' in a miscellaneous list at the end of the 1767 book; and 'Bill / £ / 120' written next to Parker's appointment with Reynolds on Saturday 16 January 1768.[27]

CAT. 20

John and Therese Parker
(1779)
oil on canvas
142.2 x 111.8 cm
Saltram, The Morley Collection (accepted in lieu of tax by H.M. Treasury, and transferred to the National Trust in 1957).

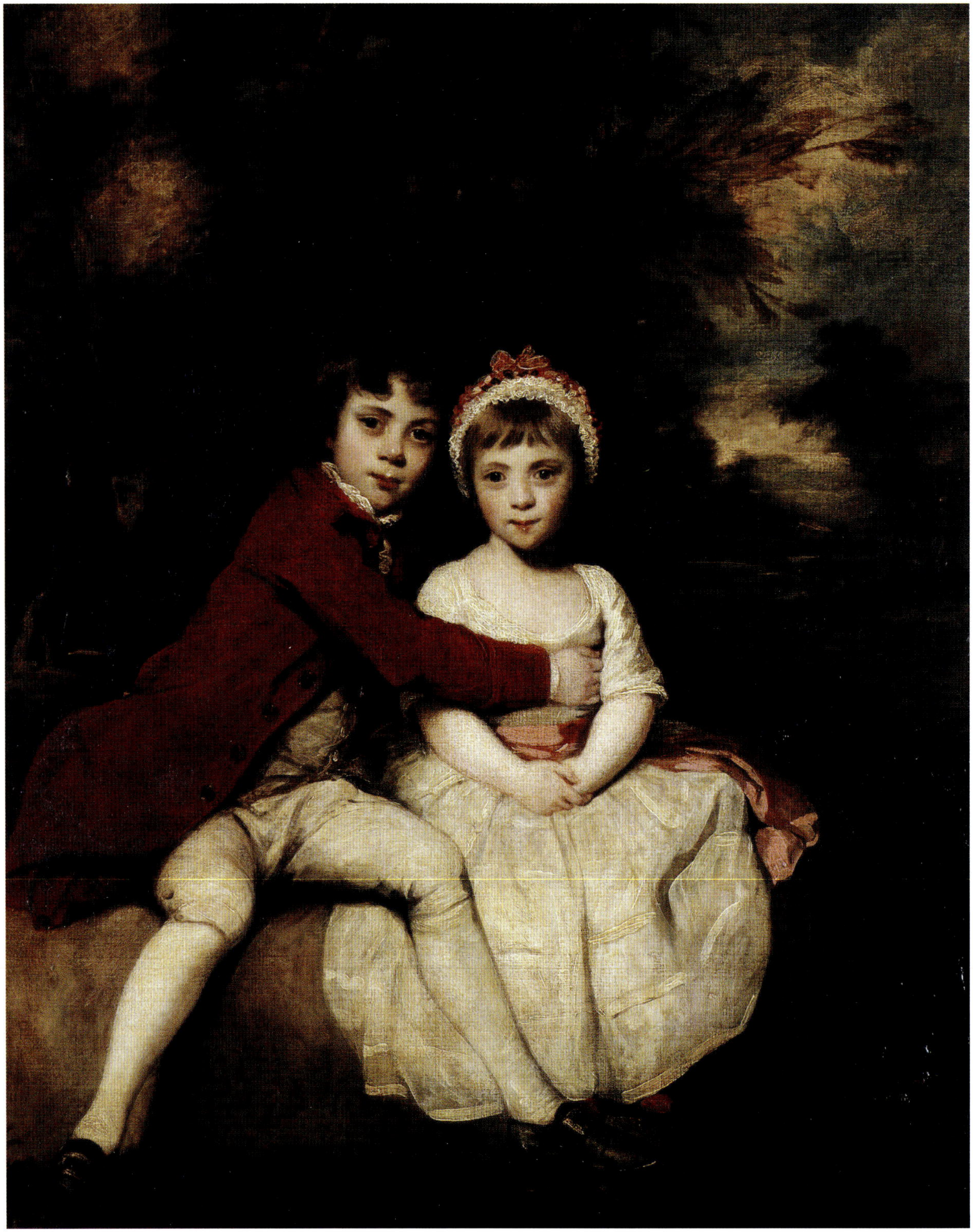

PROVENANCE: By descent to the 4th Earl of Morley (1877–1951); acquired from his executors by the National Trust, 1957.

EXHIBITION HISTORY: 1813, British Institution, London, 'Pictures by the late Sir Joshua Reynolds', no.45/122; 1867, South Kensington, 'Second Special Exhibition of National Portraits', no.787; 1876, Royal Academy, London, 'Loan Exhibition of Old Masters and Deceased Masters of the British School', no.24; 1883, Grosvenor Gallery, London, 'Works of Sir Joshua Reynolds', no.145; 1934, Royal Academy, London, 'Exhibition of British Art', no.268; 1937, 45 Park Lane, London, 'Sir Joshua Reynolds Loan Exhibition', no.31; 1951, Plymouth, 'Paintings by Sir Joshua Reynolds', no.48; 1960, Arts Council, 'Touring Exhibition', no.17; 1965, Agnew's, London, 'English Pictures 1730-1830', no.14; 1973, Brussels, 'Europalia', no.53; 1985, Paris, 'Sir Joshua Reynolds', no.54; 1986, Royal Academy, 'Reynolds', no.111.

LITERATURE: Saltram 1819, p.27, no.116; Saltram 1844, p.31 no.116; Leslie and Taylor, vol.2, p.224; Graves & Cronin, vol.2, pp.730-1; Waterhouse 1941, p.73; Neatby 1977, p.22; M Pointon, *Hanging the Head*, Yale 1993, pp.190–3; Johnson 1998, pp.9–10; Amal Asfour and Paul Williamson, *Gainsborough's Vision*, Liverpool 1999, pp.269–71; Mannings 2000, vol.1, pp.366–7, no.1398.

JOHN AND THERESE PARKER

What is beyond doubt is that Reynolds enjoyed a very close friendship with John Parker [II] in the years from 1768. In his son's words, Reynolds 'always had continued to live in habits of the greatest intimacy in my fathers family'.[28] Reynolds and Parker were from the same small town in Devon; their entry into high society was formalised at the same moment, in May 1769: Reynolds with a knighthood, Parker by marriage to Lord Grantham's daughter, Therese. With their blend of Plympton landowning wealth and Whig cosmopolitan taste-making, Reynolds found a truer home in the company of John and Therese Parker than within the often strained relationships of his actual, provincial middle-class family.

Reynolds's very frequent interactions with the Parkers are well documented in the artist's pocket books and Parker family letters.[29] For instance, he noted meetings on 3, 9, 10, 11, 14, 15, 18, 19, 29 and 30 April 1772;[30] and as many as 36 meetings are recorded in the first half of 1779, when Reynolds was working on *John and Therese Parker*. They met usually in London, either at Reynolds's house in Leicester Square or Parker's house a few hundred metres away in Sackville Street, off Piccadilly. But there were also outings to Reynolds's weekend home at Richmond-upon-Thames, and Reynolds made several visits to Saltram.

The Parker archive often enlivens the bare record of Reynolds's appointments diary. For example, Reynolds noted John Parker as his dining companion on 4 March 1771 (they also ate together on the two days following); Parker's account book adds that they visited the Star and Garter Inn on Bond Street, where Parker spent £2 9s 6d.[31] Reynolds met Parker on 24 March 1786; Parker's accounts show that he took Reynolds to the Devonshire Club.[32] Family correspondence also describes many dinners that the Parkers and other old West Country friends enjoyed with Reynolds; on a more intimate scale than the famous gatherings of literary and political men, these were like a family night in for the artist. On 9 March 1779, for example, Reynolds noted a 5pm meeting with Parker; a letter that Fritz Robinson wrote a few days later states that the dinner was 'at Sr. Joshua's with his two Nieces, my Sister, Mr Parker, Sr Charles Davies [Davers] & Mr Elliot. The Miss Palmers are both very pretty, though different. I like them both together as the little girl [Therese [II]] says when she is ask'd who she prefers. Mr Elliott is a good deal alter'd in his person, he is always very polite & very entertaining when in good Spirits, but more subject than ever to be otherwise.'[33] The Parker correspondence describes some twenty previously unrecorded meetings with Reynolds, such as a visit to his 'charming House upon Richmond Hill where I suppose Nanny told you we dined last Sunday & return'd in such a Storm' on 30 April 1775.[34]

Much of the minutiae of Reynolds's dealings with John Parker are preserved in the ledgers of Parker's two account books.[35] The most significant entries relate to a loan of £3,000 that Reynolds provided to Parker on 20 July 1777, secured on the latter's Sackville Street house.[36] Several other entries, perhaps the majority, are the results of late nights at the gaming table: on 7 April 1772 he paid Reynolds £31 10s for 'part of a bett'; on 10 March 1780, £10 was paid 'To Sir J.Reynolds lost at vignt[sic] & un':[37] on 11 June 1786 Parker lost 8gns 'To Sir Joshua at Cards'.[38] Occasionally Reynolds lost, too: Parker won £157 17s 6d from him on 5 February 1780.[39] There are tips to Reynolds's servants: a guinea to his coachman on 2 July 1777 and 20 November 1784, and another guinea to Ralph on 2 June 1787. On 1 April 1778 Parker paid £61 11s 'To Sir Joshua Reynolds for Champagne 13 ca[ses].' Only two paintings are mentioned by name, though perhaps the large round numbers – £50 on 26 June 1775, £150 on 16 July 1777 and another £50 on 12 June 1779 – were payments for portraits.[40] A few entries remain obscure.[41]

John Parker was a countryman whose spending on art was dwarfed by the cost of his stable and his best friends, Sir Thomas Acland and Sir John Chichester, were like-minded members of West Country gentry. Reynolds once invited Parker to the Literary Club, 'to dine with Dr. Johnson and the rest; but though a man of rank and also of good information, he seemed as much alarmed at the idea as if you had tried to force him into one of the cages at Exeter-'Change.'[42] In cultural matters, Parker appears to have been happy to place his trust in an expert, be it Reynolds, his cosmopolitan wife or her connoisseurial brother Lord Grantham, a friend of Reynolds in his own right. Anecdotal evidence suggests that Parker relied heavily on Reynolds's judgement on aesthetic matters. A dinner guest at Saltram c.1796 described its 'very choice and expensive collection of pictures, chiefly bought by Sir Joshua Reynolds; the old lord [ie 1st Lord Boringdon] employing him to go to any price, provided a bad picture did not come into the house.'[43] As the Parkers' constant friend and dinner companion during the 1770s Reynolds must have been privy to all of their collecting activities. This is certainly the impression given by Lord Grantham. When he wished to give a painting by Juan de Roelas (c.1560–1624) to Parker in 1778, he asked his brother Fritz to 'present it to Mr Parker but he need not put it up till Sr Joshua shall have seen it.'[44] Similarly, when a year later Grantham was sending over from Spain two just-finished copies after Murillo, he pointed out their 'freshness for the present, which will not deceive Sr Joshua.'[45] The Parkers bought portraits from other artists, but this only confirmed them in their faith in Reynolds. They spent one Saturday morning in 1779 on a tour of artists' studios, ending up at Reynolds's house in Leicester Square: 'We… wanted nothing more than the first coup d'oeil [of his paintings] to be convinced how he is at the head of his profession in this country.'[46]

'SIR JOSHUA WILL HAVE NONE BUT ORIGINAL PICTURES PUT UP'
Reynolds and the Saltram saloon

In all probability, *Walter Radcliffe* and *Thomas Harrison* were acquired by John Parker [II], but the first paintings by Reynolds that can be linked to him with certainty is a group of portraits of family and close friends, all remaining at Saltram, that he acquired in the late 1760s. His own portrait, in the costume of the Woburn hunt, bears a date of 1767 (FIG. 8, Mannings 1399, as a portrait of Montagu Parker) and was probably painted at sittings between March and June that year.[47] A portrait of Montagu Parker, also in hunting clothes, can be linked with sittings in May and June 1768 (FIG. 7, Mannings 1395, as a portrait of John Parker [II]).[48] Three other portraits depict Parker's closest friends; two, and perhaps the three, were gifts. The portrait of Sir Thomas Acland was a gift in or about 1768; in return Parker gave Acland his own portrait.[49] *Sir John Chichester* was painted in 1767 but the date of its acquisition is unknown.[50] At some point between 1767 and 1773 Parker's old university friend the Earl of Shelburne sent his portrait to Saltram.[51]

On inheriting Saltram in 1768, Parker discovered some £32,233 15s 2d secreted around the house and was very soon contemplating significant new works, commissioning designs from Robert Adam and making large payments to Reynolds, of £1,000 on 21 November and £398 on 5 December 1768.[52] These are surely linked with Reynolds's September 1768 shopping trip to Paris: Parker's meeting with the painter on 29 August was Reynolds's last appointment before setting off abroad; and, as well as the payments to Reynolds, on 3 December 1768 Parker transfered £389 16s 4d to the Paris bankers Messrs Panchaud, presumably the same 'Mr Panchaw' with whom Reynolds dined on his first full day in Paris.[53]

The new building work John Parker envisaged for Saltram was focused on the east range, and comprised a grand Saloon and a library to its north, with some minor redecoration elsewhere.[54] Adam's initial 1768 designs for the Saloon underwent some changes, and may even have remained unexecuted until Parker's marriage in May 1769 to Therese Robinson, who became a driving force behind the works at Saltram until her unexpected death in 1775. By September 1769 the rooms had made 'much progress' and were 'very forward'; Therese was asking her brother in London to inspect the paintings that Antonio Zucchi (1726–96) had completed for the library, and to send samples of damask wall hangings to help 'fix upon the best Blue for setting off the Pictures' in the Saloon.[55] When Reynolds came down to visit a year later, though, Saltram was still a building site:

> *The Great Room is ready for the Damask though the Windows are not put in, the Ceiling is the most beautifull I ever saw Sir Joshua will have*

CAT. 21

Therese Parker with her Son
(1770–75)
oil on canvas,
119.4 x 100.3 cm

Saltram, The Morley Collection (accepted in lieu of tax by H.M. Treasury, and transferred to the National Trust in 1957).
©NTPL

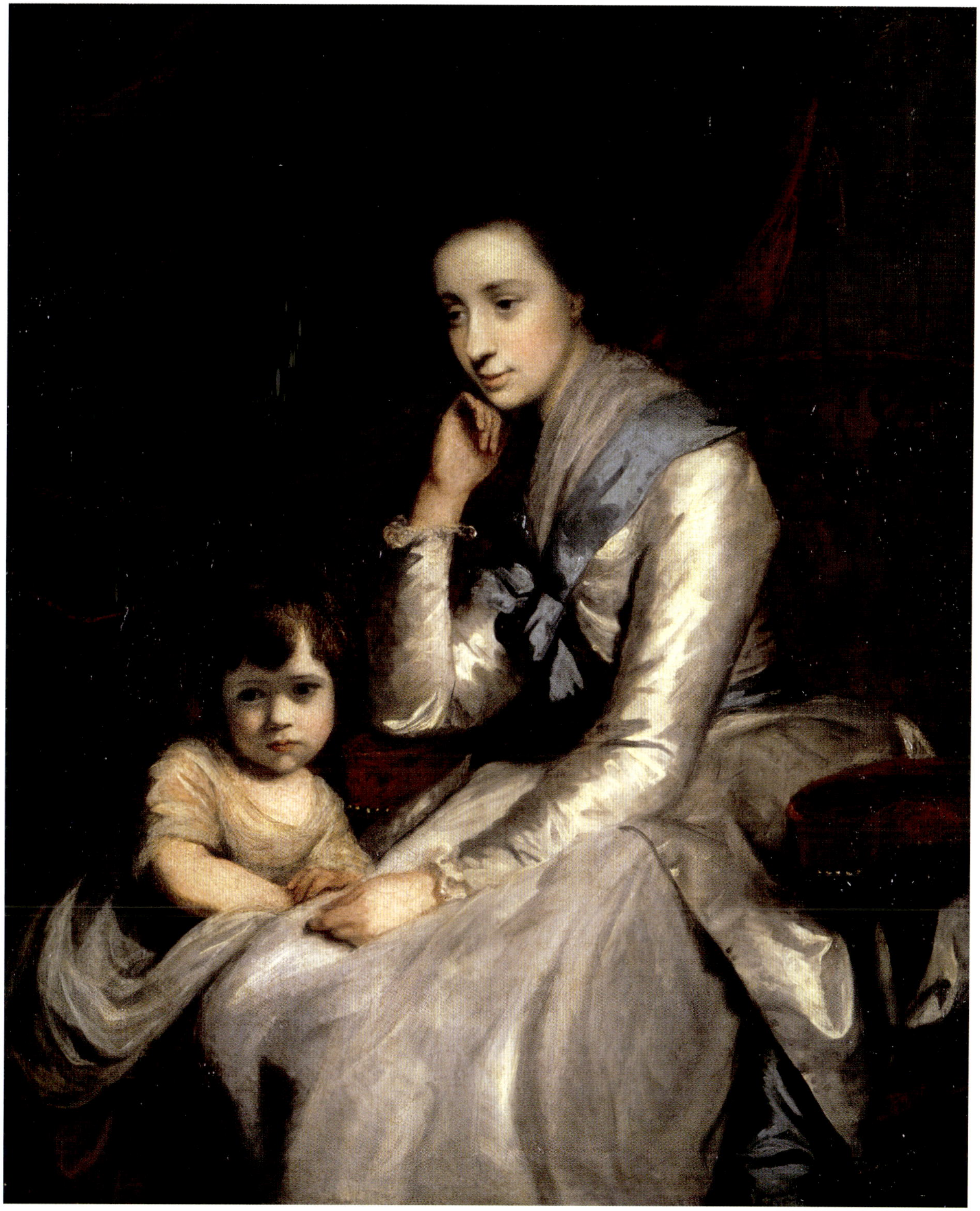

PROVENANCE: By descent to 4th Earl of Morley (1877–1951); acquired from his executors by the National Trust, 1957.

EXHIBITION HISTORY: 1878, Royal Academy, London, 'Loan Exhibition of Old Masters and Deceased Masters of the British School', no.79; 1883, Grosvenor Galleries, London,' Works of Sir Joshua Reynolds', no.163; 1905, Agnew's, London, no.10.

LITERATURE: Saltram 1819, p.28, no.123; Saltram 1844, p.31, no.119; Graves and Cronin, vol.2, pp.729–30; Waterhouse 1941, p.63, Neatby 1977, p.20; Johnson 1998, pp.9–10; Mannings 2000, vol.1 p.366, no.1397.

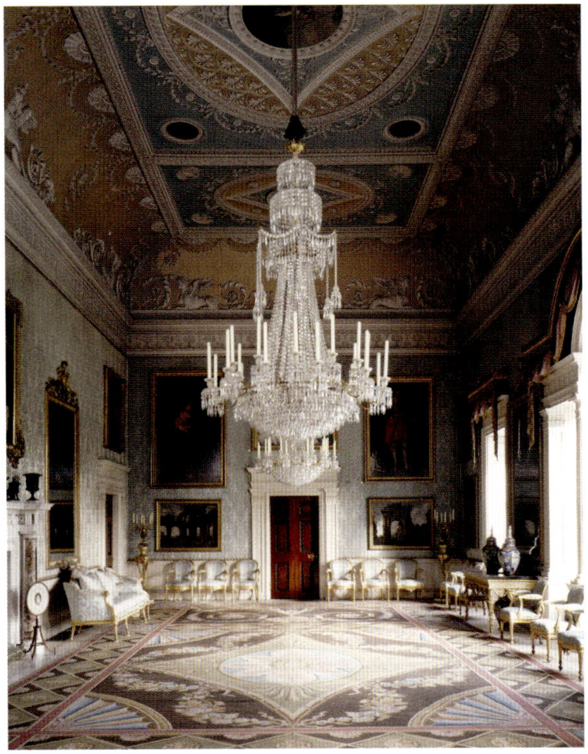

FIG. 9

The Saloon at Saltram
©NTPL/Andreas von Einsiedel

none but original pictures put up there he finds some exceeding good here. There is no describing the library, it is fitted up like a snuff box, they do not like it yet because of the noise of the workmen in the next room there are more books than I thought. Upstairs the rooms that are alterd are much improved. but their own apartment is not be known again. Theres's dressing room has a remarkable pretty colourd Green Paper & is hung with a great many drawings which Sr Joshua says are invaluable.[56]

During his visit to Saltram in September 1770, Reynolds met old friends and went hunting. But the business of the visit was to advise on the acquisition of showpiece paintings for the new Saloon, a project completed before Mrs Parker's death put a temporary stop to the collecting activities at Saltram. By spring 1770 Reynolds may already have begun work on his own contribution to the Saloon, a grand full-length portrait of Therese Parker, and during his visit he would have assessed *Sir Thomas Parker*, by Marcus Gheeraerts the Younger (1561–1635/6), whose partner it was intended to become.[57] Therese kept a close eye on the art market and Reynolds was also assisting the Parkers in their search for Old Master paintings for the room.[58] In May 1770 Reynolds had met Therese in London to discuss a Rubens.[59] Reynolds also supplied *A Virgin teaching St John* by 'Guercino',[60] and probably also the 'Baroccio' *Holy Family* which is framed as its pendant.[61] Parker's great trophy, the 'Titian' displayed over the Saloon fireplace in an elaborate Adam frame, was acquired from Reynolds, feasibly from the artist's Paris trip, as a version of the painting was sold by M de Merval at the same Paris sale from which Reynolds also acquired two landscapes by Claude Lorraine (c.1604–82) which he offered to Parker in 1771:[62] 'Mr. Parker in the Summer offer'd Sr. Joshua 800 for the two Claud Lorraines, but he would listen to nothing under 2000, he will not perhaps catch Mr. Parker again in the humour to offer even 800.'[63] By 1772, only one painting remained to be found, 'to match our Vandyke as to size & partly as to Subject.'[64] In 1773, Therese Parker visited both the Royal Academy and Society of Artists exhibitions: 'The Exhibitions are open'd bad in general. Sr Joshua shines his Comte Ugolino is charming tho' an unpleasant subject – It would match our Vandyke in every respect, but so many people have the refusal that we shall not get it.'[65] The Parkers were still searching in 1774 but eventually purchased a 'Veronese'.

Reynolds surely also advised his friend about two important groups of paintings that John Parker purchased in the years around 1770, and which formed a prominent part of the decorative schemes in the Saloon and the adjoining areas. Parker commissioned Angelica Kauffman (1741–1807) to paint the four large paintings of classical history and purchased two large paintings of Anglo-Saxon history. When she moved to London from Italy in 1766, Parker and Reynolds were soon both Kauffman's close friends;[66] indeed, J.T. Smith noted that another artist had 'for a long time flirted with Angelica Kauffman; but he found at last that that lady's glances were directed towards Sir Joshua Reynolds and Mr Parker.'[67] Parker had already sat to Kauffman in Rome, and now she and Reynolds sat to each other; Parker acquired her highly informal portrait of Reynolds, dated 1767, which he perhaps envisaged as forming part of the group of his close friends' portraits by Reynolds that was taking shape around the same time (FIG. 17, p. 85).[68] In addition to Kauffman's two portraits, which remain at Saltram, Parker continued to employ her throughout the 1770s; he acquired at least 15 paintings in total, and bought nine volumes of prints and one of drawings.

Collecting abated after Therese Parker's death at the end of 1775, but by early 1778 Parker was acquiring again, asking Lord Grantham to look out for two Murillos in Spain.[69] Damage from a fire at Saltram in November 1778 also obliged Parker to reorganise the service area, dining room and library, and in 1779 Robert Adam produced a plan for major alterations to the ground floor, which were not executed.[70] Parker commissioned several portraits of his children, including in 1779 Reynolds's *John and Therese Parker* (CAT. 20), and a group of family portraits drawn by John Downman (1750–1824), and dated 1780. A few paintings, acquired after Mrs Parker's death, can be linked to Reynolds. The 35gns payment that became due in July 1776 when Reynolds sent *Sir Charles Davers* to Saltram was surely, though, a commission that predated her death (Mannings 482a).[71] By tradition, the *Fall of Phaeton* (1777) by George Stubbs (1724–1806), which was at Saltram by 1803, came via Reynolds, though Parker had significant dealings of his own with the horse painter, as he paid him £200 on 15 November 1769 and £1,050 on 6 February 1781.[72] Reynolds is said to have received the picture in a swap with Stubbs, exchanging another example of the artist's work that had long been in his collection. On 2 June 1787 Parker bought 'a picture of a Grapes [sic]' from Reynolds, costing £10.[73] When in 1784 Parker wished to make a group of portraits of friends and family, Reynolds recommended that he ask Gilbert Stuart (1755–1828), who had himself just painted Reynolds (National Gallery of Art, Washington).[74] In 1787 Reynolds himself received a final commission from Parker (by now Lord Boringdon) to paint his daughter Therese, now at the Huntington Library in California.

Parker also picked up paintings locally in Devon. Here, too, Reynolds's influence was felt: Parker bought two portraits from Anthony de Poggi (exh. RA 1776–1781), a Corsican painter friendly with Reynolds, under whose patronage Poggi had set himself up in Plymouth in the early 1770s as a painter and drawing master.[75] The naval base at Plymouth and the country estates in its vicinity attracted landscape painters, among whom three were employed by John Parker. William Tomkins (c.1732–92) was frequently employed, not only as a painter but picture restorer and errand runner.[76] There are seven of Tomkins's paintings at Saltram from the 1770s; another pair was in Sackville Street.[77] These last two Parker gave to Nanny Robinson, and the view of Plympton by Tomkins that Reynolds owned (untraced) may well have been a gift from Parker.[78] Probably around 1784 John Parker ordered the two views at Crabtree attributed to Edmund Garvey (1740–1813) which are now at Saltram.[79] Garvey lived at Bath during the 1770s and knew the West Country well; among several Devon landscapes, he exhibited three views of Saltram at the 1798 RA. William Payne (1760–1830), who worked at the Plymouth dockyard, was employed at Saltram in the late 1780s, during his transition from Plymouth drawing master to fashionable London watercolourist.[80] Payne made a series of views for Parker in 1788, and sold drawings to other members of the family. Between 1788 and 1790 he was drawing master to Therese Parker.

'SR JOSHUA WILL NOT EASILY QUIT THIS PLACE & COUNTRY'

Reynolds's visits to Devon

Reynolds's visit to Devon in 1762 is well-known from James Boswell's anecdotes of Samuel Johnson, who accompanied the artist.[81] Reynolds's pocket book provides a detailed itinerary, which was surely influenced by Johnson and his down-to-earth 'country' values. For, in contrast to later visits, Reynolds made an extensive tour of old friends among Plymouth's middling gentry, and it appears that Reynolds and Johnson were not house guests at Saltram or Mount Edgcumbe, but instead stayed with Dr John Mudge (whom Reynolds met at the start and conclusion of the 1762 visit). Reynolds and Johnson were in Exeter on Monday 23 August and set out for Torrington the following day. Reynolds met his brother-in-law Johnson on Wednesday and Palmer on Thursday. On Friday 27 August he met Mr Morrison before travelling south to Plymouth on Saturday, via Okehampton. The next four weeks were spent in and around Plymouth. During the week commencing 30 August Reynolds noted: Mount Edgcumbe (30 Aug), Mr Mudge and Sir Nicholas Yard[? Ward?] (31 Aug), Mr Loyd (1 Sept), Mr Veal at Cofflet [sic] (2 Sept), Mr Bastard (3 Sept), Mr Veal at Cofflet (4 Sept), and 'Dr Vin[cent?]' (5 Sept). There are a few illegible notes in the account column, possibly including 'thos rennell'. During the week of 6 September 1762 Reynolds met Mr Manglis[?] (6 Sept), Mr Robinson (7 Sept), visited the Edystone [with 'Mr Redstone' crossed out] (8 Sept), Mr Redstone (9 Sept), Mr Heren (10 Sept), Mr Foot (11 Sept), and Mr Woolcomb (12 Sept). The following week Reynolds met Dr Blacket (13 Sept), visited Mount Edgcumbe (14 Sept, with 'Mr Proby' in the accounts list for that date), Miss How (15 Sept), Mr Dodge (16 Sept), and Mr Parker (17 and 18 Sept). His final appointments were with 'Mr Mangles & find at Mr Lay[?]' (20 Sept) and Mr Mudge (21 Sept, over crossed out 'Mr Mangles & sup at Mr Loyd's). He was at Plympton on 22 September, Exeter the next day, and arrived in London on Sunday 25 September.[82]

Reynolds's first lengthy stay at Saltram was in 1770. His movements are again known from his pocket book, and he features frequently in letters written by John Parker's brother-in-law, Fritz Robinson, who was also staying at Saltram.[83] Having arrived 'at about noon' on Monday 10 September, Reynolds looked over the house, pronouncing on the paintings and drawings. In the evening 'it was not a great addition to the pleasure we were enjoying' that Parker's cousins, the Bastards, were to dine at Saltram; during a walk to the Amphitheatre after dinner, the party were saluted by John Parker's cannons.[84] The following day Reynolds and the Parkers were out hunting; 'we had not much sport, but I liked it very well' wrote Fritz. On Wednesday, Reynolds and Fritz dined at Mount Edgcumbe at 3 o'clock, after riding to Plym bridge. Thursday was spent hunting again: 'the Ladys staid with us till we found a hare which afforded us good sport, but I expect better from a fox which we are soon to turn out… There never was so chearfull agreable simple a man as Sr Joshua. We have had charming weather till to day which is bad indeed, but I hope the fine will return as we have not yet been on the water or at Burrington [Boringdon].'[85] Reynolds noted 'Partridge Shooting' for the Friday, and it was perhaps then that John Parker bet 'Sir Joshua five guineas, that he does not beat Mr. Robinson – and ten guineas, that Mr. Montagu does not beat Mr. Parker, to shoot with Mr. Treby's bullet gun at 100 yards distance: and a sheet of paper to be put up, and the person who shoots nearest the centre wins.'[86] Fritz records how the following day, Saturday 15 September, passed: 'we were out hunting in the morning Mr Bastard dined here & as usual dawdled till it was too dark to return home, he engaged us to dine at Kitley on Wednesday.' On Sunday morning Reynolds accompanied the family to church. They 'drove afterwards to Burrington. Mr P & Sr Joshua & Mr Montague & I in Phaetons the Ladys in a Post…

Sr Joshua goes for a few days to morrow & we really do not know how to spare him.'[87] Reynolds noted in the pocket book that he travelled to Torrington on Monday 17 September and returned to Saltram on Thursday. Fritz explains that: 'he is gone to Torrington to see a Sister who has just lost her husband'.[88] Friday was spent hunting again and the following day, Saturday 22 September, was 'the Mayors day' at Plympton, where 'Sr Joshua dined… as a freeman of the Borough… [he] goes about to all the old weeding women & asks if they remember his Father & if he stays long he will be ruind in sixpences to them & their children.'[89] The visit to Kitley, put off because of Reynolds's absence in Torrington, was to take place in the coming week. Fritz wrote to his brother: 'Sr Joshua will not easily quit this place & country so you will not have his account of us which I hear you bespoke as soon as he should return before we are arrived [back in London].'[90] Reynolds's pocket book is blank between 23 September and his 5 October meeting with Mr Mudge. During that time he remained at Saltram; Fritz described some of their activities in a letter dated Friday 28 September: 'Mr Elliot Mrs & Miss Bonfoy came here last night in their way from London to Port Elliot they think the place as indeed every body must much improved… Sr Joshua is gone to day to Mount Edgecumbe & meets me to morrow at Dock where we are to see every thing & dine with a Mr Loyd.'[91] The pocket book records that on 6 October Reynolds finally went for a boat ride, on the *Laira*, the day before leaving Saltram. As he prepared to go, Parker paid him £24 3s, probably in settlement of that month's card-playing debts.[92]

Although he catalogued it as a work of the later 1760s, Ellis Waterhouse wondered whether Reynolds had painted *John Parker* (Mannings 1394), on loan here from Saltram, during his visit in 1770. There is much in this suggestion: its small full-length format does not fit easily into the conventional portrait types which formed the basis of Reynolds's London studio practice, and this invites some other explanation of how it came to be painted. Fritz's letters indicate that it was a holiday spent very much on John Parker's terms. Both Reynolds and Fritz Robinson were creatures of the city, neither experienced in country sports. Reynolds had even gone to church, something he never did in London. As Robinson's brother, Lord Grantham, put it: 'I hope Sr. Joshua does justice to his native Country. I suppose Mr Parker makes him do just what he pleases.'[93] Especially given the presence at Saltram of the good-humoured portrait of Reynolds by Kauffmann, it is easy to see *John Parker* as Reynolds's reply in kind to the hunting holiday Parker had taken him on; an affectionate account of Parker in all his country sports element.[94] It was clearly a holiday much enjoyed by all. Grantham, back in London, wrote good-naturedly to Fritz: 'I am almost jealous of Sr Joshua – You give yourself great Airs about hunting.' In fact, it may be that Grantham was aware that Reynolds was painting Parker in his country glory, for he added: 'I hope Sr Joshua has offerd to paint all our Pictures your's with Coke & Blakstone, Nanny like Miss – mourning her Bird, Therese with a bust of Stockman, & me with my base.'[95]

The Parkers invited Reynolds to visit them at Saltram in 1772 but, as Therese wrote to her brother: 'I dont know whether we shall be able to persuade him to come into Devonsr. this year. tho' he has been rather active in promoting a scheme of Mr. Eliots & Footes which I fear will take place, Mr. Footes proposes having a sort of Jubilee at Truro in Cornwall the place of his Birth, which he is to make out as well as he can for a week, by different amusements, I said I was afraid it would take place because I am afraid we must go there & I dont see how it is possible to make such a thing answer at that distance from London.'[96] The following year, though, Reynolds served as Mayor of Plympton and travelled to Devon to be sworn in. As the Parkers were staying at Bath because of John Parker's ill health, Reynolds met him there on 13 September, before setting out for Devon some days later.[97] Fritz wrote: 'I think the Parkers will be a great while absent from Saltram, we had a letter from Therese at Bath… I imagine she will be sorry not to have been at home whilst Sr Joshua was at Plympton.'[98] Reynolds's pocket book records that he left London on 11 September and was back there on 11 October. After his brief excursion to Bath, Reynolds dined at Plympton Guildhall on 14 September, and the following day with Lord Shelburne, when he also met 'Henderson'. On

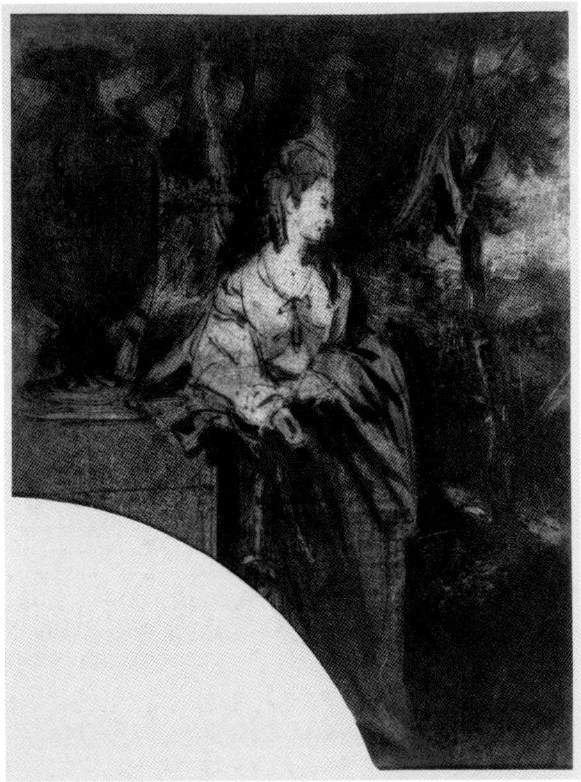

FIG. 10

Oil sketch for portrait of Therese Parker
(early 1770s)
oil on card, 14.5 x 11.5 cm
Saltram, The Morley Collection (accepted in lieu of tax by H.M. Treasury, and transferred to the National Trust in 1957)

16 September Reynolds returned to Bath, having visited Mount Edgcumbe in the morning; he dined at Escot on 17 and 18 September. Reynolds was back in Plympton on 22 September, and remained there until 5 October, when he set out for Torrington to visit his family.[99] During the Plympton fortnight he visited Mount Edgcumbe (24, 28 and 30 September), Thomas Mudge (25 September), Paul Ourry (27 September), Port Eliot (29 September), 'Dr Farr [?]' (1 October) and 'Mr Bastard' (2 October).[100]

Reynolds visited Devon in 1780 and appears to have used Saltram as his base, at any rate until going to Port Eliot on 15 September. For, although his pocket book notes only that he dined at Saltram with General Grey on 4 September and spent the following day there, a letter from Nanny Robinson on 12 September confirms that: 'Sir Joshua is with us at present, He is in High Glory today having gone to Plympton to choose Lord Cranbourn and Sir Ralph Payne for that Borough – but what he pleased himself most with the thoughts of was the walking there that he might look into every Orchard and field that he remembered at school he is in great Spirits & I never saw him better, he has touched up all the Ghosts in the Eating Room & has improved them very much.'[101] Reynolds left Exeter on Friday 31 August and spent the weekend with Lord Dunning, at [?] Ashburton. He was at Port Eliot on Monday 3 September, before arriving at Saltram. His pocket book records few other details of the trip: visits to Mount Edgcumbe on 14 September and to General Haviland on 13, 18 and 19 September ('Mrs Hale [?]' is also noted on this last date). By 20 September he was in Exeter, on his way back to London, which he reached on 22 September.

There is no pocket book for 1783, and details of Reynolds's trip to Devon that year are few; probably the visit was connected with his niece Mary Palmer's engagement to Edward Eliot. Lord Grantham wrote to his brother on 5 September that 'I called on Sr Joshua this morning – he sets out tomorrow for ye West,'[102] though his arrival at Saltram on 13 September, accompanied by Edmund Burke (1729–97) and his family, was not anticipated by Nanny Robinson: 'we were much surprised by a visit yesterday from Mr & Mrs Burch [sic] and

Sir Joshua whom we thought was at Bevoir.'[103] On 18 September Reynolds wrote from Saltram to his niece Offy, who was staying at Port Eliot, that he was 'very much mortified that I could not stay at Port-Elliot till your arrival which I hear will be on Saturday but it would disarange all our schemes' for him to travel there, as Burke 'wishes to get to Town [London] as soon as possible, I have full as great a desire to be there, [ie Port Eliot, but] if I was to quit Mr. Burke I should have no excuse left for not visiting all my friends which would take up at least a fortnight longer.'[104] Although he considered visiting Cornwall the following year, this was to be Reynolds's last visit to Devon.[105] It is fitting, then, that Reynolds's final comment in the county finds him scheming to escape from dutiful visits to old friends and family, and instead return to his beloved metropolis.

'ONE OF THE GREATEST WONDERS OF OUR ENGLISH RAPHAEL'
Reynolds's portrait of Therese Parker

Reynolds's most imposing contribution to Saltram is the full-length portrait, *Therese Parker*, in the Saloon. Reynolds's oil sketch for the portrait was at Saltram until the 1960s (FIG. 10).[106] Hanging beside two would-be ancestral portraits, *Sir Thomas Parker* and Van Dyck's *The Bolinbroke Family*, the painting is foremost a statement of Therese Parker's inclusion within the ancient Parker lineage.[107] Evidently assembling these grand family portraits was a matter of some urgency for the Parkers. In October 1772 Therese chided Reynolds for the delay in having the full-length sent to Devon: 'My Picture is not actually at Saltram Sr. Joshua is very lazy.'[108] Earlier in the year she had sat for the portrait even while heavily pregnant with her son, John, who was born in May 1772. Reynolds himself admitted that 'she is at a point of time when Ladies dont look at the best'[109] but, as Therese herself explained to her brother: 'Sir. Thos. Parker wants a companion so much in the great Room at Saltram, that it could not be delayed another year.'[110] The urgency is understandable, as the paucity of inherited family portraits at Saltram sat uncomfortably with the family's rising social rank and the grandeur of the Saloon. Saltram had itself been Parker property for only half a century, and neither of the two other family portraits were heirlooms. The *Bolinbroke Family*, which reputedly depicted John Parker's Poulett ancestors, was a gift from his aunt, Ann Poulett, who appears to have bought it on the London market. The provenance of *Sir Thomas Parker* is unknown, but it depicts the ancestor of a different Parker family so was surely also an acquisition.

As well as the full-length, Reynolds painted a half-length portrait of Therese Parker (CAT. 21). In both pictures Therese Parker is shown in contemplative poses, a theme that accorded with the sitter's own interests, for in 1773 she described 'another figure of Contemplation' that the gem engraver Edward Burch RA (1730–1814) had cut for her.[111] Therese and her siblings judged the full-length pose, in which Therese was painted 'feeling my Pulse', successful and lifelike.[112] By contrast, Nanny wrote in June 1772 that the half-length portrait was not a good resemblance, and 'looks melancholy and sick'.[113] Reynolds had by then abandoned work on the painting, which was not completed until two years after the full-length. As Therese described in 1775, because Reynolds did 'not think [it] worthy of a place in the Exhibition [it] lay by & stood no chance of being finished.'[114] Clearly the half-length was quite far advanced by the time that Lord Grantham left England for Spain in May 1771, as Therese wrote to him two years later that it 'remains just as you left it, only in bright yellow, which he [Reynolds] is very fond of at present, but I do not approve of.'[115] Probably, then, at least some of the 1770 sittings that Mannings associates with the full-length were for the smaller portrait. Therese's sittings in February and March 1772 were certainly for the larger painting, as on 2 April she wrote to her brother that 'Sr. Thos. Parkers Companion has done setting & is universally allow'd to be very like.'[116] With the full-length complete and ready for exhibition at the Royal Academy, in March 1773 Therese's thoughts returned to the unfinished portrait: 'I have some thoughts (that is) Mr. Parker talks of having the little Boy put into the half length at Sir Joshuas.'[117] As she recalled in 1775, though, the baby 'made such faces it was impossible to do any thing, however this year he [Reynolds] has consented to put him in, & tho' he sat but an hour you would be astonish'd to see how strong a likeness it is, he has caught the Character of the Child so exactly that I am quite delighted with it.'[118] Parker paid Reynolds 50 guineas for the half-length portrait in about July 1779.[119]

'THE PRINT, THE PRINT!'
Thomas Watson's mezzotint of Therese Parker

Reynolds's grand paintings were scrutinised by the London art public during the Royal Academy exhibition, but they remained highly personal artefacts for the sitter's loved ones and could help to sustain relationships between distant family members. In 1773, Lord Grantham lobbied hard to have an engraving made of Reynolds's portrait and sent to him in Spain.[120] Therese commissioned a mezzotint from Thomas Watson, and bought 50 impressions from him, which were used as gifts to family, friends and John Parker's constituents among the Devon gentry.[121] The Parkers sent one to Grantham as a surprise and involved Reynolds in the plan, but Grantham found out about it by accident: 'The Cat is out of ye bag, for Mr Draper in reckoning up the things that are coming for me, mentions two Prints of Mrs Parker, which it seems Fritz knew of from Waddilove, but kept a Secret from me. We are very impatient for the Cargo. & suspect that Sr Joshua's Letter which comes with his Speech by ye same occasion was kept back on purpose, to prevent our knowing any thing of the Print, which he most probably mentions.'[122] When it finally arrived, in December 1773, Grantham was ecstatic: 'The Print, the Print! – at last is arrived, & has paid our Impatience by it's beauty, & it's likeness. It is indeed a very fine & gracefull Figure, the Countenance very sweet & compose'd rather however too grave; the Attitude of the hands natural to her, the Hair admirable, being in a great style, yet exact; in short it gave us compleat Satisfaction.'[123] Grantham showed the print around the Spanish court, where it was admired not only as a work of art but for its engraving technique: 'Your Print is most universally admired, – let it not take

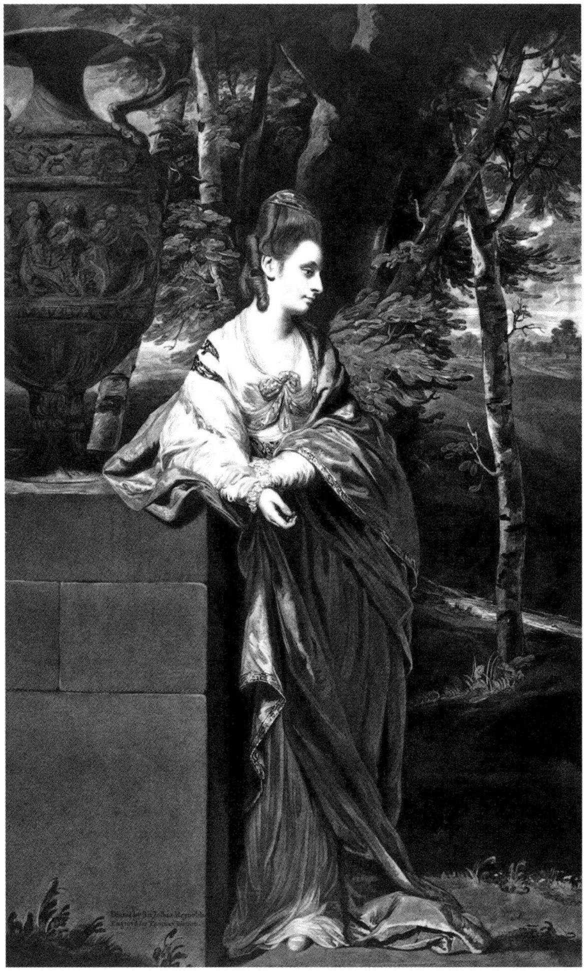

FIG. 11

Thomas Watson
(1792–1882)
after Joshua Reynolds
Therese Parker
(1773)
mezzotint, 61.5 x 38 cm
Plymouth City Museum and Art Gallery: Cottonian Collection

from its incomparable merit, to say that the People here are not Connoisseurs On the Contrary it proves the real merit of it, that it makes such an Impression; & the manner of Engraving or Mezzotinto is scarcely known here – so that a great deal of surprize is expressed at it. Indeed I am dailiy more and more pleased with it.'[124]

'AN END TO THE LIFE OF ONE OF THE MOST VALUABLE OF WOMEN'
Reynolds's obituary of Therese Parker

Therese Parker died unexpectedly in December 1775, shortly after the birth of her daughter Therese. Reynolds offered a distraught John Parker the use of his Richmond weekend house as a place of convalescence, and memorialised Therese in a tribute published in the London press:

> *...one of the most valuable of Women. Her amiable Disposition, her Softness and Gentleness of Manners endeared her to every Person that had the Happiness of knowing her. Her whole Pleasure and Ambition seemed to be centred in a Consciousness of properly discharging all the duties of a Wife, a Mother, and a Sister, and she neither sought for nor expected Fame out of her own House. As she made no Ostentation of her Virtues, she excited no Envy; but if there had existed a Being of so black and malignant a Disposition as to wish to wound so fair an Object, it must have searched in vain for a weak Part wherein to inflict its Venom. Her Virtues were habitual, uniform and quiet. They were not occasionally put on; she wore them continually; they seemed to grow to her and be a Part of herself; and it seemed to be impossible for her to lay them aside, or be other than what she was. In so exalted a Character it seems to be scarce worth mentioning her Skill and exact Judgement in the polite Arts. She seemed to possess, by a kind of Intuition, that Propriety of Taste and right Thinking which others but imperfectly acquire by long Labour and Application.*[125]

The obituary provided a focus for the grief of friends and family. Therese's close friend Lady Pelham 'read it over and over and shed many a tear over it';[126] Therese's son, who was only three when she died, transcribed it in his autobiography.[127] Frederick Hilles observed that the obituary was a literary form of Reynolds's portraiture. Just as Saltram's *Therese Parker* projected its subject as an exemplifaction of female virtues and sensibility, so Reynolds's obituary sketches an unblemished personification of domesticity, feminine softness and taste.[128] As Bishop Beilby Porteus put it: 'It was written I am told by Sir Joshua Reynolds; & it is worthy of his Pencil. He had before drawn her lovely form. He has now painted her still lovelier soul; both, with the same Elegance, Taste, & Truth.'[129]

Reynolds wrote the paragraph in a hurry and, in so doing, overlooked his readers' expectation that a description of a genteel young woman should not praise inner qualities exclusively, at the expense of her external beauty.[130] One of Therese's closest friends made the point: 'Sr Joshua Reynolds owns <u>the</u> Paragraph; a Person (I know not who) said to him, "I suppose by your Silence on that which the Lady was plain in her Person; upon my Honour said Sr. Joshua, I was so wholly engrossed by the Idea of her wonderful Merit, that I totally forgot her exterior Charms; which he is now much vexed at; as I confess I was; for altho' I would not have had it dwelt upon, I wished it to have been mentioned, especially as it was so peculiarly – what shall I say! enchanting, I have heard it called, & was struck by the Expression.'[131] When the paragraph was republished in 1776, Reynolds redressed this by stating that Therese's 'person was eminently beautiful' and adding some further words on her physical presence. His anxiety over the obituary was not at an end, though, for the printer substituted 'agreeable' for 'beautiful.'[132] Northcote related that 'In speaking of this afterwards to the late Caleb Whiteford, Sir Joshua complained of the absurd alteration, and said it had quite destroyed the simplicity of the whole.'[133]

'THE LIKEST AND MOST BEAUTIFULL PICTURE I EVER SAW'
John and Therese Parker

On 4 February 1779, Reynolds came away from 'an Excellent & comfortable dinner' with the Parkers in

Sackville Street with a new commission from his old friend, as Fritz Robinson reported the following day: 'Sr. Joshua is to paint the two little Children together & will I have no doubt make a charming Picture.'[134] The resulting painting (Mannings 1398) is one of Reynolds's great representations of childhood; Reynolds himself claimed that the head of young John Parker was 'the best he ever did.'

As elsewhere, Reynolds's pocket books and the Parker archive combine to provide a very detailed account of the sittings, which were more numerous even than those recorded by Mannings. The first meeting was on the morning of 11 February, when Fritz 'met Nanny at Sr Joshuas where the Children went to set for the first time. I have no doubt but it will make a very pretty picture & as Sr Joshua has so many opportunitys of seeing them he will catch their true natural countenances.'[135] After two further sittings on 13 and 17 February the children's faces were painted sufficiently for Fritz to report that 'the likeness in both is at present very strong.' The day after their 22 February sitting he added: 'our dear little children will be very like indeed, he has caught the exact expression of their countenances & is himself much pleasd with the picture.'[136] There was a sitting on 24 February but appointments on 1 and 6 March were probably missed, as a few days later Fritz wrote that 'The Children have not lately sat for their pictures on account of a little sniveling cold which made their noses red.'[137] By 16 March they had 'quite recover'd from their colds & are in every respect fit to set for their pictures,'[138] but it was not until 26 March that they sat again 'because they had not recovered their good looks,' explained Nanny, adding 'it will not be finished for some time but will be a very fine picture and very like, I cannot very well describe the composition of it, but they are very near kissing an attitude that they are very often in.'[139] During the sittings Lord Grantham sought repeatedly to have the portrait engraved by John Powell, but Fritz chided him at the end of March: 'You must not be in a hurry about the copy of the little Childrens picture. Sr. J. has not yet finishd it. Powells time is much taken up & he is besides a very lazy man; but as soon as anything is settled I will let you know.'[140] Reynolds made such slow progress that Grantham had returned to England by the time the painting was finished, making an engraving unnecessary.

By April Reynolds was busy preparing for the Academy exhibition; there was a sitting on 30 March, but the next one did not take place until 24 or 27 April.[141] Nanny reported during April that Reynolds had said: 'that the Boy's Head was the finest he had ever done.'[142] There were further sittings on 1, 4 and 7 May, by which point Fritz considered that one sitting 'more will finish it; it is most exceedingly like & very pretty.'[143] After their appointment on 13 May, Fritz reported to Lord Grantham: 'Sr Joshua is much pleas'd with his Portrait of the Children & says the boys head is the best he ever did. I hope the colours will not fade before you see it, they are to have one more setting.'[144] However, at least six further sittings ensued, on 18, 22, 27 May and 2, 8, 9 June. On 18 June Fritz 'was this morning at Sr Joshuas who says that he shall finish the picture without loss of time'[145] but it was still incomplete on 6 July, when Fritz dined with Reynolds, 'who promisd to finish the picture of the Children in the course of next week.'[146] Nanny wrote from Saltram on 27 July that 'the picture is set out – we expect it in the course of the week' and again on 8 August: 'Sir Joshua's picture is come down & I think the likest and most beautifull picture I ever saw.[147] Reynolds noted a payment of 200 guineas for the painting in July 1779: 'Mr Parker, for His two Children.'

As well as Reynolds's portrait, the two children were at the same time sitting separately for other artists. John Parker's gouache portrait by Daniel Gardner (c.1750–1805), painted in February or March 1779, remains at Saltram. Fritz outlined the commission to Lord Grantham: 'Mr Gardner in Bond Street draws in Crayons in the manner of Hamilton (but in generall full length figures) with a great deal more taste & spirit, but perhaps with less truth; the little boy is to set or rather stand to him.'[148] Amid widespread fears of a French invasion, John had been given a child's 'suit of Regimentals Red faced with Green Silver Epaulets & Buttons with Devon Jo Regt written on the latter, they become him much & he is not a little pleas'd with them.'[149] Gardner portrayed the boy 'in his Regimentals with a Spontoon & all his Accoutrements a full length' with military tents in the background.[150] His sister Therese was sitting to Angelica Kauffman for an oval portrait commissioned by her uncle Fritz, as a pair with the portrait Kauffman had painted some years earlier of Therese's brother, which he also owned.[151] This busy round of sittings in spring 1779 prompted comparisons between the work of the three artists. Fritz's appraisals show how concerned clients were with the accuracy of a likeness, and invariably Reynolds was praised at the expense of the other two. Fritz considered that Kauffman 'wants force & truth. Sr J. says she does not paint from nature but the stage. She is now doing the dear little girls Picture. it will be something like exceedingly pretty, but will have the same fault as the boys to which it is to be the companion, viz. the head is too large.'[152] A month later the portrait had become 'more like than the boys, & has in a great measure the true character of her countenance, but is not like Sr Joshua the truth the whole truth & nothing but the truth.'[153] Similarly, 'The little boys picture by Gardner will be like & pretty. Sr. Joshua's Capital.'[154]

The unusual pose that Reynolds chose for the Parker children's portrait has a religious source. Mannings attributed it to Reynolds's knowledge of Old Master paintings of the infant Christ with St John the Baptist. Indeed, this was first suggested in 1779, while the children were still sitting to Reynolds. In June 1778 John Parker had asked his brother-in-law Lord Grantham to commission two copies after Murillo: one, a *Holy Family*, and the other, an *Infant Christ and St John the Baptist*.[155] The copies were begun in January 1779; by mid-March one of them was 'very near finished & the other will be soon'; they arrived at Saltram, where they remain, around the end of the year.[156] In one of many reports on two copies, Lord Grantham wondered (without having even seen Reynolds's portrait) whether the Christ and St John composition 'is something [like] Sr Joshuas of the Children.'[157] Perhaps some discussion of the Murillos had taken place between Reynolds and Parker, which inspired Reynolds's treatment of the two children, though Murillo's *Infant Christ and St John the Baptist* cannot have been a direct source. Feasibly Reynolds was guided by a Guido Reni etching which shows the infant Jesus in a pose very close to young John Parker's.[158] Closer still are the figures in *Amoris Securitas*, a seventeenth-century Dutch emblematic engraving with which Reynolds was familiar.[159] The print, which shows two young cherubs hugging each other while beset by evils and danger, represents the mutually protective love of two innocents. Recent events in the Parker children's lives, both public and private, would have made this an appropriate theme. In 1779 invasion fears were at their height, especially among the landowners of maritime Devon, who would have been among the first to repel any attack; John Parker had spent much of 1778 preparing his militia regiment for such an event.[160] The Parkers were also still adjusting to the loss of their mother, whose absence from Reynolds's portrait must have been obvious to contemporary viewers familiar with the family's history. Nevertheless young John Parker was growing up; in spring 1779 his education was a matter for debate within the family and he started at Plympton school that June.[161] At the outset of his training for adult life, Reynolds shows him in the manly role of caring for his more passively posed sister.

'IT IS MUCH THE SHORTEST ROAD TO GET AT SALTRAM BY THE WAY OF MADRID'[162]
Lord Grantham, Saltram and Reynolds

Reynolds painted Therese Parker's older brother, Thomas Robinson, 2nd Baron Grantham, in the late 1750s, and the two men became friends.[163] Grantham was closely interested in art by the time he visited Italy in 1758, where he studied architecture and befriended Anton Raphael Mengs (1728–79) and Benjamin West (1738–1820), the American painter who succeeded Reynolds as President of the Royal Academy. On his return to London Grantham became an active member of the Dilettanti Society, to which Reynolds was elected in 1766. Between 1771 and 1779 Grantham and his brother worked in Spain, where Grantham became interested in Velázquez.[164] On their return to London, the brothers' letters provide colourful snapshots of Reynolds at work and play, and describe projects such as the New College windows, Royal portraits and *Sarah Siddons as the Tragic Muse*.[165] Grantham's correspondence also outlines his deal-ings with West, Romney, Gainsborough, Bacon, Downman and Flaxman.[166] Reynolds painted Grantham's children in 1788.[167]

Reynolds corresponded with Grantham in Spain about the Academy's annual exhibitions and the London art world, sending him copies of his latest *Discourse* as they were published.[168] Grantham, in turn, kept Reynolds informed about artists in Spain, including Mengs and Goya.[169] Only four of Reynolds's letters are known but the correspondence is nevertheless 'among the fullest and most interesting of all the letters by the artist to have survived.'[170] The July 1773 letter (*Letters*, 35) is a typical example, in which Reynolds gives Grantham a highly informative account of his own activities and paintings, as well as anecdotes of the royal family. It is easy to understand Grantham's eagerness to hear more from Reynolds. He instructed his sister in 1773: 'Pray tell Sr Joshua I expect to hear from him, & press him to write before ye Exhibition, for then he will surely write again';[171] In 1777 Grantham mentions that Reynolds had written (*Letters*, 65), but it was 'much too short for which I shall scold him.'[172]

Reynolds and Grantham often transacted their friendship via the Parkers. In 1775, for instance, Therese forwarded a manuscript from Reynolds to her brother: 'I do not know whether Sir Joshua has wrote to you, I should rather think not, as he is now busy from nine in the morning till four o Clock, & has sent me a paper he wrote a few years ago, to convey to you, if I think it worth your reading, I shall certainly take the first opportunity of sending it, as it will please you much not only from its real merit, but from the ridicule it thro[ws] upon a silly Book that I know you de[test], I mean Barettis Travels through Spain. This is a journey to Brentford through Turnham Green, supposed to be a Continuation of his Travels, but as Baretti lived a good deal with Sir Joshua, you must not betray him indeed he has ventured to shew it only to a very few particular Friends in England.'[173] A month later, Therese passed on a letter from Grantham to Reynolds: 'I shall send your Postscript about Mr. Jennings to Sir Joshua, he will be delighted with it, as he has the highest esteem for your opinion & besides, hates (as much as he can hate) Mr Jennings, he was attacked by him last winter before a large company with very false arguments to prove that it was impossible Sir Joshua as a Painter could be the least judge of Pictures, & affirmed he knew nothing of the matter, which has dwelt a little upon Sir Joshua's mind nor can he hear of any body being amused in his Company but by considering him as a Character, not a Companion.'[174]

Therese Parker frequently looked to her brother for advice about Saltram and asked him to source paintings in Spain for the Saloon.[175] Such was Grantham's influence that a friend quipped: 'it is much the shortest Road to get at Saltram by the way of Madrid.'[176] Grantham visited Saltram in 1769 and expressed his approval of the new Adam room; during Reynolds's visit the following year, Grantham wrote: 'I am very glad Sr Joshua confirms my Opinion of the Drawings. I quite agree with him; that the Drawing Room should admit none but good & original Pictures.'[177] Lord Grantham designed a garden building at Saltram, conceived in 1769 and built 1771–72.[178]

JOHN PARKER [III], 1ST EARL OF MORLEY

John Parker [III] spent much of his early childhood with Reynolds, but he was still a minor when his father died in 1788, and Reynolds's contact with the family was thereafter limited chiefly to the visits of Fritz Robinson.[179] As an Oxford undergraduate Parker followed Reynolds in the newspapers, and his letters betray a respectful concern for the artist over the opposition he suffered in 1790 to his preferred candidates for Academy positions.[180] Parker did see Reynolds occasionally, and called on him in October 1791, a few months before his death, when he reported that the ailing painter was 'a good deal out of spirits & with a painful inflammation in his well eye. Miss Palmer however afterwards assured me that it was in no way likely to affect his sight.'[181] The copy after Correggio's *Marriage of St Catherine*, which Reynolds bought in 1790 and which was at Saltram by 1803 (untraced), was surely Reynolds's final direct contribution to the collection.[182]

Although Reynolds died before Parker came of age, Saltram's links with the artist were strengthened during Parker's long tenure of the estate. *Mrs Abington*, now at Yale, was at Saltram as early as 1803.[183] In the 1830s Parker tried to acquire Plympton Corporation's Reynolds self-portrait (FIG. 11, p. 36).[184] One portrait which remains at Saltram was almost certainly acquired in this period: *Francesco Bartolozzi* was at Saltram by 1844, but is absent from the 1819 catalogue.[185] *Paul Henry Ourry* (FIG. 10, p. 36) is the most recent acquisition, having arrived in the early 20th century.[186] One Reynolds portrait left the collection under John Parker [III], when he gave *General Guise* to Christ Church, Oxford, in 1796.[187]

Like his father and grandfather, Parker married a woman who would oversee Saltram's art collection and make lasting changes to the house. After his first marriage ended in divorce, in August 1809 Parker married Frances Talbot (d.1857). Only a few months later, she was taking 'much interest in His Lordship's pictures, & Has placed 11 or 12 pictures by Sir Joshua Reynolds in one room, the Library, making a collection of His works'.[188] According to Talbot herself, the pictures 'which were before never seen or heard of, appear to the greatest advantage. This is the first great act I have performed since the commencement of my reign.'[189] By 1819 the Library held 14 paintings by Reynolds.[190]

Displaying most of Reynolds's work within one room emphasised the painter's connection with the family. In 1829 the family's Reynoldses were 'believed to constitute the finest collection of his works that exists', and Reynolds came to form an intrinsic part of descriptions of Saltram that appeared in nineteenth-century guidebooks.[191] John Parker [III]'s life linked the era of Reynolds's supremacy as a practising artist of the 1770s, and the period of his apotheosis by the scholars and artists of Victorian England. During Parker's lifetime, the status of the Reynolds paintings at Saltram also changed, in a way that reflects the artist's more general absorption within the historical record. By the removal of the Saltram Reynoldses from long-established positions thoughout the house and their assembly instead as a single gallery within the library, the Reynoldses began their inevitable transformation from portraits of cherished friends and relatives to the ancestral paintings, evocative of a remote past, that we see today.

CAT. 22

The Honorable Commodore Augustus Keppel
(1749)
127 x 101.5 cm

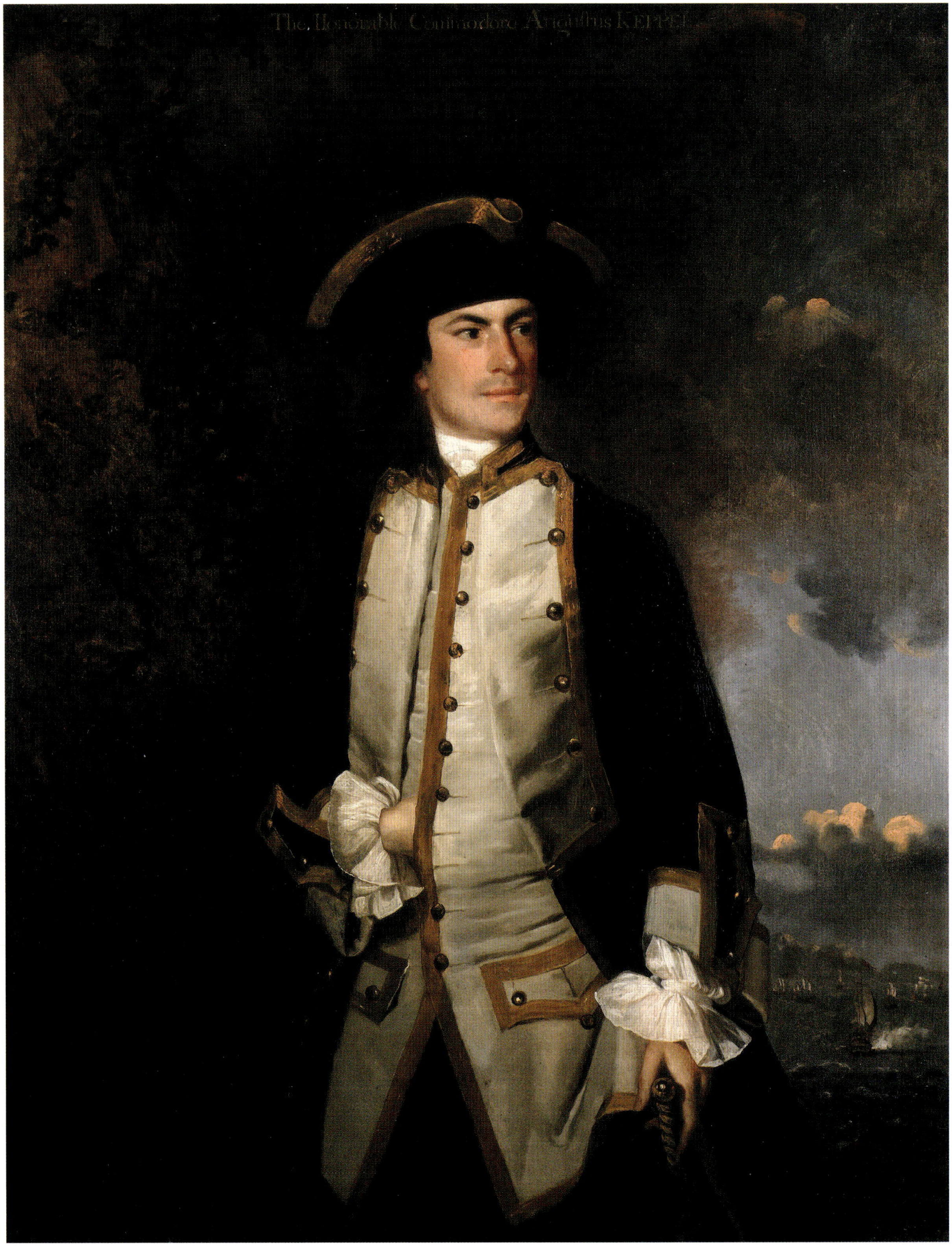

PROVENANCE: Frederick Keppel, Bishop of Exeter (sitter's brother); by descent to BWA Keppel who sold it at Christies' 19 June 1911 (19) bt Shepherd; Lionel Robinson collection, Old Buckenham Hall; bought for National Maritime Museum in 1956 with the Caird fund.

EXHIBITION HISTORY: Rome 1959; Birmingham 1961 (8); Plymouth 1973 (23).

LITERATURE: O'Malley 1912; Duleep Singh 1928, i, 405; Waterhouse 38; Archibald 1961, 77; Greenwich 1988, 321, Mannings 2000, 287 (1036).

AUGUSTUS KEPPEL

THE SECOND SON OF THE EARL OF Albemarle, and a member of a powerful Whig family, in 1749 the young Keppel (1725–86) was already an experienced mariner. In 1740 he had served under Commodore Anson in the *Centurion* on his four-year voyage round the world; in 1744 he was promoted first to Lieutenant and then to Captain. Promoted to Commodore in 1749 he was sent to the Mediterranean to negotiate with the Barbary corsairs whose activities were threatening trade. Reynolds had been introduced to Keppel by Lord Edgcumbe early that year and sailed with him from Plymouth on 11 May, 1749. He spent the autumn and winter at Port Mahon, Menorca, and this portrait was probably painted there. Keppel wears his Captain's uniform and his ship the *Centurion*, 54 guns, flying his Commodore's pendant, is shown behind him. In January 1750 Reynolds travelled on to Italy by himself, staying there two years to study. Reynolds developed a life-long friendship with Keppel and painted him seven times in his career. His second portrait (FIG. 12) was painted after Reynolds had returned from Italy to London in 1752. By all accounts it was a calculated effort to attract attention and did indeed make his name.

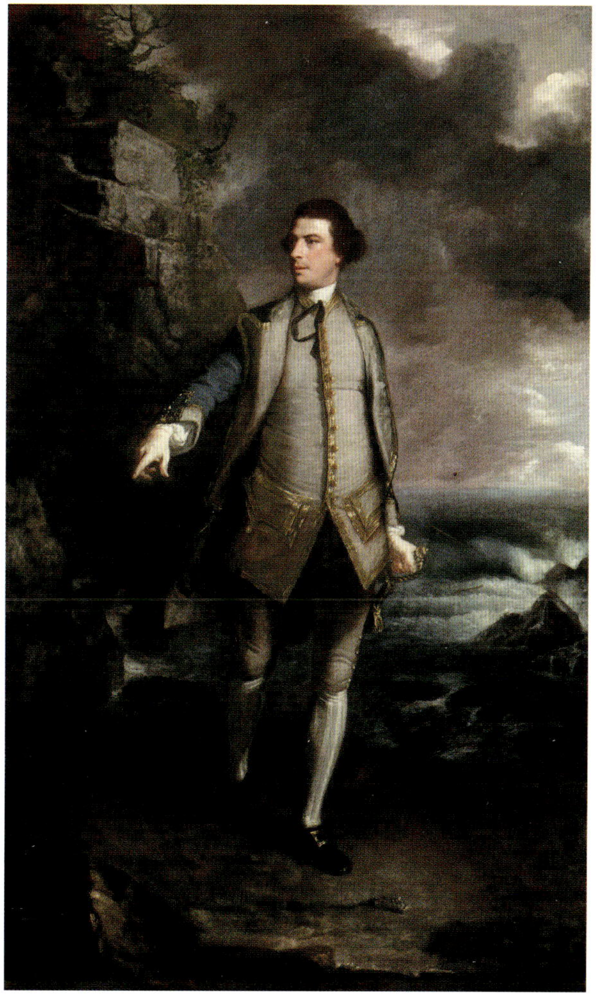

FIG. 12

Augustus Keppel
(1752–53)
oil on canvas,
238.8 x 147.5 cm
© National Maritime Museum, Greenwich, London

MRS ORCHARD

BETTINA ORCHARD (1738–1833) WAS THE daughter of Sir Robert Lawley, 4t Bt. Canwell, Staffs. She married Paul Orchard (1739–1812) on 17 July 1764. Her husband was the MP for Callington and Colonel of the Northern Regiment of the Devon militia. Paul Orchard inherited Hartland Abbey from his father and carried out major alterations in the middle of the eighteenth century, hiring the London architect John Meadows to transform the remnants of the original medieval abbey into a modern Gothick house in the style of Batty Langley. The remodelling was complete by 1779 and it is tempting to see Paul Orchard's commissioning of three portraits by Reynolds earlier in that decade – himself, his wife, and, posthumously, his father – as part of a bid to emulate the most advanced taste of the time in what is still a remote area of north Devon.

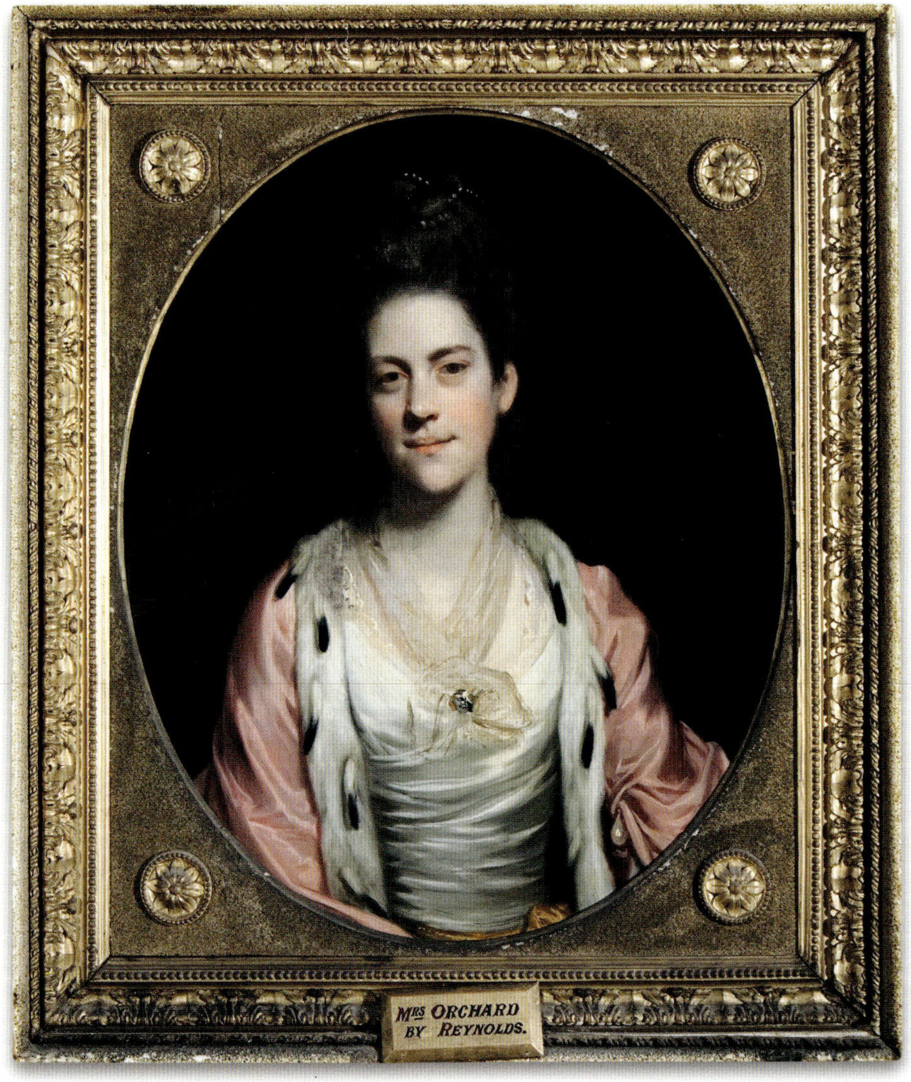

CAT. 23

Mrs Orchard
(1772)
76.2 x 63.5 cm
Hartland Abbey

PROVENANCE: By descent. In the Stucley family.
EXHIBITION HISTORY: Plymouth 1951 (61).
LITERATURE: Graves & Cronin ii, 709; Mannings 2000, 357 (1365).

THE ROAD TO THE ROYAL ACADEMY

REYNOLDS RETURNED FROM EUROPE in October 1752.[1] After a brief visit to Devon to see friends and family, he re-established his portrait practice in St Martin's Lane, at the heart of the capital's artistic community.[2] Among the first works Reynolds painted at this time was a bust-length portrait of his Italian pupil and studio assistant, Giuseppe Marchi (FIG. 13, p. 77). While the painting in some respects resembled Reynolds's work of the 1740s, it also demonstrated a daring breadth of handling and a penchant for vivid colour that was quite new. Reynolds's former master, Thomas Hudson, did not like it.[3] The painting had an even more dramatic impact on the portraitist, John Ellys, who, upon seeing it, cried out in rage, 'Shakespeare in poetry, and Kneller in painting, damme!', before storming out of Reynolds's studio.[4] Others were more supportive. His patron, Richard, 1st Baron Edgcumbe (FIG. 2, p. 30), who had advised him that London was 'the only place where his fame could be established and his fortune advanced',[5] also provided practical assistance, persuading 'many of the first nobility to sit to him for their pictures'.[6] For many years Lord Edgcumbe had been among the most active supporters of the governing Whig oligarchy via his control of important Parliamentary seats in Devon and Cornwall. He was therefore well placed to introduce Reynolds to the big hitters within the corridors of power: the Devonshires, Pelhams, Russells and Townshends. It comes as no surprise that these families provided Reynolds with the backbone of his lucrative portrait business. And, by the summer of 1753, Reynolds was able to report:

> *I have finishd the head of the Duke of Devonshire he himself and all the family say it is the only like picture he ever had of himself there are many copies bespoke, I have drawn a whole lenght [sic] of Comodore Kepple [sic] and his brother Ld Bury: Ld & Lady Kildare who is thought the handsomest woman in England. Lord & Lady Carisfort Mr Fox the Secretary at war [and] The Ld Godolphin and this week the Duke of Grafton is to sit I am told that the Prince of Whales [sic] intends to come and see my Pictures.*[7]

Among these paintings, the most celebrated and most successful was the full-length portrait of Augustus Keppel (FIG. 12, p. 73); a work which established Reynolds, in the words of his friend, Edmond Malone, as 'the greatest painter that England had seen since Vandyck'.[8] The brilliance of Reynolds's portrait of Keppel lay in its innovative combination of the Italian Renaissance Old-Master tradition and the antique. Stylistically, Reynolds referred back to Tintoretto, while for the pose of Keppel he relied upon a drawing he had made of a statue of Apollo holding a lyre by the seventeenth-century French sculptor, Pierre Legros the Younger, which was in turn based loosely upon a celebrated classical statue, the Apollo Belvedere.[9]

Throughout the 1750s, and beyond, Giuseppe Marchi was the mainstay of Reynolds's workshop practice. In larger commissions, where elaborate formal costume and regalia were required, he increasingly tendered out paintings to specialist drapery-painters such as Peter Toms and George Roth. At the time Reynolds was charging forty-eight guineas for a full-length portrait. Out of this total, Toms received fifteen guineas although, according to Marchi, Reynolds was wholly unappreciative of his skills.[10] Reynolds's sitter-books, which survive (with the exception of a few gaps) from 1755 to 1790, provide a detailed record of his daily routine over a period of thirty-five years.[11] They also reveal the enforced pliability of the society portraitist, sittings for individual commissions spanning weeks, months, and even years, owing to the various commitments, caprices, and whims of Reynolds's clientele. Even so, while sitters were at times irregular in their attendance, Reynolds was a creature of habit, beginning his working day at 9 or 10 in the morning and working until 4 or 5 p.m., often seven days a week. On average a portrait head required five or six separate one-hour sittings, although it is not unusual to find up to a dozen recorded in Reynolds's sitter books.[12] It is a measure of the base upon which he sought to build his reputation, that from the moment of his return to London, Reynolds had the confidence to charge as much for his portraits as his elders, Thomas Hudson and Allan Ramsay.[13] In 1753 Reynolds moved from apartments in St. Martin's Lane to a house in Great Newport Street.[14] This new residence provided a home (which Reynolds shared with his youngest sister, Frances), a work place, and a gallery space, or 'shew room', in which he displayed examples of his work to potential clients. He used it also to entertain friends and members of fashionable, polite, and intellectual society.

Around 1755 Reynolds met Samuel Johnson, the man who was to change, or at least modify, the course of his life. The attraction of Johnson, aside from his compelling personality, was the extent and quality of his social network. Dogged by an obsessive need for company, Johnson had already formed a wide-ranging literary acquaintance including Giuseppe Baretti, Thomas and Joseph Warton, and Bennet Langton; all of who became life-long friends of Reynolds. In 1756 Reynolds painted Johnson's portrait, a wonderfully idiosyncratic image picture, which at once celebrated his *magnum opus*, *A Dictionary of the English Language*, and his unconventional, and somewhat uncouth, demeanour. Reynolds, influenced perhaps by the example of Johnson, did not aspire to personal gentility either. A few years later, in June 1759, the Honourable John West reported to his friend, Lord Harcourt, on his recent visit to Reynolds's studio: 'I really am not in the least surpriz'd at your dislike to him: I think, in my life, I never saw so vulgar & so familiar a forward fellow, really worse than you described him'.[15] Indeed, Reynolds did not appear to have been in the habit of addressing aristocratic patrons by their titles, his pupil, James Northcote, recalling that he had 'never hear the words "your lordship or your ladyship", come from his mouth'.[16] 'His pronunciation', as one female acquaintance observed, 'was tinctured with the accent of Devonshire; his features coarse, his outward appearance slovenly'.[17] Reynolds's unbuttoned appearance was, it would seem, cultivated quite deliberately to flaunt his disdain for courtly etiquette, puncture the pretensions of social superiors, and confront fashionable society on his own terms.

Around the time that Reynolds met Johnson he painted the portrait of Horace Walpole (CAT. 28, p. 93), a supremely well-mannered individual who believed himself to be a class above any living painter, regarding even Reynolds *de haut en bas*. Although they were never on close terms, Walpole kept a watchful eye on Reynolds's career, discussing his work in witty and at times sardonic missives to a network of correspondents at home and abroad. One of his earliest observations appeared early in 1759, in the context of a now celebrated comparison between Reynolds and Allan Ramsay:

> *He and Mr Reynolds are our favourite painters and two of the very best we ever had… Mr Reynolds and Mr Ramsay can scarce be rivals; their manners are so different. The former is bold, and has a kind of tempestuous colouring; yet with dignity and grace; the latter is all delicacy. Mr Reynolds seldom succeeds in women; Mr Ramsay is formed to paint them.*[18]

FIG. 13

Giuseppe Marchi
(1752–53)
oil on canvas,
77.2 x 63.6 cm

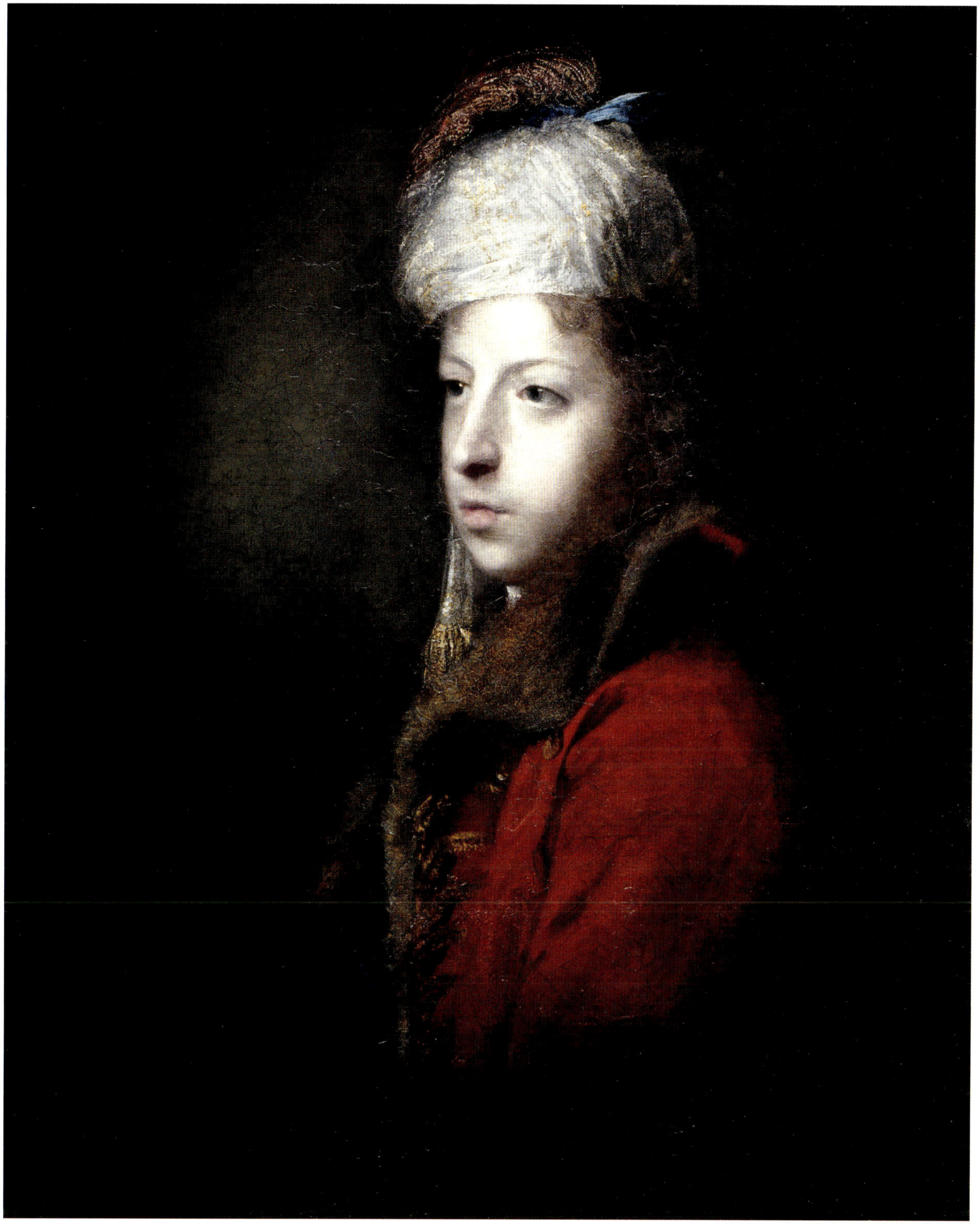

FIG. 14

Anne, Countess of Albemarle
(1760)
oil on canvas,
126.5 x 101 cm

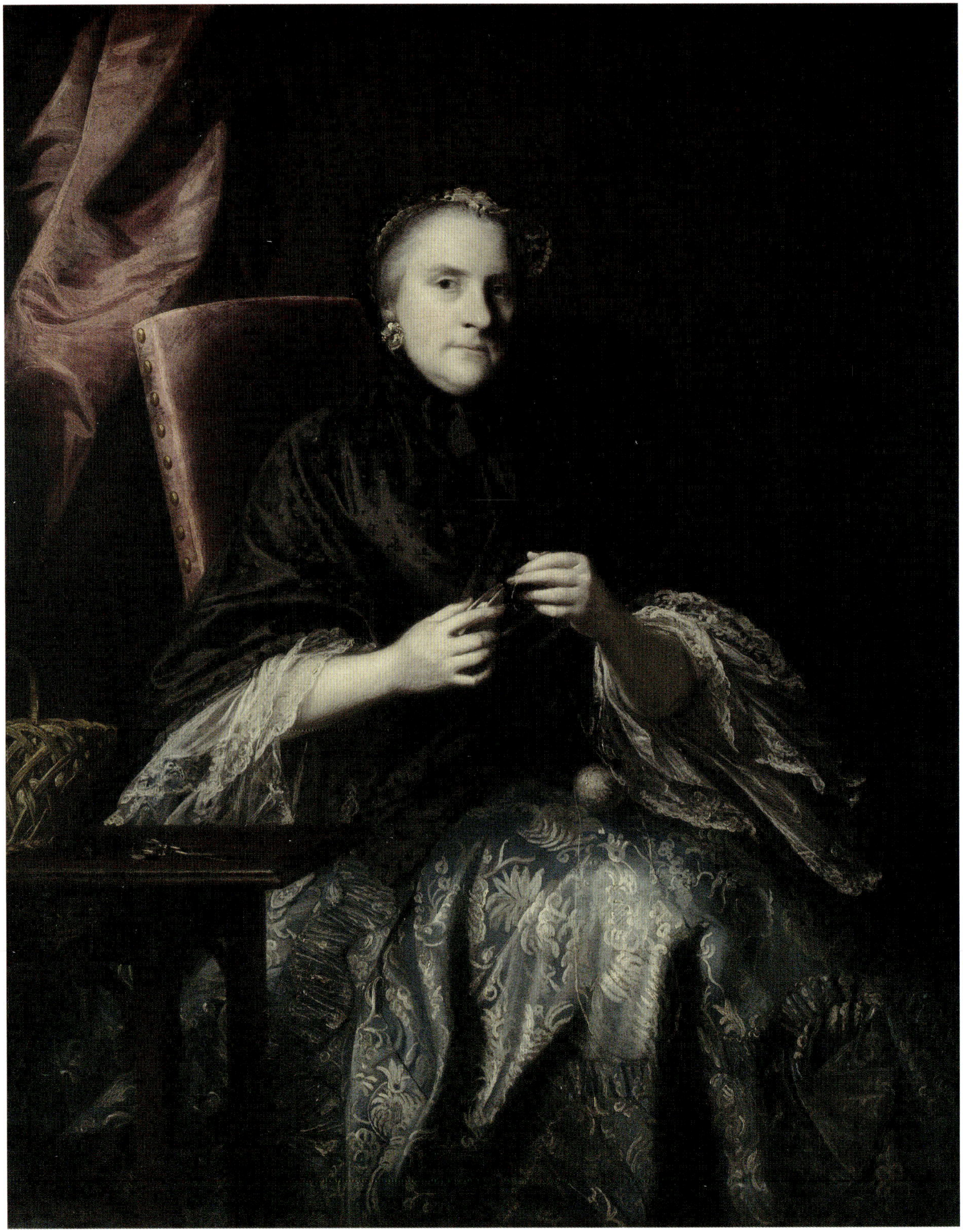

Ramsay had taken up residence in London in late August 1757, following a three-year sojourn in Italy. By mid-October he and Reynolds were on personal terms, an association which lasted until Ramsay's death in 1784.[19] Reynolds had been familiar with Ramsay's art since the 1740s, and may have known him slightly at that time. However, it was only when his physical presence in London marked him out as a rival that Reynolds took a closer interest in his art, unashamedly assimilating aspects of his style into his own practice. In late September 1757, barely a month after Ramsay's return to London, Reynolds began sittings for his three-quarter-length portrait of Anne, Countess of Albemarle (FIG. 14) Her reticent expression, the detailed attention to costume, and her eloquent hand gestures, indicate the influence of Ramsay. Indeed, a whole series of female portraits by Reynolds of the late 1750s took their lead from Ramsay. His desire to compete was actuated principally by Ramsay's favoured position within the court-in-waiting of the Prince of Wales (later George III). Between October 1757 and September 1758 Ramsay was commissioned to paint full-length formal portraits of Prince George and John Stuart, 3rd Earl of Bute. Through Bute's future influence as Prime Minister, these portraits, as it has been noted, helped to facilitate Ramsay's appointment in 1761 as 'one of His Majesty's Principal Painters in Ordinary'.[20] Several years later, Reynolds painted a formal full-length portrait of another Prime Minister, the Marquess of Rockingham. His desire to rival Ramsay's *Earl of Bute* was made clear by his witty remark that he wished to 'show a leg with Ramsay's Lord Bute'; a reference to Bute's vanity over the elegant shape of his legs and, I would suggest, to Rockingham's position as a successor to Bute's political position.[21] In 1759, shortly after Ramsay had painted him, Reynolds also painted the Prince of Wales. Here, too, Reynolds clearly sought to compete with Ramsay on his own terms, the portrait of the Prince being as close as Reynolds ever came to replicating Ramsay in male portraiture. And yet, Reynolds failed in his attempt to gain the patronage of the Prince of Wales, whose indifference was, on his succession to the throne, to develop into a strong personal antipathy. As for the portrait of the Prince, it remained in Reynolds's studio until 1815, when it was presented by his niece to another Prince of Wales, the future George IV.[22]

In July 1760 Reynolds took a long lease on a large house on the west side of Leicester Square.[23] Immediately he set about refurbishing and enlarging the property, ripping out staircases, installing custom-built fireplaces and acquiring fashionable furniture. He added studios and a picture gallery to the rear of the premises where he exhibited his own work in the context of his expanding collection of Old-Master paintings.[24] To ensure that his improvement in circumstances did not go unnoticed to the outside world, Reynolds 'gave a ball and refreshments to a numerous and elegant company on the opening of his gallery to the public', and purchased an ornate coach with gilded wheels and painted panels.[25] Reynolds now lived in some style. Yet, he still had to graft in order to maintain his improved ménage and enhanced public *persona.* As a self-employed businessman Reynolds was personally responsible for overseeing a range of routine tasks beyond his portrait practice; keeping accounts, taking care of the packaging and delivery of commissions, liaising with waggoners, colourmen, frame-makers, drapery painters, professional copyists and miniaturists.[26] He also worked closely with engravers, to whom he distributed commissions, gave instructions on inscriptions required, and from whom he requested copies of their mezzotints to send on to interested parties. ('Get 3 Prints of Garrick when finished fram'd Glazed & Cased for Mr Redstone to be sent to Plymouth'.) A memorandum book of the early 1760s (not to be confused with his sitter-books) included reminders to 'wait on the Duchess of Beaufort', or 'wait on Mrs Clevland and carry my Book with me'.[27] In the same memorandum book Reynolds recorded the poses required by clients, their clothing (even down to the manner in which they wished to be dressed), and the preferred style of picture frame. And while Reynolds now employed others to paint the draperies in his portraits, he still needed to keep track of particular requirements; to 'unbutton' Colonel Irwin's waistcoat, to give Mrs Smith 'the same dress as Mrs Brudnell', or ensure that Lord Brome was 'finished by November', even retaining a lock of his hair as an *aide-mémoire.*[28]

Despite the obvious collaborative nature of Reynolds's portrait business, the intricacies of his practice were clearly something of a mystery to his sitters. On 15 October 1761 William Pulteney, Earl of Bath, reported triumphantly to Mrs Montagu:

> *I was yesterday with Mr Reynolds, & have fixed Fryday next at twelve, to finish the picture. I have discovered a secret by being often at Mr Reynolds, that I fancy, he is sorry I should know. I find that none of these great Painters finish any of their Pictures themselves. The same Person, (but who he is, I know not) works for Ramsey [sic], Reynolds & another, calld [sic] Hudson, my Picture will not come from that Person till Thursday night, and on Fryday it will be totally finished.*[29]

Lord Bath's final appointment with Reynolds was at noon on Friday 16 October. Before he added the finishing touches, the portrait had probably been in the hands of Peter Toms, who had been painting Reynolds's draperies since 1755 (and who had also been a pupil of Hudson).[30] Given the quantity of canvas covered by Toms in Lord Bath's portrait, as well as other contributions by pupils (who may have painted the silver standish, books, and background details), it is not surprising that Lord Bath wondered about the extent of Reynolds's involvement in the commission.

While Reynolds often dealt with official commissions in a dispassionate and piecemeal fashion, he took a hands-on role in works which he painted of his own volition; not least the portraits of the elite band of Georgian celebrities who crossed his threshold with the express aim of enhancing their public *personae*. In 1759 Reynolds made two paintings of Kitty Fisher, who was currently enjoying the fame generated by her sensual allure and extravagant mode of living. In one portrait Reynolds portrayed Kitty leaning forward over a stone sill, arms folded, relying on the visual vocabulary of Allan Ramsay (who had in turn learnt it in France). Here, Kitty the courtesan, *billet-doux* at her elbow, returns the admiring gaze of her would-be suitors.[31] In the other portrait (FIG. 16, p. 83), in the guise of the libidinous Egyptian queen, Cleopatra, Kitty suspends a large pearl above a goblet of wine, the motif taken from Francesco Trevisani's *Banquet of Antony and Cleopatra*, which Reynolds had seen in the Galleria Spada in Rome.[32] The suggestive 'O' gesture of the hand exhibiting the jewel is a nuanced allusion to the potency of Kitty's sexuality; a point which would not have been lost on her many male admirers.[33] The comparison between Kitty Fisher and Cleopatra was in other ways particularly apt, since Kitty's celebrated party-trick of eating a large bank note between two pieces of bread could be regarded as a modern-day version of Cleopatra's legendary consumption of a pearl dissolved in wine.[34]

During the 1760s Reynolds exhibited a series of portraits of people who were newsworthy. They included courtesans, actors, soldiers, statesmen, writers, and beautiful young women. Reynolds's particular skill was to define a leading characteristic of the individual in question, whether it was the sex appeal of the courtesan, the valour of the soldier, or the 'genius' of the writer. Reynolds selected his exhibits carefully. In 1760, at the inaugural exhibition of the Society of Artists, he showed five portraits: *General Charles Vernon* (Museo de Arte de Ponce, Puerto Rico), *General Kingsley* (private collection), *Lady Elizabeth Keppel* (National Trust, Ascott), *Elizabeth Gunning, Duchess of Hamilton and Argyll* (Lady Lever Art Gallery, Port Sunlight), and *Rebecca, Viscountess Folkestone.*[35] All these people were either already in the public eye, or belonged to families with whom Reynolds was personally acquainted, and whose patronage he especially valued. Lady Elizabeth Keppel was the sister of Augustus Keppel, while Rebecca, Viscountess Folkestone, was the wife of William Bouverie, later Earl of Radnor. General Kingsley and General Vernon were both high-ranking officers in the British army, while Elizabeth Gunning was considered to be the most beautiful woman in London. The following year Reynolds once again showed five works, including a three-quarter-length portrait of Laurence Sterne, who only months before the exhibition had published the first two volumes of his hugely popular novel *The Life and Opinions of Tristram Shandy, Gentleman*. The portrait of Sterne (begun in March 1760) was destined to remain with Reynolds until his death, although this was probably because it had been painted on his own initiative, as a speculative venture. Certainly, Reynolds was eager to see it reproduced, because Edward Fisher's mezzotint was published the same year as the painting was exhibited.[36] As has been observed, Sterne's physiognomy and the gesture of the forefinger pressed against the temple were derived from a painting of John the Baptist by the school of Leonardo da Vinci (Ashmolean Museum). But whereas John the Baptist points to heaven as the source of his divine inspiration, the subversive Sterne gestures towards his own spotlit cranium.[37]

As his portraits of the 1760s attest, Reynolds enjoyed melding the *personae* of his celebrated sitters with classical and mythological characters. Sometimes, as in the case of *David Garrick between Tragedy and Comedy* (CAT. 26, p. 90), he did so by alluding to a particular topos or narrative. At other times he forged the link between sitter and subject by way of reference to a particular Old-Master painting, print, or piece of sculpture. One of the most illuminating accounts of the process occurs in an autobiographical note by David Steuart Erskine, 11th Earl of Buchan, who befriended Reynolds towards the end of 1764:

> *One morning in his painting room I observed that beautiful portrait of Pontius the Engraver by Sir Anthony Vandyke which was then his property & having greatly praised its spirit only to be matched by the portrait of the Earl of Denbigh by Rubens at Hamilton Reinholds [sic] Said that he meant to attempt a portrait in the same Style as a Studio & wish'd me to sitt for the Mask of the head. – So at his request I sate nine times enjoying all my hours of sitting in the agreeable company of Reynholds [sic] & his interesting friends, who at these times by my desire were freely admitted.*[38]

Reynolds had modelled his portrait of Lord Buchan (then Lord Cardross) on Van Dyck's *Paul Pontius*, reversing the image, probably by reflecting it in a mirror.[39] The most interesting revelation, however, is that the picture was conceived not as a routine portrait but as a 'studio'; Lord Buchan sitting at

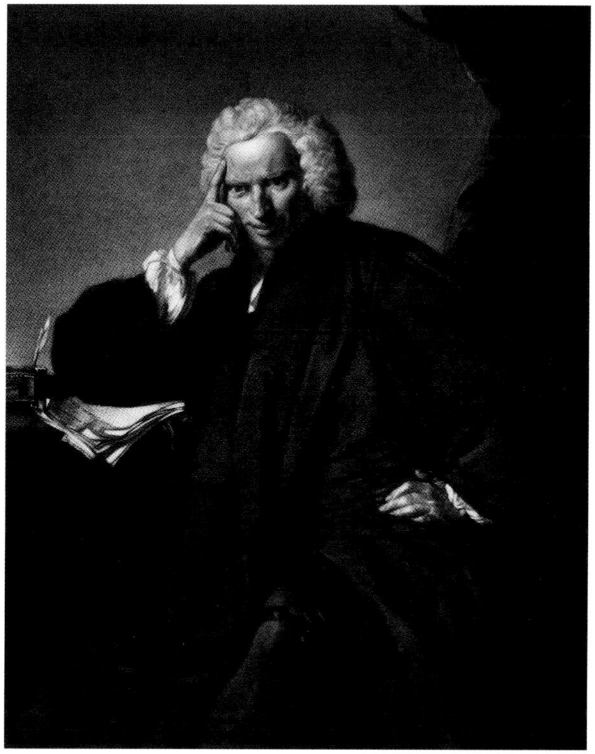

FIG. 15

Edward Fisher
(c.1722–82)
after Joshua Reynolds
Laurence Sterne
(1760)
mezzotint, 37.9 x 27.7 cm
British Museum, London (PD 1902, 1011.2189)

Reynolds's request as his model – albeit one who took an unusually active interest in the matter.

Reynolds was successful in virtually all arenas of public portraiture. Royal patronage, however, continued to elude him, especially when, in December 1761, Ramsay was appointed His Majesty's Principal Painter in Ordinary to George III. Like a number of Reynolds's supporters and acolytes, the young artist, Ozias Humphry, believed that Reynolds would feel snubbed by George III's refusal to patronize him. Although Reynolds probably was piqued, Samuel Johnson provided the official, Reynoldsian, response:

> *Mr. Reynolds has too much good sense to be affected by it: when he was younger he believed it would have been agreeable; but now he does not want their favour. It has ever been more profitable to be popular among the people than favoured by the King: it is no reflection on Mr. Reynolds not to be employed by them; but it will be a reflection on the Court not to have employed him. The King, perhaps, knows nothing but that he employs the best painter; and as for the Queen, I don't imagine she has any other idea of a picture but that it is a thing composed of many colours.*[40]

As Johnson and Reynolds knew, the Hanoverian Court was by now far from omnipotent in the cultural sphere. Indeed, by this time Reynolds was far more interested in attracting the attention of the King's detractors, the influential Whig families of Lennox, Fox, Townshend and Pelham. In addition he was also cultivating his own personal circle of influence.

In February 1764 Reynolds suggested the formation of a dining club in order to regularise the gatherings of his immediate friends.[41] Outsiders referred to this organization as the 'Literary Club', since members were united by their scholarly interests: to its members it was known simply as the Club. The original membership was restricted to nine individuals: Samuel Johnson, Edmund Burke, Christopher Nugent, Topham Beauclerck, Bennet Langton, Oliver Goldsmith, Anthony Chamier, John Hawkins, and Reynolds. According to Thomas Percy (who was later admitted to the Club), members were chosen so 'that if only Two of them chanced to meet, they shd. be able to entertain each other sufficiently without wishing for more Company with who to pass an evening'.[42] They were also – with the exception of Beauclerk (grandson of the Earl of St Albans and son-in-law of the Duke of Marlborough) – resolutely bourgeois; the sons of clerics, solicitors and booksellers. Reynolds remained on intimate terms with all members of the Club. However, he was particularly close to Edmund Burke and Oliver Goldsmith, both of whom he painted during this period. Goldsmith sat to Reynolds probably in the late 1760s.[43] Reynolds's sister, Frances (who did not like Goldsmith) referred to it as 'the most flattered picture she ever knew her brother to have painted'.[44] By this time Reynolds had also begun a double portrait of the Whig grandee Lord Rockingham and Edmund Burke, who then acted as Rockingham's private secretary. The composition, abandoned owing to Rockingham's abrupt resignation as Prime Minister in July 1766, was based upon Titian's famous portrait of George d'Armagnac with Guillaume Philandrier (Duke of Northumberland collection), which Reynolds must have seen often at Northumberland House.[45] It also had a number of more recent antecedents (which in turn looked back to Titian). The most important was Van Dyck's *Thomas Wentworth, 1st Earl of Strafford, with Sir Philip Mainwaring*, which also belonged to Lord Rockingham. Given that Rockingham was a direct descendant of the Earl of Strafford, Reynolds's painting was probably conceived as a 'companion' to the Van Dyck at Wentworth Woodhouse.[46] Both the Titian in the Duke of Northumberland's collection and Lord Rockingham's Van Dyck had been copied extensively in England, and as recently as 1752 John Shackleton had used them as the basis for his double portrait of the prime minister, Henry Pelham, and his secretary, John Roberts. The portrait of Lord Rockingham and Edmund Burke, despite the status of the sitters, languished among Reynolds's stacks of incomplete and rejected commissions until, following the death of his niece and heiress, Mary Palmer, in 1821, it was auctioned off as part of a job-lot for less than eleven guineas.[47]

During the 1760s, as the annual exhibitions held in London by the Society of Artists gained increasing

FIG. 16

Kitty Fisher as Cleopatra
(1759)
oil on canvas,
76.2 x 63.5 cm
© The Iveagh Bequest Kenwood (English Heritage)

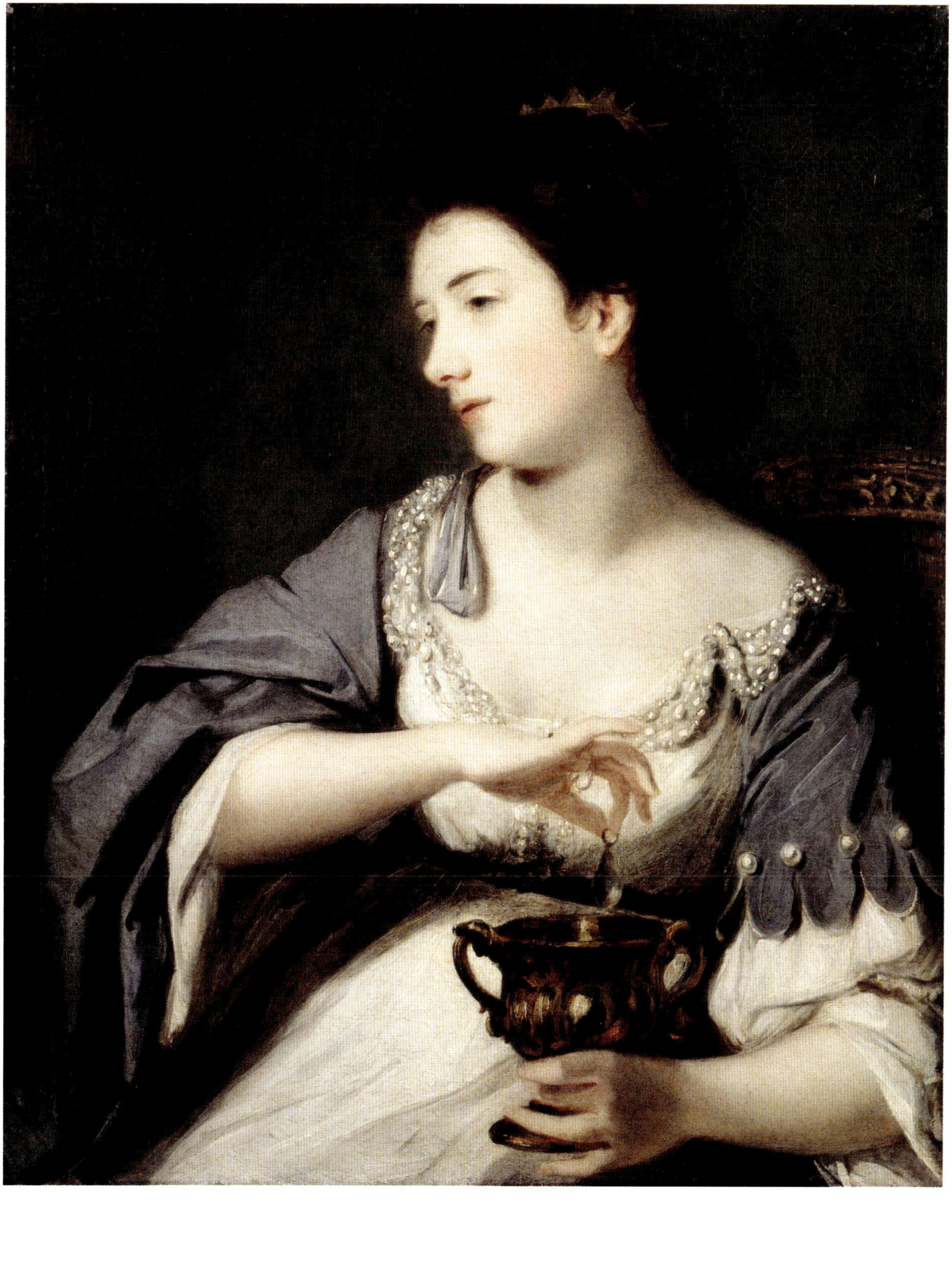

public notice, competition between the capital's artists intensified. Reynolds's portraiture was brought into direct competition with his fellow portraitists, notably Thomas Gainsborough, Allan Ramsay and Francis Cotes. At this time Gainsborough was based in Bath, although he visited London from time to time for business and pleasure. He knew Reynolds slightly, and they had mutual friends, including the actor David Garrick, and the painter Ozias Humphry. Reynolds and Gainsborough, who were to become arch-rivals in the 1770s, were very different in character, temperament, and in their respective attitudes towards portraiture. Gainsborough gave the impression of approaching his art as a pastime, painting fitfully, and largely without assistance. Reynolds, on the other hand, ran a busy workshop, suggesting that painting was hard work. Reynolds assiduously courted a wide range of celebrities, painting their portraits as speculative ventures, which would advance his own status as well as their respective careers. Gainsborough was more select in his friendships, forming strong personal attachments to those who shared, in particular, his love of music as well as art. Reynolds and Gainsborough were familiar with the notable Old-Master collections of Bowood, Wilton, Corsham Court, Longford Castle, and Stourhead, which lay between London and the West Country. The artists admired by Gainsborough, such as Van Dyck, Rubens and Watteau, were those with whom he had an instinctive sympathy. Reynolds's role models, by way of contrast, tended to be artists whom tradition had taught him to respect. Gainsborough, who relished painting drapery and the potential of paint to recreate the textures of silks, satin, and lace, ransacked the art of the past to realize particular pictorial effects. Reynolds studied past masters and schools of art from a taxonomic perspective, intent upon understanding and preserving prevailing hierarchies. Received wisdom, which Gainsborough treated with scant respect, was the touchstone of Reynolds's *modus operandi*. Unlike Reynolds, Gainsborough did not go out of his way to promote his portraits through the medium of engraving, or use assistants to replicate his work. And, while he participated in the annual exhibitions of the Society of Artists, Gainsborough distrusted the strictures which the public exhibition placed on his art, forcing his more reticent style of painting to compete for attention with Reynolds's often lurid portraits. In 1766 Gainsborough confided to Garrick, surely with Reynolds in mind, that there was 'certainly a false taste & an impudent stile prevailing, which if Vandyke was living would put him out of countenance; & I think even his work would appear so, opposed to such a Glare'.[48]

Reynolds's portraiture had a limited impact on the independently minded Gainsborough. Others were less able to resist Reynolds's influence. They included Francis Cotes and the London-born portraitist, Tilly Kettle, whose early career was based on his gift for imitating Reynolds's style. Cotes had emerged from the same 'stable' as Reynolds, having been guided by Arthur Pond and Thomas Hudson, as well as his own master George Knapton. Until the late 1750s Cotes had worked almost exclusively as a pastellist, drawing inspiration from the example of Jean-Etienne Liotard and Allan Ramsay, whose soft-focused naturalism he successfully emulated. In the 1760s, with the increasingly lucrative market for large-scale exhibition pictures in oils, Reynolds became Cotes's main role-model. As if to announce his new-found status, in 1763 Cotes moved to an imposing house in Cavendish Square, where, in common with Reynolds, he employed Peter Toms to paint his draperies.[49] Cotes's slick professionalism, combined with a pleasing overtly ornamental style clearly appealed to those who either disliked Reynolds's more robust style or were unable to afford his prices. As the *Public Advertiser* stated on 2 May 1764, Cotes's 'portraits may justly vie with those of Reynolds; and greatly to his Honour be it said, that he generally preserves a beautiful Correctness in his Pictures, which the latter Master too often ignores'. Cotes's portrait style certainly appealed to the King, who granted him the unique privilege of exhibiting a pastel portrait of Queen Charlotte and Princess Caroline at the Society of Artists in 1767. It was an honour not previously accorded to any artist and may, as it has been suggested, have contributed towards Reynolds's decision not to show his own work at the exhibition that year (although, as I suggest below, other factors may have been involved).[50] Reynolds may also have

FIG. 17

Angelica Kauffman
(1741–1807)
Sir Joshua Reynolds
(1767)
oil on canvas,
127 x 101.5 cm
Saltram, The Morley Collection (accepted in lieu of tax by H.M. Treasury, and transferred to the National Trust in 1957).
©NTPL/Rob Matheson

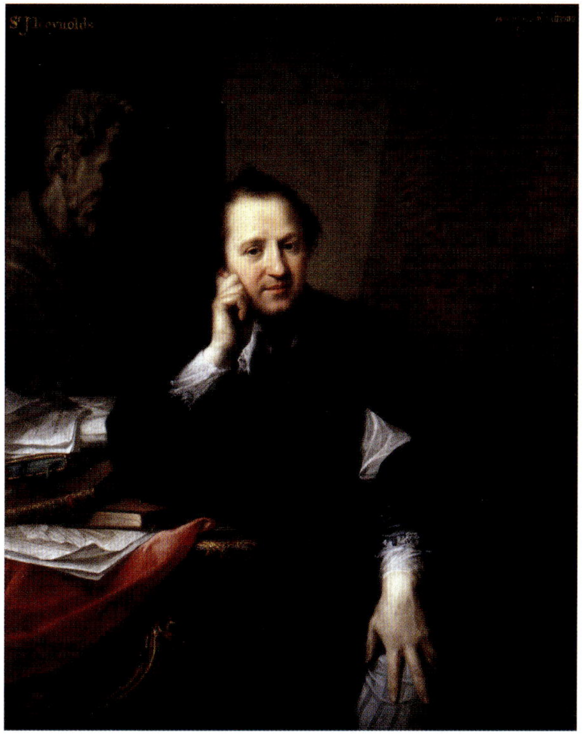

FIG. 18

Giuseppe Marchi
(c.1735–1808)
after Joshua Reynolds
The Honourable Miss Cholmondeley
(1768)
mezzotint,
49.8 x 35.3 cm
British Museum, London (PD 1840, 0808.56)
© The Trustees of the British Museum

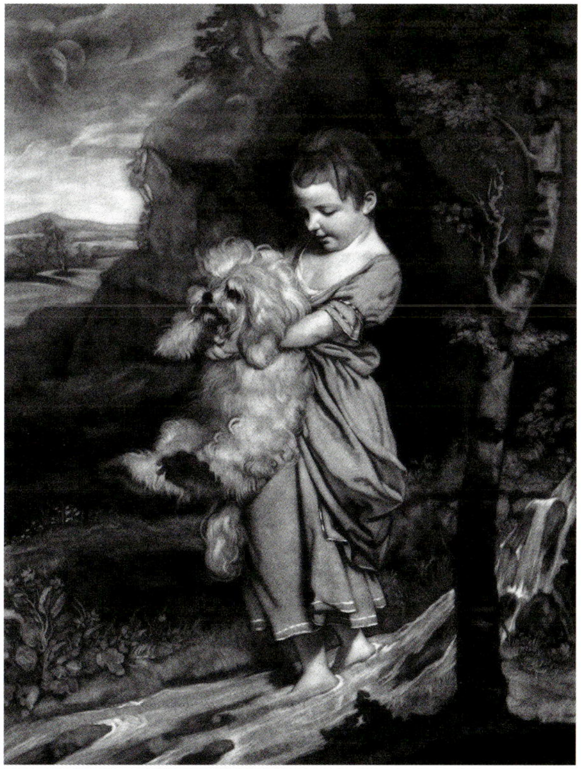

been vexed at Cotes's knack of securing the best spaces for his portraits at the annual exhibition – one of the perks, no doubt, of being a leading figure on the Society's committee.

Reynolds influenced Cotes, but did not encourage him. Indeed, as a rule, he tended to lend assistance to those who were either considerably younger than himself or whose practice did not conflict with his own. Reynolds also made a special point of welcoming artists from abroad, valuing the contribution they made to maintaining the cosmopolitan nature of the British art world. They included, during the 1760s, the American artist Benjamin West, who arrived in London, via Italy, in 1763. In England West continued to emulate the style of Batoni and Mengs, whose work he had copied in Rome. However, he too was influenced by Reynolds's classical portrait compositions. In general, those artists from abroad who succeeded best in London were those who, rather than disturbing patterns of existing patronage, extended the range of options open to patrons. West is one example. Another is the Swiss painter, Angelica Kauffman, who, upon arriving in England in June 1766, was immediately introduced to Reynolds by Brownlow Cecil, 9th Earl of Exeter. Within a matter of months she could boast that Reynolds was 'one of my kindest friends, and is never done praising me to everyone. As a proof of his admiration for me, he has asked me to sit for my picture to him, and, in return, I am to paint his.'[51]

There is no doubt that Kauffman captivated Reynolds, who, by the autumn of 1766, referred to her in his sitter book as 'Miss Angel'.[52] She, in turn, showered affection upon Reynolds, as demonstrated by the intimate portrait she painted of him for John Parker, who was then employing her at Saltram.[53] In Kauffman's portrait of Reynolds he sports a Van Dyck costume, a mode of dress he is unlikely to have ever adopted beyond the realm of the masquerade, if at all. The table at his side is strewn with books, including Goldsmith's *The Traveller*, Burke's *Philosophical Enquiry*, and essays from Johnson's *Rambler* and *Idler*.[54] Behind and to the left is a plaster cast of Daniele da Volterra's bust of Michelangelo; the same bust that appears in the self-portrait he painted for the Royal Academy around 1780.

To the right, resting on an easel, is a blank canvas; an allusion, perhaps, as it has been observed, 'to the first part of creation, the invention that takes place within the mind'.[55] Collectively, the emblems assembled in the portrait reveal the sources of Reynolds's inspiration: the writings of his friends, their company and conversation (to which he apparently lends an ear), and the legacy of the 'Great Style', exemplified by Michelangelo.[56]

By the later 1760s Reynolds was regarded justifiably as the leading portrait British painter of the age. As a result, he was entangled in the art politics of the period; not least the deliberations of the Society of Artists. Reynolds had been a key figure in the establishment of the Society, heading the committee to organize the first exhibition in 1759, and playing an instrumental role in drafting its policy documents. He continued to be an active member of the Committee during the early 1760s. Yet, in 1765 Reynolds abruptly distanced himself from the Society of Artists, ostensibly remaining aloof from its internal affairs, which over the next few years were characterized by fierce internecine strife. By the spring of 1767 the Society of Artists had reached crisis point, and in March 1767 the rump of the Society, led by the outspoken Irish painter, William 'Blarney' Thomson, resolved to petition the Directors to establish a 'proper form for instituting a public Academy'. Early in June George Michael Moser, on behalf of the Directors, stated that this resolution was to be repealed owing to George III's 'royal intention of taking the Academy under his protection'.[57] The principal consequence of the announcement was the removal by the Directors of the complete apparatus of the St Martin's Lane Academy to Richard Dalton's print warehouse in Pall Mall, over which was placed a makeshift sign reading 'the royal academy'.[58] It may not, therefore, have been a coincidence that in 1767 Reynolds decided to abstain, for the only time in his career, from exhibiting work at the annual summer exhibition. He was, possibly, honouring the promise made to 'some friends of the society' not to become involved in any way.[59] According to his friend Edmund Burke, the reason was more straightforward, noting that Reynolds 'does not think mere heads sufficient and having no piece of fancy sends in nothing this time'.[60] Exactly what Burke meant by a 'piece of fancy' is unclear; not least since Reynolds had not yet exhibited any 'fancy pictures'; the sort of imaginative character studies of children which he began to produce over the next few years. His comment does, however, suggest that Reynolds was no longer content to be regarded simply as a society portrait painter, albeit the best of them.

At the annual exhibition of the Society of Artists in 1768 Reynolds exhibited one work only, the portrait of a young girl, Miss Hester Cholmondeley, struggling across a stream with a large dog (FIG. 18, p. 85), which, it has been observed, may have been a 'humorous adaptation' of Hercules lifting Antaeus.[61] Perhaps this was the sort of painting that Reynolds regarded as a 'piece of fancy'. Later in the year, at a special exhibition to mark the state visit to England by the king of Denmark, he showed three pictures, including his earlier portrait of Laurence Sterne (who had died that spring), and a double portrait of the architect, James Paine, and his son, poring over the architect's designs for Worksop Manor, Nottinghamshire, which he had painted some two years earlier. Paine had been a close friend of Reynolds for some years, and had designed a chimneypiece and probably also his gallery and painting room in Leicester Square.[62] However, his decision to exhibit the portrait may have been linked to his tacit support for Paine's position within the Society of Artists. In marked contrast to most of the nation's leading artistic figures Paine had conspicuously allied himself with the rank and file of the Society of Artists who objected to what they regarded as the abuse of power by the Society's Directors, including his principal political rival, William Chambers.[63] In promoting Paine at the exhibition, perhaps Reynolds was sending out a signal to both sides that he retained his old allegiances, and was not to be counted among those who sought to destroy the Society of Artists.

The exhibition for the King of Denmark provided only a brief respite to the hostilities within the Society of Artists, which was by now irredeemably divided in its ranks. Already, in June the Fellows of the Society of Artists had gained a ruling from the Attorney General allowing them to replace eight of the twenty-four Directors. In an extended coup during October 1768 the Fellows removed sixteen of the existing Directors. The following month, the remaining Directors tendered their resignation.[64] Reynolds, who was on a visit to France for most of this time, remained aloof, remote from the clique of court artists (including William Chambers, Benjamin West and Francis Cotes) who sought the patronage of the King for their new 'royal' academy. Nor was Reynolds's name included among the twenty-two signatures appended to the Memorial presented to the King on 28 November 1768, requesting his 'gracious assistance, patronage, and protection'. Reynolds, who had still to make up his mind whether to remain with the Society of Artists, chose to discuss the situation with 'a particular friend' within the Society; almost certainly James Paine.[65] Indeed, Reynolds's sitter book confirms that on Sunday 20 November, just over a week before the Memorial was presented to the King, he had met Paine, perhaps to discuss the possibility of taking up one of the vacant Directorships – or even the Presidency – of the Society of Artists.[66] In the event, on 25 November 1768, he wrote to resign his place as a Director, 'the doing of which', he stated, 'I hope will not be understood as proceeding from any want of respect'.[67] Shortly afterwards, Reynolds apparently corresponded with Gainsborough. Although the contents of the letter are unknown, it was probably more than mere coincidence that just over two weeks later Gainsborough also tendered his resignation.

By the end of 1768, from a position on the periphery of London's institutional art world, Reynolds moved rapidly to assume centre stage. Although William Chambers coveted the presidency of the Royal Academy, it was decided to offer the post to Reynolds, Benjamin West being deputed to liaise with him on the matter.[68] Initially, Reynolds resisted West's offer, informing him that the scheme 'would come to nothing'.[69] However, a few hours later, realizing that West's cohort had the royal ear, he accepted. Within twenty-four hours George III signed the Instrument of Foundation of the Royal Academy.[70] On 14 December 1768 Reynolds was formally elected President.[71] It has been suggested that Reynolds's reluctance to become involved with plans to form the Royal Academy may have been connected with his unsuccessful attempts to gain the King's patronage during the 1760s.[72] Whatever his motives, before he assumed the Presidency, Reynolds had signalled his independence from the King by consulting with his close friends, Edmund Burke and Samuel Johnson. 'This hesitation,' stated West, 'was mentioned by Sir Wm. Chambers to the King, who from that time entertained a prejudice against Reynolds, for both Johnson & Burke were then disliked by the King, the latter particularly on political accounts'.[73] George III disliked Burke, who was outspoken in his attacks on the King's position and policies, culminating in his skilful *Thoughts on the present Discontents* of 1770. The King had little reason to distrust Johnson, who was an ardent monarchist.[74] Even so, while he respected the Crown, Johnson was no courtier, and like Reynolds, felt that any allegiance he owed to the King should not compromise his own independence.

George III's principal ally within the Royal Academy was William Chambers, who assumed the post of Treasurer. However, while Chambers courted the King assiduously, Reynolds demonstrated a conspicuous lack of deference towards his Royal patron. In April 1769, only four months after his election, Reynolds reportedly threatened to resign the Presidency, despite a personal plea from the King: 'Reynolds returned that he owed his Majesty the duty of a subject, but no more; and that, as his Majesty had never sat to him, as he had to many others, he desired to adhere to his resolution. The King then said he *would* sit to him'.[75] The sittings did not take place until some years later.[76] On 21 April 1769 George III knighted Reynolds at St James's Palace.[77] From now on, like the famous people who paraded through his studio, Sir Joshua Reynolds, President of the Royal Academy, was confirmed as a celebrity in his own right.

CAPTURING CELEBRITY

WILLIAM BECKFORD

THIS SMALL PORTRAIT WAS PAINTED IN 1782, at a time when the young William Beckford (1760–1844), as entries in Reynolds's sitter books indicate, was making frequent visits to the artist's home in Leicester Square; only some of which were evidently related to this modestly scaled work. Beckford, heir to a large fortune accrued by his father from sugar plantations in the West Indies, was passionate in both his personal affections and his love of art. A phenomenally wealthy young man, Beckford could easily have afforded a much larger, and more imposing, portrait by Reynolds. However, he appears to have chosen the present format for particular reasons, not least because the picture's size – around 28 by 23 inches – does not conform to the standard dimensions used in similar head-and-shoulders portraits by Reynolds. It is significant, therefore, that the dimensions and format of Beckford's portrait are almost identical to another portrait commissioned by him from Reynolds that year; namely, Beckford's fifteen year-old cousin, Alexander Hamilton, eldest son of the 9th Duke of Hamilton – and Beckford's future son-in-law (National Gallery of Scotland). Beckford, who was at that time engaged in an illicit sexual relationship with the teenager, William Courtney, heir to Powderham Castle and later the 9th Earl of Devon, was evidently also attracted to his young cousin, whose portrait was surely commissioned as a pendant to his own by Reynolds.

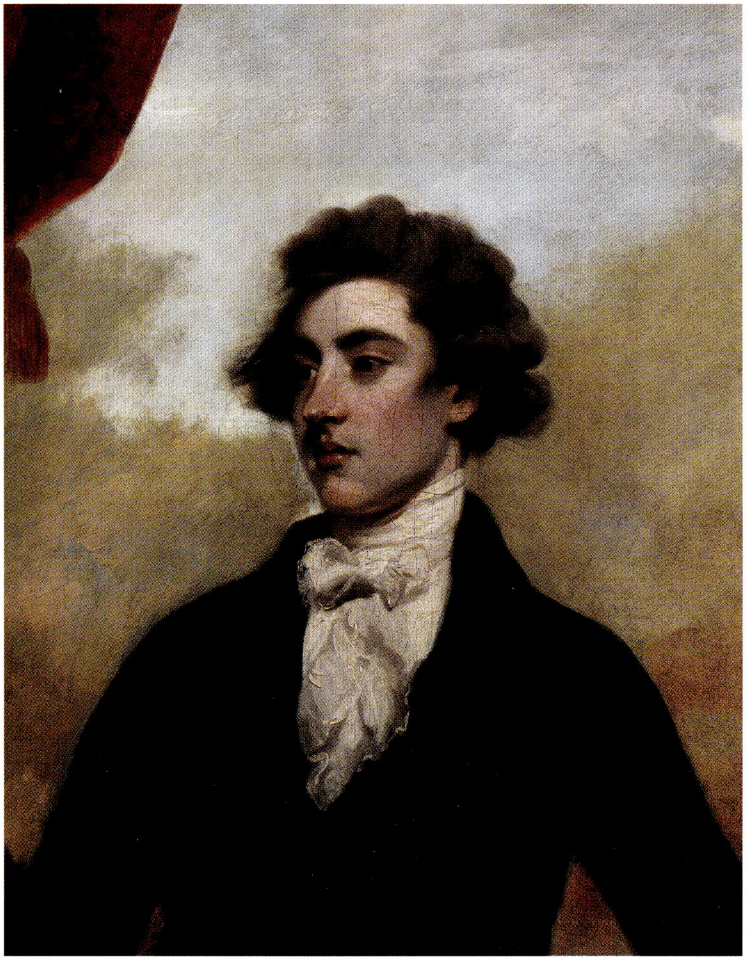

CAT. 24

William Beckford
(1782)
oil on canvas, 71.5 x 58.5 cm
National Portrait Gallery, London

PROVENANCE: Commissioned by William Beckford; bequeathed to his daughter, Susannah, Duchess of Hamilton; Hamilton Palace sale, Christie's, 6 November 1919 (52); bought Knoedler who sold it 7 June 1920 to Mrs George Elkins of Chestnut Hill, Philadelphia; sold by her estate after 1977; purchased in 1980.

EXHIBITION HISTORY: RA 1782 (10); Edinburgh 1883 (110); Grosvenor 1883 (186); New Gallery 1891 (115); 25 Park Lane 1931 (31); Manchester 1988 (96); Bonn 1992.

LITERATURE: Graves & Cronin i, 74–75; Waterhouse, 1941, 73; Mannings 2000, 83 (149).

WILLIAM CHAMBERS

THIS IS THE EARLIEST OF THREE KNOWN portraits by Reynolds of William Chambers (1723–96). It has been suggested, on stylistic grounds, and the age of the sitter (who would then have been in his early thirties), that this portrait dates from the mid-1750s. It is characteristic of a series of portraits of friends that Reynolds painted at this time, in which he sought to depict the sitters in contemplative or intellectual attitudes; another notable instance being the idiosyncratic image of Samuel Johnson (National Portrait Gallery). Reynolds had befriended Chambers probably in Rome some years earlier, in the course of his Grand Tour. Certainly, Chambers was among his principal companions in Paris in 1752, where he made a portrait of Chambers's fiancée, Catherine More. Although Chambers and Reynolds remained on good terms in the 1750s and sixties, relations between them deteriorated in the years following the foundation of the Royal Academy, where Chambers served as Treasurer, and where, as Reynolds maintained, 'Sir William was viceroy over him'. Nevertheless, following the transference of the Royal Academy to the elegant surroundings of Chambers's New Somerset House in 1780, Reynolds once more painted Chambers' portrait, which was installed in the Assembly Room alongside Reynolds's own self-portrait.

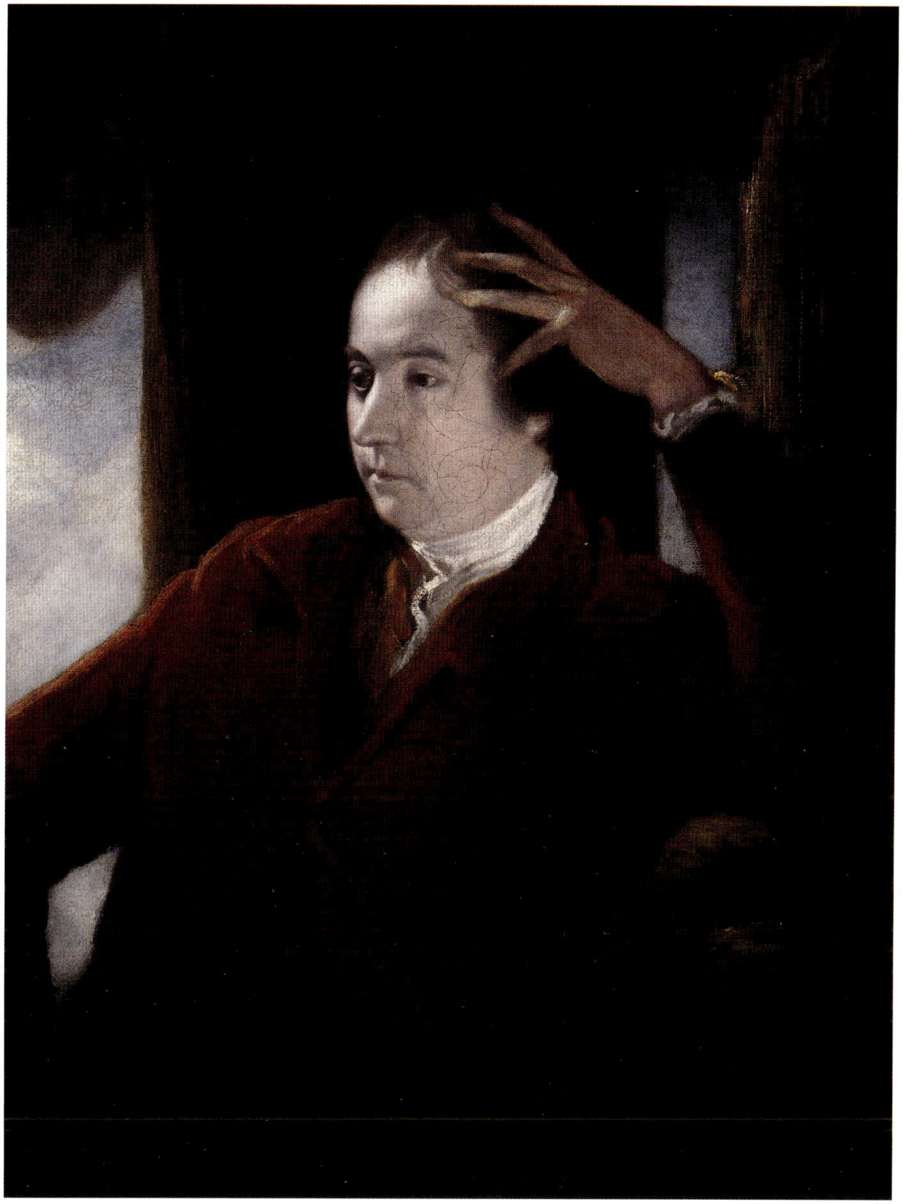

CAT. 25

Sir William Chambers
(c.1756)
oil on canvas, 88.9 x 68.6 cm
National Portrait Gallery, London

PROVENANCE: Acquired from the sitter's son by West; sold West, Christie's, 24 May 1845 (51); bought B S Smith, from whom purchased in 1858.

EXHIBITION HISTORY: Courtauld Institute 1996 (3).

LITERATURE: Graves & Cronin i, 163; Yung 1981, 104; Mannings 2000, 128 (344).

CAT. 26

David Garrick between Tragedy and Comedy
(1760–61)
oil on canvas, 148 x 183 cm

Waddesdon, The Rothschild Collection (Rothschild Family Trust).
Accession no. 102.1995. Photo Mike Fear.

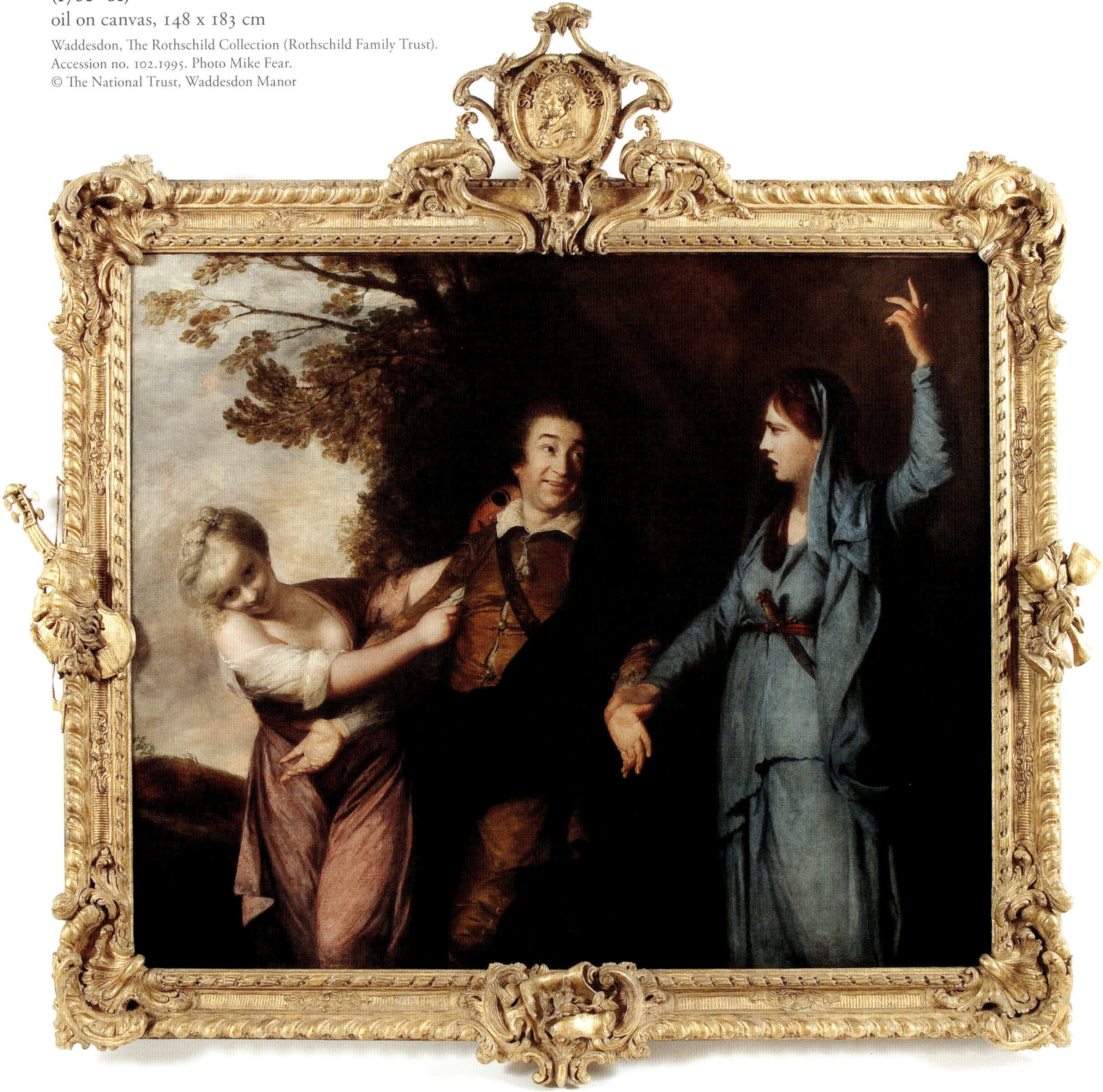

DAVID GARRICK

PROVENANCE: Bought from the artist by George Montagu-Dunk, 2nd Earl of Halifax; Earl of Halifax (deceased) sale, Christie's 20 April 1782 (75); bought by John Julius Angerstein, in whose family it remained until 1872; bought from Wertheimer by Agnew's 11 June 1885 for Sir Nathaniel de Rothschild 1885; thence by descent.

EXHIBITION HISTORY: SA 1762 (88); BI 1813 (32), 1843 (26), 1851 (70); South Kensington 1867 (594); RA 1872 (78); 45 Park Lane 1937 (88); RA 1951 (18); Paris 1985 (21); RA 1986 (42); Holburne Museum of Art, Bath 2003.

LITERATURE: Malone, in Reynolds 1798, i, lxii; Edwards 1808, 188; Northcote i, 105; Hamilton 1831, i, n.p.; Beechey 1835, i, 156–57; Cotton 1856, 70; Leslie & Taylor i, 205; Graves & Cronin i, 350–51; Panofsky 1930, note 1, 133; Waterhouse 12, 48, 50; Waterhouse 1973, 21–22; Mannings 1984, 259–83; Busch 1984, 82–99; Wind 1986, 35–39; Postle 190, 306–11; APS 4; Mannings 2000, 209–10 (700).

AMONG REYNOLDS'S FINEST ACHIEVEMENTS, the allegorical portrayal of David Garrick (1717–79)poised between the muses of Tragedy and Comedy, under-lined the artist's credentials as the most inventive and ambitious portraitist of his age, as well as Garrick's supreme acting skills. As Horace Walpole stated, when the portrait was exhibited at the Society of Artists in 1761, 'the thought [was] taken by Garrick from the judgement of Hercules'; an observation which suggests that Reynolds was responding to an idea supplied by the eminent actor, who wished evidently to draw attention to his versatility. The tale of Hercules at the Crossroads, where the hero encounters Virtue and Pleasure, was told by the classical author, Prodicus, although Reynolds relied evidently upon the parodic account in Ovid's *Amores*, where the eponymous author – like Garrick – opts for pleasure rather than duty. Reynolds's pictorial sources for the portrait were varied, including, it has been suggested, a *Triumph of Silenus* from the studio of Rubens, Guido Reni's *Lot and his daughters*, and William Dobson's portrait of the artist with Nicholas Lanier and Sir Charles Cotterell. As well as adverting to the choices open to Garrick as a stage actor, Reynolds's composition also alluded to his own artistic options; for while Tragedy is painted in the public style of the Bolognese master, Guido Reni – who exemplifies the intellectual sphere of drawing, or 'disegno' – the soft-focussed figure of Comedy is inspired by the art of Correggio, which appeals to the private sphere of the senses.

CHARLES ROGERS

CHARLES ROGERS'S (1711–84) CAREER WAS spent at the Customs House in London, where he began work in 1731, rising to Clerk of the Certificates in 1746 and holding that post until his retirement in 1780. Although not born into wealth, in 1740 he inherited property from his friend and patron William Townson and again, in 1742 and 1755, from Townson's unmarried sisters. Starting in the late 1730s Rogers became a notable collector of works of art. Contacts with influential figures at the Customs House provided him with a network of fellow enthusiasts who helped him purchase from abroad. His wide circle of friends included artists and aesthetes, among them Horace Walpole, Sir Joshua Reynolds, Paul Sandby and George Romney. The nucleus of Rogers's collection was passed on to him by Townson but he enlarged it substantially over the next 40 years, becoming one of the best known collectors of the age. He left his collection to his brother-in-law William Cotton, whose grandson, also called William, bequeathed it to Plymouth in 1853 as part of the Cottonian Collection (Plymouth City Museum and Art Gallery).

Rogers complained to Walpole that Reynolds had made him look too young. Walpole replied that 'posterity will not know at what age the Likeness was taken'. The portrait was engraved by William Wynne Ryland (1733–83) in 1778 and appeared as the frontispiece in both volumes of Rogers's *A Collection of Prints in Imitation of Drawings* published in that year and comprising 112 prints after Old Master drawings

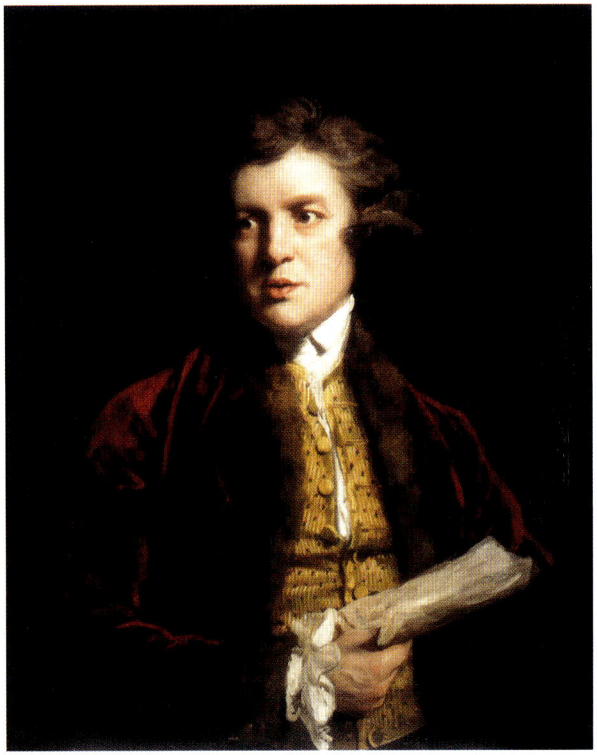

CAT. 27

Charles Rogers
(1777)
oil on canvas, 75.7 x 63.3 cm
Plymouth City Museum and Art Gallery: Cottonian Collection

PROVENANCE: By descent to William Cotton of Ivybridge, 1816. Bequeathed with Cotton's collection to the City of Plymouth, 1853.

EXHIBITION HISTORY: British Institution, 1855 (102); 45 Park Lane, 1937 (38); Plymouth, 1951 (45), 1953, 1973 (47).

LITERATURE: Jewitt, 1853, p.vii; Cotton, 1856, p.130; Graves and Cronin, vol.2, p.841–42; Cottonian Collection, 1953, p.9; Mannings, 2000, p.398.

and 463 pages of text. As Rogers announced, the prints were 'faithful Imitations, they are engraved the same way, as well as of the same size, as the Originals are drawn; and printed, as nearly as possible, in the same colours.' His pioneering book is a testament to the eighteenth-century enthusiasm for Old Master drawings.

HORACE WALPOLE

REYNOLDS'S PORTRAIT OF THE WEALTHY connoisseur and collector, Horace Walpole (1717–97), depicts the sitter in contemplative mode, his elbow resting upon a table with an engraving of a large stone eagle which he had acquired from the Boccapadugli Gardens in Rome. The quill, positioned nearby, refers to Walpole's scholarly aspirations, which were to reach fruition in 1758 with the publication of his *Catalogue of Royal and Noble Authors of England.* Walpole evidently admired Reynolds's portrait as he commissioned two further replicas, which he presented to his relations. The portrait was also engraved by James McArdell, although Walpole seized from the engraver not only all the impressions but also the copper plate itself, in order to control the distribution of the image. The youngest son of the Prime Minister, Robert Walpole, Horace had travelled to Europe in 1739, following an education at Eton and King's College, Cambridge. As a youth, he had been surrounded by the magnificent Old-Master collection assembled by his father at Houghton Hall, Norfolk. In 1747, at the age of thirty, Walpole acquired his own property in Twickenham, where over the ensuing years he created his celebrated Gothic residence, Strawberry Hill. Walpole kept a critical eye on the development of Reynolds's career, and although Walpole did not commission further portraits of himself from Reynolds, in 1780 he requested a portrait of his 'three fair nieces', the daughters of James, 2nd Earl Waldegrave, and Maria Walpole, the illegitimate daughter of Horace's elder brother.

CAT. 28

Horace Walpole
(1756)
oil on canvas,
127 x 101.6 cm
National Portrait Gallery, London

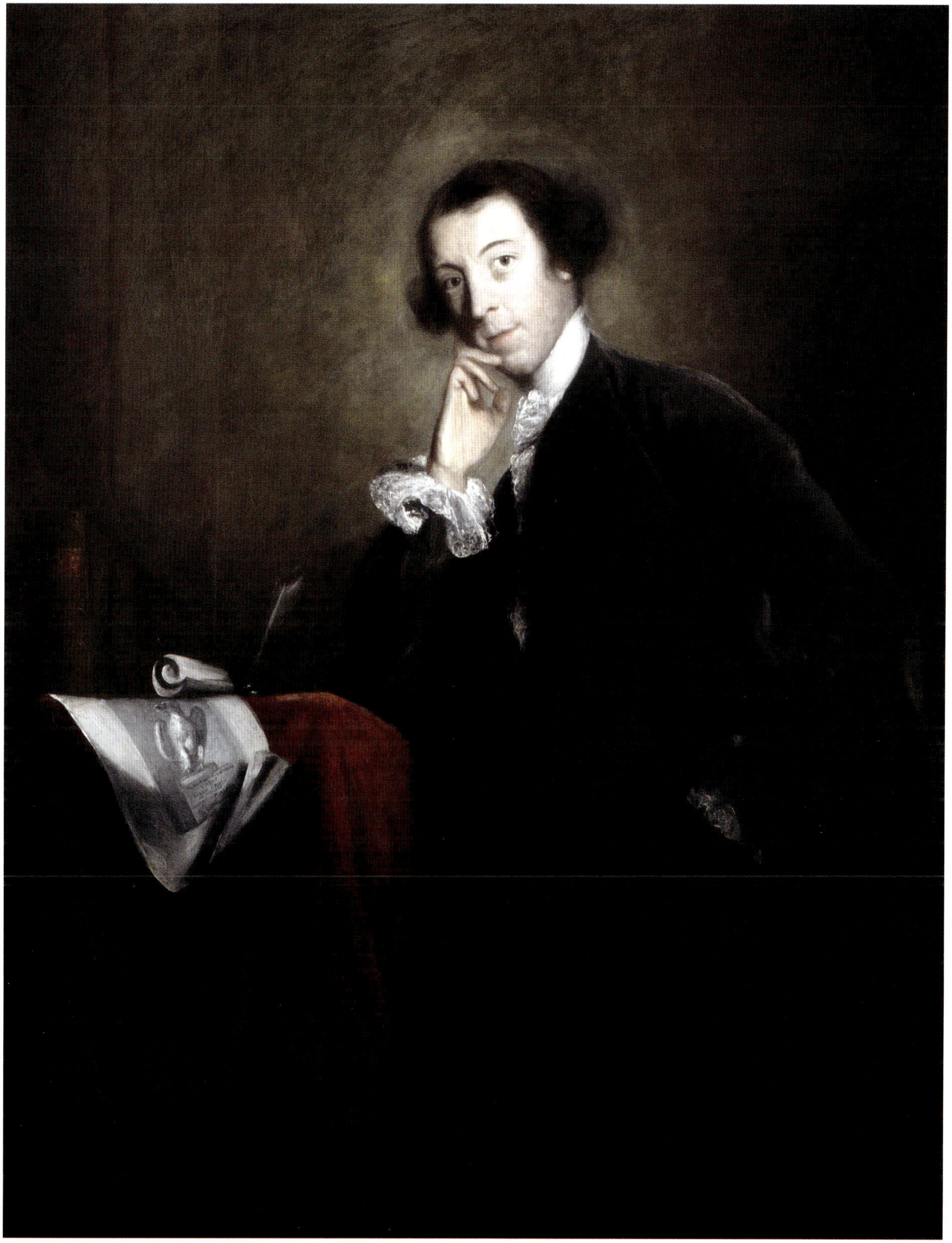

PROVENANCE: Painted for Grosvenor Bedford, Walpole's London agent; Lady Colum Crichton-Stuart; bought by the 3rd Marquess of Lansdowne before the Grosvenor Bedford sale of 1861; by descent until 1999, when purchased from Lord Lansdowne through a private treaty sale in 1999, with the assistance of the Heritage Lottery Fund, the Art Fund and the Dame Helen Gardner Bequest.

EXHIBITION HISTORY: 45 Park Lane 1937 (80); Agnews 1954 (Lansdowne) (41); Edinburgh 1962 (83); Twickenham 1966 (15); York 1973 (42); Orleans House 1980 (9); Tate Britain 2005 (32).

LITERATURE: [Ambrose] 1897, no.40; Graves & Cronin, iii, 1024–25; Waterhouse, 41; Adams and Lewis 1970, no.A.13.2; Miller 1982, 15; Mannings 2000, 459 (1819); Postle 2005.

CAT. 29

James McArdell
(1729–65)
after Joshua Reynolds
Edward Boscawen
(1757)
mezzotint engraving,
51 x 35 cm
National Portrait Gallery, London

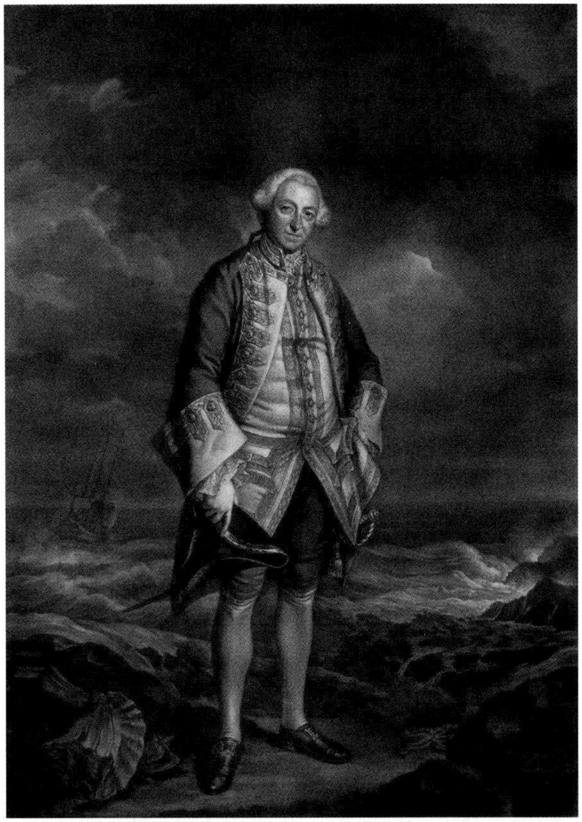

CAT. 30

James McArdell
(1729–65)
after Joshua Reynolds
Dr John Reynolds
(1757)
mezzotint engraving,
35.6 x 25.5 cm
National Portrait Gallery, London

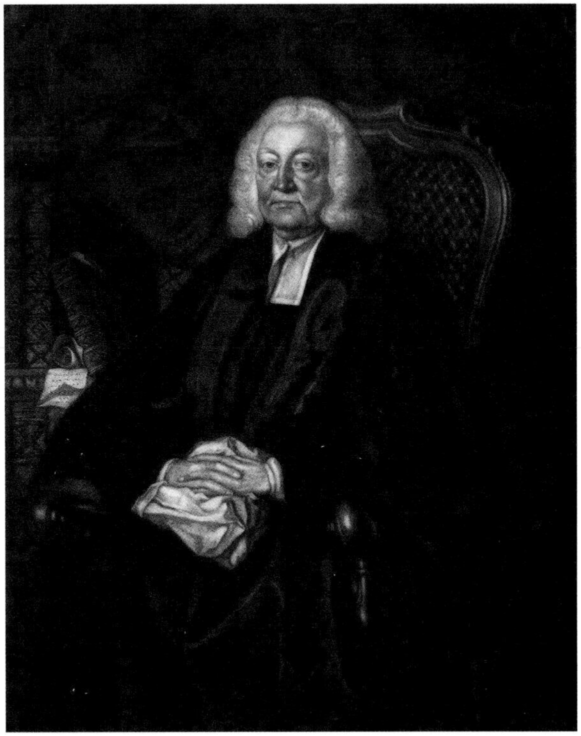

JAMES MCARDELL

THE PORTRAIT OF THE IRISH COPPER-plate engraver, James McArdell (1729–65), was probably painted by Reynolds of his own volition, rather than as a commission. As its whereabouts are unknown prior to 1836, it is quite possible that the portrait was either sold, or presented to McArdell in recognition of his skills in replicating Reynolds's portraits in print form. Reynolds's awareness of the importance of McArdell's contribution to his burgeoning reputation was revealed in his reputed exclamation, 'by this man I shall be immortalized'. McArdell made the very first recorded mezzotint after Reynolds in 1754, based upon the portrait of the eight-year old, Lady Charlotte Fitzwilliam. Reynolds was so proud of the portrait that he wrote to the sitter's mother 'to beg the liberty of having a Mezzotinto Print from it, which will be finish'd whilst the Picture is drying, so that it will not be detain'd on that account'. McArdell continued to make engravings of some of Reynolds's most prestigious portraits until his untimely death in his mid-thirties. They included, notably, prints after Horace Walpole, Admiral Boscawen, Laurence Sterne, and Anne Bonfoy, eldest daughter of his important early patron, Richard Eliot.

James McArdell's mezzotint of John Reynolds (CAT. 30) was made in 1757, probably the same year in which Reynolds painted the original portrait. The portrait is among the most formal and austere of Reynolds's portraits, an indication of the respect which he had for his uncle, and his clerical office.

John was the half-brother of Reynolds's father, Samuel, being the only son of their father's first marriage. A distinguished cleric and scholar, he was a Fellow of Eton College (where Reynolds's portrait now hangs), and Fellow of King's College, Cambridge, as well as rector of Stoke Charity, Hampshire, and canon of St Peter's Cathedral, Exeter. During his apprentice years in London, Reynolds evidently stayed from time to time with his uncle, who, according to Joseph Farington, at that time 'resided in the Temple'.

Reynolds's full-length portrait of Admiral Edward Boscawen (CAT. 29) was among his most prestigious commissions of the 1750s, as indicated by the decision to enlist McArdell's services to produce this magnificent mezzotint engraving. In the portrait, which Reynolds evidently painted between 1756 and 1757, Boscawen wears the undress uniform of a flag officer, standing impassively on the shore against a storm-tossed sea. A Cornishman by birth, Boscawen had already enjoyed a distinguished naval career, seeing action at Porto Bello, the siege of Cartagena, Madras, and the first battle of Finisterre. Shortly after Reynolds began work on his portrait, Boscawen gained further plaudits following his interception of a French squadron bound for South America, and the capture of several vessels, for which he was thanked formally by Parliament. As his public profile grew steadily during the the Seven Years War, the reproduction of Reynolds's portrait in print form was an excellent commercial proposition.

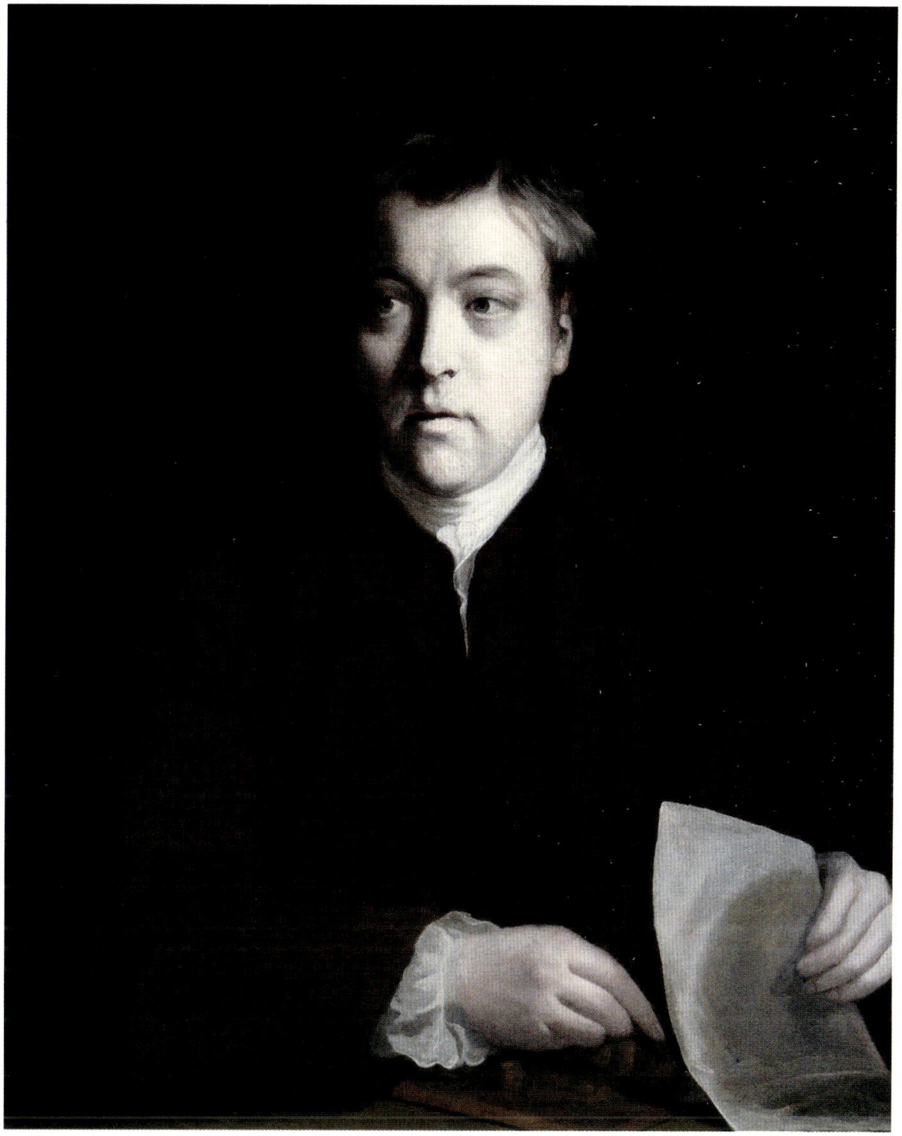

CAT. 31

James McArdell
(c.1756)
oil on canvas, 75 x 62 cm
National Portrait Gallery, London

PROVENANCE: Probably Meade sale Christie's 12 March 1836 (12); bought in; Sir Gilbert Greenall, Bt., 1884; by descent to the Dowager Lady Daresbury, from whom acquired 22 October 1942, via Agnew's, by the National Art Collections Fund, who presented it to the National Portrait Gallery.

EXHIBITION HISTORY: RA 1884 (19); Birmingham 1961 (39).

LITERATURE: Graves & Cronin ii, 101; Kerslake 1977, 175–76; Yung 1981, 361; Mannings 2000, 330 (1235).

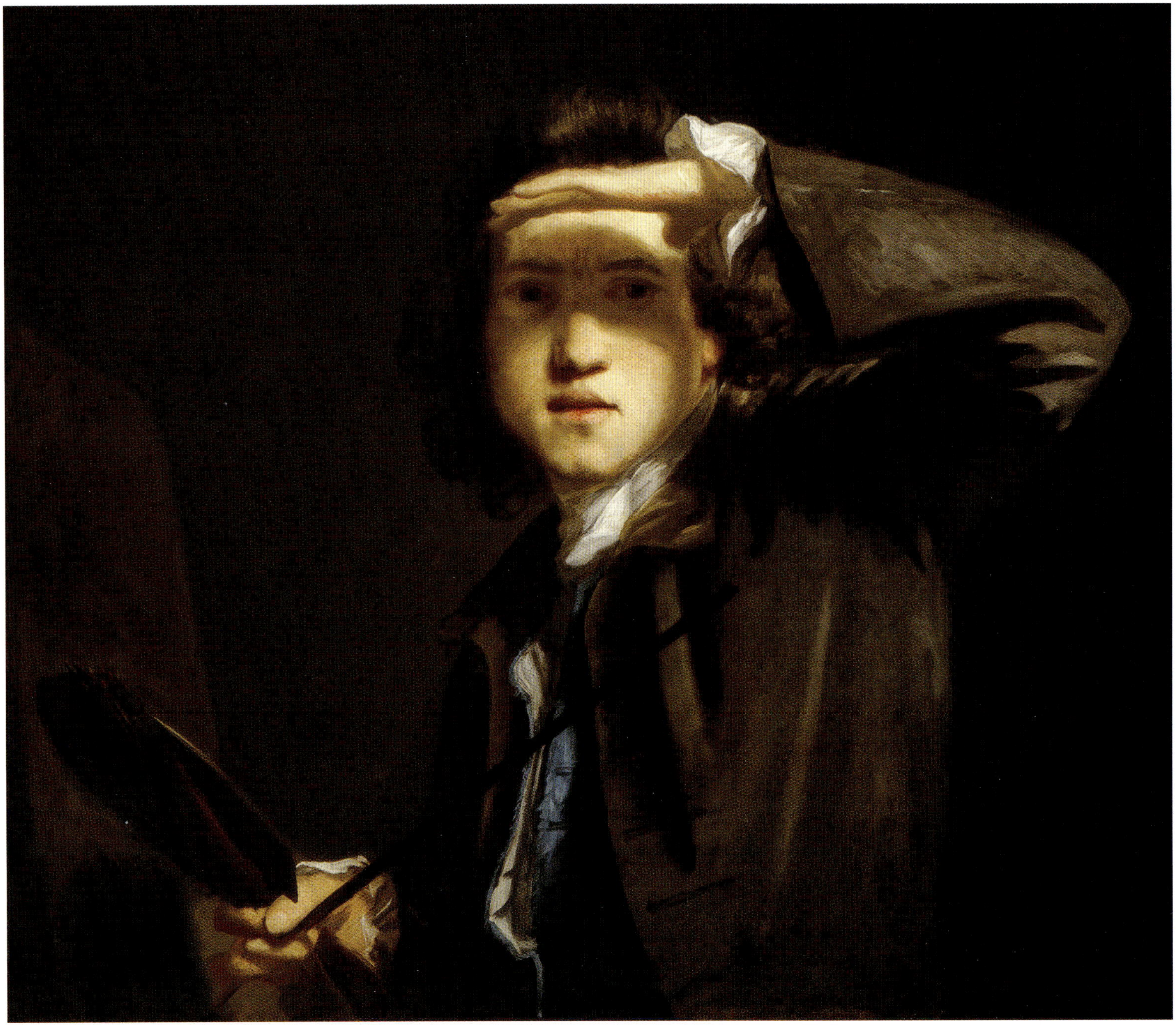

CAT. 32

Self-portrait Shading the Eyes
(c.1747–49)
oil on canvas, 63 x 40 cm
National Portrait Gallery, London

PROVENANCE: Thomas Lane of Coffleet by 1795; Christie's, 24 May 1845 (62); Joseph Sanders of Johnston Hall; his sale, Christie's, 15 May 1858 (40); from whom purchased in 1858.

EXHIBITION HISTORY: South Kensington 1867 (517); British Council 1967; Plymouth 1973 (27); Royal Academy 1986 (13).

LITERATURE: Northcote 1818, vol.I, note p. 304; Cotton 1856, pp.59–60, 272; Leslie & Taylor 1865, vol.I, p.34; Graves & Cronin 1899–1901, vol.II, pp.790–1; Whitman 1903, pp.3, 78; Waterhouse 1948, p.39; Mannings 1975, p.219; White 1983, p.34; Penny *et al.* 1986, pp.175–6; Mannings 2000, 46 (2).

SELF-PORTRAITS

REYNOLDS WAS A MAN OF VARIED talents and remarkable achievements. In his self-portraits, he depicts himself almost exclusively in the context of his impressive academic status and gentlemanly aspirations rather than in his profession as an artist. There is only a single self-portrait (CAT. 32) in which Reynolds, in his mid-twenties, presents himself at work with brushes and palette. Here, he is seen shading his eyes, alluding to his innate faculty of observation, and drawing attention to his hands that are illuminated by a vivid light, reminiscent of Rembrandt's chiaroscuro technique. He is dressed in casual unbuttoned garments as befit the character of the artist and his hair is painted in loose thin strokes that frame the masculine features of the face. Particularly noteworthy is the intense and uneven red of the lips aligned diagonally with the touch of red paint on the brushes and reinforced by the maulstick. In this manner, Reynolds perhaps underscores a reference to painting's mute character: an art that communicates without words. The powerful diagonal between his brush and his lips in fact concludes at his ear, which is also red, and ultimately indicates how he employed all of his senses, including that of hearing, in the service of his art. The empty canvas at the easel stands as a metaphor for his life suggesting that his best work is yet to be completed and that while his technical painting skills may already be established, other complex facets of his character are being developed: the sights he is setting for himself are not merely on his future as a painter but also on his life aspirations beyond the canvas.

Throughout his career, Reynolds amassed an extraordinary collection of honours. He was designated first President of the Academy in 1768, graced with the distinction of knighthood in 1769, elected Alderman of the borough of Plympton in 1772, and voted Mayor a year later. Reynolds was also awarded in 1773 an honorary degree of Doctor of Civil Law by the University of Oxford and, three years later, a degree of Doctor of Laws from Trinity College (Dublin). Among English artists, we find very few with such a roster of achievements and perhaps fewer still who would so candidly acknowledge their ambitions and assert their pride:

> *I do not feel my self possessed of that grandeur of soul sufficient to give me any pretensions of looking down with such philosophical contempt upon titles. Distinction is what we all seek after, and the world does set a value on them, and I go with the great stream of life.*[1]

There is no doubt that the knighthood bestowed upon Reynolds was very gratifying to him, as was his appointment as Court Painter in August 1784. He would not have despised such an honour, which surely elevated his social standing, but he seemed to have favoured his intellectual achievements over his royal appointments, preferring, as the official portraits he painted for the Corporation of Plympton,

CAT. 33

Self-portrait in doctoral robes

(1773)
oil on canvas,
76 x 63.5 cm
Phillip Mould

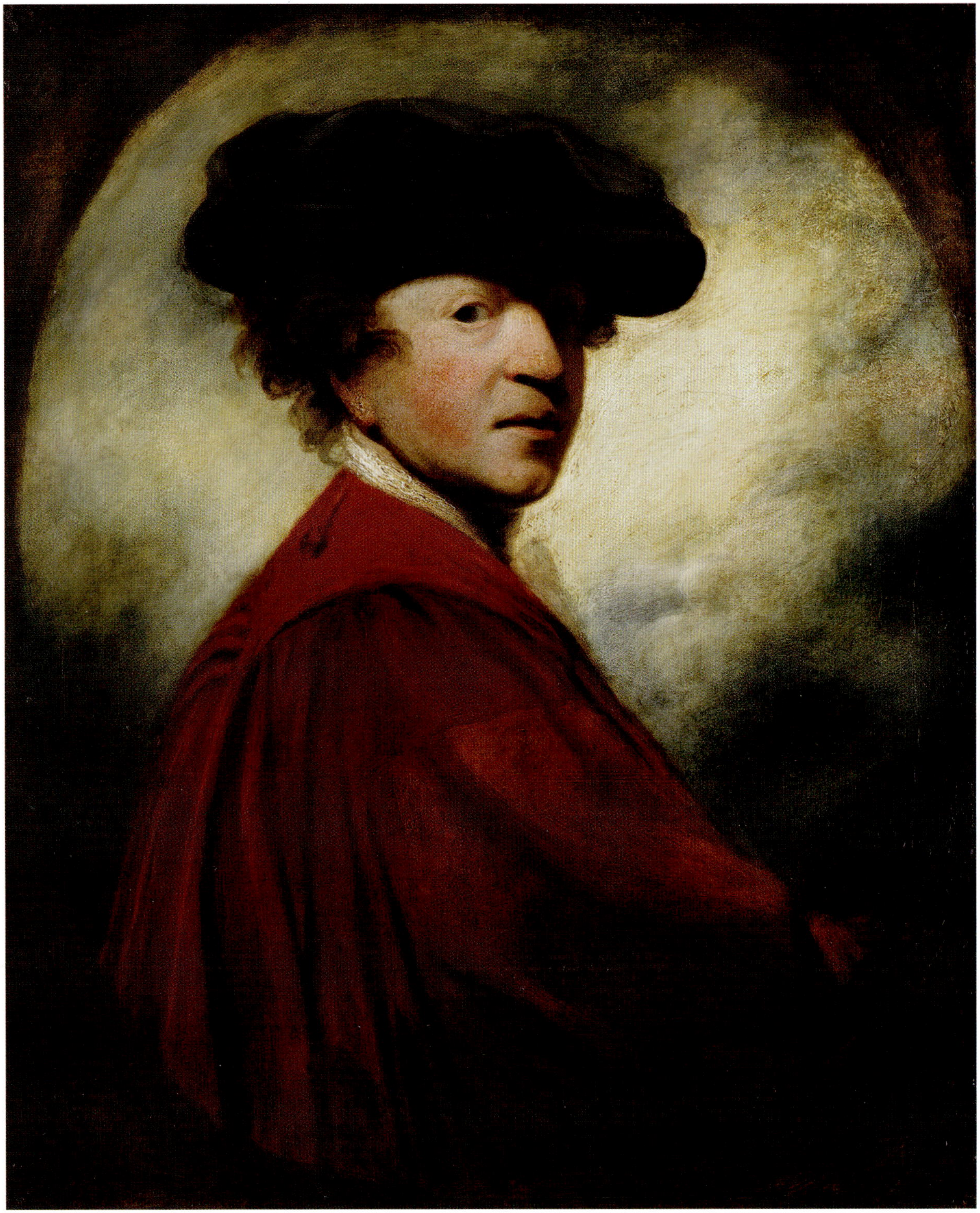

PROVENANCE: Private collection, New York; Philip Mould Ltd.

EXHIBITION HISTORY: None.

LITERATURE: None.

the Uffizi Gallery in Florence, and the Royal Academy, demonstrate, to represent himself as a man of law. Reynolds was acutely aware of the way others perceived him and cared greatly about his appearance. The crimson robes and cap of a Doctor of Civil Law allowed him to project an image of social prestige and importance. In the manner and mode of his Italian predecessors Raphael and Titian, Reynolds ostentatiously shows the large bell-sleeve, traditionally worn by Venetian nobles, as a means of asserting his position in both the preliminary study (CAT. 33) and full-length self-portrait for the Royal Academy. He takes occasion to celebrate his academic status and advertise his authorial stance. The self-assured gaze, like the pose, commands a respectful distance and accentuates the message that Reynolds was the Academy's leader and chief.

As his career progressed, Reynolds's self-portraits increasingly reflected his professional pre-eminence and higher social status. His self-portrait from c.1788, in the Royal Collection (CAT. 34), conveys an image of respect and dignified elegance. In contrast to his more casual self-portrait of around 1747, Reynolds portrays himself as a cultivated and accomplished gentleman. Although his posture seems to imply that he is engaged in the act of painting, significantly, he omits any reference to his profession and conceals his hands. Reynolds lays emphasis on his face and penetrating eyes.[2] Elegantly dressed and wearing spectacles, he looks straight at us with his mouth slightly open. The portrait testifies to the artist's vitality and reflects his ambitions as a man of learning and gentle manners. 'He always evinced a desire to pay a due respect to persons in superior stations,' James Northcote observed, 'and certainly contrived to move in a higher sphere of society than any other English artist had done before him.'[3] He became acquainted with statesmen, intellectuals, and others of significance in society and sought to gain for artists something of the status enjoyed by the sitters he was employed to paint. Reynolds's influence, both from his example and his directives, helped to raise the art of painting into a position of prominence. 'He was the first Englishman,' wrote Edmund Burke, 'who added the praise of the elegant arts to the other glories of his country'.[4]

CAT. 34

Self-portrait
(c.1788)
oil on panel,
75.2 x 63.2 cm
Royal Collection,
H.M. Queen Elizabeth II

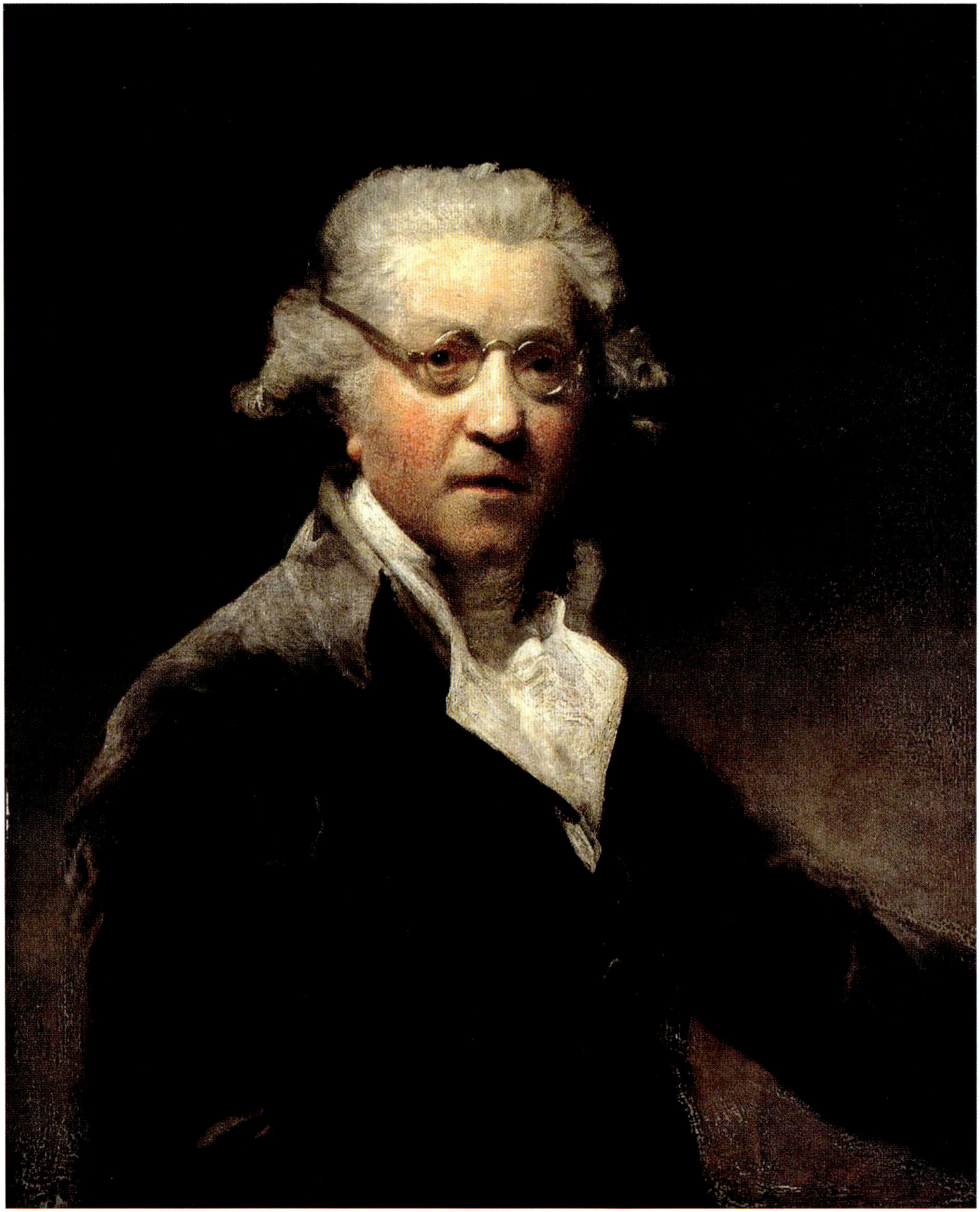

PROVENANCE: Given to George IV in June 1812 by Reynolds's niece, Mary Palmer, Marchioness of Thomond.

EXHIBITION HISTORY: British Institution 1820 (30), 1826 (4); 1827 (67), 1833 (1); Manchester 1857 (307); Royal Academy 1986 (149).

LITERATURE: Malone, in *Reynolds* 1798, vol.I, note 45 p.lxxvii; Northcote 1818, vol.II, p.245; Waagen 1854, vol.II, p.24; Graves & Cronin 1899–1901, vol.II, pp.804–5; Waterhouse 1941, p80; Steegman 1942, p.34; Millar 1969, pp.98–9, no.1088; Waterhouse 1973, p.48; Penny *et al.* 1986, pp.320–22; Mannings 2000, 51 (22).

SIR JOSHUA REYNOLDS COLLECTOR

'CARE, TASTE AND JUDGEMENT': REYNOLDS'S COLLECTION OF WORKS ON PAPER

REYNOLDS'S GRAPHIC ART COLLECTION was large and numbered approximately 3,000 sheets.[1] In many ways its complexity and size make it difficult to fully grasp; it ranged widely in date, geographical reach and concentration. The collection was eclectic and provides a valuable insight into Reynolds's aesthetic preferences. It included drawings by the greatest Italian, Dutch and Flemish draughtsmen such as Raphael, Leonardo da Vinci, Michelangelo, Rembrandt, Rubens and Van Dyck. Painters whose surviving graphic *oeuvre* is small also featured in the collection: Titian, for example, is represented by a small study of Saint Peter for the famous altarpiece *The Assumption* in the Frari, Venice. Reynolds had many examples from prodigious draughtsmen such as Luca Cambiaso or Giulio Romano, a talented pupil of Raphael. Drawings by the Spaniard Bartolomé Estabán Murillo accompanied northern European work by Dürer and Lucas van Leyden (FIG. 19), mural designs by Sir James Thornhill, early drawings by Lorenzo di Bicci (c.1350–1427) and prints, made four centuries later, by Thomas Cheesman (1760–c.1834/5). Stunning red chalk studies of Adam for *The creation of Man* by Michelangelo (FIG. 21), sat next to topographical views of Plymouth (FIG. 20).[2] Reynolds also collected notable drawings in their own right, such as a metalpoint on vivid pink paper by Filippino Lippi (1457–1504) (FIG. 22).[3]

Reynolds owned examples depicting Saint Luke, the patron saint of painters and painting. However, his high-minded nature was counterbalanced by the inclusion in his graphic collection of a surprising number of caricatures and humorous drawings. His early painted parody of Raphael's *The School of Athens* is well known (National Gallery of Ireland, Dublin) and is proof of his witty sense of humour. Later in life, he owned satirical drawings by Guercino and Carlo Maratti. Guercino's caricature of a canine mother and child is one such example.[4] Some of these satires even poke fun at the hallowed art of portraiture itself, such as a sheet by Giovanni Bonatti (1635–81).[5]

Reynolds was doubtless aware of the personal, artistic and stylistic affinities that connect one artist's drawings to another's. He owned drawings by Jacopo da Pontormo (1494–1557), his pupil Agnolo Bronzino (1503–72) and Bronzino's pupil Alessandro Allori (1535–1607). These were among the premier artists in sixteenth-century Florence so vividly described by Giorgio Vasari in his popular *Lives of the most eminent painters, sculptors, and architects (Le vite de' più eccellenti pittori, scultori e architettori).* Reynolds's copy of the first edition of 1550 of Vasari's *Lives* is now fittingly in the library of the Royal Academy of Arts, bearing his sparing annotations in pencil.[6] Pontormo was himself a pupil of Andrea del Sarto, and both he and his fellow student Rosso Fiorentino (1494–1540) were strongly affected by Michelangelo. Rosso was a friend of Vasari and in later life worked for the French King Francis I at Fontainebleau with other Italians, such as Primaticcio. Reynolds owned examples of all their work. He also owned work by

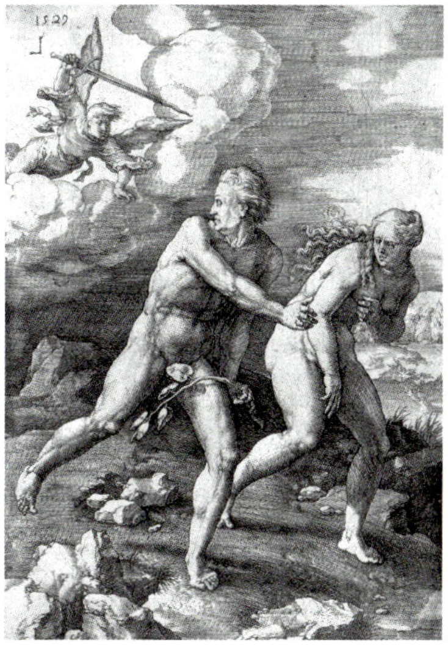

FIG. 19

Lucas van Leyden
(c.1494–1533)
The Expulsion from Paradise
(1529)
engraving, 16.3 x 11.6 cm
Private collection

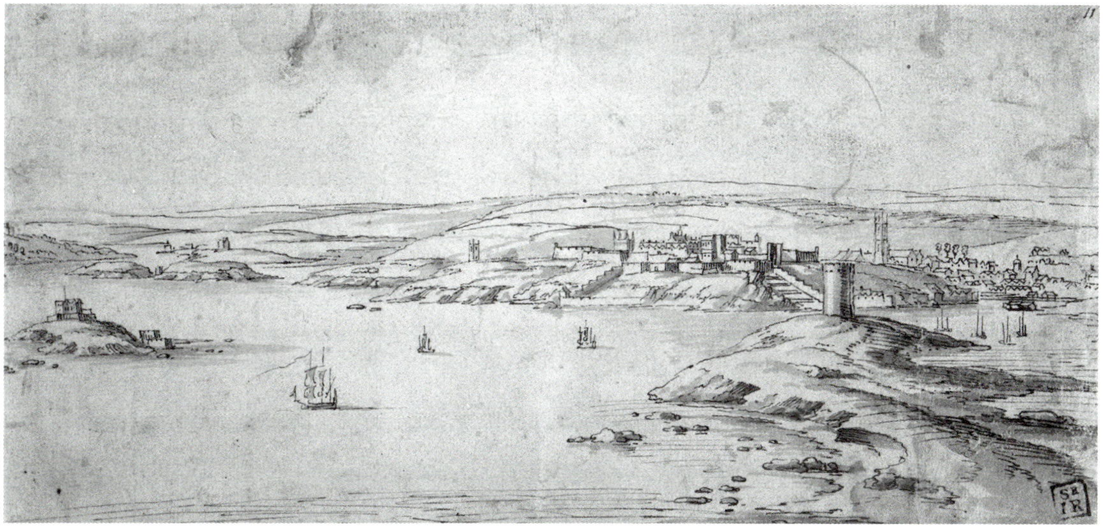

FIG. 20

Anonymous
British School, late seventeenth century
Plymouth Sound
pen and brown ink, with brown wash, 13.3 x 28.3 cm
The Huntington Library, Art Collections, and Botanical Gardens, San Marino, California (acc.no.63.52.178)

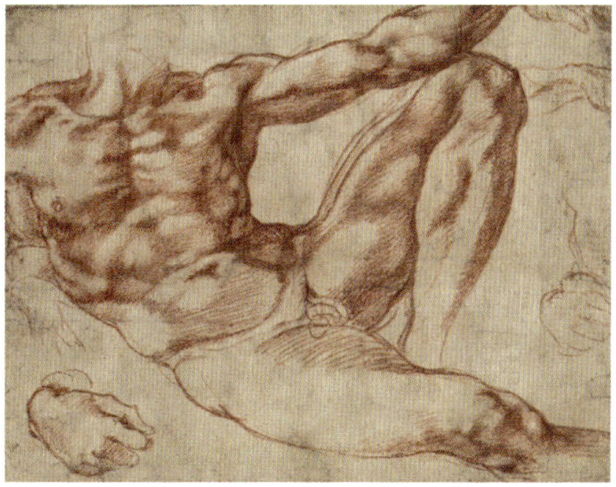

FIG. 21

Michelangelo
(1475–1564)
Study of Adam for the fresco 'The Creation of Man'
(c.1511)
red chalk, 19.3 x 25.9 cm
British Museum, London (PD 1926, 1009.1)

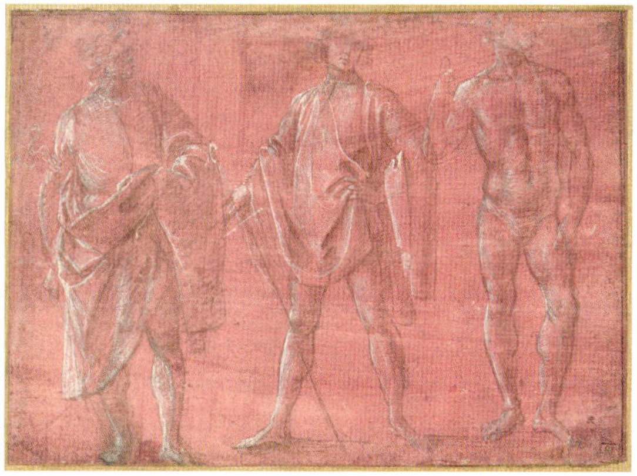

FIG. 22

Filippino Lippi
(c.1457–1504)
Three standing male figures
(c.1480)
metalpoint on pink prepared paper, 19.6 x 27.8 cm
Kunsthalle, Hamburg (inv.no.21044)

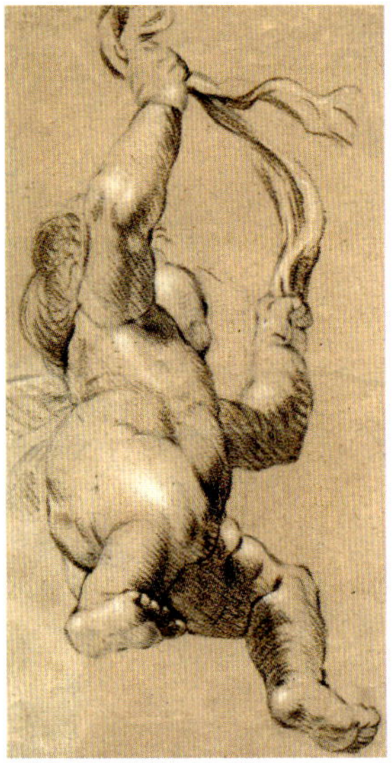

FIG. 23

Sketch of a putto holding a sash
black and white chalk on brown paper, 42.5 x 24.7 cm
British Museum, London (PD 1911, 0517.22)

Michelangelo's friend Sebastiano del Piombo (c.1485–1547), for whom Michelangelo supplied drawings for difficult passages in his enormous canvas *The Raising of Lazarus* (c.1517–19; National Gallery, London) which in the eighteenth century was in the Duc d'Orléans collection. Reynolds owned some of Sebastiano's own drawings for the picture, one large example of which is now in Frankfurt.[7]

Reynolds's collection of drawings also allowed him to make inter-generational connections. Perhaps in an effort to better understand if artistic 'genius' was nurtured or innate, he owned the work of the masters of famous artists. Thus he collected work by Michelangelo's master, Domenico Ghirlandaio, and a drawing connected with *The Birth of the Virgin* in one of his masterpieces, the frescoes for the Tornabuoni Chapel in Santa Maria Novella, Florence (1485–90). Reynolds might have been thinking of his own training in the studio of Hudson in the early 1740s. Hudson's master was Jonathan Richardson I, who in turn was a pupil of John Riley.

Both Richardson and Hudson were important collectors of Old Master prints and drawings. Reynolds was introduced to auctions during his studentship with Hudson. Northcote describes an occasion when Reynolds was 'sent by his master to make a purchase for him at a sale of pictures' and bid on his behalf.[8] Carol Gibson-Wood records the fever occasioned by the release onto the market of the connoisseur Jonathan Richardson's collection, following his death in 1745. The most ardent purchaser was Hudson, who particularly sought out drawings by Rembrandt, which numbered around 120. The prices paid for the Rembrandt drawings were the highest of the sale. Hudson bought *Christ carried to the Sepulchre* for £11-5s[9] and *An Old Woman Rocking a Cradle* for £12. The dealer Arthur Pond paid the highest price of all – £18-5s – for an unidentified drawing.[10] At this stage of his career Reynolds was probably not in a position to compete for prestigious sheets with wealthier collectors with greater resources. Nonetheless, when his financial position was more secure he was later able to buy works that both Pond and Hudson had once previously owned. In following their lead, Reynolds was working in a tradition of collecting graphic works that went back at least to Vasari. He would have been aware of Vasari's glowing reference to Giulio Romano's drawings in which he 'always expressed his ideas better in [these] drawings than in finished work or in paintings, displaying more vivacity, boldness, and expression.'

Broadly put, Reynolds's graphic art collection overlapped his collection of paintings.[11] Many artists were represented in both prints and drawings (Andrea Schiavone, Annibale Carracci, Rembrandt, Rubens, Titian and Barocci) or in drawings and paintings (Guercino, Rembrandt, Rubens and Poussin). Reynolds sometimes owned paintings and drawings for the same composition, giving his collection unusual depth. For example, Rembrandt's painting *The Lamentation over the Dead Christ* (c.1635; National Gallery, London) has a label stuck on the back by Reynolds in which he had copied an inscription from a drawing he owned, now in the British Museum.[12]

Reynolds had his favourites. For example, Guercino (1591–1666) seems to have been an important artist for him, to whom he had been exposed from his earliest training under Hudson. Years later, following his master's death, he acquired choice examples of Guercino drawings from Hudson's collection. In between, visits to Italy had exposed him to countless of his works in Bologna and elsewhere. Reynolds owned an early copy of Guercino's *Madonna and Child with the Infant Saint John*, engraved by John Hamilton Mortimer in 1766 as in Reynolds's collection, and later sold it to Lord Boringdon for Saltram House, where it remains.[13] Reynolds seems to have responded to Guercino's depictions of children and *putti*, as well as his technique. In one drawing of a child with raised arms, Guercino prefigures Reynolds's own depictions of children. The drawing had once belonged to Hudson, in whose studio Reynolds would have seen it in his formative years, and later he came to own it himself (private collection).[14] One drawing by Reynolds of a *putto* with a sash is heavily influenced by Guercino (FIG. 23), and bears close resemblance to a sheet he once owned, now attributed to a follower of Guercino (FIG. 24).[15]

Northcote describes Hudson's advice to Reynolds, recommending the young student to make elaborate copies of Guercino drawings he had in his collection, usually in pen and brown ink, the same medium

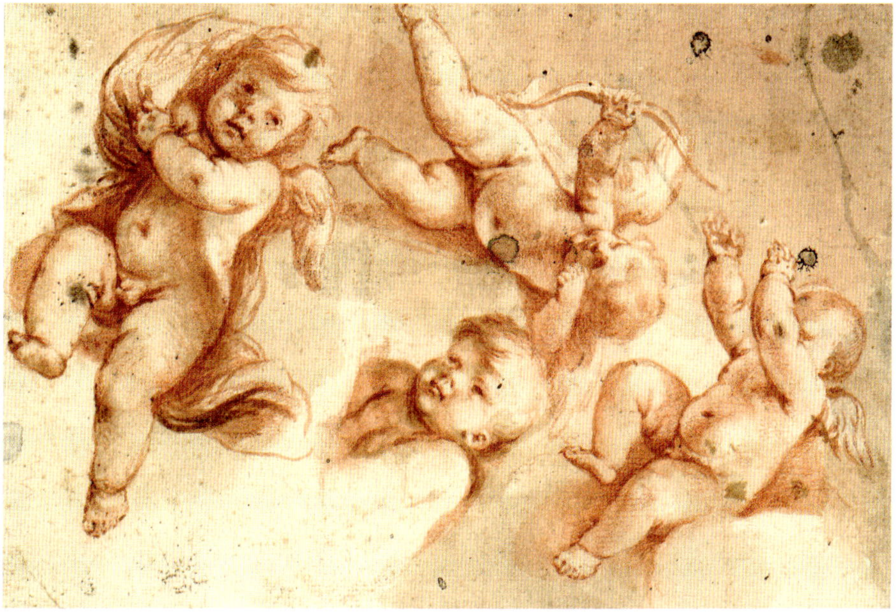

FIG. 24

After **Guercino**
(1591–1666)
Four putti
red chalk with red-brown wash, 24.9 x 17.1 cm
British Museum, London (PD Pp, 4.43)

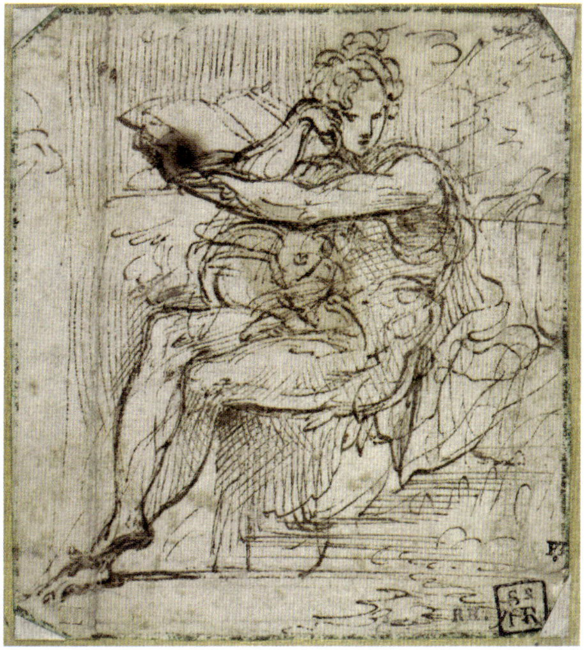

FIG. 25

Parmigianino
(1503–40)
Saint John the Baptist in the wilderness
pen and brown ink, 10.4 x 9.6 cm
British Museum, London (PD 1947, 1108.1)

employed by the Italian. These were executed 'with such skill, that many of those early productions [of Reynolds]... are actually considered as masterly originals by Guercino himself.'[16] After he left Hudson's tutelage Reynolds continued the practice of making drawings. On one sheet he made two separate recordings, in a fast and annotated fashion, after two Rembrandt drawings that he owned.[17] Reynolds was attracted by these drawings' unusual poses: the first of a seated male with his hands resting on his knees, and the other of a male with his hand to his head, deep in thought. The speedy economy of Rembrandt's small study was matched by Reynolds's swift, adept recording in the same medium.

Reynolds's elevated social position and wide friendships brought him into contact with other important collections of Old Master prints and drawings. Prominent was the customs official Charles Rogers (1711–84). His fame now rests upon his splendid two-volume publication *A collection of prints in imitation of drawings* (1778). Reynolds painted his portrait in 1777 (CAT. 27, p. 92), which served as the model for the frontispiece to his work, engraved by William Wynne Ryland. Rogers had a good group of drawings by Maratti and Farinati, artists whose work coincided with Reynolds's taste. In 1799 most of Rogers's collection was sold, too late to benefit Reynolds. However, Rogers seems to have given at least one drawing to Reynolds, a pen-and-ink by Parmigianino, perhaps in gratitude for having so generously offered his collection up for reproduction, since it was included in *Imitation of drawings* as Rogers's but does not bear his collector's mark (FIG. 25). The Spencer family at Althorp and the Devonshires at Chatsworth also had superb collections, to which Reynolds is likely to have had access, especially at their London residences. He certainly painted many portraits of members of both these families. Lesser collections included the Bouverie family from Northamptonshire, who owned 'hundreds of drawings by Guercino'.[18] They also owned a superb Guido Reni of *Saint Francis* that came from Jonathan Richardson I,[19] as well as five genuine Correggio drawings, which were highly prized in eighteenth-century Britain.[20] Reynolds

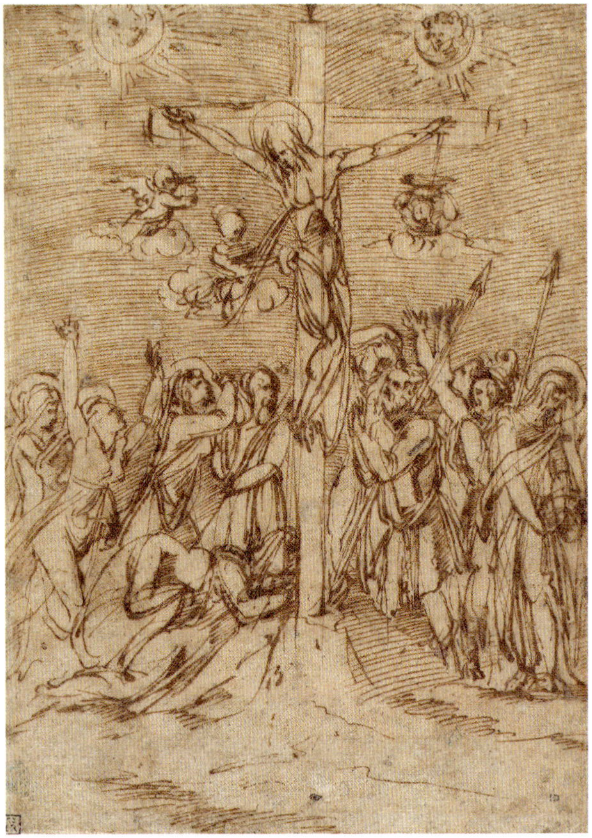

FIG. 26

Baccio Bandinelli
(1493–1560)
The Crucifixion
pen and brown ink, 37.4 x 20 cm
National Gallery of Canada, Ottawa (no.30718)

painted members of the family so may well have been acquainted with their collection.

Northcote was keen to stress Reynolds's busy and productive attitude to his professional practice; evenings spent alone at home were never 'spent in idleness, or lost in dissipation', as in 1762 when:

> *...after his daily occupation was past, he employed himself in looking over, and studying from, the prints of the Old Masters, of which he had procured a fine collection.*[21]

Reynolds occasionally made specific reference to his graphic collection in his lectures, as he also did with paintings he owned. For example, in December 1778 he mentions his celebrated Rubens panel *Moonlit Landscape*[22] in Discourse VIII. In another lecture (Discourse XII) from December 1784 he describes:

> *This figure [with her head thrown back in emotion] Baccio Bandinelli, in a drawing that I have of that Master, of the* Descent from the Cross, *has adopted, (and he knew very well what was worth borrowing,) for one of the Marys, to express frantick agony of grief. It is curious to observe, and it is certainly true, that the extremes of contrary passions are with very little variation expressed by the same action.*

Many drawings by Bandinelli were in Reynolds's collection, and the sheet described might be that now in the National Gallery of Canada (FIG. 26).[23] Reynolds bequeathed his collection to his niece, Mary Palmer. In 1794, parts of it were offered for sale. The catalogue by Reynolds's friend, art dealer and print publisher, Antonio Cesare Poggi, described the lots:

> *Among them will be found drawings by...[many Old] Masters, of the greatest beauty, both for genius and execution; others, which are sketches (or as Italians call them,* primi pensieri*), may not have the same fascination for the general observer; but the well-informed connoisseur will easily discern, that if they possess not the same magical attraction to the eye, the mind is as much entertained, and oftentimes more powerfully instructed, by these performances, than by more laboured efforts.*[24]

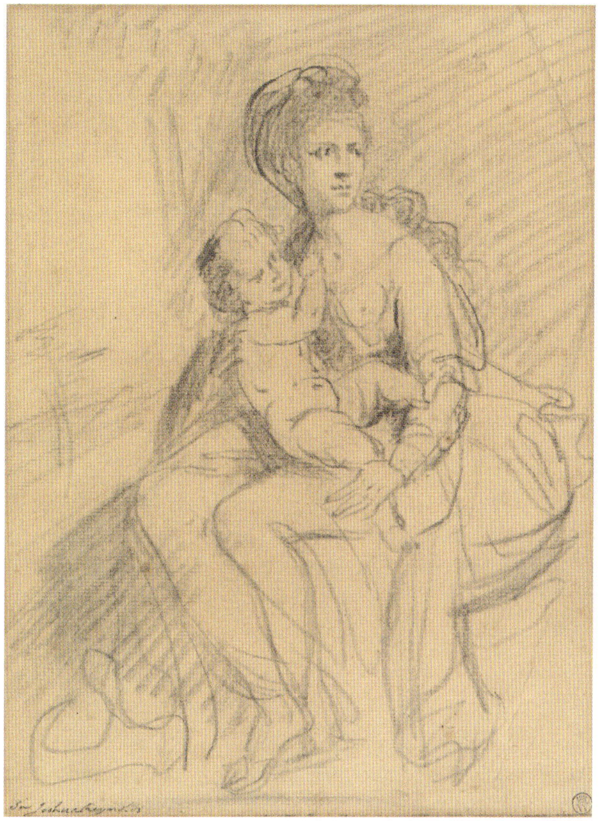

FIG. 27

Study of a woman and child
black chalk, 26.6 x 18.3 cm
Metropolitan Museum of Art, New York (2000.285)

Reynolds' drawings soon ended up in the collection of his fellow Royal Academicians, including Paul Sandby, Benjamin West and Thomas Lawrence. The latter arguably formed the greatest such British collection. Throughout the nineteenth century, many sought to emulate their illustrious predecessors in this field, most notably Frederic Leighton and Edward John Poynter. But the growth of public collections and the diversification of private collectors, meant that future collections could not hope to match those formed in previous centuries, in range, depth or number. It was the burgeoning public collections founded from the eighteenth century onwards that benefited most from the dispersal of collections such as Reynolds's. In many ways these public institutions are 'collections of collections'. Reynolds's own collection has long been found in these public collections, beginning in 1799, just a few years after his collection began to be dispersed, with the bequest to the British Museum of the art collection of The Revd. Clayton Mordaunt Cracherode (1730–99). The arrival of choice drawings that had once belonged to Reynolds by Giulio Romano, Carlo Maratti, Battista Franco, Parmigianino and Guercino – all represented in the exhibition at Plymouth by other examples from other collections – laid the foundations of the largest (and growing) residue of Reynolds's former graphic collection.

The next largest holding of Reynolds's prints and drawings is in the Szépművészeti Múzeum in Budapest, which obtained most of these via Poggi. He sold his collection, some obtained from Reynolds after his death, to the Hungarian Prince Nicholas Esterházy (1765–1833) in 1810, and this became the founding collection of the Museum of Fine Arts in Budapest when purchased by the Hungarian State in 1870. Countries as far apart as Canada, Australia, Greece, Norway, Russia and Romania contain remnants of Reynolds's collection, though the greater part remains in the United Kingdom, principally in the many museums in London, and those in Oxford, Cambridge and Edinburgh. Some of Reynolds's collection has also found its way into prestigious and entirely appropriate collections: a chalk drawing by Van Dyck of the infant Charles II has been acquired by the Royal Collection (Royal Library) at Windsor, a Dürer drawing by the Kupferstichkabinett in Berlin, a Rembrandt drawing by the Rembrandthuis in Amsterdam, Poussin drawings by the Cabinet des Dessins at the Musée du Louvre and many Italian drawings have 'returned' to Italy.

Many more of Reynolds's sheets continue to find their way into public collections across the world. In 2003 the first Michelangelo to enter a Canadian collection occurred when Kenneth Thomson (1923–2006) presented the Art Gallery of Ontario in Toronto with one of the very few Michelangelo drawings remaining in private hands.[25] The following year the National Gallery of Canada in Ottawa made two purchases of items that had once belonged to Reynolds. Firstly, Niccolò della Casa's engraved portrait of Bandinelli, circa 1544.[26] Secondly, a double-sided black chalk drawing which, when in the collection of Sir Thomas Lawrence, was attributed to Michelangelo and connected with the sleeping Adam in *The Creation of Eve* on the Sistine chapel ceiling. This would have complemented Reynolds's red chalk drawings for the same scheme.[27] Items from Reynolds's collection continue to appear on the market from time to time, and many Old Master drawing sales in London or New York offer something that once belonged to Reynolds.[28] In 2000, in another example, the Metropolitan Museum of Art purchased a drawing by Reynolds, heavily indebted to the Old Masters, complementing their rich holdings of his former collection (FIG. 27).

In 1978 the British Museum's broadly conceived exhibition *Gainsborough to Reynolds in the British Museum* dealt with Reynolds as a collector of Old Master drawings in some depth. Recent scholarship has considered the role of collecting in monographic surveys of the work of Reynolds's contemporary colleagues such as Richard Cosway by Stephen Lloyd (1995) and Thomas Banks by Julius Bryant (2006).[29] In addition, the theme of artists as collectors has been treated in its own right in the exhibition *A House of Art: Rubens as Collector* (2004) at the Rubenshuis, Antwerp.[30] Happily, a few items from the British Museum's unmatched collection that were included in the 1978 exhibition are being shown in Plymouth. These sheets, by Cigoli, Zuccaro, Palma Giovane, Mola, Rosso Fiorentino and Perugino, are reunited with other examples from Reynolds's former collection for the first time since 1792. Plymouth's offering provides a mere glimpse of the depth and quality of the prints and drawings Reynolds owned; nonetheless, the impress of his taste is found as much in each sheet, as in the enormous sum of the collection's many parts.

PRINTS AND DRAWINGS ACQUIRED BY REYNOLDS

REYNOLDS OWNED WORKS BY A succession of Mantuan court painters, from Mantegna, through Lorenzo Leonbruno to Giulio Romano. Mantegna's prints were relatively unknown in Reynolds' time, but he might have known some of his drawings at first hand. For example, Mantegna's *St. James Led to Execution* and *Studies of St. John the Baptist and a Suppliant* were both formerly in the Spencer Collection, while his *Virgin and Child*, *Bird on a branch with fruit*, and *Bird on a branch catching a fly* had all three once belonged to Richardson the Elder.[1]

Mantegna was the first painter to engage seriously with printmaking, and did so during engraving's infancy. This impression in blue ink, rather than in the normal black, is highly unusual. Unfortunately no corresponding impression in blue of the right hand is known to complete this allegory of human envy – note the old hag on the left brandishing a tablet inscribed with 'Invid[ia]' (Latin for envy). The Devonshire Collection has another copy of this left-hand section, which until the mid-twentieth century was thought to have been Mantegna's own preparatory drawing for the print. Reynolds is likely to have known at first hand both this drawing and the complete example of the print in black ink in the same collection. Mantegna has long been admired by many artists. Dürer made a drawing of the right half of *Battle of the Sea Gods* during his trip to Italy in 1494.[2]

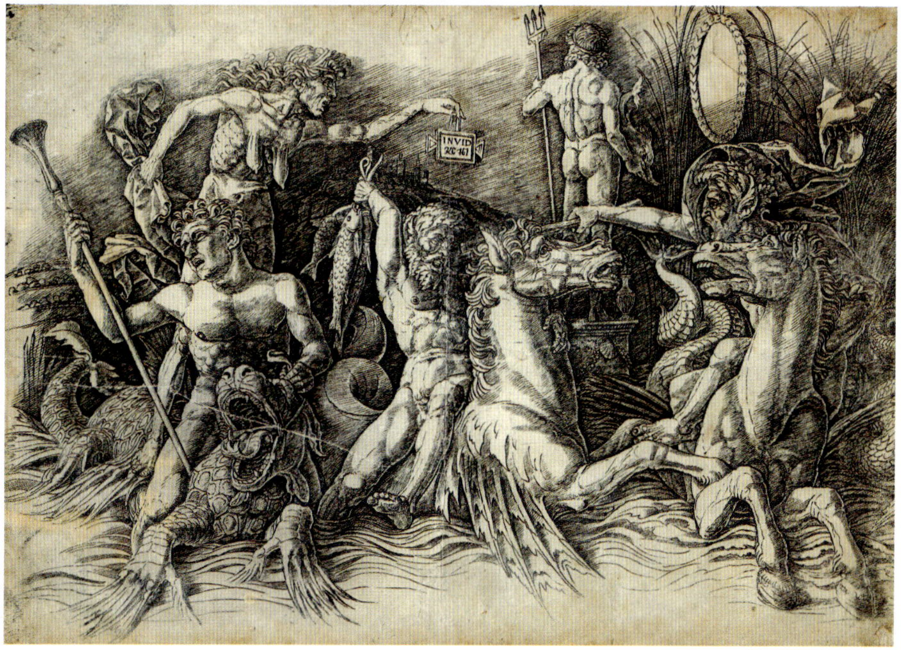

CAT. 35

Andrea Mantegna
(1431–1506)
Battle of the Sea Gods
(left half)
engraving in blue ink, 29.6 x 43 cm
British Museum, London (PD 1922,0410.251)

PROVENANCE: Sir Joshua Reynolds (1723-92; Lugt 2364 verso); Nan Ino Cooper, Baroness Lucas of Crudwell and Lady Dingwall (1880–1958), from whom purchased in 1922.

EXHIBITION HISTORY: None.

LITERATURE: Adam Bartsch, *Le peintre graveur: Les vieux maîtres Italiens* (Vienna: J V Degen, 1811), vol.XIII, p.239, no.18; William Lefroy, 'Andrea Mantegna', *The Portfolio*, XII, 1881, pp.79–84 (84); A M Hind, *Early Italian engraving: A critical catalogue with complete reproduction of all the prints described* (London: Bernard Quaritch, 1948), vol.V, p.15, no.5, vol.VI, plate 494; Paul Kristeller, *Andrea Mantegna* (London: Longmans, Green & Co, 1901), pp.393–98, fig.145; Erika Tietze-Conrat, *Mantegna: Paintings, drawings, engravings* (London: Phaidon Press, 1955), pp.242–43, fig.100; Jay A Levenson, Konrad Oberhuber and Jacquelyn L Sheehan, *Early Italian engravings from the National Gallery of Art* (Washington: National Gallery of Art, 1973), pp.188–93, no.75; David Landau in Jane Martineau (ed.), *Andrea Mantegna* (London and New York: Royal Academy of Arts and Metropolitan Museum of Art, 1992), pp.285–87, no.79; David Landau and Peter Parshall, *The Renaissance print, 1470–1550* (New Haven and London: Yale University Press, 1994), p.79, fig.67; Shelley Fletcher, 'A closer look at Mantegna's prints', *Print Quarterly*, XVIII (1), 2001, pp.3–41 (31–34 and *passim*), fig.45; Alison Wright, *The Pollaiuolo Brothers: The arts of Florence and Rome* (New Haven and London: Yale University Press, 2005), pp.180–81, fig.139; Andrea Canova in Giovanni Agosti and Dominique Thiébaut (eds), *Mantegna 1431–1506* (Paris: Musée du Louvre Éditions and Hazan, 2008), pp.273–76, no.108; Laura Aldovini, 'The Prevedari print', *Print Quarterly*, XXVI (1), 2009, pp.38–45 (45).

CAT. 36

Pietro Perugino
(c.1450–1523)
Head of a young woman
c.1480-90
metalpoint on grey prepared paper,
37.7 x 24.3 cm
British Museum, London
(PD Pp, 1.26)

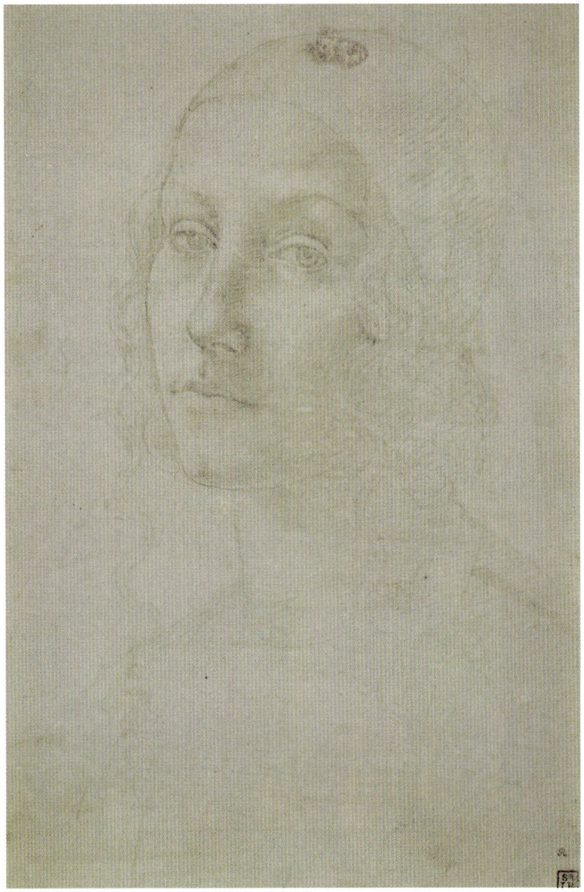

PROVENANCE: Jonathan Richardson I (1665–1745; Lugt 2184); Arthur Pond (1701–58), Langford's, London, 3 June 1759, lot 25; Sir Joshua Reynolds (1723–92; Lugt 2364), Harry Phillips, London, 23 March 1798, lot 1683 as '1 [drawing], Dom.Grillandaio [sic]'; Richard Payne Knight (1751–1824), by whom bequeathed in 1824.

EXHIBITION HISTORY: 1962–63, London, British Museum, 'Raphael and his circle'; 1978, London, British Museum, 'Gainsborough and Reynolds in the British Museum', no.206; 1995, Hull, Ferens Art Gallery and London, Whitechapel Art Gallery, 'Drawing the line', no. 156; 2001-2, Washington, National Gallery of Art, 'Virtue and beauty: Leonardo's 'Ginevra de' Benci' and Renaissance portraits of women', no.32.

LITERATURE: Gerald Stanley Davies, *Ghirlandaio* (London: Methuen, 1908), p.143, plate XLIX (as Ghirlandaio); Oskar Fischel, *Die zeichnungen der Umbrer* (Berlin: G Grote, 1917), p.112, no.46, fig.115 (as Perugino); Bernard Berenson, *The drawings of the Florentine painters: Amplified edition* (Chicago: Chicago University Press, 1938), vol.II, p.92, no.880; Charles De Tolnay, *History and technique of Old Master drawings* (New York: H Bittner & Co, 1943), p.110, no.38; A E Popham and Philip Pouncey, *Italian drawings in the Department of Prints and Drawings in the British Museum: The fourteenth and fifteenth centuries* (London: Trustees of the British Museum, 1950), vol.I, p.117, no.191, vol.II, plate CLXXIII; David Alan Brown in David Alan Brown (ed.), *Virtue and beauty: Leonardo's 'Ginevra de' Benci' and Renaissance portraits of women* (Washington: National Gallery of Art, 2001), pp.198–99, no.32.

ITALIAN FIFTEENTH-CENTURY DRAWINGS (especially in metalpoint) are rare in Reynolds's collection; less than half a dozen can be traced. This is perhaps the most impressive survivor from that period. In 1917 Oskar Fischel (1870–1939) was the first to propose an attribution to Perugino, Raphael's master. However, Reynolds believed the drawing was by Domenico Ghirlandaio (1449–94), who had been the master of Michelangelo. Nonetheless the arresting immediacy of the portrait is apparent, and was undoubtedly drawn from life. Reynolds owned another 'Perugino' drawing on green prepared paper, in fact copied from Perugino's altarpiece *The Ascension* (1496; San Pietro, Perugia).[3] Reynolds also owned a metalpoint on pink prepared paper of a standing male figure, now in the Walker Art Gallery in Liverpool and attributed to the workshop of Ghirlandaio.[4]

In addition to Leonardo da Vinci, Reynolds owned a few drawings by his close contemporary and associate, Lorenzo di Credi (1456/9–1537). One of these is a metalpoint portrait of a boy with a cap on vivid yellow prepared paper and another an impressive *Madonna and Child Enthroned*, flanked by figures.[5] Two other notable early drawings that once belonged to Reynolds, both now in the Institut Néerlandais (Fondation Custodia) in Paris, include one by Lorenzo di Bicci (c.1340–1427) that was previously owned by the great Florentine Renaissance artist Giorgio Vasari (1511–74) and came from his celebrated *Libro de' Disegni*. The other drawing, *Saint Bartholomew*, though anonymous, was likely drawn in Florence; it is on pale blue paper and pricked for transfer.[6] Reynolds also owned a metalpoint by Raphael, now in the Szépművészeti Múzeum, Budapest.[7]

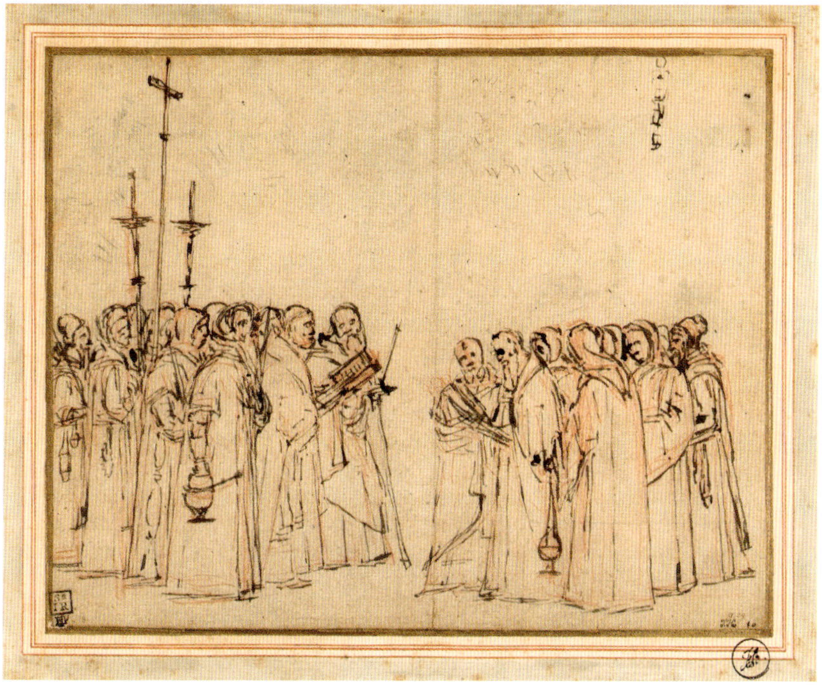

CAT. 37

Vittore Carpaccio
(c.1460/65–c.1525/26)
Two groups of ecclesiastics, facing one another
(c.1502)
pen and brown ink over red chalk, 21.4 x 27.8 cm
Fitzwilliam Museum, Cambridge (PD.3-1979)

PROVENANCE: Padre Sebastiano Resta (1635–1714); Giovanni Matteo Marchetti, Bishop of Arezzo (1647–1704); by descent to his nephews Felice and Cesare Marchetti, sold through John Talman (1677–1726) in 1710 to John, Lord Somers (1651-1716; Lugt 2981); Thomas Hudson (1701–79; Lugt 2432), Langford's London, March 1779; Sir Joshua Reynolds (1723–92; Lugt 2364); Thomas Banks (1735–1805; Lugt 2423), by descent to his daughter Lavinia Forster, née Banks (1774–1858); by descent to her son-in-law Ambrose Poynter (1796-1886; Lugt 161 verso); by descent to his son Sir Edward John Poynter (1836–1919; Lugt 874), Sotheby's, London, 24–25 April 1918, lot 23; Henry Lascelles, 6th Earl of Harewood (1882–1947); by descent to his eldest son George Lascelles, 7th Earl of Harewood (b.1923), Christie's, London, 6 July 1965, lot 118; Col. Norman Colville (1893–1974); by descent to Diana Colville, née Legh (1924–2000), accepted by Her Majesty's Treasury in lieu of estate duty and allocated at the request of Diana Colville in 1979.

EXHIBITION HISTORY: 1963, Venice, Palazzo Ducale, 'Carpaccio', no.19 (drawings); 1980, Cambridge, Fitzwilliam Museum, 'Venetian drawings'; 1989–90, 'Treasures from the Fitzwilliam', no.57; 1991, Cambridge, Fitzwilliam Museum, 'Venetian drawings'; 1992, Venice, Fondazione Giorgio Cini, 'Da Pisanello a Tiepolo: Disegni Veneti dal Fitzwilliam Museum di Cambridge', no.5.

LITERATURE: Tancred Borenius, 'Two unpublished North Italian drawings', *The Burlington Magazine*, XXIX, 1916, pp.271–72 (271), plate A; Detlev von Hadeln, *Venezianische zeichnungen des Quattrocento* (Berlin: Paul Cassirer, 1925), no.18, pp.57–58; Giuseppe Fiocco, *Carpaccio: 201 riproduzioni in fototipia* (Rome: Casa Editrice d'Arte Valoria Plastici, 1931), p.72, plate C; A E Popham, 'Vittore Carpaccio, The Death of St Jerome', *Old Master Drawings*, XXXVII (10), June 1935, pp.10–11 (11); Raimond van Marle, *The development of the Italian schools of painting* (The Hague: Martinus Nijhoff, 1936), vol.XVIII, p.344; Giuseppe Fiocco, *Carpaccio* (Milan: Hoepli, 1942), p.74; Hans Tietze and Erika Tietze-Conrat, *The drawings of the Venetian painters in the 15th and 16th centuries* (New York: J J Augustin, 1944), p.61, no.254 (as Lazzaro Bastiani); Edoardo Arslan, 'Due disegni e un dipinto di Carpaccio', *Emporium*, CXVI, 1952, pp.109–13; Giuseppe Fiocco, *Carpaccio* (Novara: Istituto geografico de Agostini, 1958), p.29, no.4; Rodolfo Pallucchini, con appendice di Guido Perocco, *I teleri del Carpaccio in S Giorgio degli Schiavoni* (Milan: Rizzoli, 1961), p.44, no.23; Jan Lauts, *Carpaccio: Paintings and drawings* (London: Phaidon, 1962), pp.272–73, no.D32, pl.VIIa; Terisio Pignatti, 'Jan Lauts, Carpaccio: Paintings and drawings' [review], *Master Drawings*, I (4), Winter 1963, pp.47–54 (51); Manlio Cancogni and Guido Perocco, *L'opera completa del Carpaccio* (Milan: Rizzoli, 1967), p.98; Alessandro Bettagno, *Da Pisanello a Tiepolo: Disegni Veneti dal Fitzwilliam Museum di Cambridge* (Milan: Electa, 1992), pp.28–29, no.5; Maria-Cristina White, *The drawings of Vittore Carpaccio*, unpublished Ph.D., University of Oxford, 1994, pp.68–70, fig. 34; David Scrase, *Italian drawings at the Fitzwilliam Museum* (Cambridge: Fitzwilliam Museum, 2009), forthcoming.

THE DRAWING'S HISTORIC MOUNT IS inscribed in brown ink in an eighteenth-century hand 'Frate Bartolomeo' (possibly by Reynolds).[8] Reynolds's genuine drawings by Fra Bartolommeo (1472–1517) include a splendid one in the Victoria and Albert Museum in black chalk on pink prepared paper and two in the British Museum.[9]

Two groups are set against one another, with the dense lower area contrasting with blankness above. In 1916 Tancred Borenius (1885–1948) first published this sheet by Carpaccio for *Obsequies of Saint Jerome* (1502; Scuola degli Schiavoni, Venice). Maria-Cristina White notes that the 'tiny squiggles in the top right-hand corner are short horizontal lines crossing the rounded, sketchy outlines of a figurine.' She demonstrates that Carpaccio followed Alberti's advice regarding the use of the head as a unit of measurement for proportions of the human figure. On the other hand, more prosaically, the upper area to the right besides other faint markings could have been where the artist tested his nib before setting down his pen. The drawing's penmanship has a varied character; long thinly drawn out lines made without recharging the nib with ink contrast with thick, blotchy lines.

REYNOLDS HAD MANY PRINTS FROM sixteenth-century Italy. Nicholas Penny has identified two impressions of Marcantonio's engraving *Parnassus* after Raphael in Reynolds's collection, sold in March 1798 (both untraced).[10] He owned, besides Marcantonio, work after him, such as Eneo Vico's repetition of his *Bacchanal*, work by one of his pupils in Rome, Marco Dente da Ravenna's *Vulcan,* and work after another pupil, Agostino Veneziano's *Apollo*.[11]

Marcantonio was the leading engraver of the High Renaissance. He was born in Bologna and was a pupil of Francia's there, before he set off first for Venice and then Rome, where he arrived about 1510. He found fame collaborating with Raphael who saw the lucrative possibility of disseminating his work across Europe and made designs expressly for him to engrave. Francia was a painter and goldsmith active in his native Bologna, and was much influenced by both Raphael and Perugino.

Saint Catherine is shown leaning against the spiked wheel, her traditional attribute to which she was strapped. Lucy had her eyes removed to avoid the unwanted attentions of a suitor, and they can be seen in the dish in her left hand; her blindness is indicated by the closed book she holds, never to be read again. However, God later restored her sight. The withered tree, with broken branches, and the young though poorly formed example at the left, can both be taken as symbols of martyrdom. The treatment of the drapery on both figures is strongly reminiscent of that by Reynolds in some of his full-length portraits.

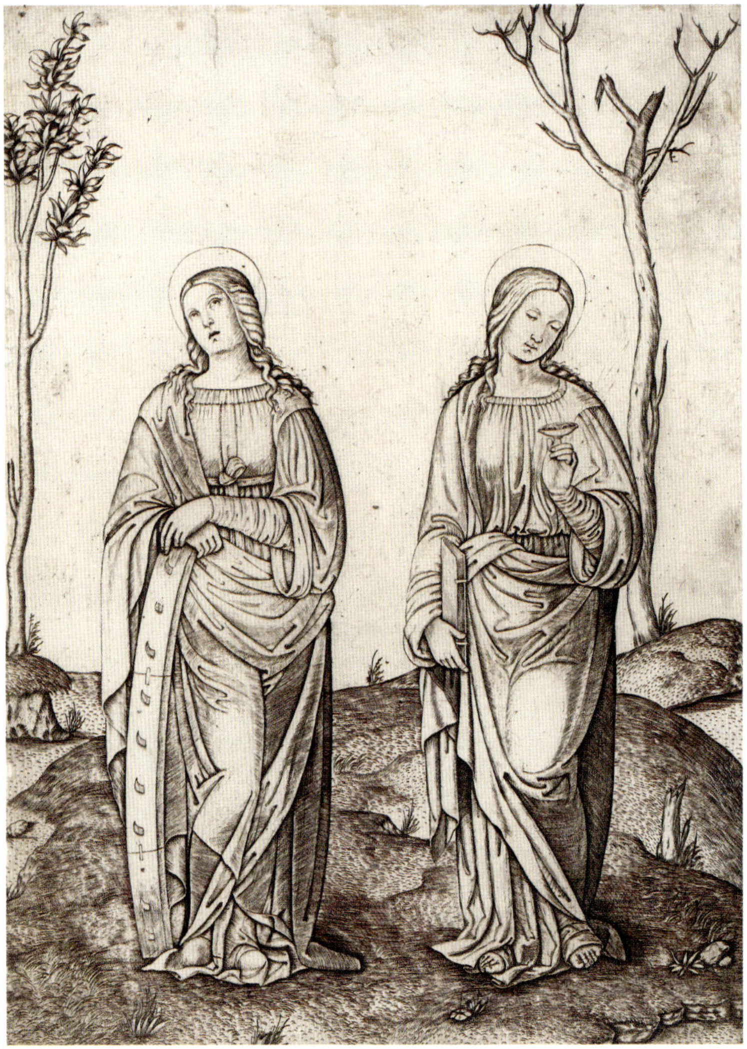

CAT. 38

Marcantonio Raimondi (1470/82–1527/34)
after Francesco Francia (1450–1517)
Saint Catherine and Saint Lucy
(c.1504-08)
engraving, 28.5 x 20.8 cm
Fitzwilliam Museum, Cambridge (P.5263-R)

PROVENANCE: Sir Joshua Reynolds (1723–92; Lugt 2364 verso); Richard Fitzwilliam, 7th Viscount Fitzwilliam (1745–1816), by whom bequeathed in 1816.

EXHIBITION HISTORY: None.

LITERATURE: Adam Bartsch, *Le peintre graveur: Oeuvres de Marc-Antoine [Raimondi], et de ses deux principaux élèves Augustin de Venise, et Marc de Ravenne* (Vienna: J V Degen, 1813), vol.XIV, p.108, no.121.

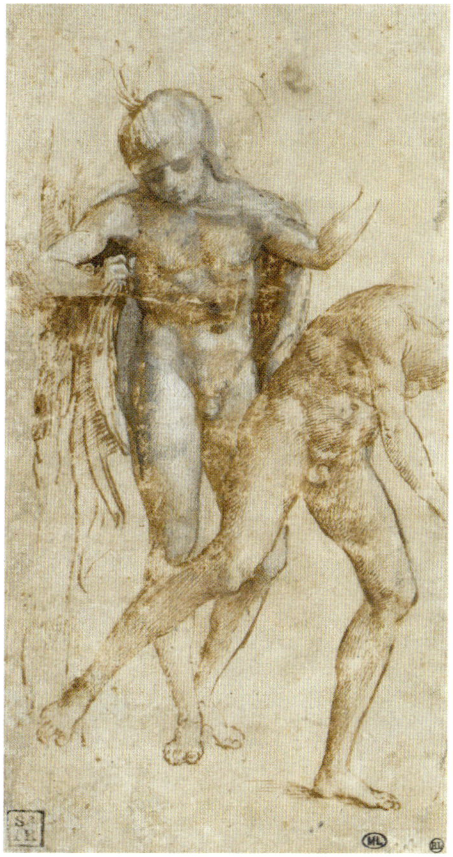

CAT. 39

Lorenzo Leonbruno
(1477–1533)
Two male nudes
pen and brown ink, brown wash with white heightening (partly oxidised), 20.4 x 10.9 cm
Musée du Louvre, Paris (RF 442)

PROVENANCE: Sir Joshua Reynolds (1723–92; Lugt 2364); Aimé Charles Horace His de la Salle (1795–1878; Lugt 1333), by whom bequeathed in 1878.

EXHIBITION HISTORY: 1881, Paris, Musée du Louvre, 'Dessins de la collection His de la Salle', no.138.

LITERATURE: Both de Tauzia, *Notice des dessins de la collection His de la Salle exposés au [Musée du] Louvre* (Paris: Charles de Mourgues Frères, 1881), p.97, no.138 (as anonymous Lombard or Ferrarese School, beginning of sixteenth century).

REYNOLDS SEEMS TO HAVE OWNED NO other work by this obscure Mantuan painter, who worked at the court in Mantua between his more celebrated predecessor Andrea Mantegna and successor Giulio Romano. Leonbruno's style is slightly awkward and laboured, with a strong trace of Mantegna. His style also bears the trace of Lorenzo Costa (1460–1535), who worked in Mantua from 1506 until his death. Reynolds probably thought this drawing was by Mantegna, though no trace of the original mount survives.

Leonbruno's drawing might have inspired Reynolds in his important and daring double-portrait *Colonel Acland and Lord Sydney: The Archers* (1769; Tate, London).[12] The tangle of legs and the play of silhouette, seen in both this drawing and the double-portrait, seems to have engaged Reynolds more than the capture of the two sitters' likenesses. During his lifetime Reynolds's contemporaries noted his Old Master 'borrowings'. His young friend Frederick Howard, 5th Earl of Carlisle (1748–1825), said of his *Lady Sarah Bunbury sacrificing to the Graces* in 1768:

> *I saw, in a cupola at Piacenza, an angel very like...; I am sure Reynolds must have taken the idea of his picture from it. You may easily fancy that such a resemblance would not escape me.*[13]

Leonbruno's graphic *oeuvre* is at present small, extending slowly from a core group.[14] The attribution was made comparatively recently – in 1999 – by Dominique Cordellier; the former mount was inscribed 'sans doute de Leonbruno'.

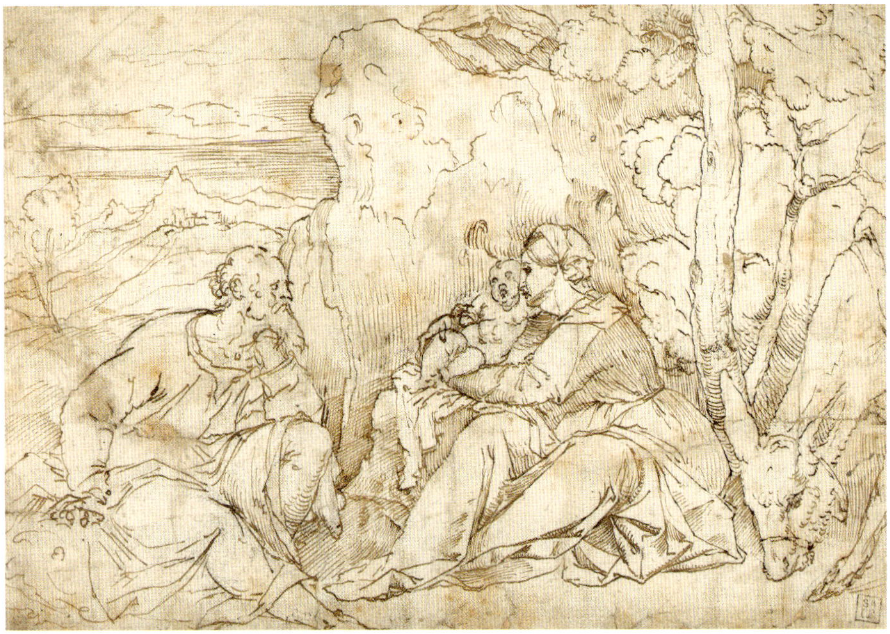

CAT. 40

Palma Vecchio
(?1480–1528)
The rest on the Flight into Egypt
(c.1520–24)
pen and brown ink over black chalk, 21.6 x 31.1 cm
Fitzwilliam Museum, Cambridge (no.954)

PROVENANCE: Sir Joshua Reynolds (1723–92; Lugt 2364); Joseph Prior (1834–1918), by whom bequeathed in 1918.

EXHIBITION HISTORY: 1960, Cambridge, Fitzwilliam Museum, 'Fifteenth- and sixteenth-century drawings', no.39; 1983–84, London, Royal Academy, 'The genius of Venice, 1500–1600', no.D.35; 1992, Venice, Fondazione Cini, 'Da Pisanello a Tiepolo', 1992, no.9.

LITERATURE: Giovanni Mariacher, *Palma il Vecchio* (Milan: Bramante Editrice, 1968), p.116; Alessandro Ballarin, 'Tre disegni: Palma il Vecchio, Lotto, Romanino (e alcune osservazioni sul ruolo del Romanino al Buonconsiglio)', *Arte Veneta*, XXIV, 1970, pp.47–62 (47–48), fig.67; William R. Rearick, *Tiziano e il disegno Veneziano del suo tempo* (Florence: Olschki, 1976), p.71; Philip Rylands in Jane Martineau and Charles Hope (eds), *The genius of Venice, 1500–1600* (London: Royal Academy of Arts amd Weidenfeld & Nicholson, 1983), pp.267–68, no.D35; Philip Rylands, *Palma Vecchio* (Cambridge: Cambridge University Press, 1992), pp.117, 119, 252, no.D5; William R. Rearick, *Il disegno Veneziano del Cinquecento* (Milan: Electa, 2001), p.71; David Scrase, *Italian drawings at the Fitzwilliam Museum* (Cambridge: Fitzwilliam Museum, 2009), forthcoming.

MORE FULLY RESOLVED THAN MOST drawings in Reynolds's collection, this sheet reveals the Venetian's love of charming and harmoniously arranged figural compositions. Reynolds's occasional forays into religious painting are strongly indebted to works by Palma Vecchio and other painters working in Venice. Close connections may be made with Reynolds's late *The Holy Family* (1788–89; Tate, London).[15] Reynolds was noted for his judicious re-use of motifs from past art, declaring that 'invention, strictly speaking, is little more than a new combination of those images which have been previously gathered and deposited in the memory' (Discourse II). Reynolds owned many depictions of the Holy Family, including one in the Musée Calvet in Avignon (formerly given to Correggio)[16] and another by Ludovico Cigoli (CAT. 59, p. 133). He turned to these for his secular portraiture of aristocratic families likewise set out of doors, framed by woodland in grassy clearings.

Drawings by Palma Vecchio are rare, with Rylands listing a mere eleven known anywhere, and no others from Reynolds's collection are known. On the other hand, Reynolds formed a large collection of works by his great-nephew Palma Giovane, who was a prodigious draughtsman (CAT. 65, p. 139). The famous Rembrandt scholar Otto Benesch (1896–1964) was the first to make the attribution to Palma Vecchio in 1939. Rylands in his monograph on Palma Vecchio dates the drawing towards the end of the painter's life, to around 1522–24.

CAT. 41

Giulio Romano
(1499–1547)
Study of a dragon
(c.1526–27)
pen and ink with brown wash, with later framing lines, 14.9 x 18.8 cm
Private collection, London

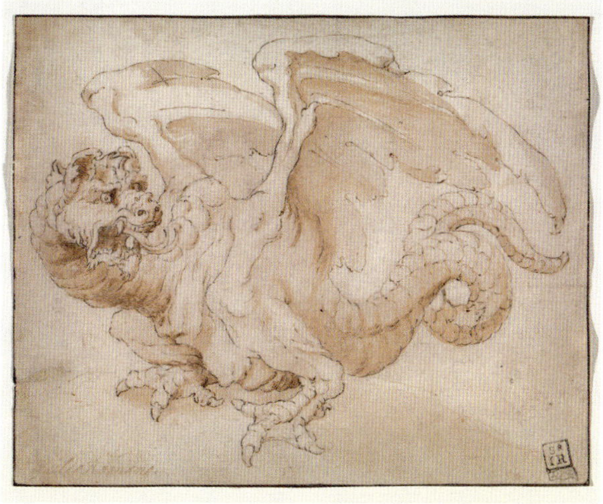

PROVENANCE: Jan Pietersz. Zoomer (1641–1724; Lugt 1511); Sir Joshua Reynolds (1723–92; Lugt 2364).
EXHIBITION HISTORY: None.
LITERATURE: None.

FIG. 28

Giulio Romano
(1499–1547)
Architectural grotesque (study of a dog and serpent in combat)
pen and brown ink, brown wash, over black chalk, 18.2 x 27.9 cm
Fitzwilliam Museum, Cambridge (no.2998)

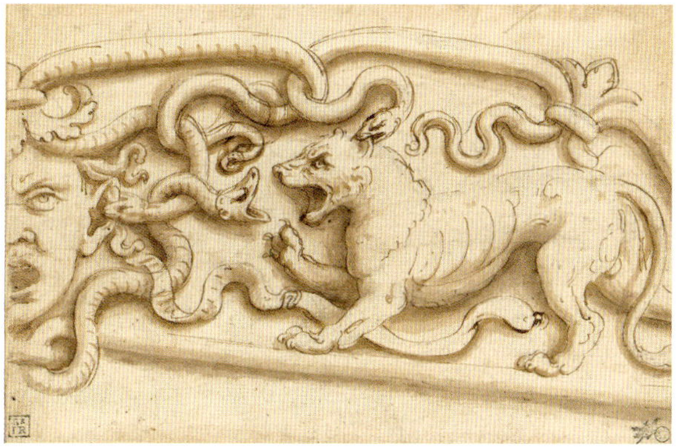

THE DRAUGHTSMANSHIP OF GIULIO Romano was well represented in Reynolds's collection with dozens of superb examples, now scattered all over the world in collections in Melbourne, Los Angeles, Washington, New York, Paris, Budapest and London. Many of them were later owned by Sir Thomas Lawrence and remained together until the spectacular sale in London in 1972 of the Ellesmere Collection, where 11 Romano drawings that had once belonged to Reynolds were sold.[17] Reynolds had no problem citing Romano in close proximity to Raphael (his master) and Michelangelo as 'those three great painters' and concurred with Charles Alphone Du Fresnoy (1611–68) in considering that this trio 'all justly deserve that high rank.' Reynolds went on to assert that Romano had the 'true poetical genius of painting, perhaps in a higher degree than any other painter whatever' (*Notes on Du Fresnoy's The Art of Painting*, 1783).

Reynolds owned so many drawings by Romano that distinct groups of related material can be traced. Romano's work for his principal patrons, the Gonzaga family in Mantua, for example, is represented by many sheets. The present drawing appears to be an early rejected study for one of the dragons in *Psyche receiving water from the Styx*, the central lunette on the west wall of the Camera di Psiche, in the Palazzo Te, dating from 1526–27. Reynolds owned a study of a river god for another section of the west wall in the same room, *The Marriage Feast of Cupid and Psyche*, which is now in the National Gallery of Art, Washington.[18] He also owned a study for the *Allegory of the Virtues of Federico Gonzaga*, for the vault of the Camera di Attilio Regolo, Appartamento del Giardino Segreto in the same building, c.1530–34, which is now in the British Museum. In the Getty Museum in Los Angeles is one of Reynolds's drawings related to the later scheme to decorate the vault in the Camera dei Giganti, also in the same building, in around 1530.[19] Romano also designed the coat of arms of Cardinal Ercole Gonzaga (1505–63) and Reynolds owned two preparatory studies, one now in the Snite Museum of Art, University of Notre Dame in Indiana and another in the Morgan Library, New York.[20] However, many other drawings by Romano cannot be identified with any known projects or commissions.

CAT. 42

Jacopo Caraglio
(c.1500-1565)
after Parmigianino
(1503-1540)
The Martyrdom of Saint Peter and Saint Paul
(c.1527)
engraving,
26 x 46 cm
National Gallery of Scotland, Edinburgh

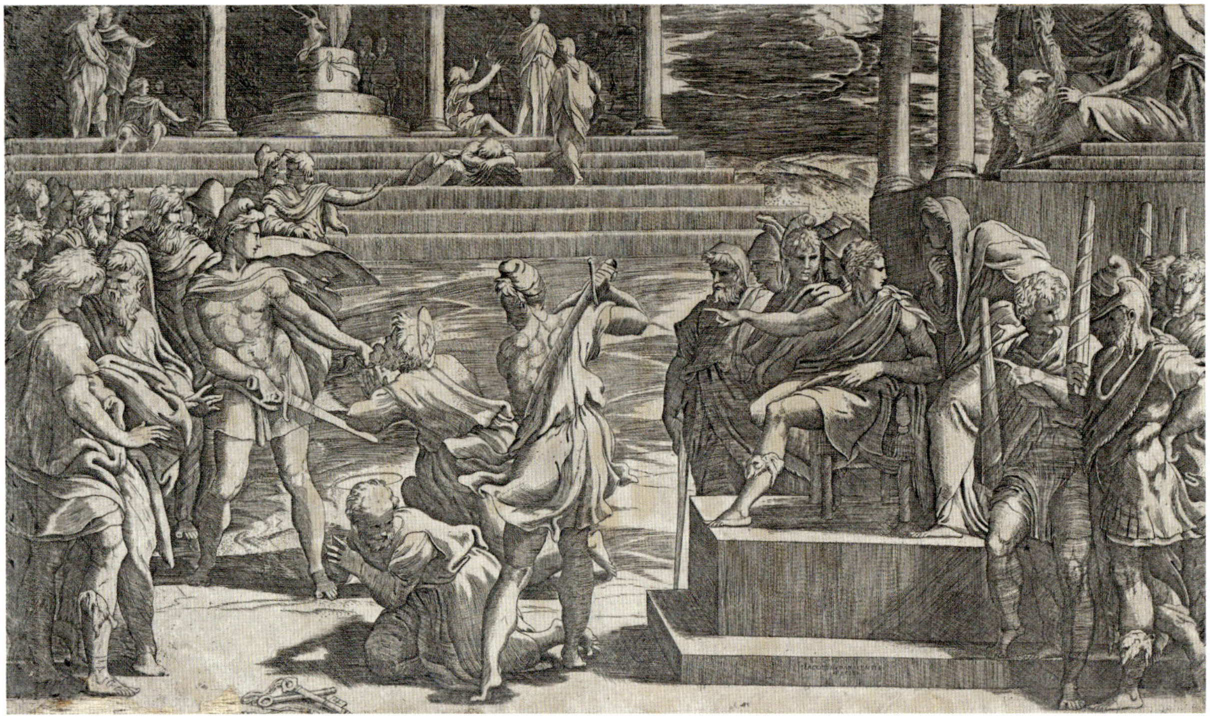

PROVENANCE: Sir Joshua Reynolds (1723–92; Lugt 2364 verso); date acquired unknown.

EXHIBITION HISTORY: None.

LITERATURE: Adam Bartsch, *Le peintre graveur: Les graveurs de l'école de Marc-Antoine Raimondi (Estampes de differens graveurs anonymes qui semblent être de l'école de Marc-Antoine Raimondi)* (Vienna: J V Degen, 1813), vol.xv, p.71, no.8; David Landau and Peter Parshall, *The Renaissance Print, 1470–1550* (New Haven and London: Yale University Press, 1994), p.154, fig.161; David Franklin and David Ekserdjian, *The art of Parmigianino* (New Haven and London: Ottawa: Yale University Press and National Gallery of Canada, 2003), pp. 147–52, no.35; David Ekserdjian, *Parmigianino* (New Haven and London: Yale University Press, 2006), p.216, fig.230; Achim Gnann, *Parmigianino und sein kreis: Druckgraphik aus der sammlung Baselitz* (Ostfildern: Hatje Cantz, 2007), pp.110–12, no.34.

REYNOLDS SINGLED OUT THE DRAWINGS of Parmigianino (and Correggio) as 'very skillful' (Discourse XI) and they have always been widely collected, Peter Lely once owning more than 75 by Parmigianino alone. Etchings and chiaroscuro woodcuts by Antonio Maria Zanetti (1680–1767) after Parmigianino's work were found alongside dozens of his drawings in Reynolds's collection. In Popham's 1971 *catalogue raisonné* of Parmigianino's drawings, he identified 26 drawings that once belonged to Reynolds, nine of which are now in the British Museum. Since 1971, many more have come to light and Gnann's *catalogue raisonné* of 2007 has identified 35.[21] Reynolds's Parmigianino drawings are widely scattered across the world, including examples in Munich, Frankfurt, Budapest, Los Angeles,[22] New York and Philadelphia.

Parmigianino became interested in printmaking because of the success of such partnerships as Marcantonio Raimondi and Raphael, for which the latter designed compositions with the express purpose of making printed images. Parmigianino teamed up with Caraglio, who had had notable previous successes with Rosso Fiorentino (CAT. 45) and was a leading member in the circle of Marcantonio, another printmaker collected by Reynolds (CAT. 38). The print derives in part from Marcantonio's print after Raphael of *The martyrdom of Saint Cecilia* and is signed by Caraglio on a step at the lower right: 'Jacobvs Parmensis / Fecit' [Jacopo from Parma/Made this']. Reynolds also owned a chiaroscuro woodcut of Parmigianino's *The martyrdom of Saints Peter and Paul* by Antonio da Trento, now in a private collection.[23]

CAT. 43

Giorgio Gandini
(c.1489–1538)
Study for the painting 'Mystic Marriage of Saint Catherine'
(c.1530)
red chalk, 11.9 x 9.5 cm
Musée du Louvre, Paris (RF 500)

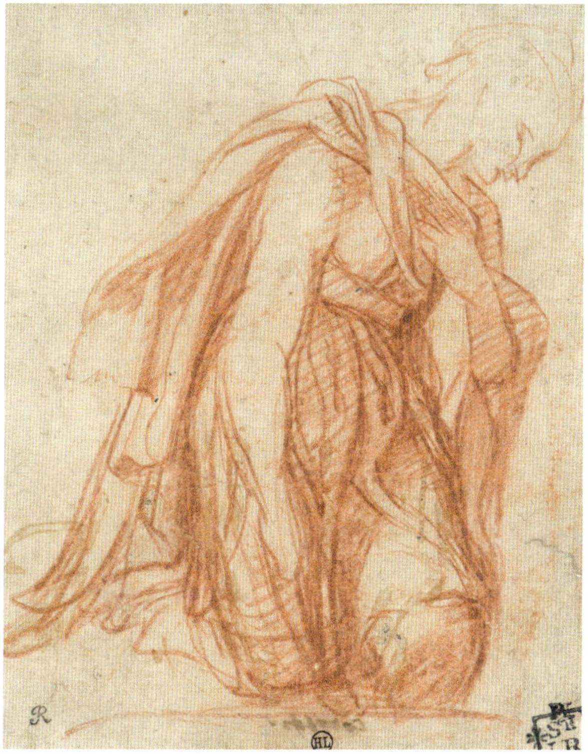

PROVENANCE: Nicholas Lanier (1588–1666; Lugt 2908); Sir Peter Lely (1618–80; Lugt 2092); Jonathan Richardson I (1665–1745; Lugt 2184); John Barnard (1709–84; Lugt 1419), Greenwood's, London, 16 February 1787; Sir Joshua Reynolds (1723–92; Lugt 2364); Sir Thomas Lawrence (1769–1830; Lugt 2445); Aimé Charles Horace His de la Salle (1795–1878; Lugt 1333), by whom bequeathed in 1878.

EXHIBITION HISTORY: 1836, London, Woodburn's Gallery, 'The Lawrence Gallery: Fourth Exhibition', no.52; 1881, Paris, Musée du Louvre, 'Dessins de la collection His de la Salle', no.9; 1934, Paris, Musée de l'Orangerie, 'Hommage au Corrège', no.25; 1964, Paris, Musée du Louvre, 'Dessins de l'école de Parme: Corrège/Parmesan', no.34.

LITERATURE: Both de Tauzia, *Notice des dessins de la collection His de la Salle exposés au [Musée du] Louvre* (Paris: Charles de Mourgues Frères, 1881), p.18, no.9 (as Correggio); Jean Vergnet-Ruiz, *Hommage au Corrège : Catalogue des dessins du maître, de ses élèves et des artistes qui ont subi son influence, exposés à l'occasion du quatrième centenaire de sa mort, 1534* (Paris: L'Orangerie des Tuileries, 1934), p.25, no.25 (as Correggio); A E Popham, *Correggio's drawings* (London: Oxford University Press, 1957), p.192, no.A109 (as Gatti); Roseline Bacou and Françoise Viatte, *Dessins de l'école de Parme: Corrège/Parmesan: XXXIIIe exposition du Cabinet des Dessins, Musée du Louvre* (Paris: Réunion des musées nationaux, 1964), p.40, no.34 (as Gatti).

GANDINI WAS BORN IN PAVIA, WORKED IN Parma and later in Cremona, where he died. He was an exact contemporary and former pupil of Antonio Correggio (1489–1534), and outlived him by only a few years. Two other studies are known for the same painting in the British Museum, one of which was formerly owned by Reynolds, and both previously by Lely too (FIG. 29).[24] Reynolds must have taken delight in reconstructing projects from his many drawings related to identical schemes. He could also do this with his mass of drawings by Giulio Romano (CAT. 41).

Graceful and seductive, the red chalk freely handled on this sheet is among Gandini's closest works to those of his master Correggio, for whose style it has been mistaken in the past until quite recently. Many Old Master drawings, usually in red chalk, once hopefully attributed to 'Correggio' (and bearing conspicuous inscriptions) were in Reynolds's collection; they include a *Leda and the Swan* by Camillo Boccaccino (1504/05–46) sold in 2001.[25] Reynolds owned many genuine Correggios, which sometimes, as in this example by Gandini here, are littered with collectors' marks. The drawing has lost its original mount and Reynolds's mark is now left incomplete. Nonetheless, careful scrutiny of the present example reveals the ghostly offset of an historic attribution, from another sheet, to Correggio, which can be seen in the lower centre; therefore the drawing was once kept in a 'Correggio' sequence.

FIG. 29

Giorgio Gandini
(c.1489–1538)
Study for the painting 'Mystic Marriage of Saint Catherine'
(c.1530)
red chalk, 14.8 x 11.1 cm
British Museum, London
(PD 1895,0915.734)

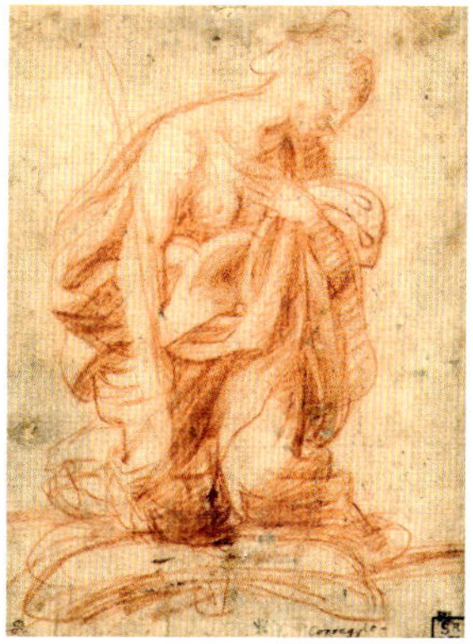

CAT. 44

Guido Ruggieri
(fl.1540s)
after Primaticcio
(1504–70)
Vulcan and the Cyclopes forging arrows (Vulcan's forge)
engraving,
31.6 x 41.2 cm
Fitzwilliam Museum, Cambridge (P.6115-R)

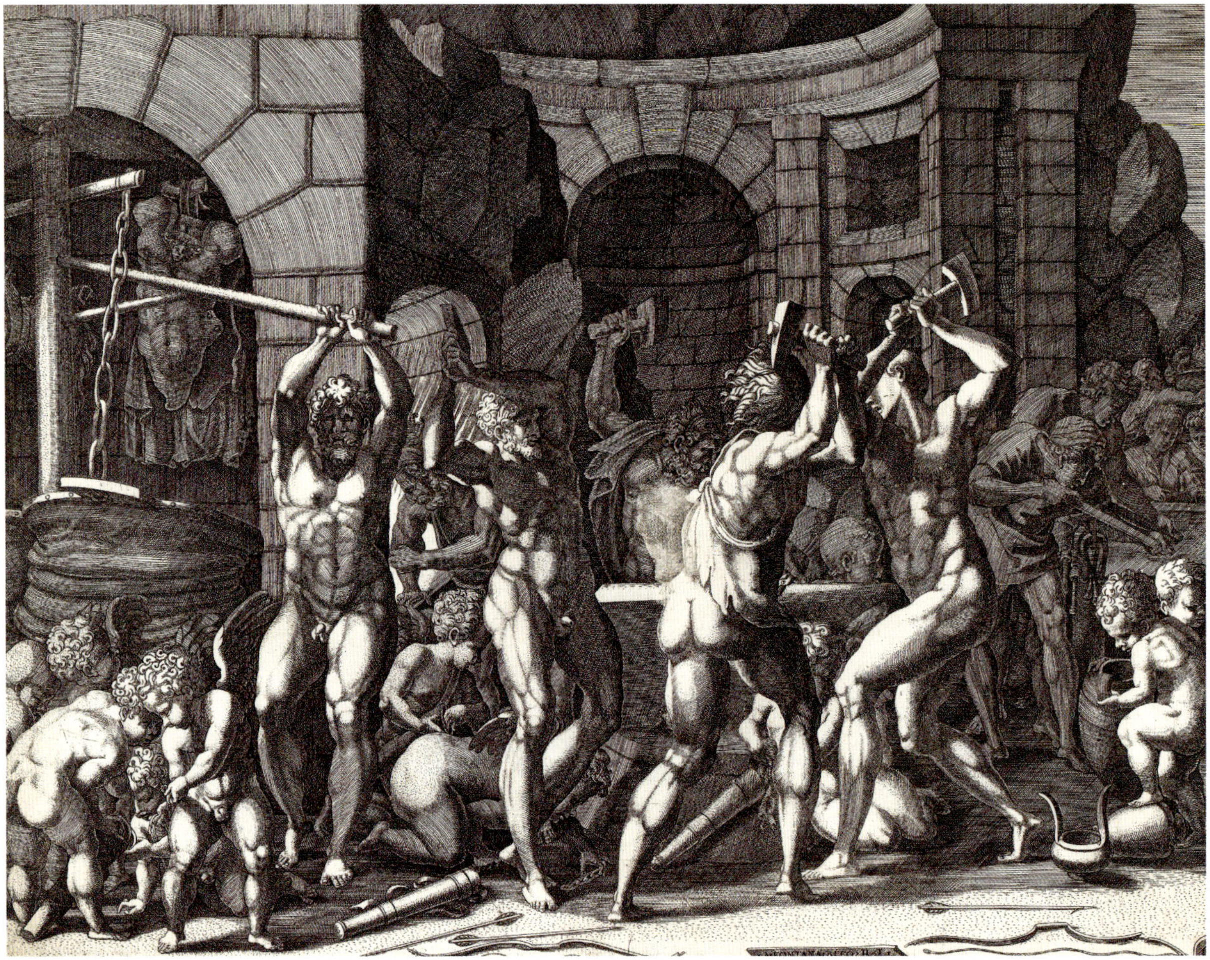

PROVENANCE: Sir Joshua Reynolds (1723–92; Lugt 2364 verso), Greenwood's, London, 16–18 April 1792; Sir Mark Masterman Sykes (1771–1823; Lugt 1897 verso), Sotheby's, London, 29 March 1824 (and 11 days), lot 519 (with one other), from whom bought through Samuel Woodburn (1786–1853) in 1824.

EXHIBITION HISTORY: None.

LITERATURE: Adam Bartsch, *Le peintre graveur: Les vieux maîtres Allemands* (Vienna: J V Degen, 1808), vol.IX, pp.25–26, no.4; Maria Biasini, 'Le incisioni del Maestro F G Italiano (Guido Ruggieri?)', *Grafica d'arte*, 30, 1997, pp.2–9, no.4 i/v, fig.4.

THE WORK OF ARTISTS KNOWN collectively as the School of Fontainebleau was well represented in Reynolds's graphic collection with prints and drawings by or after Rosso Fiorentino (CAT. 45), Luca Penni, Master L D, Primaticcio as here and others. This example was an early acquisition by the newly founded Fitzwilliam Museum and on a note on the verso Sykes records the source of the print, allowing some completeness in the provenance unusual for prints: 'Sir Joshua's sale 1792'.

Primaticcio's straining muscular figures are arranged frieze-like across the print and recall the famous engraving of the *Battle of nude men* by Antonio de Pollaiuolo of the previous century. This impression is the first state (of five) which carries the lettering: 'A.FONTANA.BLEO.BOL' and a monogrammed 'FG'. In the second state the lettering is supplemented with 'Ant Lafreri Sequani formis/expressa Romae', which refers to the French-born Italian publisher Antoine Lafréry (d.1577). The Italian printmaker Enea Vico (1523–67) also engraved the composition.[26] The printmaker responsible for this work had long been thought to be Guido Ruggieri, who worked with Primaticcio in Fontainebleau, but recently Suzanne Boorsch has given the work to Girolamo Fagiuoli instead.[27]

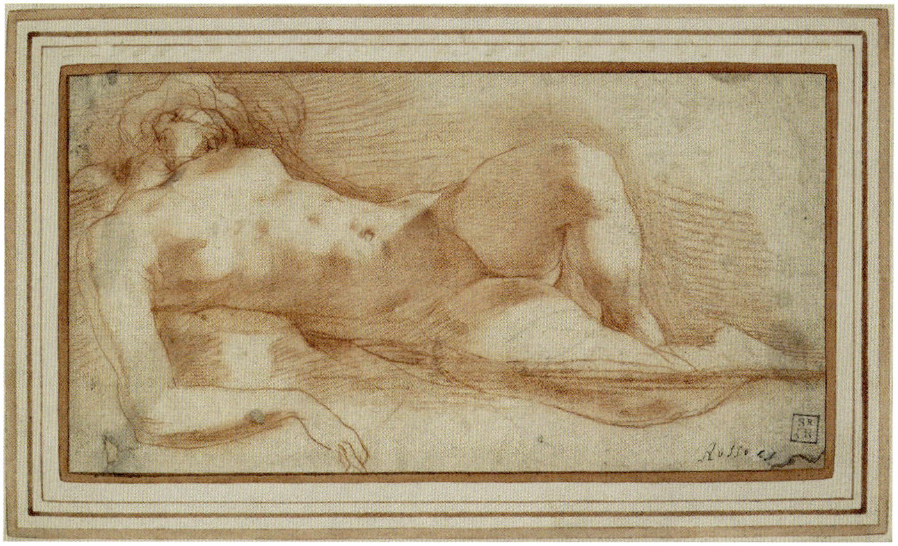

CAT. 45

Rosso Fiorentino
(1494–1540)
Recumbent nude female figure asleep
(c.1530–40)
red chalk with traces of underdrawing in black chalk, 12.6 x 24.4 cm
British Museum, London (PD Pp, 5.132)

PROVENANCE: Sir Joshua Reynolds (1723–92; Lugt 2364); Richard Payne Knight (1751–1824), by whom bequeathed in 1824.

EXHIBITION HISTORY: 1972–73, Paris, Grand Palais and Ottawa, National Gallery of Canada, 'L'école de Fontainebleau', no.207; 1978, London, British Museum, 'Gainsborough and Reynolds in the British Museum', no.221; 1977, Saint Petersburg, State Hermitage Museum and Moscow, State Pushkin Museum of Fine Arts, 'Italian Renaissance', no.53; 1980, Adelaide, Art Gallery of South Australia and Melbourne, National Gallery of Victoria, 'Leonardo, Michelangelo and the century of genius: Master drawings from the British Museum', no.53; 1986, London, British Museum, 'Florentine drawings of the sixteenth century', no.111.

LITERATURE: Kurt Kusenberg, *Le Rosso* (Paris: Albin Michel, 1931), p.142, no.51; Paola Barocchi, *Il Rosso Fiorentino* (Rome: Gismondi, 1950), p.227; Sylvie Béguin in Michel Laclotte *et al.*, *L'école de Fontainebleau* (Paris: Éditions des musées nationaux, 1972), pp.182, 185, no. 207; Nicholas Turner and Martin Royalton-Kisch, *Leonardo, Michelangelo and the century of genius: Master drawings from the British Museum* (Adelaide: Art Gallery of South Australia, 1980), pp.108–9, no.53; Nicholas Turner, *Florentine drawings of the sixteenth century* (London: British Museum Publications, 1986), p.154, no. 111; Eugene A. Carroll *Rosso Fiorentino: Drawings, prints and decorative arts* (Washington: National Gallery of Art, 1987), p.338; Hugo Chapman, *Michelangelo drawings: Closer to the master* (London: British Museum Press, 2005), p.189, fig.79; Claire van Cleave, *Master drawings of the Italian Renaissance* (London: British Museum Press, 2007), p.172.

REYNOLDS HAD A LARGE COLLECTION OF prints and drawings of the School of Fontainebleau, named after the French royal palace on the outskirts of Paris, where French and Italian artists worked in the middle of the sixteenth century. These included another drawing by Rosso, attributed now to his circle, which is in the British Museum; and the highly unusual *Bust of a woman with an elaborate coiffure* by Primaticcio.[28]

Rosso was, with Primaticcio, the leading painter and designer at the court of Francis I. He came to France in 1530 to work on the remodelling of Fontainebleau, and died ten years later. The sensual subject is matched by the deft handling of red chalk, deliberately rubbed in several places to create delicate modulation of light over the nude figure. Carroll and Béguin have both noted the subject's similarity to the sleeping figure at the bottom left of Rosso's fresco *Fountain of Youth* in the Gallery of Francis I at Fontainebleau, and therefore date the drawing to Rosso's time in France. Its strong Michelangeloesque qualities derive from his famous sculpture *Dawn*, on the Medici tombs in Florence.[29] The historic mount, dating from at least the eighteenth century, with its red pen lines and wash borders complements the tonality of the drawing.

Martin Postle has recently suggested that this drawing was, in part, the inspiration for Reynolds's sleeping female figure in *Cimon and Iphigenia* (Royal Collection). Contemporary critics of the picture in 1789 noted the skill with which 'the artist has imitated Luca Giordana [sic] with success'.[30] Reynolds owned work by Giordano, such as a drawing in the Victoria and Albert Museum, London[31] but in fact the depiction seems much closer to a work by Guercino, now in Truro (CAT. 69).

REYNOLDS'S COLLECTION WAS STRONG in work of the School of Fontainebleau. Besides Primaticcio, he owned work by Rosso Fiorentino, as well as many fine prints. Other drawings by Primaticcio include two drawings in red chalk in the British Museum: a male reclining nude and *The flaying of Marsyas*.[32] Oxford's Ashmolean Museum also has an example that has passed through the collections of a succession of painters including Lely, Lankrink, Reynolds and Sandby.[33]

This is a finished study or *modello* for the thirty-ninth fresco in the series in the Galerie d'Ulysse which was commissioned by King Francis I of France for his palace at Fontainebleau. Fifty-eight scenes relating to the story of Ulysses were produced in total, though all were lost in the palace remodeling of 1738–39. The numerous drawings that survive for the scheme give vital clues to the subjects chosen for depiction. Here Ulysses wins the hand of Penelope, having demonstrated his prowess in firing an arrow through a series of twelve hoops. The drawing is typical of Primaticcio's usual high technical refinement and the highlights, picked out in white heightening, are delicately rendered. The composition was engraved in 1633 by the Flemish printmaker Theodor van Thulden (1606–69) as plate 39 in *Les travaux d'Ulysse*.

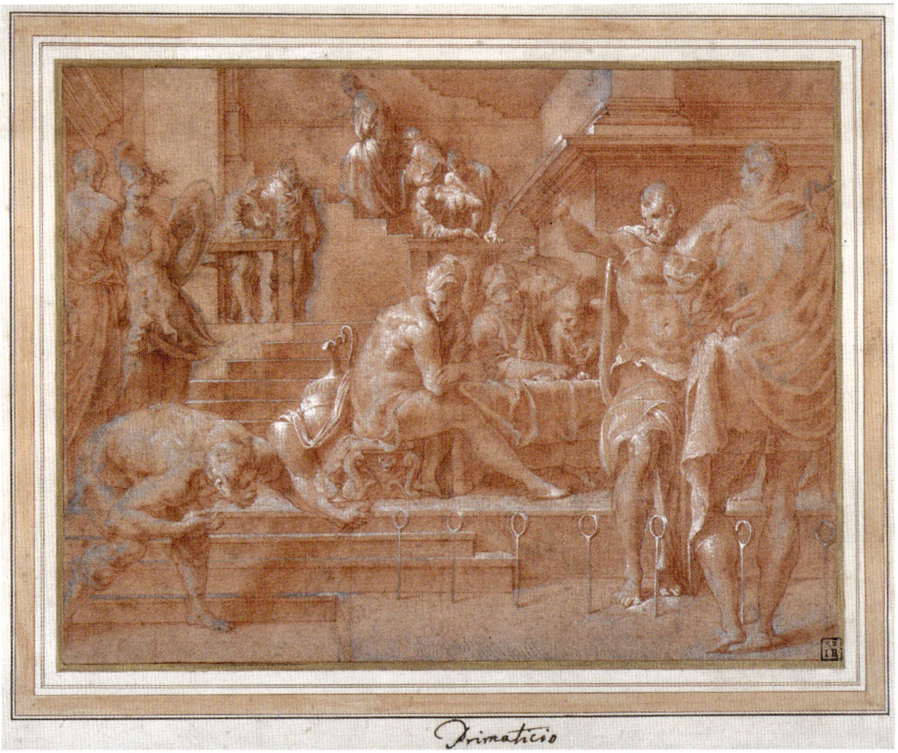

CAT. 46

Primaticcio
(1504–70)
Ulysses shooting through the rings
red chalk and white heightening on pink prepared paper, 24.3 x 32.4 cm
Walker Art Gallery, Liverpool (WAG10843)

PROVENANCE: Sir Joshua Reynolds (1723–92; Lugt 2364); William Roscoe (1753–1831), Thomas Winstanley's, Liverpool, 23 September 1816, lot 346; bought Slater; Charles Robert Blundell (1761–1837), by descent in the family, Christie's London, 11 December 1990, lot 62; export stopped, purchased with the aid of The Art Fund in 1991.

EXHIBITION HISTORY: 1969, Edinburgh Merchant's Hall, 'Italian sixteenth-century drawings from British private collections', no.69; 1998–99, Liverpool and London, Walker Art Gallery and British Museum, 'Mantegna to Rubens: Drawings from the Liverpool Weld-Blundell collection revealed', no.43; 2003–04, London, Hayward Gallery, 'Saved! 100 years of the National Art Collections Fund', no.163; 2004–05, Paris, Musée du Louvre, 'Primatice: Maître de Fontainebleau', no.170.

LITERATURE: Sylvie Béguin, Jean Guillaume, Alain Roy, *La galerie d'Ulysse à Fontainebleau* (Paris: Presses Universitaires de France, 1985), pp.284–86, no.39, fig.299; David Ekserdjian, 'Francesco Primaticcio: An Old Master Drawing returns to Merseyside', *NACF Review*, 1992, pp.10–11; Xanthe Brooke, *Mantegna to Rubens: The Weld-Blundell drawings collection* (London: Merrell Holberton, 1998), pp.90–91, 151, no.43; David Ekserdjian in Richard Verdi (ed.), *Saved! 100 years of the National Art Collections Fund* (London: Scala, 2003), p.229, no.163; Dominique Cordellier in Dominique Cordellier (ed), *Primatice: Maître de Fontainebleau* (Paris: Réunion des musées nationaux, 2004), pp.332–33, 334, no.170.

CAT. 47

Battista Franco
(c.1510–61)
Study of God the Father in 'The Baptism of Christ with Saints Bernardino of Siena and Francis'
(c.1552–54)
black, red and white chalk on blue paper, 29.2 x 24.3 cm
National Gallery of Scotland, Edinburgh (D1590)

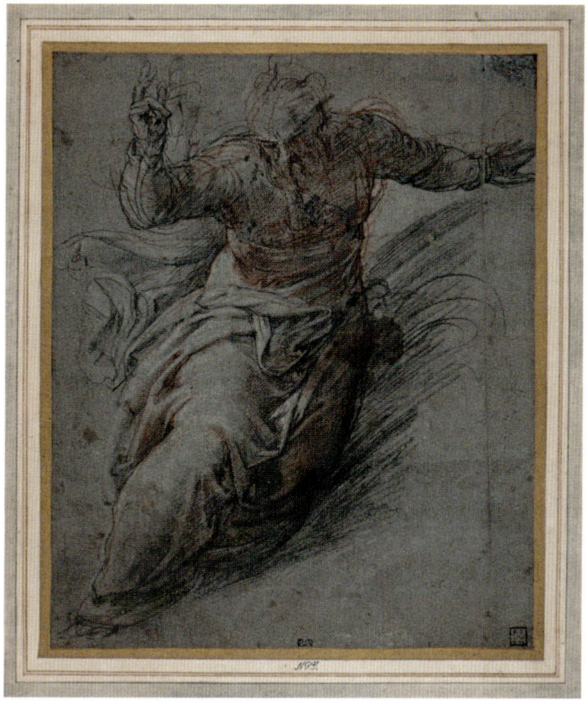

PROVENANCE: Jonathan Richardson I (1665–1745; Lugt 2184); Sir Joshua Reynolds (1723–92; Lugt 2364); Sir Thomas Lawrence (1769–1830; Lugt 2445); David Laing (1793–1878) bequeathed to Royal Scottish Academy, Edinburgh in 1878; transferred in 1910.

EXHIBITION HISTORY: 1990–91, Washington, National Gallery of Art and Fort Worth, Kimbell Art Museum, 'Old Master drawings from the National Gallery of Scotland', no.8; 2004, Edinburgh, Royal Scottish Academy, 'The age of Titian: Venetian Renaissance art from Scottish Collections', no.97.

LITERATURE: Keith Andrews, *Catalogue of Italian drawings in the National Gallery of Scotland* (Cambridge: Cambridge University Press, 1968), vol.I, p.52, vol.II, fig.372; Hugh Macandrew, *Old Master drawings from the National Gallery of Scotland* (Washington: National Gallery of Art, 1990), pp.36–37, no.8; Anne Varick Lauder, 'Un nuovo disegno di Battista Franco per il 'Battesimo di Cristo' della cappella Barbaro', *Arte Veneta*, 50, 1997, pp.98–107 (98), fig.4; Carol Gibson-Wood, '"A Judiciously Disposed Collection": Jonathan Richardson Senior's cabinet of drawings', in Christopher Baker *et al.* (eds), *Collecting prints and drawings in Europe, c.1500–1750* (Aldershot and Burlington, VT: Ashgate, 2003), pp.155–71 (167), figs.10.6 (recto) and 10.7 (verso); Aidan Weston-Lewis in Peter Humfrey *et al.*, *The age of Titian: Venetian Renaissance art from Scottish collections* (Edinburgh: National Galleries of Scotland, 2004), pp.236–37, no.97.

REYNOLDS OWNED MANY FRANCO drawings, including another in Edinburgh,[34] also acquired from Richardson the Elder, and several more in the British Museum. Individual sheets are scattered in the Institut Néerlandais (Fondation Custodia), in the Walker Art Gallery, Liverpool and the Szépművészeti Múzeum, Budapest.[35]

The Richardson mount has two red ink lines and a blue wash area to complement the predominant tonality of the sheet: the electric red chalk on the vivid blue paper. Richardson's mount is seen too on a drawing by Barocci (CAT. 53). Franco experimented with the position of God the Father's right arm, with rapid strokes at the right suggesting many alternatives. Richardson gives an account of the commission on the verso, much lengthier than Reynolds's annotations, which are extremely brief. Most of this drawing is in black chalk with later additions in red and white chalk, making the combined effect extremely beautiful (and unique) in his drawn *oeuvre*. Franco's drawings are usually in pen and ink; their fluidity is matched by those of Giulio Romano, another artist whom Reynolds admired (CAT. 41). The figure, as painted, has lost much of the vitality of the drawing, the drapery has been simplified and the facial expression muted.

REYNOLDS OWNED LITTLE GERMAN work in any medium. Albrecht Dürer (1471–1528) is the notable exception, though only a handful of works can be traced to Reynolds's collection. In the Kupferstichkabinett in Berlin is a pen and ink *Madonna and Child*, exactly of the type that Reynolds seems to have particularly admired and collected in large numbers.[36] He also owned some graphic work by Dürer, including the woodcut *The Flight into Egypt*, of about 1504, which is now in the Saint Louis Art Museum, Missouri,[37] and the artist's first engraving *The Ravisher* (c.1495).[38] Reynolds also owned a delicate metalpoint study of a full-length female in profile by the Flemish artist Jacques de Gheyn II (1565–1629), which, though once thought to be by Dürer, was stamped with Reynolds's mark on the verso of the sheet, indicating its 'inferior' status.[39]

Hopfer made a number of prints based on etchings by the German printmaker Albrecht Altdorfer, dating from the 1520s. This particular example reverses a smaller work by Altdorfer,[40] and the three goblets have here been rearranged to give more space between each vessel, and topped by a banderol proclaiming Hopfer's pride in the splendid work. It is the only traceable work by Hopfer in Reynolds' collection, one of his very few German prints and certainly his most exuberant.

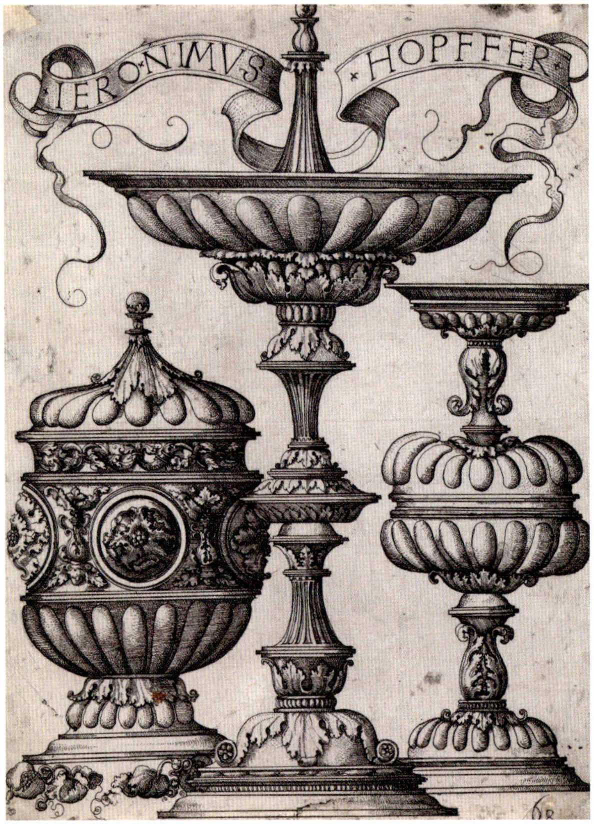

CAT. 48

Hieronymus Hopfer
(c.1500–63)
after Albrecht Altdorfer (1482/5–1538)
Three goblets
etching, 28.5 x 21.2 cm
Private collection, London

PROVENANCE: Sir Joshua Reynolds (1723–92; Lugt 2364 verso); anonymous (circular red stamp undescribed by Lugt; fig.30); Xavier Seydoux, Paris, from whom purchased by present owner in April 2008.

EXHIBITION HISTORY: None.

LITERATURE: Robert Zijlma, *Hollstein's German engravings, etchings and woodcuts 1400–1700, vol.XV* (Blaricum: A L van Gendt, 1986), p.242, no.72 ii/ii.

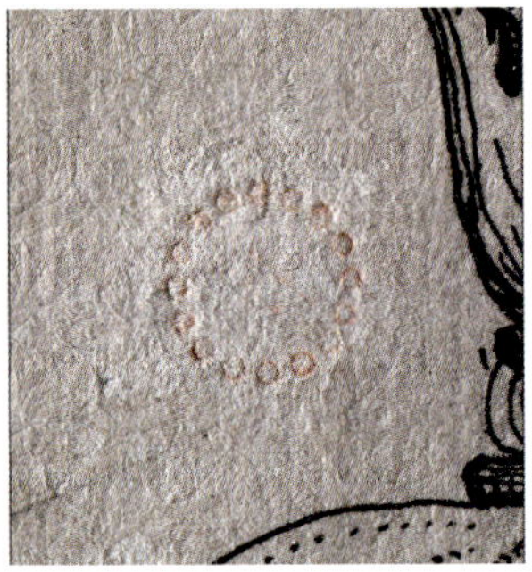

FIG. 30

Unidentified collector's mark (detail of CAT. 48).

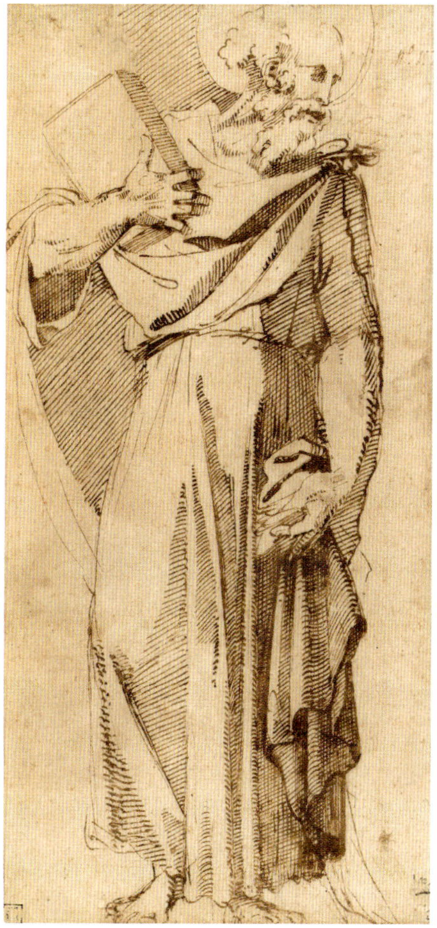

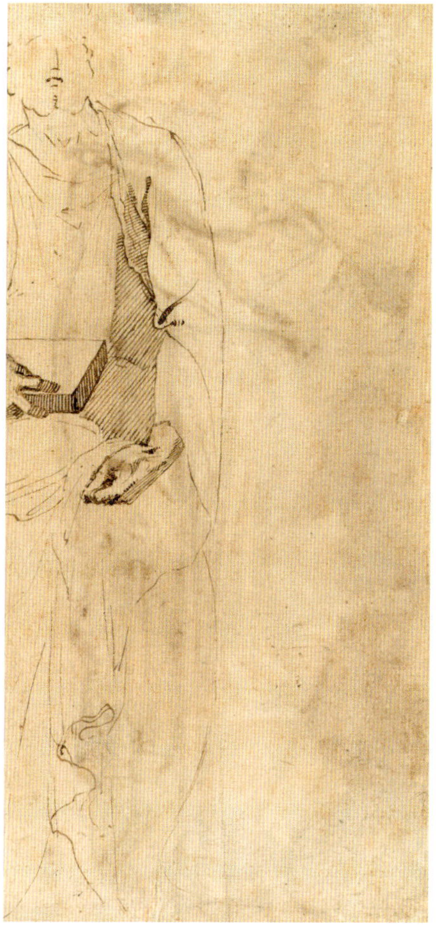

ALTHOUGH IT WAS CATALOGUED IN THE nineteenth century as a Donatello (1386/7–1466), Reynolds probably knew this drawing as by Bandini's master Baccio Bandinelli (1493–1560).[41] Hudson owned a superb Bandinelli drawing, which Reynolds probably knew at first hand.[42] Reynolds owned two versions of Bandinelli's *The Crucifixion*, one in the National Gallery of Canada in Ottawa (FIG. 26, p. 106) and the other in a private collection in New York.

Both the recto and the verso were drawn in preparation for the standing male figures, which decorate the bas-reliefs of the choir in the Duomo in Florence. This was a project begun by Bandinelli in 1547 on which Bandini worked from 1560–72 following his master's death. Bandini's regular hatching and dry handling set his drawings apart from the more expressive examples by Bandinelli. Bandini was rediscovered as a draughtsman by Ulrich Middeldorf (1901–83) in 1939, when he connected some of the surviving group of studies for this project. The Courtauld Institute Gallery has another study by Bandini relating to the Duomo project that had also been in Reynolds's collection.[43]

CAT. 49

Giovanni Bandini
(1540–99)
A figure of a standing saint
(recto)
and
Another figure of a standing saint
(verso)
pen and brown ink, 40.4 x 19.4 cm
Fitzwilliam Museum, Cambridge (PD.3-2004)

PROVENANCE: Sir Joshua Reynolds (1723–92; Lugt 2364), Harry Phillips, London, 5 March 1798, (?) part of lot 117 as '3 [drawings], Parmegian[in]o, Donatello'; Sir Thomas Lawrence (1769-1830; Lugt 2445); William Mayor (d.1874; Lugt 2799); private collection, Switzerland; Phillips, London, 13 December 2000, lot 116; Crispian Riley-Smith, from whom purchased by the Cunliffe Fund with a contribution from The Art Fund in 2004.

EXHIBITION HISTORY: None.

LITERATURE: Roger Ward, *Baccio Bandinelli, 1493–1560: Drawings from British collections* (Cambridge: Fitzwilliam Museum, 1988), pp.78–79 (79) as 'untraced'; Anna Forlani Tempesti, 'Disegni di "Apostoli" di Giovanni Bandini', *Prospettiva*, April 1989–October 1990, 57–60, pp.66–73 (66, 71–72); David Scrase, *Italian drawings at the Fitzwilliam Museum* (Cambridge: Fitzwilliam Museum, 2009), forthcoming.

CAT. 50

Taddeo Zuccaro
(1529–66)
Soldier walking down a step
red chalk, 35.7 x 13.4 cm
British Museum, London
(PD 1895,0915.814)

PROVENANCE: Sir Joshua Reynolds (1723–92; Lugt 2364); William Mayor (d.1874; Lugt 2799); Sir John Charles Robinson (1824–1913); John Malcolm (1805–93), by descent to Col John Wingfield Malcolm (1833–1902), from whom purchased in 1895.

EXHIBITION HISTORY: 1978, London, British Museum, 'Gainsborough and Reynolds in the British Museum', no.229.

LITERATURE: John Charles Robinson, *A descriptive catalogue of drawings by the Old Masters, forming the collection of John Malcolm of Poltalloch, Esq.* (London: privately printed, 1876), p.132, no.367 (as Sebastiano del Piombo); Luitpold Dussler, *Sebastiano del Piombo* (Basel: Holbein-Verlag, 1942), pp.181–82, no.183 (as Sebastiano del Piombo); Rodolfo Pallucchini, *Sebastian Viniziano (fra Sebastiano del Piombo); Con 113 tavole fuori testo di cui una a colori* (Milan: Mondadori, 1944), p.192 (as Sebastiano del Piombo); Martin Royalton-Kisch in Timothy Clifford, Antony Griffiths and Martin Royalton-Kisch, *Gainsborough and Reynolds in the British Museum* (London: British Museum Publications, 1978), p.80, no.229 (as Zuccaro); John Gere and Philip Pouncey, *Italian drawings in the Department of Prints and Drawings in the British Museum: Artists working in Rome c.1550 to c.1640* (London: British Museum Publications, 1983), vol.I, pp.207–8, no. 332, vol.II, plate 318 (as Zuccaro).

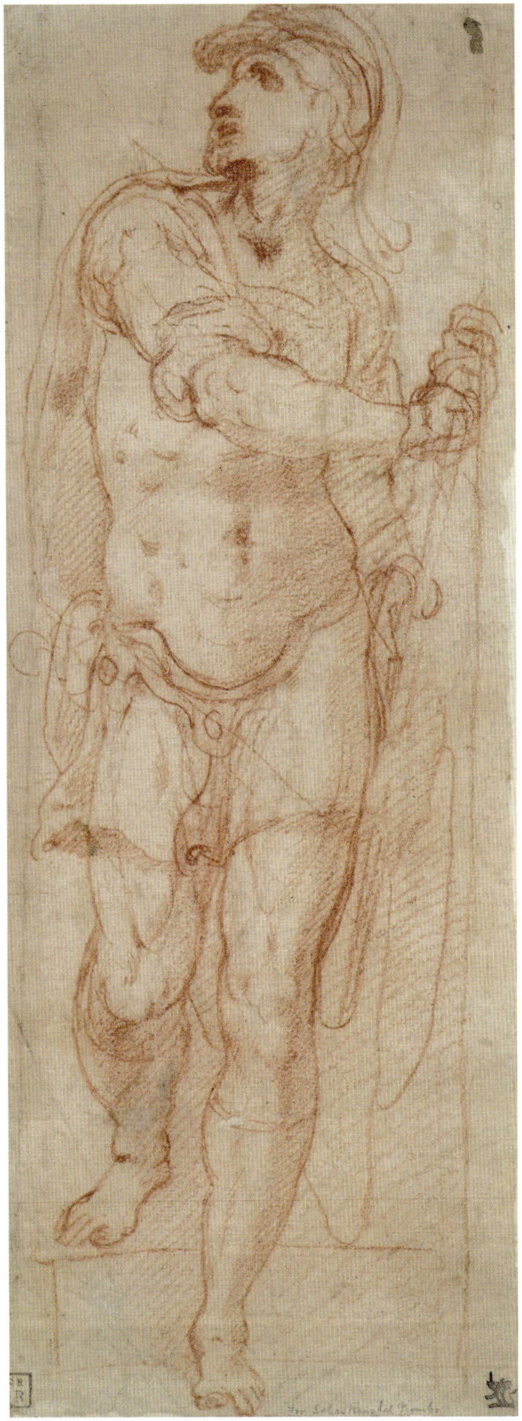

REYNOLDS HAD FEW DRAWINGS BY THIS artist. There are two others in the British Museum, both very different from the present example. One is on blue paper with white heightening and is a copy of a figure from Correggio (a favourite of Reynolds) and the other is a double-sided sheet with *The Foundation of Orbetello* in pen and brown ink with brown wash.[44]

In this drawing the soldier's pose is very inventive, and Reynolds seems to have adapted the stance of this figure for two of his full-length male portraits. The crossed arm over the chest might have been considered impolite, so in the portrait of his friend *Frederick Howard, 5th Earl of Carlisle* (1769; Castle Howard, Yorkshire) Reynolds has extended the young aristocrat's right arm outwards in a gesturing pose, but the lower half of his body is exactly as in Zuccaro's drawing. Reynolds also used the device of a figure descending a staircase in his portrait *Peregrine Bertie, 3rd Duke of Ancaster* (1758–61; Grimsthorpe Castle).[45] The drawing was until the late twentieth century thought to be by Sebastiano del Piombo (c.1485–1547), a painter in the circle of Michelangelo, who was one of Reynolds's greatest favourites.

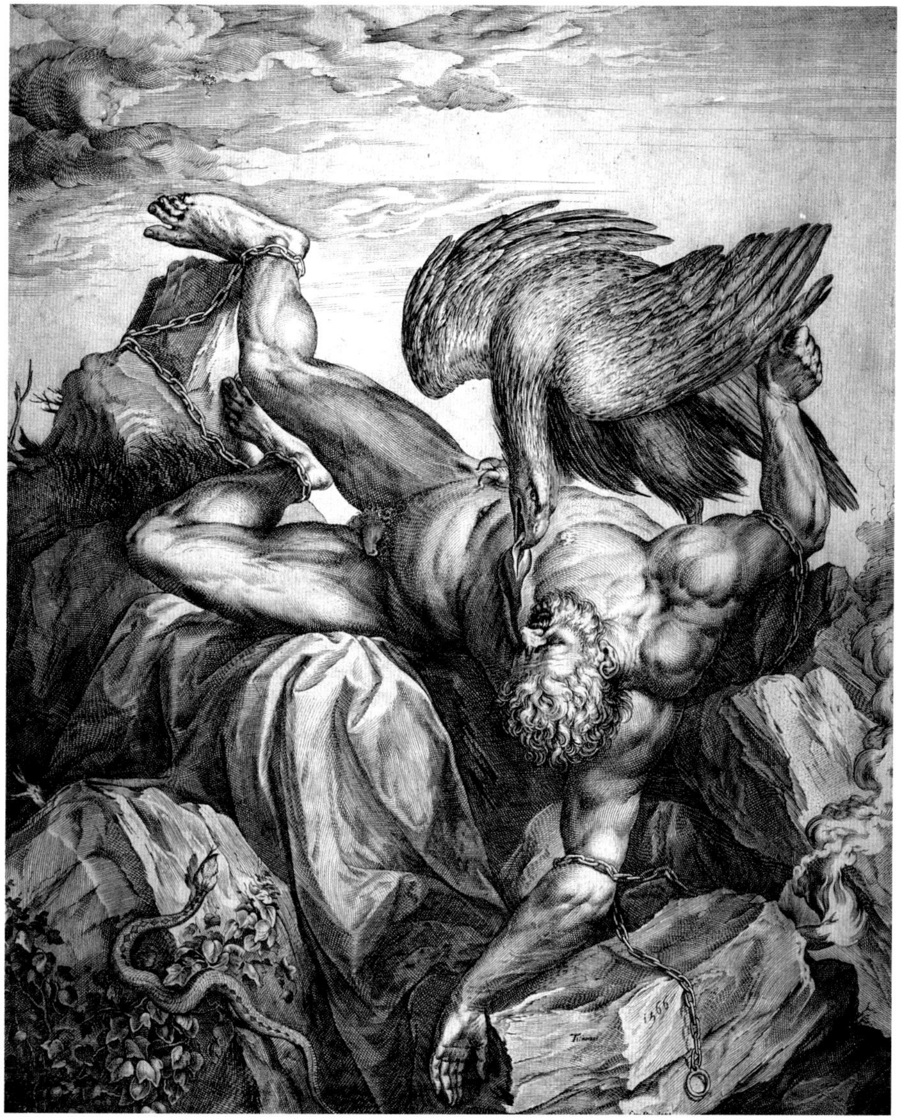

TITIAN WAS REPRESENTED IN REYNOLDS'S collection with both prints and drawings. The drawings included a small chalk study for the famous altarpiece *The Assumption* (1516–18), painted for the church of the Frari, which Reynolds saw during his visit to Venice in 1752; the study is now in the British Museum.[46] He also owned a sheet *Cupid with Quiver* (possibly after Titian), now in New York, which had previously belonged to Lely and Mariette.[47] Reynolds also owned a 'Titian' (now at the Fogg Museum of Art in Harvard and considered a copy), related to the famous canvas *The Venus of Urbino* (1538; Uffizi, Florence). Reynolds had obtained this drawing from Richardson the Elder.[48] Reynolds also owned an anonymous Italian print after Titian's famous *Venus and Adonis* (1553–54; Prado, Madrid) which is also now in Edinburgh.[49] However, Reynolds's greatest Venetian treasures were his dozens of drawings by Tintoretto.

Cort made six engravings in a short period from 1565 to 1566 under Titian's supervision in Venice, who supplied him with drawings of his paintings specifically for printmaking. This handsome engraving reverses the composition of Titian's painting (now in Madrid) upon which it is based. Titian, worried about inferior piracies, obtained a 15-year privilege from the Venetian Senate to protect his compositions, hence the dated Latin inscription, with Titian's name: 'Titianus 1566' and 'Cum Privilegio' ('with privilege, or permission').

CAT. 51

Cornelis Cort
(c.1533–78)
after Titian
(c.1490–1576)
Tityus (Prometheus)
(1566)
engraving,
38.2 x 31.4 cm
National Gallery of Scotland, Edinburgh

PROVENANCE: Sir Joshua Reynolds (1723–92; Lugt 2364 verso); acquired at an unknown date.

EXHIBITION HISTORY: 2004, Edinburgh, Royal Scottish Academy, 'The age of Titian: Venetian Renaissance art from Scottish collections', no.144.

LITERATURE: Johann Catharius Justus Bierens de Haan, *L'oeuvre gravé de Cornelis Cort, graveur Hollandais, 1533–1578* (The Hague: Martinus Nijhoff, 1948), pp.174–75, no.192 i/ii; Manfred Sellink, *The new Hollstein, Dutch and Flemish etchings, engravings and woodcuts 1450–1700: Cornelis Cort (Part III)* (Rotterdam: Sound and Vision, 2000), pp.77–79, no.190 i/iii; Michael Bury, *The print in Italy, 1550–1620* (London: British Museum Press, 2001), pp.189–90, no.126; Michael Bury in Peter Humfrey *et al.*, *The age of Titian: Venetian Renaissance art from Scottish collections* (Edinburgh: National Galleries of Scotland, 2004), p.302, no.144.

CAT. 52

Luca Cambiaso
(1527–85)
The Annunciation
(c.1568)
pen and brown ink, with brown wash, 29.8 x 21 cm
Courtauld Institute Gallery (Samuel Courtauld Trust), London (D.1952.RW.1956)

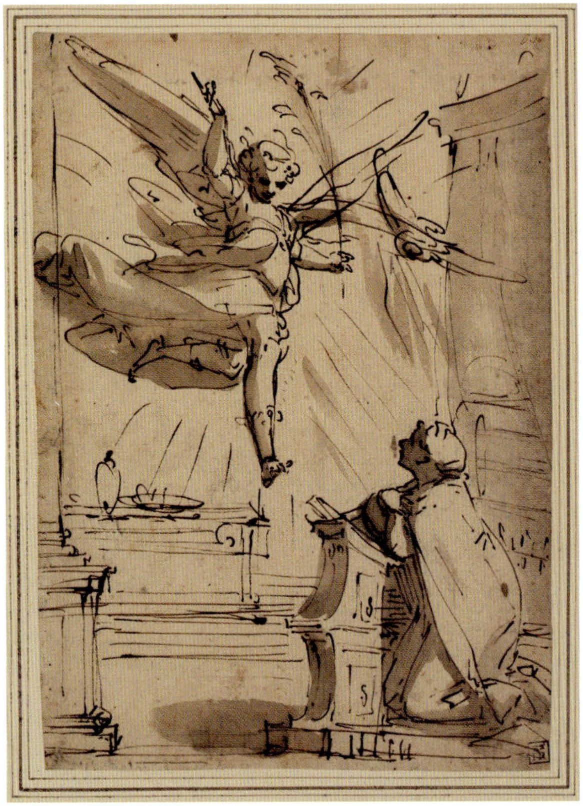

PROVENANCE: Sir Joshua Reynolds (1723–92; Lugt 2364); Sotheby's, London; F Parsons & Son, London; from whom purchased by Sir Robert Witt (1872–1952; Lugt 2228b), by 1936 (? through Leonard G Duke) and by whom bequeathed in 1952.

EXHIBITION HISTORY: 1936, London, R E A Wilson, 'Drawings by Luca Cambiaso (1527–1585)', no.14; 1937–38, London, Burlington Fine Arts Club, 'Exhibition of pictures, drawings, furniture and other objects of art', no.80; 1943, London, Victoria and Albert Museum, 'Drawings of the Old Masters from the Witt collection'; 1965, Manchester City Art Gallery, 'Between Renaissance and Baroque: European art, 1520–1600', no.288.

LITERATURE: Bertina Suida Manning and William Suida, *Luca Cambiaso: La vita e le opere* (Milan: Ceschina, 1958), p.180, plate CXLIV, fig.233; Fritz Grossmann, *Between Renaissance and Baroque: European art, 1520–1600* (Manchester: Manchester City Art Gallery, 1965), p.88, no.288.

REYNOLDS OWNED AT LEAST TWENTY-five drawings by the prolific Genoese painter and draughtsman Cambiaso. Recent scholarship has revealed that the dispersal of Reynolds' Cambiaso drawings was begun by his friend Antonio Cesare Poggi on 26 May 1794 and was completed at the death of Reynolds's niece and heir Mary Palmer, Marchioness of Thomond (1750–1820) at Christie's, London, 16–17 May 1821.[50] Those Cambiaso drawings are now widely dispersed throughout the world, with one in Copenhagen, one in Venice, one in Budapest, two at the Blanton Museum of Art at the University of Texas at Austin, as well as other fine examples in London, at the Courtauld Institute Gallery and the British Museum.[51]

The archangel Gabriel here fulfils Isaiah's prophecy: 'Behold a virgin shall conceive and bear a son, and shall call his name Emmanuel' (Isaiah 7.14). The Cleveland Museum of Art in Ohio has another version of the subject in the same medium and approximate size.[52] Both these drawings are related to Cambiaso's 1568 commission for SS Annunziata di Portoria, Genoa. Reynolds himself seldom painted religious subjects but *The Annunciation*, now lost, was one of those he did.[53]

CAT. 53

Federico Barocci
(1535–1612)
Study for the painting 'Martyrdom of San Vitale'
(c.1580)
coloured chalks on blue paper, with stylus underdrawing, squared for transfer, 26.6 x 23.2 cm
National Gallery of Scotland, Edinburgh (D1589)

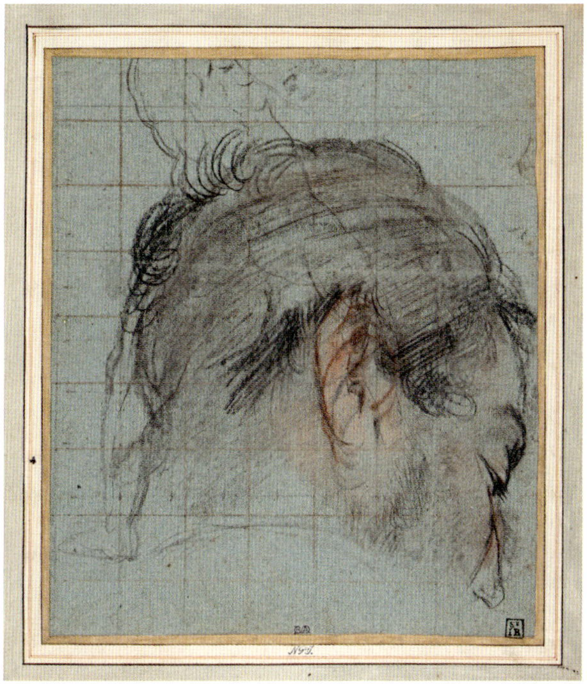

PROVENANCE: Jonathan Richardson II (1694–1771; Lugt 2170), Langford's, London, February 1772; Sir Joshua Reynolds (1723–92; Lugt 2364); David Laing (1793–1878) bequeathed to Royal Scottish Academy, Edinburgh in 1878; transferred in 1910.

EXHIBITION HISTORY: 1978, Cleveland (Ohio), Cleveland Museum of Art and New Haven, Yale University Art Gallery, 'The graphic art of Federico Barocci: Selected drawings and prints', no.46; 1990–91, Washington, National Gallery of Art and Fort Worth, Kimbell Art Museum, 'Old Master drawings from the National Gallery of Scotland', no.12; 2006, Cambridge, Fitzwilliam Museum, 'A Touch of the Divine': Drawings by Federico Barocci in British collections', no.50.

LITERATURE: Harald Olsen, *Federico Barocci: A critical study in Italian Cinquecento painting* (Stockholm: Almqvist & Wiksell, 1955), p.136; Harald Olsen, *Federico Barocci* (Copenhagen: Munksgaard, 1962), p.174; Keith Andrews, *Catalogue of Italian drawings in the National Gallery of Scotland* (Cambridge: Cambridge University Press, 1968), vol.I, p.12, vol.II, fig.112; Edmund Pillsbury in Edmund Pillsbury and Louise Richards, *The graphic art of Federico Barocci: Selected drawings and prints* (New Haven: Yale University Art Gallery, 1978), pp.69–70, no.46; Andrea Emiliani, *Federico Barocci (Urbino 1535–1612)* (Bologna: Banca Popolare Pesarese, 1985), vol.I, pp.169–87, fig.363; David Scrase, *'A Touch of the Divine': Drawings by Federico Barocci in British collections* (Cambridge: Fitzwilliam Museum, 2006), pp.150–51, no.50.

REYNOLDS OWNED A NUMBER OF Baroccis (in a variety of media), including another drawing in Edinburgh,[54] two in the British Museum, and one in Cambridge. Others include *Head of a young girl* in Vienna, formerly in Jonathan Richardson the Younger's collection, and a study for the same altarpiece.[55] One of the British Museum drawings, a large study for the head of Christ in *The Last Supper* (1590–99) in the cathedral at Urbino,[56] is found on exactly the same mount as the present sheet, which had previously belonged to Richardson. Reynolds also owned prints after Barocci, including an engraving by Cort, now in Cambridge (FIG. 31). He also owned paintings attributed to Barocci including an untraced *The Marriage of the Virgin*.[57]

Barocci was a talented pupil of Battista Franco. The painting related to this drawing was commissioned in 1580 for the church of San Vitale in Ravenna. The drawing has been squared for transfer to the canvas and uses black accents to delineate the eyelashes, and elsewhere *pentimenti* related to an ear. The outlined figure picked out with the stylus is about to hurl a rock at the saint. Though some areas of the sheets are rubbed, the area around the eye is pristine. The red ink parallel lines and blue wash area of the historic mount, like the Franco also in Edinburgh (CAT. 47), set off the dominant tones of the sheet: red chalk on blue paper.

FIG. 31

Cornelis Cort
(c.1533–78)
after Federico Barocci
(1535–1612)
La Madonna del Gatto (The Holy Family with a Cat)
(1577)
engraving,
33 x 24.1 cm
Fitzwilliam Museum, Cambridge (P.1605–1991)

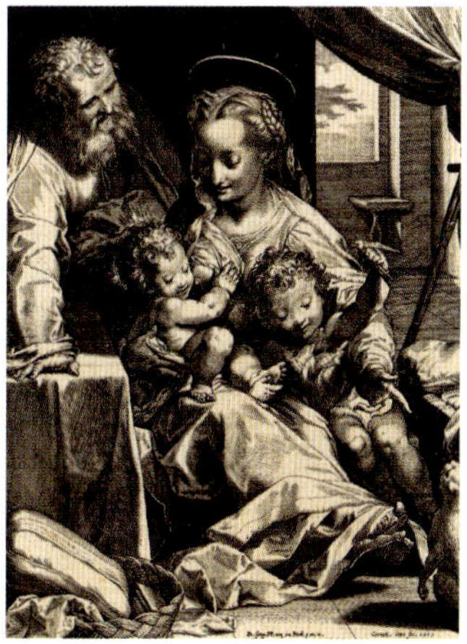

FARINATI'S EXUBERANT STYLE OF drawing appealed to Reynolds. One sheet in the British Museum depicts Tamerlane mounting his horse from the back of a captive king.[58] One of the finest is a large drawing of two prophets, bequeathed to the Bibliothèque Municipale de Rouen by the painter, print historian and collector Jules Hédou (1833–1905); one prophet supports an open book and the other a stone tablet.[59] The sheet in Rouen bears the historic attribution (to Farinati) in what seems Reynolds's hand. One other Farinati that belonged to Reynolds is now in the Snite Museum of Art, University of Notre Dame in Indiana.[60]

David Scrase notes that the elaborate contortion of the figures, the heavy use of wash and abundance of white highlights are characteristic of Farinati's later work. Unusually for Old Master drawings, it is dated: May 1588. Farinati had painted the subject for a ceiling in the Palazzo Murari in Verona in 1588, but appears to have re-used the design elsewhere. There is no evidence as to where the original subject was intended. But a similar drawing, *Mercury and Psyche*, now in the Ashmolean Museum in Oxford and which had once belonged to Reynolds, is also for an octagonal ceiling painting.[61]

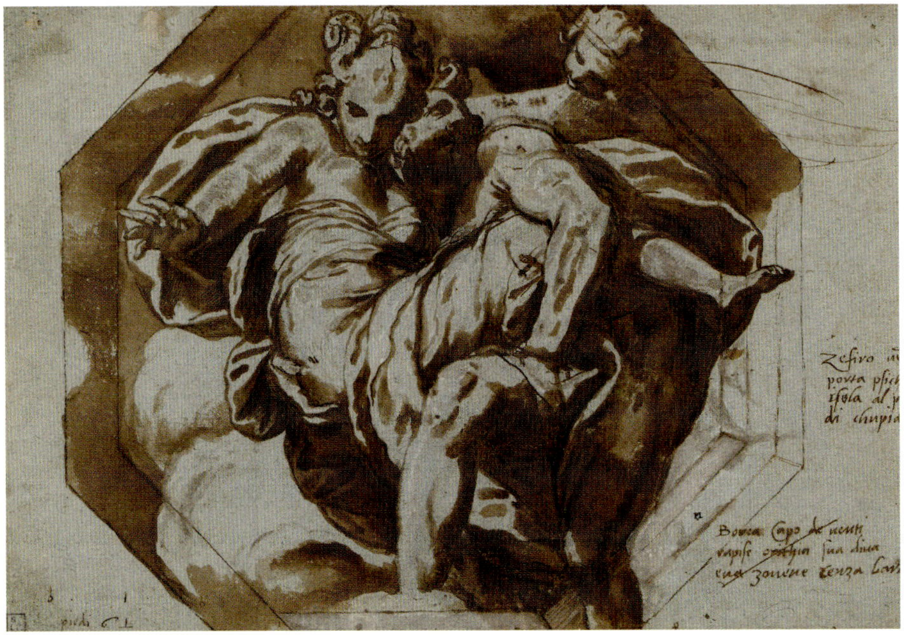

CAT. 54

Paolo Farinati
(1524–1606)
Boreas raping Orizia
(1588)
pen and brown ink, brown wash, heightened with white on faded blue paper, 28.5 x 41.6 cm
Fitzwilliam Museum, Cambridge (no.2956)

PROVENANCE: Sir Peter Lely (1618–80; Lugt 2092); William Gibson (d.1703; Lugt suppl. 2885); Sir Joshua Reynolds (1723–92; Lugt 2364); Rev. Dr. Henry Wellesley (1794–1866), Sotheby's, London, 27 June 1866, lot 529; Sir James Thomas Knowles (1831–1908), Christie's, London, 28 May 1908, part of lot 232; G T Clough (1839–1928), by whom presented in 1913.

EXHIBITION HISTORY: 1868, Leeds, Leeds General Infirmary, 'National exhibition of works of art', no.2601; 1960, Cambridge, Fitzwilliam Museum, 'Fifteenth and sixteenth-century drawings', no.27; 1983–84, London, Royal Academy, 'The genius of Venice, 1500–1600', no.D15; 1992, Venice, Fondazione Giorgio Cini, 'Da Pisanello a Tiepolo', no.30.

LITERATURE: Hugh Macandrew, *Catalogue of the collection of drawings in the Ashmolean Museum, Oxford: Volume III (Italian Schools: Supplement)* (Oxford: Oxford University Press, 1980), p.261; Giuliana Ericani, 'Tra Padova e Verona: Dipinti e disegni inediti di Paolo Farinati e Felice Brusasorci', *Verona Illustrata* (9), 1996, pp.69–86; David Scrase in Jane Martineau and Charles Hope (eds), *The genius of Venice, 1500–1600* (London: Royal Academy of Art and Weidenfeld and Nicolson, 1983), p.255, no.D15; Alessandro Bettagno, *Da Pisanello a Tiepolo: Disegni Veneti dal Fitzwilliam Museum di Cambridge* (Milan: Electa, 1992), pp.78–79, no.30; Giorgio Marini *et al.*, *Paolo Farinati 1524–1606* (Venice: Marsilio, 2005), p.148; David Scrase, *Italian drawings at the Fitzwilliam Museum* (Cambridge: Fitzwilliam Museum, 2009), forthcoming.

REYNOLDS HAD MANY DRAWINGS BY each member of the Carracci family. Others of his sheets by Annibale, who was cousin of Ludovico (CAT. 56), include one in red chalk of a youthful male, now in the collection of Jak Katalan in the USA.[62] This had previously belonged to Richardson the Elder, and might have been given by Reynolds to the Royal Academician Samuel Woodforde (1763–1817). Reynolds also owned a tender pen and brown ink study of the *Madonna and Child*, a subject that might have appealed to him, given his numerous depictions of eighteenth-century aristocratic mothers with their children.[63] Reynolds also owned more sketchy pen and ink drawings by Annibale, such as *Seated nude male*, now in Bremen.[64] The study of *Two Putti* in red chalk by him is now in the British Museum.[65] Annibale's drawings have long been collected, especially among artists. Both the Italians Domenichino and Carlo Maratti, and the French painter Antoine Coypel, formed large groups of them.[66]

The model in this study might be the same as that seen in a sheet (also owned by Reynolds) by the Bolognese painter Pietro Faccini (c.1562–1602), who studied under the Carracci family at the academy in Bologna. Faccini's drawing displays the wild curly hair and large eyes that closely match these features seen in this study.[67] Reynolds owned other drawings by Faccini, such as the sheet in red chalk with *The Mystic Marriage of Saint Catherine*, now in the British Museum.[68]

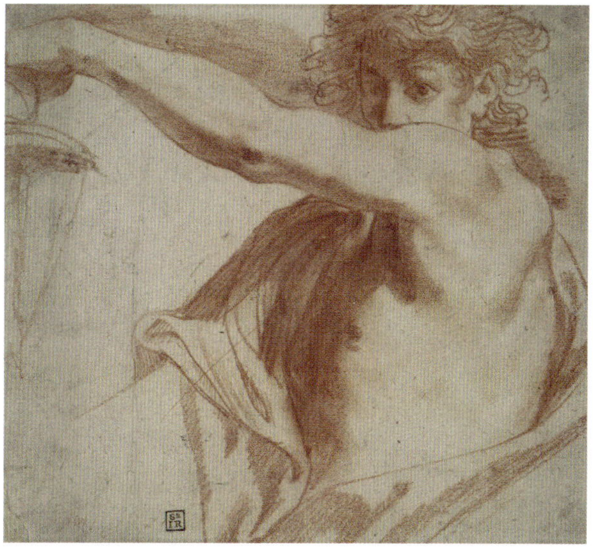

CAT. 55

Annibale Carracci
(1560–1609)
Study of a male figure (? holding a censer)
red chalk, 24.2 x 27.4 cm
British Museum, London (PD Pp, 3.14)

PROVENANCE: Sir Joshua Reynolds (1723–92; Lugt 2364); Richard Payne Knight (1751–1824), by whom bequeathed in 1824.

EXHIBITION HISTORY: 1978, London, British Museum, 'Gainsborough and Reynolds in the British Museum', no.250.

LITERATURE: Martin Royalton-Kisch in Timothy Clifford, Antony Griffiths and Martin Royalton-Kisch, *Gainsborough and Reynolds in the British Museum* (London: British Museum Publications, 1978), p.83, no.250; Catherine Loisel, *Musée du Louvre, Département des Arts Graphiques: Inventaire Général des dessins Italians, no.VII: Ludovico, Agostino, Annibale Carracci* (Paris: Réunion des musées nationaux, 2004), p.31, fig.33.

CAT. 56

Ludovico Carracci
(1555–1619)
Study of Pluto for the fresco 'Ceres searching for Proserpina'
(c.1593–94)
black chalk on faded blue-grey paper,
25 x 13.8 cm
Fitzwilliam Museum, Cambridge (PD.21-1956)

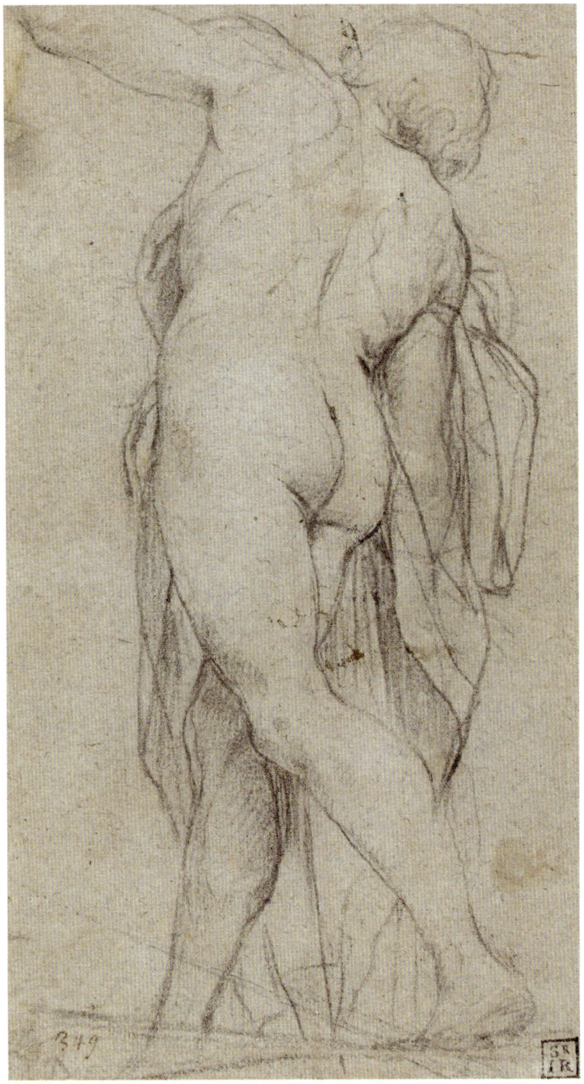

PROVENANCE: Sir Joshua Reynolds (1723–92; Lugt 2364); Col. Norman Colville (1893–1974); Charles Clarke (d.1935); bequeathed to his brother Dr. Louis Clarke (1881–1960), by whom presented in 1956.

EXHIBITION HISTORY: 1959, Fitzwilliam Museum, Cambridge, 'Seventeenth-century Italian drawings', no.59; 1981–82, Fitzwilliam Museum, Cambridge, 'Drawings from the collection of Louis C G Clarke, LLD'; 1989–90, Fitzwilliam Museum, Cambridge, 'Italian Old Master drawings, c.1550–c.1620'.

LITERATURE: Babette Bohn, *Ludovico Carracci and the art of drawing* (Turnhout: Harvey Miller, 2004), pp.235–36, no.108; David Scrase, *Italian drawings at the Fitzwilliam Museum* (Cambridge: Fitzwilliam Museum, 2009), forthcoming.

REYNOLDS DEEPLY ADMIRED LUDOVICO Carracci and considered that his art 'appears to me to approach the nearest to perfection' (Discourse II). He owned a number of other drawings by Ludovico, including studies of the risen Christ and a man in pensive mood, both now in the Ashmolean Museum, Oxford,[69] a large multi-figure sheet *Judith and Holofernes*,[70] a pen and brown ink *Madonna and Child with St. John*, set in a wooden landscape,[71] and another *Madonna and Child*.[72] Old Master depictions of the Madonna such as these informed Reynolds's informal portraits of mothers and their children, similarly set in shady glades.

This graceful drawing on blue paper was once attributed to Guido Reni, who was taught by Ludovico; the mount (now lost) was inscribed in an eighteenth-century hand: 'di Guido Reni'. Subsequently Philip Pouncey (1910–90) proposed an attribution to the circle of Giuseppe Baglione (1571–1644), whose drawings Reynolds collected, such as the sheet now in the University of Princeton.[73] James Byam Shaw (1903–92) noted the inspiration for the stance of the youth from Correggio's frescoes in the cupola of Parma Cathedral. Reynolds owned Correggio drawings for this very scheme. Recently, David Scrase observed that the drawing's style and technique are characteristic of the Carracci Academy and can be directly related to Ludovico's fresco depicting *Ceres searching for Proserpina* on the chimneypiece in the Palazzo Sampieri-Talon in Bologna (1593–94).

CAT. 57

Cherubino Alberti
(1553–1615)
after Baccio Bandinelli
(1493–1560)
Winged figure on a sphere with a tablet (frontispiece to 'Mythological Scenes')
engraving, 23.4 x 15.2 cm
Courtauld Institute Gallery (Samuel Courtauld Trust), London (G.1990.WL.3327)

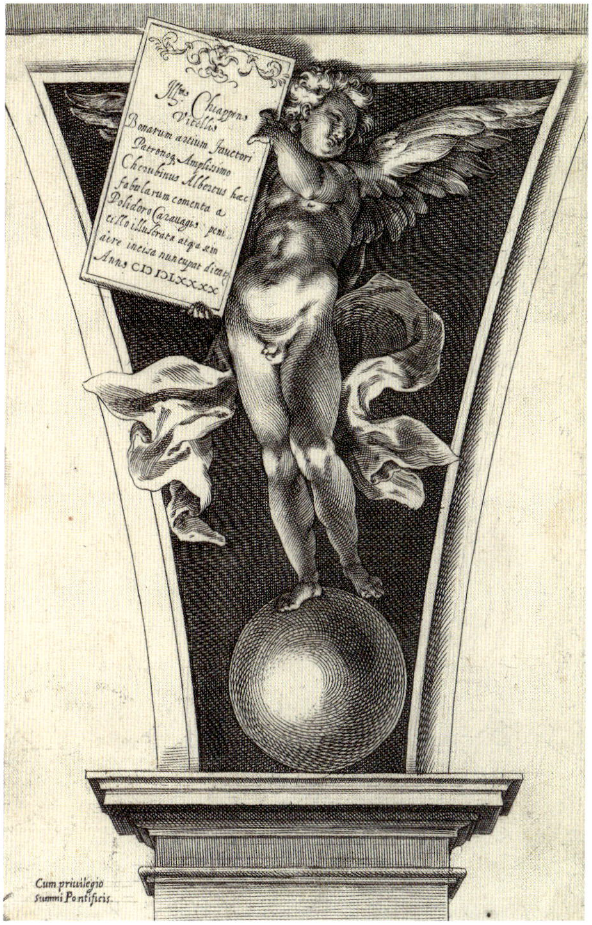

PROVENANCE: Sir Joshua Reynolds (1723–92; Lugt 2364 verso); Sir Robert Witt (1872–1952), by whom presented to the Witt Library, Courtauld Institute of Art, London in 1945; transferred in 1990.

EXHIBITION HISTORY: None.

LITERATURE: Adam Bartsch, *Le peintre graveur: Peintres ou dessinateurs Italiens, maîtres du seizième siècle, seconde partie* (Vienna: Pierre Machetti, 1818), vol.XVII, p.78, no.78.

LARGE DECORATIVE MOTIFS, SUCH AS antique vases, were favourites of Reynolds in his more ambitious portraits. He used them to dazzling effect in such works as *Mary Monckton* (c.1777–78; Tate, London)[74] and Timothy Clifford has identified the source of the vase in Reynolds's *Therese Parker* (FIG. 11, p. 66) as a print after Polidoro da Caravaggio.[75] Reynolds also owned drawings by Alberti, such as a spirited copy he made after Raphael.[76]

Alberti was a painter and engraver, working mostly in Rome. Noted especially for his ceiling decorations, he and his brother Giovanni undertook work in the Sala Clementina at the Vatican for Pope Clement VIII. He was taught printmaking by the Dutchman Cornelis Cort (CAT. 51, p. 125), when the latter was in Rome, and by 1571 had begun printmaking in earnest. The attribution of the design of this print has recently been changed from Polidoro da Caravaggio to Baccio Bandinelli (1493–1560). In the Courtauld Institute Gallery itself is a related pen and ink drawing (in reverse) by Bandinelli for the winged figure, complete with wings and a tablet, whose drapery closely matches Alberti's engraving.[77]

REYNOLDS OWNED SEVERAL DRAWINGS by Boscoli, including two now in the British Museum.[78] Other examples include a drawing of bacchantes with goat and deer in the form of an antique frieze (Fitzwilliam Museum, Cambridge) and Boscoli's copy of a section of the Palazzo Gaddi decoration in Rome by Polidoro da Caravaggio (University of Leiden).[79]

Boscoli excelled in monochromatic studies and here, using brown washes alone, he produces an intense scene of devotion around the prostrate figure of Saint Catherine. The whiteness of the sheet provides the luminosity of the celestial light above, and the surrounding candlelight. The drawing is one of Boscoli's finest efforts in Reynolds's collection. A drawing of the *Adoration of the Shepherds* (Academia Română, Bucharest) is in the same medium as the present example, but lacks its high technical accomplishment.[80] It is thus unsurprising that Reynolds's mark is found on the verso of the Bucharest drawing, to indicate its inferior quality. Reynolds's close friend Charles Rogers owned eight Boscoli drawings: one now in the Courtauld Institute Gallery in London, one in Milwaukee Art Museum, Wisconsin, three in Oxford and others elsewhere. In 2009 a sudy of clasped hands by Boscoli, in red and black chalk, was sold which had previously belonged to Jonathan Richardson the Elder and Thomas Hudson.[81]

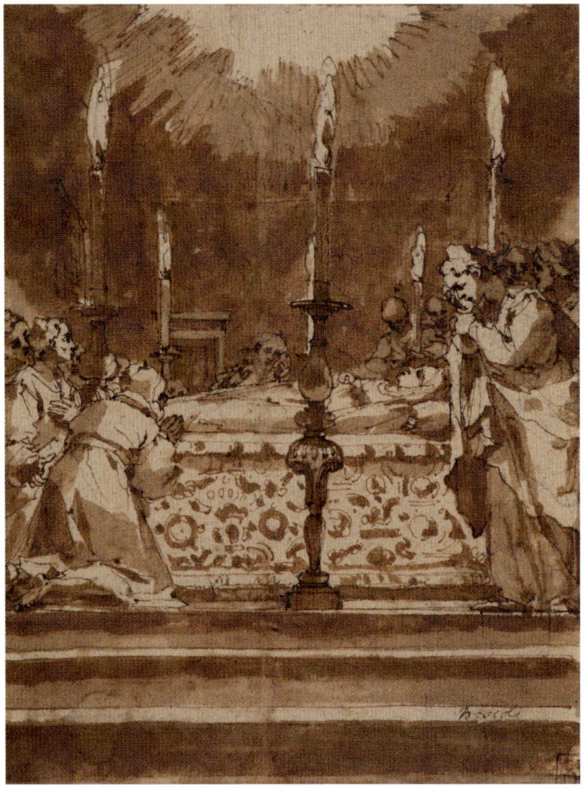

CAT. 58

Andrea Boscoli
(c.1560–1608)
The death of St Catherine of Siena
pen and brown ink with brown wash,
19 x 14.8 cm

Courtauld Institute Gallery (Samuel Courtauld Trust), London (D.1952.RW.4565)

PROVENANCE: Sir Joshua Reynolds (1723–92; Lugt 2364); Colnaghi, London in 1951; Sir Robert Witt (1872–1952), by whom bequeathed in 1952.

EXHIBITION HISTORY: None.

LITERATURE: Anthony Blunt, *Hand-list of the drawings in the Witt collection* (London: University of London, 1956), p.64; Anna Forlani, 'Andrea Boscoli', *Proporzioni*, IV, 1963, pp.85–208 (155), no.200; Julian Brooks, *The drawings of Andrea Boscoli (c.1560–1608)*, Unpublished Ph.D., University of Oxford, 1999, p.347.

CAT. 59

Ludovico Cigoli
(1559–1613)
The Holy Family with a putto *(recto)*
and
The Holy Family with the Infant Saint John the Baptist *(verso)*
pen and brown ink, with brown wash, over black chalk,
25.5 x 20 cm
British Museum, London
(PD 1946,0713.318)

PROVENANCE: Sir Joshua Reynolds (1723–92; Lugt 2364 verso); William Young Ottley (1771–1836), Thomas Philipe, London, 9 June 1814, lot 386; Sir Thomas Lawrence (1769–1830; Lugt 2445); Samuel Woodburn (1786–1853), Christie's, London, 7 June 1860, part of lot 673; Sir Thomas Phillipps (1792–1872), by descent to Thomas Fitzroy Fenwick (1856–1938); Count Antoine Seilern (1901–78), by whom presented (anonymously) in 1946.

EXHIBITION HISTORY: 1978, London, British Museum, 'Gainsborough and Reynolds in the British Museum', no.233.

LITERATURE: A E Popham, *Catalogue of drawings in the collection formed by Sir Thomas Phillipps, Bart., F.R.S., now in the possession of his grandson, T Fitzroy Phillipps Fenwick of Thirlestaine House, Cheltenham* (London: privately printed, 1935), p.50, no.1; Martin Royalton-Kisch in Timothy Clifford, Antony Griffiths and Martin Royalton-Kisch, *Gainsborough and Reynolds in the British Museum* (London: British Museum Publications, 1978), p.80, no.233; Miles L Chappell, *Gabinetto disegni e stampe degli Uffizi, vol.74: Disegni di Ludovico Cigoli (1559–1613)* (Florence: Leo S Olschki, 1992), p.124.

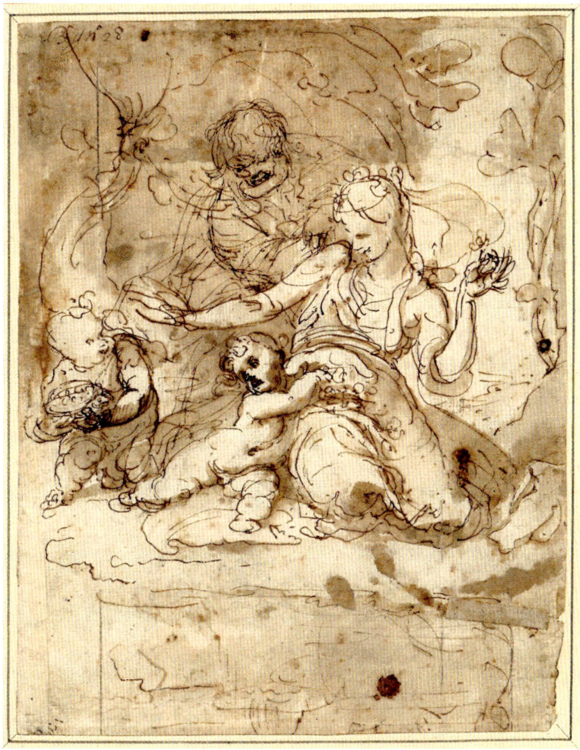

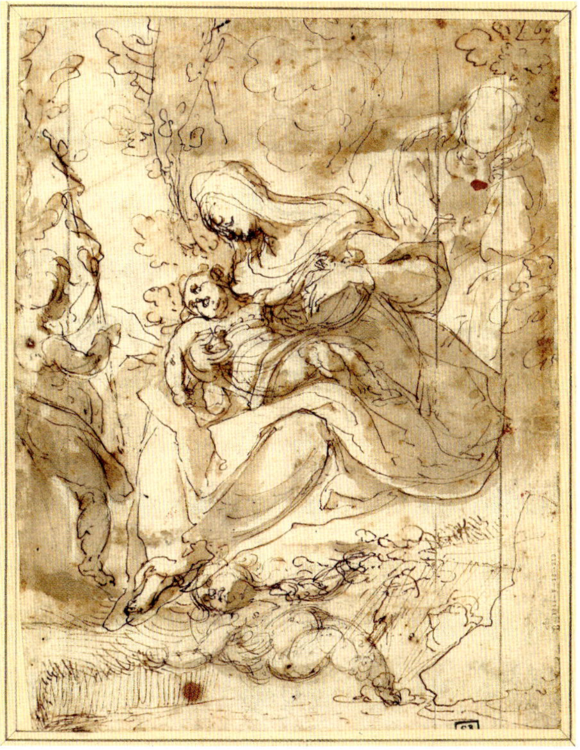

CIGOLI WAS A PUPIL OF ALESSANDRO Allori (1535–1607), an artist whom Reynolds also collected, such as the sheet in the Institut Néerlandais (Fondation Custodia), Paris.[82] Cigoli's superb draughtsmanship must have stood out in Reynolds's collection. He owned another Cigoli of the *Martyrdom of St Sebastian*, also in the British Museum.[83] Smith College Museum of Art, Northampton, Mass. has a double-side sheet related to Cigoli's painting *The Dream of Jacob* (1593; Musée des Beaux-Arts, Nancy).[84] One other of Reynolds's 'Cigoli' drawings, now attributed to his circle, is in the Art Institute of Chicago.[85]

This double-sided sheet of studies of the Holy Family, with its harmoniously arranged figural compositions, would have served as models for Reynolds's occasional forays into religious painting. He used such tender groupings for portraiture and allegorical work, too, in such paintings as *Caroline, Duchess of Marlborough and Daughter* (1764–67; Blenheim Palace, Oxfordshire), *Susanna Hoare and Child* (1763; Wallace Collection, London) and *Hope Nursing Love* (CAT. 11, p. 43).

Cigoli's drawing is today in the distinctive Ottley mount, with bright red ruled lines: Ottley acquired much of Reynolds's former collection, including his celebrated red chalk study by Michelangelo for *The Creation of Man* in the British Museum (FIG. 21, p. 103).

REYNOLDS OWNED MANY WORKS BY Reni, including paintings, prints and drawings (CAT. 61). In the eighteenth century his fame extended all over Europe, and prints after his work were very popular; numerous reproductive prints after his work were published in London. However, this example by him is after the Genoese painter Luca Cambiaso, whom Reynolds also collected (CAT. 52, P. 126), and would have appealed to Reynolds for its possible use in his portraiture. The Old Master references in Reynolds' work were frequent. The glory of angels seen here was repeated in the sumptuous portrait *Elizabeth Billington* (1789; Beaverbrook Art Gallery, Fredericton). Contemporaries, such as a critic in *St James's Chronicle*, thought the picture had much of the 'sweetness and beauty of Parmigianino' but the art historian Ellis Waterhouse (1905–85) was closer to the mark when he thought that 'Rubens and Guido [Reni] are amusingly combined'.[86]

Reni was in Rome between 1601 and 1614, and made this print in 1607 when he had begun working full-time for the Borghese family, one of the most powerful in Italy. Like the etchings by Rembrandt and Canuti (CAT. 73, P. 147 and CAT. 75, P. 149), the print is an example of an engraving not by a professional printmaker but a *peintre graveur* and sought after because of its 'painterly' qualities.

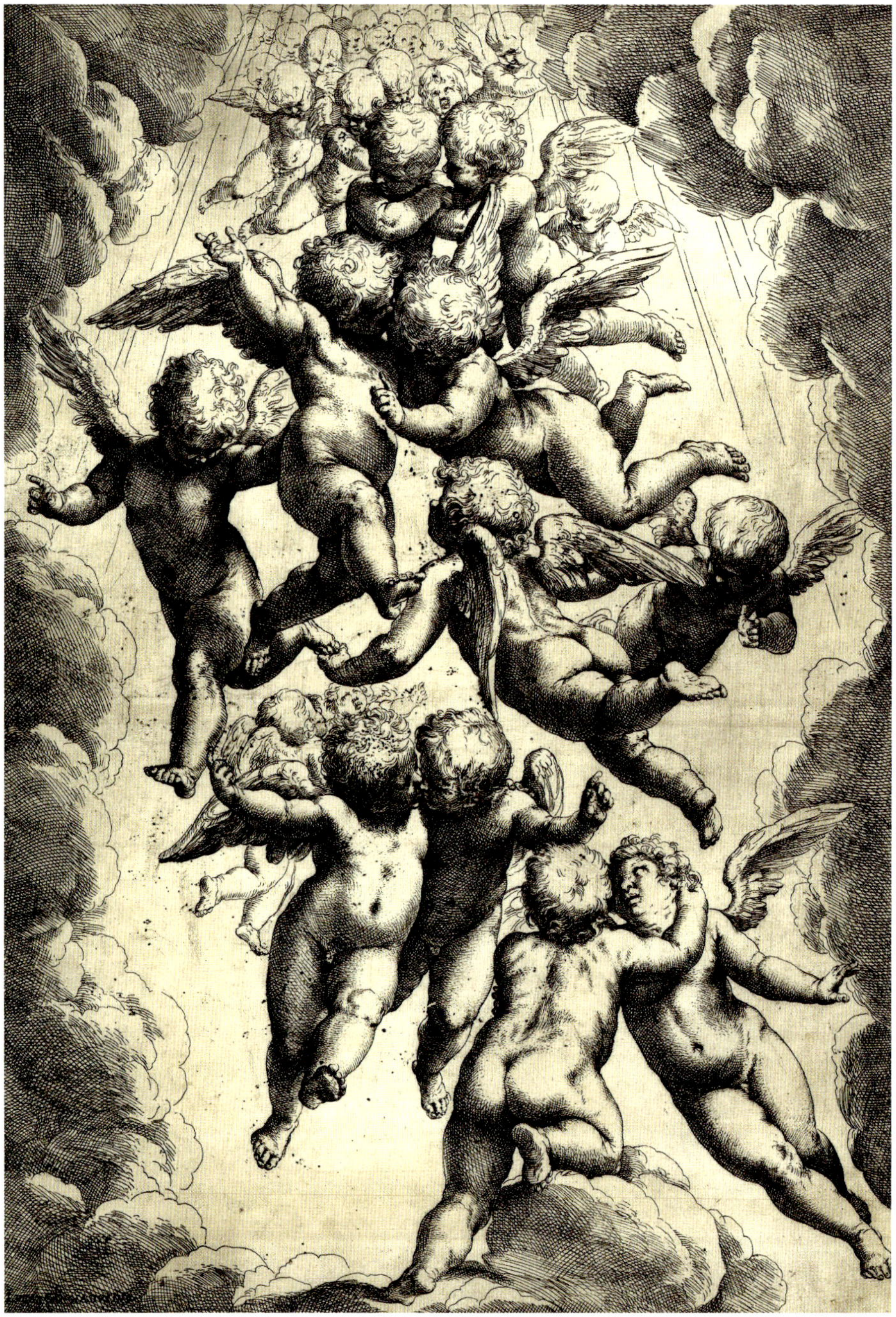

CAT. 60

Guido Reni
(1575–1642)
after Luca Cambiaso
(1527–85)
Angels in Glory
(1607)
etching, 40.4 x 27.2 cm
British Museum, London (PD 1868,0822.78)

PROVENANCE: Sir Joshua Reynolds (1723–92; Lugt 2364 verso); Felix Slade (1790–1868), by whom bequeathed in 1868.

EXHIBITION HISTORY: None.

LITERATURE: Adam Bartsch, *Le peintre graveur: Peintres ou dessinateurs Italiens, maîtres du seizième siècle, troisième partie* (Vienna: Pierre Mechetti, 1818), vol.XVIII, p.299, no.45; Bertina Suida Manning and William Suida, *Luca Cambiaso: La vita e le opere* (Milan: Ceschina, 1958), pp.172, 284–85, plate CCXX, fig.359.

CAT. 61

Guido Reni
(1575–1642)
Head of Saint Crispin
(c.1620–21)
black, red and white chalk, on brown paper, 36.1 x 23.1 cm
British Museum, London
(PD Pp, 3.23)

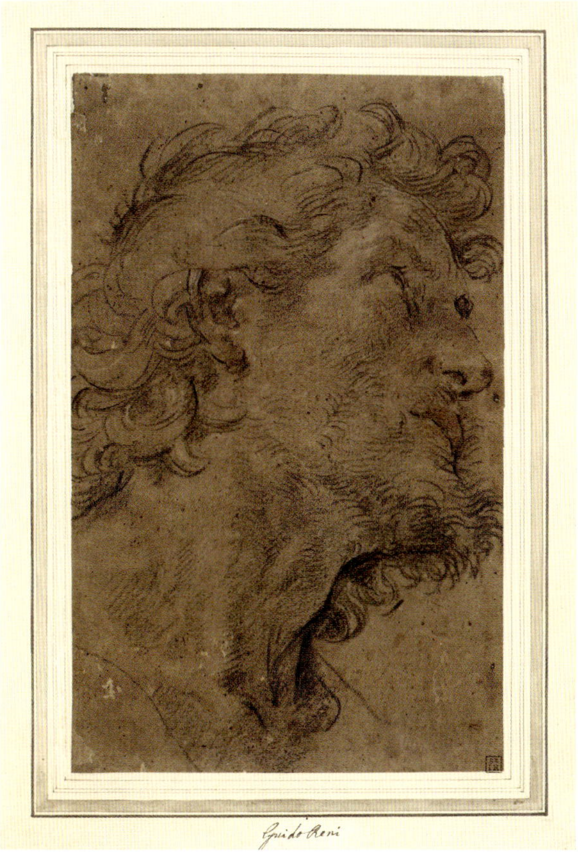

PROVENANCE: Sir Joshua Reynolds (1723–92; Lugt 2364); Richard Payne Knight (1751–1824), by whom bequeathed in 1824.

EXHIBITION HISTORY: 1981, Vienna, Albertina, 'Guido Reni: Zeichnungen', no.91; 1996, Tokyo, National Museum of Western Art and Nagoya, Aichi Prefectural Museum of Art, 'Italian 16th- and 17th-Century drawings from the British Museum', no.66.

LITERATURE: Karl T Parker, *Catalogue of the drawings in the Ashmolean Museum: Volume II (Italian Schools)* (Oxford: Oxford University Press, 1956), p.473; Nicholas Turner, *British Museum prints and drawings series: Italian Baroque drawings* (London: British Museum Publications, 1980), pp.98–99, no.40; Veronika Birke, *Guido Reni: Zeichnungen* (Vienna: Albertina, 1981), p.131, no.91; D Stephen Pepper, *Guido Reni: A complete catalogue of his works with an introductory text* (Oxford: Phaidon Press, 1984), pp.242–43 (242), no.79; Michiaki Koshikawa and Hidenori Kurita (eds), *Italian 16th- and 17th-Century drawings from the British Museum* (Tokyo: National Museum of Western Art, 1996), [English Supplement], pp.38–39, no.66.

REYNOLDS USUALLY ACQUIRED HIS drawings in the mounts that previous collectors had made for them, such as the famous blue decorated ones of the French amateur Pierre Jean Mariette (1694–1774) or the brown wash-line mounts from Richardson the Elder. Some mounts were extremely elaborate and were decorated with gold ornamental borders, such as those by John Talman (1677–1726), some of which Reynolds later owned, including one now in Chicago.[87] However, sometimes Reynolds had his own mounts made up, and the present drawing is one of the rare examples found in its 'Reynolds' mount, together with a large Pietro da Cortona drawing (CAT. 68, p. 142). Comparisons with known handwriting on letters allow us to identify the handwriting of the attribution (for the first time) to Reynolds. The mount is simple, with no gold edging common to Richardson or Mariette and framed by simple pen lines in brown ink and bordered with grey wash.

Reynolds's other Reni drawings include a superb example in pen and brown ink with wash, of Saint Peter's crucifixion, in the Szépművészeti Múzeum, Budapest.[88] Reynolds also owned a self-portrait canvas by Reni described in his posthumous sale catalogue as 'particularly valuable, as it is the only authentic one known, painted at that early period in his life.'[89] Richardson the Elder owned Reni's dashing self-portrait in red chalk.[90]

Reni was born in Bologna, where he studied and became one of the leading Italian painters of the early seventeenth century. This drawing is a study for the head of St Crispin in the painting of the *Virgin and Child with Saints Crispian, Crispin and Jerome*, painted in 1620–21 for the altar of the Arte de'Calzolari (Shoemakers' Guild) in the church of San Prospero, Reggio Emilia, and now in the Gemäldegalerie, Dresden.[91] Reynolds characterised Reni's art as one in which his figures 'are often engaged in subjects that required great expression' (Discourse V). The present example with its imploring piety seems to confirm this view.

CAT. 62

Peter Paul Rubens
(1577–1640)
after Adriaen Thomasz. Key
(c.1544–c.1589)
Abel slain by Cain
(c.1608–10)
red chalk, with brush and red ink and wash,
21.4 x 21 cm
Fitzwilliam Museum, Cambridge (PD.43-1961)

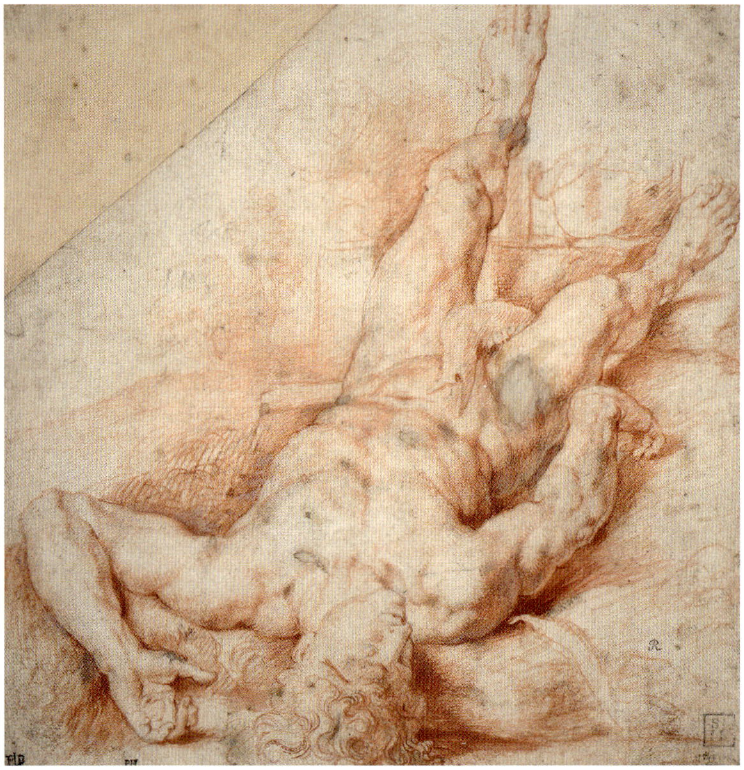

RUBENS HELD A GREAT FASCINATION for Reynolds. His work was represented with prints (CAT. 76, p. 150), drawings and several paintings. Among the latter are the celebrated *Moonlit Landscape* (Courtauld Institute Gallery, London) that Reynolds owned by at least 1778, when he mentioned the picture in his Discourse VIII in relation to colour and light. Reynolds also owned Rubens's *A Forest at Dawn with a Deer Hunt* (Metropolitan Museum New York) which he sold before 1790.[92] He emulated, Rubens's light effects, and particularly sunlight through tree cover, in his allegorical work *A contemplative youth* dating from before 1786.[93] The connection is closest when these two landscapes by Rubens are compared to the contemporary mezzotint made after Reynolds's work by Charles Howard Hodges (1764–1837) in 1786, especially colour impressions printed *à la poupé* which record Reynolds's work in pristine condition. Reynolds might also have quoted from Rubens for his rare foray into history painting in his *Continence of Scipio* (Hermitage),[94] which resembles his Rubens drawings of the same subject, now in Berlin's Kupferstichkabinett.[95]

PROVENANCE: Prosper Henry Lankrink (1628–92; Lugt 2090),London, 22 February 1694; Jonathan Richardson I (1665–1745; Lugt 2184); Sir Joshua Reynolds (1723–92; Lugt 2364); Sir Thomas Banks (Lugt 2423); by descent to his daughter Lavinia Forster (1774–1858); by descent to her son-in-law Ambrose Poynter (1796–1886; Lugt 161 verso); by descent to his son Sir Edward John Poynter (1836–1919; Lugt 874), Sotheby's London, 25 April 1918, lot 189; Charles Clarke (d.1935); bequeathed to his brother Dr. Louis Clarke (1881–1960), by whom bequeathed in 1960, received 1961.

EXHIBITION HISTORY: 1870, London, Royal Academy of Arts, 'Exhibition of the works of the Old Masters, associated with a collection from the works of Charles Robert Leslie RA and Clarkson Stanfield RA', no.477; 1938, London, Royal Academy of Arts, 'Exhibition of seventeenth-century art in Europe', no.596; 1950, London, Wildenstein, 'Peter Paul Rubens', no.49; 1956, Antwerp, Rubenshuis, 'Tekeningen van Peter Paul Rubens', no.19; 1958, Cambridge, Fitzwilliam Museum, 'Seventeenth-century Flemish drawings and oil sketches', no.29; 1977, Antwerp, Royal Museum of Fine Arts, 'P.P. Rubens: Paintings – oil sketches – drawings', no.125; 1981, Cambridge, Fitzwilliam Museum, 'Drawings from the collection of Louis C G Clarke, LLD'; 1991–92, Bristol Museum and Art Gallery, Stoke-on-Trent, City Museum and Art Gallery, and Sheffield, Graves Art Gallery, 'The primacy of drawing: An artist's view', no.122; 1995, Cambridge, Fitzwilliam Museum, 'Rubens and his Influence'.

LITERATURE: Ludwig Burchard and Roger Adolf d'Hulst, *Rubens drawings* (Brussels: Arcade Press, 1963), vol.I, pp.60–61, no.33, vol.II, pl.33 (as Rubens after Coxcie); Michael Jaffé, *Rubens and Italy* (London: Phaidon, 1977), p.49 (as Rubens after Coxcie); Deanna Petherbridge, *The primacy of drawing: An artist's view* (London: South Bank Centre, 1991), pp.21, 72, fig.12, no.122 (as Rubens after Coxcie); Koenraad Jonckheere, 'Two drawings by Peter Paul Rubens after Adriaen Thomasz. Key', *Master Drawings*, 44 (2), Summer 2006, pp.213–20 (as Rubens after Key).

CAT. 63

Peter Paul Rubens
(1577–1640)
after Adriaen Thomasz. Key
(c.1544–c.1589)
Cain cursed by the Lord
(c.1608–10)
red chalk, with brush and red ink and wash, heightened with white, 27.2 x 17.3 cm
Courtauld Institute Gallery (Samuel Courtauld Trust), London (D.1978.PG.322)

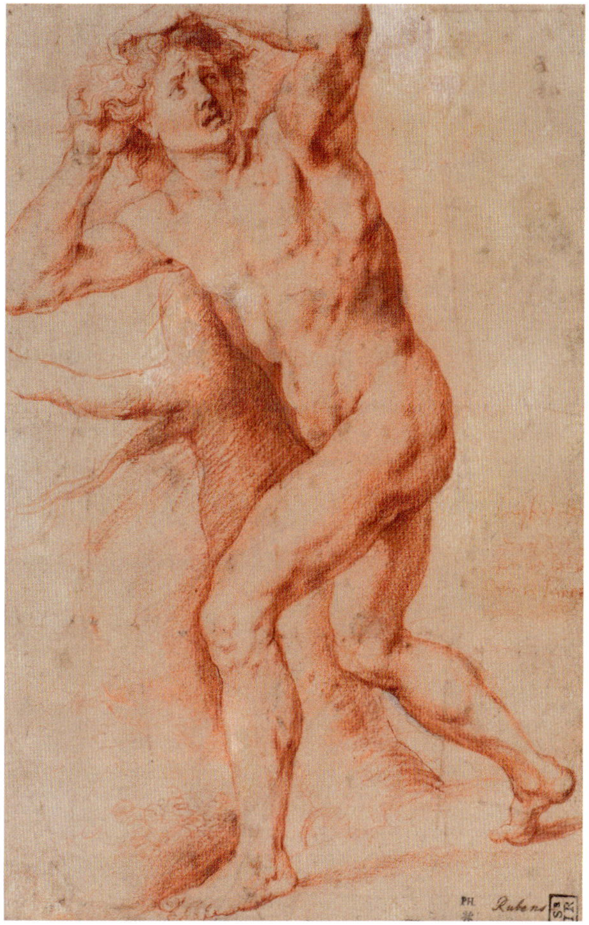

PROVENANCE: Nicholas Lanier (1588–1666; Lugt 2908); Prosper Henry Lankrink (1628–92; Lugt 2090), London, 22 February 1694; Sir Joshua Reynolds (1723–92; Lugt 2364); Marie Jeanne Josèphe Claessens-Bartholeyns (1774–1858); W Ivan Lake, Christie's, London, 28 November 1927, lot 56 (bought in), re-sold Christie's, London, 7 July 1959, lot 96, bought through Colnaghi, London by Count Antoine Seilern (1901–78), by whom bequeathed in 1978.

EXHIBITION HISTORY: 1988–89, London, Courtauld Institute Gallery, 'Rubens: Paintings, drawings, prints in the Princes Gates Collection', no.25; 1999, London, Courtauld Institute Gallery, 'The value of art'.

LITERATURE: Ludwig Burchard and Roger Adolf d'Hulst, *Rubens drawings* (Brussels: Arcade Press, 1963), vol.I, pp.58–60, no.32, vol.II, pl.32 (as Rubens after Coxcie); Michael Jaffé, 'Rubens as a draughtsman', *The Burlington Magazine*, CVII (748), July 1965, pp.372, 374–381 (379); Justus Müller Hofstede, 'Beiträge zum zeichnerischen werk von Rubens', *Wallraf-Richartz-Jahrbuch*, XXVII, 1965, pp.259–356 (264, 265, 268); Antoine Seilern, *Flemish paintings and drawings at 56 Princes Gate, London SW7: Addenda* (London: Shenval Press, 1969), pp.54–55, no.322, plate XXXVII; Helen Braham, *Rubens: Paintings, drawings, prints in the Princes Gate collection* (London: Courtauld Institute of Art, 1988), pp.21–22, no.25 (as Coxcie retouched by Rubens); Koenraad Jonckheere, 'Two drawings by Peter Paul Rubens after Adriaen Thomasz. Key', *Master Drawings*, 44 (2), Summer 2006, pp.213–20, fig.1 (as Rubens after Key).

Many of Reynolds's drawings by Rubens (and Van Dyck) had previously belonged to Hudson, and before him to Richardson the Elder.[96] Recent scholarship has perhaps unfairly dismissed Reynolds's holdings as 'about twenty sheets… though as a whole his collection [of Rubens' drawings] seems a little dull.'[97] *Cain* and *Abel* are exceptions to this summation. Both drawings had once belonged to Lely's assistant Lankrink, who died in London in 1692 and owned over 120 drawings (or retouched designs) by Rubens.[98] These two sheets became separated, probably immediately following Lankrink's drawing sale in February 1694, since *Abel* belonged to Richardson the Elder but not *Cain*. Reynolds therefore reunited the pair.

For a long time the two drawings have been linked with the work of the Flemish painter Michiel Coxcie (1499–1592) and his painting of the *Death of Abel* (after 1539) now in the Prado, Madrid.[99] It was generally considered that the drawings were either by Coxcie and reworked by Rubens (which he did often) or were by an anonymous draughtsman after Coxcie and reworked by Rubens. Recent research by Koenraad Jonckheere has demonstrated conclusively that the drawings are in fact by Rubens himself and based on a copy of Coxcie's work by Adriaen Thomasz Key.

Abel was included as a stipple engraving by Conrad Martin Metz (1749–1827) in *Imitations of ancient and modern drawings* (1789) and printed in red ink, to match the original drawing. The drawing retains its historic mount with gold border and red parallel lines, probably Richardson the Elder's. The sheet has suffered a loss to the top left corner, which has not been replaced but toned in with the mount to make it look less glaring.

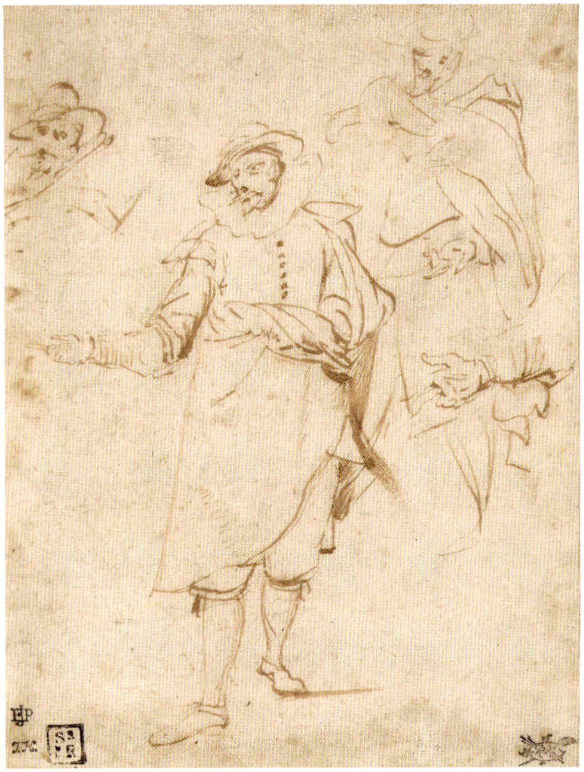

CAT. 64

Anthony van Dyck
(1599–1641)
A sheet of studies for a male figure
pen and brown ink, with brown wash,
17.7 x 13.8 cm
Fitzwilliam Museum, Cambridge (PD.31-1961)

PROVENANCE: Jonathan Richardson I (1665–1745; Lugt 2183); Thomas Hudson (1701-1779; Lugt 2432) [? Langford's, London, 15–26 March 1779]; Sir Joshua Reynolds (1723–92; Lugt 2364); Sir Edward John Poynter (1836-1919; Lugt 874), Sotheby's, London, 25 April 1918, lot 291 (as by Rubens), bought Charles Clarke (d.1935) through Thomas Agnew & Sons, London; by descent to his brother Dr. Louis Clarke (1881–1960), by whom bequeathed in 1960.

EXHIBITION HISTORY: 1958, Cambridge, Fitzwilliam Museum, 'Seventeenth-century Flemish drawings and oil sketches', no.18; 1981, Cambridge, Fitzwilliam Museum, 'Drawings from the collection of Louis C G Clarke, LLD'.

LITERATURE: None.

REYNOLDS ADORED VAN DYCK AND IN addition to finished paintings and oil sketches he also amassed a varied group of his drawings. Most of these comprise black and white chalk studies on blue or grey paper. Reynolds also owned some of his studies in pen and ink, including landscapes and decorative designs. This sheet has much to attract portraitists, and was once owned by four prominent British painters, including Reynolds's master (Hudson) and in turn Hudson's master (Richardson the Elder). Richardson and Hudson owned portrait drawings for Van Dyck's famous *Iconography*, but none of them seem to have entered Reynolds's collection, although he did once have a portrait of Lucas Vorsterman (1595–1675) from the series, now untraced.[100]

Hudson owned forty-two Van Dyck drawings, including the present sheet, one in New York, and another in Edinburgh that later passed to Reynolds (CAT. 66).[101] Hudson also owned delicate sheets by Lely, including three chalk studies of hands and arms in the Courtauld Institute Gallery, London.[102] Reynolds would have seen these in his collection and later would own more stunning examples of his own (CAT. 78, p. 152).

This drawing was last sold in 1918 as by Rubens, Van Dyck's master. It might be an early Van Dyck. The historic mount no longer survives, and there are no inscriptions anywhere; we therefore cannot ascertain by whom Reynolds thought it was drawn.[103] Numerous *pentimenti* or revisions frame the central full-length figure, the artist experimenting with alternative gestures.

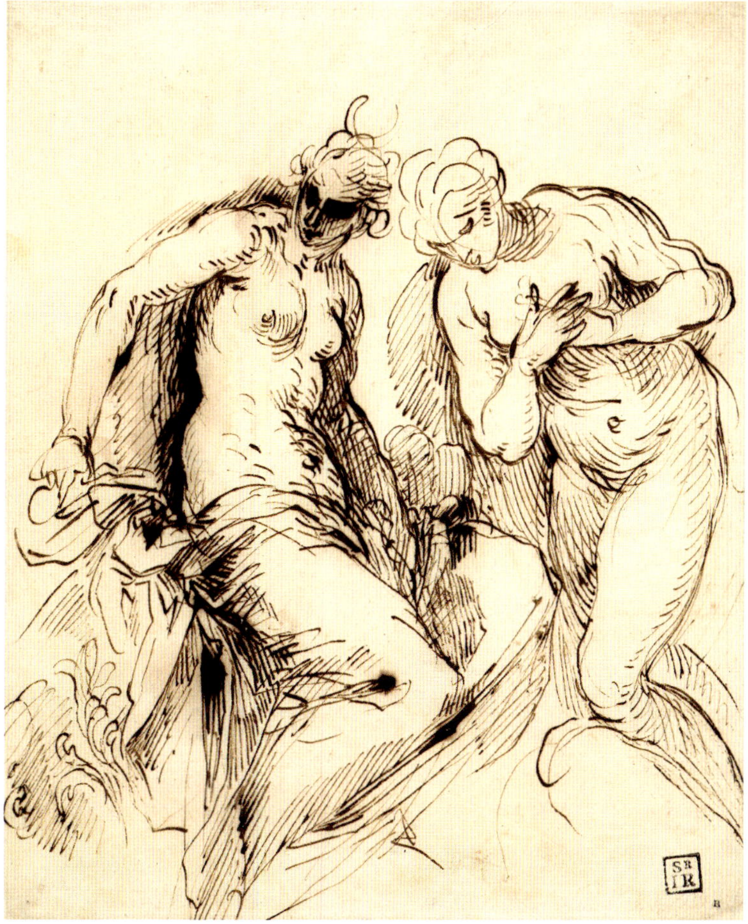

CAT. 65

Palma Giovane
(1544–1628)
Diana with a kneeling companion
pen and brown ink, 21.9 x 18.3 cm
British Museum, London (PD Pp, 3.195)

PROVENANCE: Jonathan Richardson II (1694–1771; Lugt 2170), Langford's, London, February 1772; Sir Joshua Reynolds (1723–92; Lugt 2364); Richard Payne Knight (1751–1824), by whom bequeathed in 1824.

EXHIBITION HISTORY: 1977, Saint Petersburg, State Hermitage Museum and Moscow, State Pushkin Museum of Fine Art, 'Italian Renaissance', no.35; 1978, London, British Museum, 'Gainsborough and Reynolds in the British Museum', no.232; 1980, Adelaide, Art Gallery of South Australia and Melbourne, National Gallery of Victoria, 'Leonardo, Michelangelo and the century of genius: Master drawings from the British Museum', no.34.

LITERATURE: Martin Royalton-Kisch in Timothy Clifford, Antony Griffiths and Martin Royalton-Kisch, *Gainsborough and Reynolds in the British Museum* (London: British Museum Publications, 1978), p.80, no.232; Nicholas Turner and Martin Royalton-Kisch, *Leonardo, Michelangelo and the century of genius: Master drawings from the British Museum* (Adelaide: Art Gallery of South Australia, 1980), pp.70–71, no.34.

THE VENETIAN PAINTER WAS KNOWN AS Palma Giovane ('Palma the Younger') to distinguish him from his famous great-uncle, the painter Palma Vecchio. He worked in Titian's studio and after Tintoretto's death, in 1594, was the leading painter in Venice. Palma Giovane's draughtsmanship is close in style to that of Reynolds, and his drawings might have appealed because of this affinity. Unlike his famous predecessor, Palma Giovane was a prolific draughtsman and large numbers of his drawings survive. Reynolds came to own dozens of examples. From Hudson, for instance, Reynolds obtained an exuberant sheet of *The Madonna in Glory appearing to five saints*, now in the University of Princeton in New Jersey.[104] Two other drawings are in the Art Institute of Chicago.[105] The British Museum also has *The Assumption of the Virgin*, which was later owned by Sir Thomas Lawrence.[106]

Here the goddess of hunting Diana, with her attribute of a crescent moon on her head, is relaxing with one of her retinue. The subject of Diana bathing was often based on the Roman poet Ovid's *Metamorphoses*, which was much treated in art. Reynolds also owned an etching of Diana with her bow by Andrea Schiavone (c.1522–63), now in the British Museum.[107] In the eighteenth century female portraits were sometimes posed with the attributes of goddesses. Reynolds's rival Francis Cotes (1726–70) had painted *The Hon Lady Stanhope and the Countess of Effingham as Diana and her Companion* (1765; York Art Gallery). Reynolds himself had painted the double-portrait of *Elizabeth, Duchess of Manchester and her Son as Diana and Cupid*.[108]

CAT. 66

Anthony van Dyck
(1599–1641)
Study of Henriette de Lorraine
(c.1634)
black chalk heightened with white on (faded) blue paper, 57.3 x 30.2 cm
National Gallery of Scotland, Edinburgh (D1738)

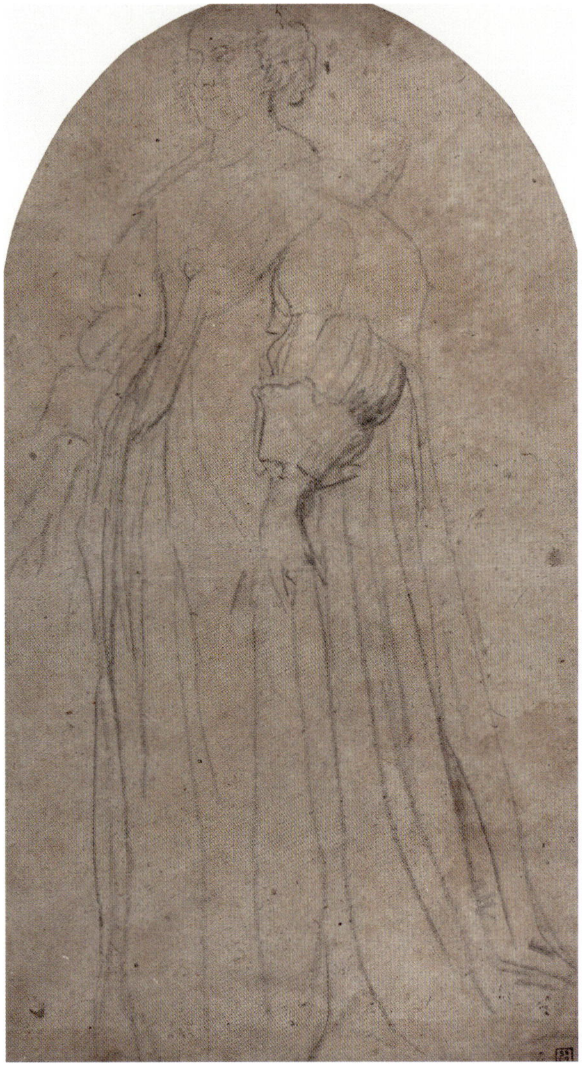

PROVENANCE: Thomas Hudson (1701–79; Lugt 2432); Sir Joshua Reynolds (1723–92; Lugt 2364); David Laing (1793–1878) bequeathed to Royal Scottish Academy, Edinburgh in 1878; transferred in 1910.

EXHIBITION HISTORY: 1949, Antwerp, Koninklijk Museum voor Schone Kunsten, 'Van Dyck tentoonstelling', no.104; 1960, Antwerp, Rubenshuis and Rotterdam, Museum Boymans-van Beuningen, 'Antoon van Dyck, tekeningen en olieverfschetsen', (no.107).

LITERATURE: Horst Vey, *Die zeichnungen Anton van Dycks* (Brussels: Verlag Arcade, 1962), vol.I, pp.265–66, no.195, vol.II, fig.234; Keith Andrews, *Catalogue of Netherlandish drawings in the National Gallery of Scotland* (Edinburgh: National Galleries of Scotland, 1985), vol.I, p.24, vol.II, p.38, fig.158.

RICHARD GIBSON (1615–90) RECOUNTED a story to his friend Lely that Van Dyck 'would take a little piece of blue paper upon a board before him, & look upon the Life & draw his figures & postures all in Suden lines, as angles with black chalk & heightened with white chalk.'[109] Reynolds might not have known this anecdote but he certainly would have known that Van Dyck was a prodigious draughtsman, and Reynolds came to own over thirty of his drawings. The British Museum has fifteen of them; others are in Windsor, Rotterdam, Ottawa, Princeton (New Jersey) and the Morgan Library and Museum in New York.[110]

Reynolds owned paintings by Van Dyck, too, such as the engaging portrait of *George Gage with two men* (National Gallery, London),[111] the full-length portrait of *Margaret Carey*, later Lady Herbert, that was bought from him by Charles-Alexandre de Calonne (Dukes of Bedford),[112] and an oil sketch for a crucifixion in Antwerp where in 1781 Reynolds complained that the 'sketch for this picture is said to be within the convent, but I could not see it.'[113] Reynolds occasionally took from Van Dyck's work, such as his quotation *verbatim* of the greyhound from Van Dyck's *James Stuart, Duke of Richmond and Lennox* in his *Sir Richard Piers Symons* (1769–70; Cincinnati Art Museum, Ohio).[114]

This drawing is related to Van Dyck's portrait of *Henriette de Lorraine* (1605–60), now at Kenwood House in London, and dated 1634.[115] It would have served to assist in the pose of the figure and her elaborate puffy dress and, though cursorily drawn and faint, the sheet retains a strong sense of presence. The sheet was once folded, and the original mount is now lost, for both the Hudson and Reynolds stamps are incomplete. Dark areas, in contrast to the lighter main body of the sheet, indicate differential fading, possibly during the nineteenth century when it might have been over-mounted.

CAT. 67

Nicolas Mignard
(1606–68)
after Annibale Carracci
(1560-1609)
Perseus killing Medusa
(1637)
etching, 24.9 x 43.6 cm
Courtauld Institute Gallery
(Samuel Courtauld Trust),
London (G.1990.WL.35)

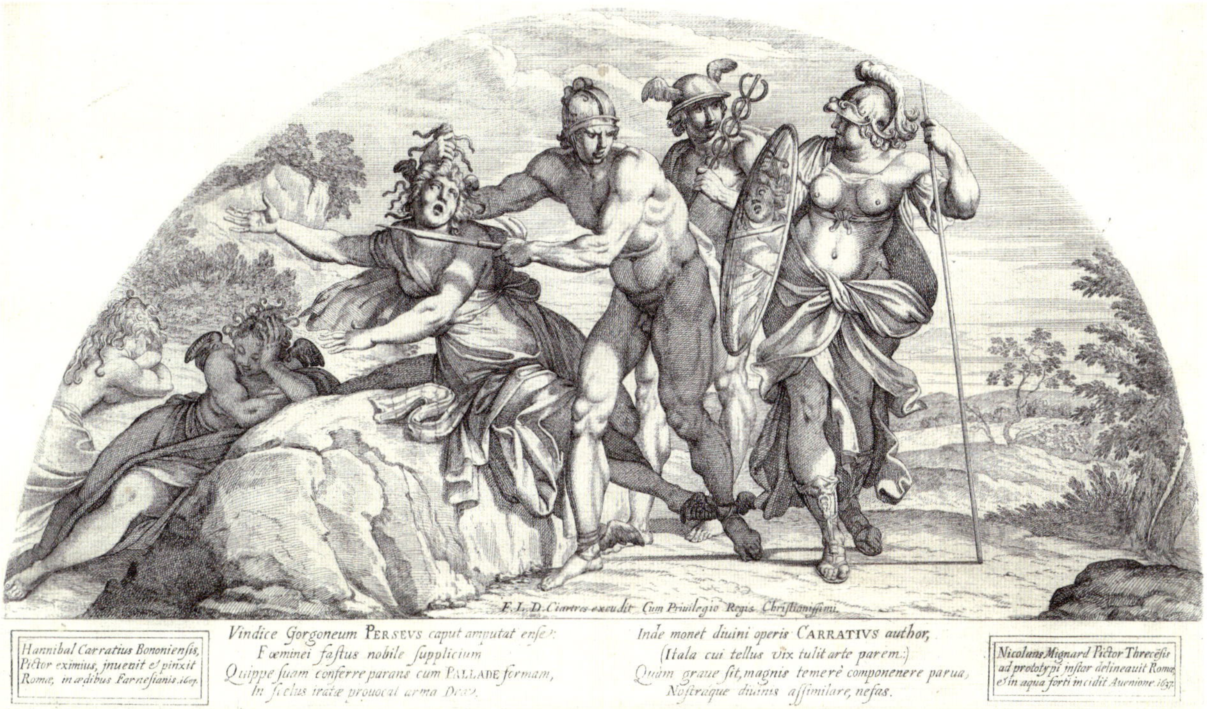

PROVENANCE: Sir Joshua Reynolds (1723–92; Lugt 2364 verso); Sir Robert Witt (1872–1952), by whom presented to the Witt Library, Courtauld Institute of Art, London in 1945; transferred in 1990.

EXHIBITION HISTORY: None.

LITERATURE: A P F Robert-Dumesnil, *Le peintre graveur Français: Artistes du dix-septième siècle* (Paris: Gabriel Warée & Huzard, 1835), vol.1, pp.105–6, no.7 i/iii; Evelina Borea and Ginevra Mariani, *Annibale Carracci e i sui incisori* (Rome: Istituto nazionale per la grafica, 1986), Section XXVIII, series A, p.72, no.5.

FRENCH PRINTS WERE SOMEWHAT scarce in Reynolds's graphic collection. He did though own five prints from the series *Capital Sins* after Luca Penni (1500/04–57), and two prints by Étienne Picart (1631–1721) after Eustache Le Sueur (1616–55), *Saint Paul* and *Saint Gervase*, both now in the British Museum.[116] This print announces the work of 'Hannibal Carratius' (Annibale Carracci) and Reynolds complemented the engravings after his work with many fine drawings by him, including one of a male figure in red chalk (CAT. 55, p. 129). Nicolas Mignard's brother Pierre Mignard (1612–95) had a collection of hundreds of drawings 'by the Carracci', especially Annibale.[117]

This print is one of six prints after the frescoed work in the Palazzo Farnese in Rome done from 1595–96, despite the print announcing on the left tablet that this work was done in 1607: 'Hannibal Carratius Bononiensis/Pictor eximius, invenit et pinxit/Romae, in aedibus Farnesianis.1607'. Mignard was the first to produce the set in full in Avignon from drawings he had made in Rome: 'Nicolaus Mignard Pictor Threcesis/ad prototypi instar delineavit Romae/et in aqua forti incidit Avenione. 1637'. Pietro Aquila (1650–92) made his own set slightly later, and other printmakers followed, making individual plates of particular compositions. The print was first published (as here) by the Frenchman François Langlois 'Il Ciartres' (1588–1647), but in the eighteenth century this print was reissued by Mariette: 'F.L.D. Ciartres excudit Cum Privilegio Regis Christianissimi'.

CAT. 68

Pietro da Cortona
(1596–1669)
Study of the 'Medici Prince defends Temple of Peace' (Sala di Marte, Palazzo Pitti, Florence)
(c.1646–47)
black chalk,
28.1 x 43.1 cm
British Museum, London
(PD 1954,0213.2)

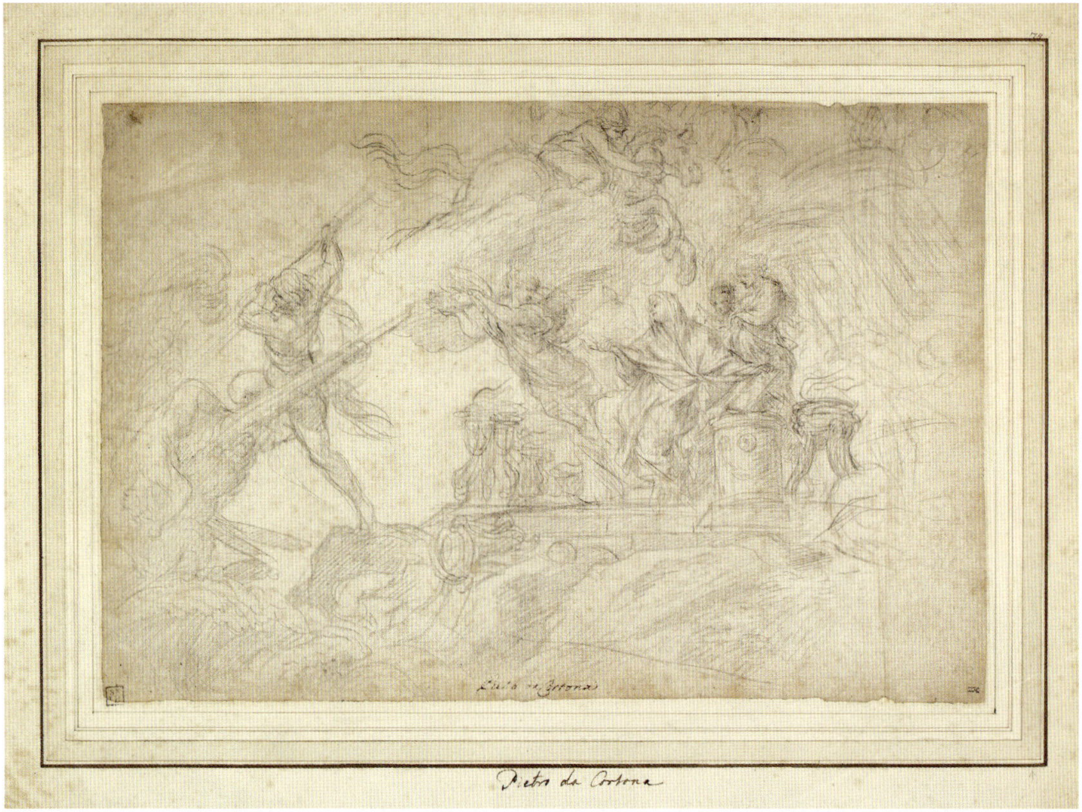

PROVENANCE: ?Cavaliere Francesco Maria Niccolò Gabburri (1676–1742); ?William Kent (fl.1742–62); Thomas Hudson (1701–79; Lugt 2432); Sir Joshua Reynolds (1723–92; Lugt 2364); Sir Jeffery Wyatville (1766–1840); ?Rev S Moore; Mrs Knapp; Colnaghi, London, by whom presented in 1954.

EXHIBITION HISTORY: None.

LITERATURE: Malcolm Campbell, *Mostra di disegni di Pietro Berrettini da Cortona per gli affreschi di Palazzo Pitti* (Florence: Leo S Olschki, 1965), p.61; Walter Vitzthum, 'Pietro da Cortona's drawings for the Pitti Palace at the Uffizi', *Burlington Magazine*, CVII (751), October 1965, pp.522–26 (525), fig.46; Walter Vitzthum, *Il barocco a Roma* (Milan: Fratelli Fabbri, 1971), plate xvi; Malcolm Campbell, *Pietro da Cortona at the Pitti Palace: A study of the planetary rooms and related projects* (Princeton, NJ: Princeton University Press, 1977), pp.125, 279, no.119; Jörg Martin Merz, *Cortona-Studien*, unpublished Ph.D., Eberhard-Karls University, Tübingen, 1985, vol.III, p.145; Nicholas Turner, *Italian drawings in the Department of Prints and Drawings in the British Museum: Roman Baroque drawings, c.1620–c.1700* (London: British Museum Press, 1999), vol.I, p.49–50, no.73.

REYNOLDS'S OTHER CORTONA DRAWINGS are dispersed across collections in Paris,[118] New York,[119] Ottawa[120] and elsewhere. This large drawing is on a 'Reynolds' mount, here identified for the first time, and is a rare survival (see also Guido Reni, CAT. 61, p. 135). In the Nationalmuseum in Stockholm is a splendid black chalk *Study of Justice, Honour and Generosity* for the same commission as this sheet, but for another space, the Sala di Giove (Jupiter Room).[121] The Stockholm drawing has lost its historic mount.[122] The drawings in Paris and Ottawa appear to be on the same mount, but not Reynolds's, since the attribution is in a different hand; but like the one here, all three came from Hudson's collection; the mounts therefore could be by Hudson. Other splendid ceiling designs that Reynolds owned include one in red chalk of *Saint Cecilia in Glory*, by Francesco Baldassare (1611–89), now in the Courtauld Institute Gallery, London.[123] Reynolds also had drawings by Cortona's studio assistants, such as *Male nude seated on the ground* by Ciro Ferri, now in the British Museum.[124]

Reynolds has inscribed on the verso of his mount, 'Painted in the Palazzo Piti [sic] – in Camera Martis' (Mars Room). Cortona worked on the commission from 1646–47 following an earlier commission for the same building in 1641–42. Nicholas Turner has fully described this complex drawing. From the left of the drawing, a ship nears a rocky shore on which stands the Temple of Peace, on the opposite side of the sheet. A warrior, personifying the young Medici prince, repels the attack by engaging the vessel and taking out one of its crew with his spear. In front of the temple, a seated priestess, accompanied by two attendants, holds a book or tablet on a round altar with her left hand and with her right hand commands the winged figure of Fame to crown the warrior with a laurel wreath, ancient symbol of victory; Fame's trumpet may be seen in a *pentimento* drawn to the right of this figure.

REYNOLDS OWNED AN ASTONISHING range of drawings by Guercino, from landscapes and caricatures to figure studies for both biblical and mythological paintings. One unusual aspect of Reynolds' collection is the number of humorous or satirical subjects by Guercino. The caricature of a canine mother and child in Besançon is one such example.[125] The multi-figured *The Mocking of a Village Madman* in the Morgan Library and Museum in New York is similarly treated with bawdy humour.[126] Reynolds' apprenticeship with Hudson exposed him to the riches of his master's collection. There he learned to make beautiful copies of Guercino drawings, many of which survive (CAT. 80, p. 154 and 81, p. 155). In the eighteenth century Guercino's drawings were widely published, including the British publication to which the printmaker Francesco Bartolozzi contributed plates, *Seventy-three prints, engraved…from the original pictures and drawings… in the collection of His Majesty* (undated), as well as the Italian *Raccolta di alcuni disegni del… Guercino* (Rome, 1764), which Reynolds might have known.

The original mount of *Cleopatra* no longer survives, and seems to have been lost by at least the early part of the twentieth century when donated by De Pass to Truro in 1928. Truro's Guercino seems to be connected with his canvas *Dying Cleopatra* (1648; Galleria di Palazzo Rosso, Genoa). The drawing closely resembles another drawing, in red chalk, at Windsor Castle.[127] Reynolds seems to have based the pose of the female protagonist in his painting *Cimon and Iphegenia* (Royal Collection)[128] upon this drawing by Guercino, suggesting that Reynolds had owned this drawing from at least 1789, when the picture was first exhibited at the Royal Academy.

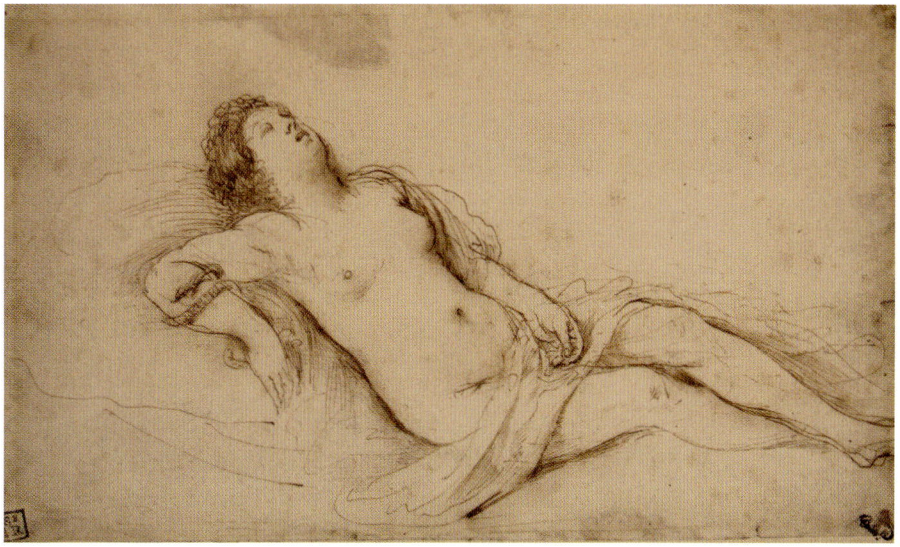

CAT. 69

Guercino
(1591–1666)
Cleopatra
(c.1648)
pen and brown ink,
16.2 x 28 cm
Royal Cornwall Museum,
Truro (1928.349)

PROVENANCE: Sir Joshua Reynolds (1723–92; Lugt 2364); Alfred de Pass (1861–1953; Lugt 108a), by whom presented in 1928.

EXHIBITION HISTORY: 1957, London, Arts Council; Nottingham University Gallery; Bristol Art Gallery; Liverpool, Walker Art Gallery, Birmingham Museum & Art Gallery; Cambridge, Fitzwilliam Museum, 'Drawings from the De Pass collection', no.10; 1994, London, Phillips and Truro, Royal Cornwall Museum, 'Master drawings from the De Pass collection, Royal Cornwall Museum, Truro', no.18.

LITERATURE: George Penrose, *Catalogue of Paintings, drawings and miniatures in the Alfred A de Pass Collection* (Truro: Royal Cornish Institution, 1936), p.21, no.169; A E Popham, *Drawings from the De Pass collection* (London: Arts Council, 1957), p.5, no.10; Marianne Joannides, *Master drawings from the De Pass Collection, Royal Cornwall Museum, Truro* (London: Phillips, 1994), pp.46–47, no.18.

CAT. 70

Nicolas Poussin
(1594–1665)
Study for the painting 'Landscape with the funeral of Phocion'
(c.1648)
black chalk,
10.6 x 12.5 cm
Musée du Louvre, Paris
(RF 34519)

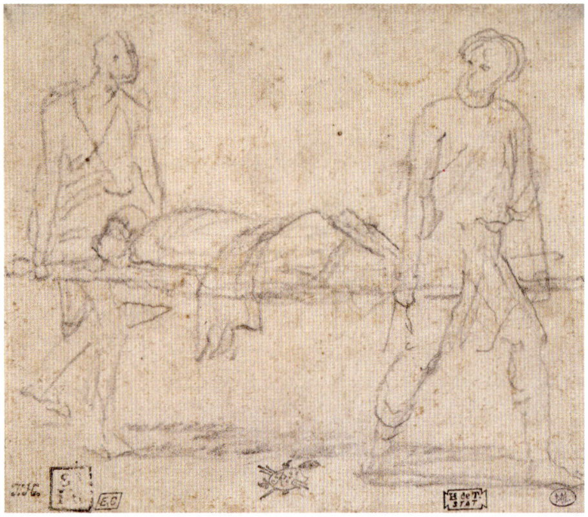

PROVENANCE: Jonathan Richardson I (1665–1745; Lugt 2183); Thomas Hudson (1701–79; Lugt 2432); Sir Joshua Reynolds (1723–92; Lugt 2364); Sir Thomas Lawrence (1769–1830; Lugt 2445); Henri de Triqueti (1802–74; Lugt 1304); Émile Louis Calando (1840–98; Lugt 837), by descent through his family, from whom acquired in 1970.

EXHIBITION HISTORY: None.

LITERATURE: Jonathan Richardson, *Traité de la peinture et de la sculpture par Messrs Richardson, père et fils* (Paris, 1728), vol.III, p.312; Walter Friedlaender and Anthony Blunt (eds), *The drawings of Nicolas Poussin: Catalogue raisonné* (London: Warburg Institute [University of London], 1974), vol.V, p.126, no.458; Pierre Rosenberg and Louis Antoine Prat, *Nicolas Poussin 1594–1665: Catalogue raisonné des dessins* (Milan: Leonardo Editore, 1994), vol.I, pp.630–31, no.324; Pierre Rosenberg, *From drawing to painting: Poussin, Watteau, Fragonard, David and Ingres* (Princeton, NJ: Princeton University Press, 1996), p.51, fig.60.

POUSSIN WAS AN ARTIST CENTRAL TO Reynolds's hierarchical view of past art; he was (with Claude Lorrain) the supreme Classical landscape painter. Consequently, Reynolds amassed his works in great numbers and counted many superb canvases in his collection, such as Poussin's *The Adoration of the Shepherds* (c.1633–34; National Gallery, London)[129] and, by 1766, *Venus and Adonis* (Rhode Island Museum of Art, Providence), which was published by John Boydell (FIG. 32). Reynolds once owned dozens of drawings by Poussin but recent scholarship by Prat and Rosenberg has reduced the number of autograph sheets to a mere handful, of which the present sheet is the finest. Moreover, it is littered with distinguished collectors' marks. Two other Reynolds 'Poussin' drawings, rejected by Rosenberg and Prat in their *catalogue raisonné* of 1994, are found in Budapest; these had later belonged to Reynolds's close friend Poggi, and were bought from him in Paris in 1810 by Prince Nicholas Esterházy (1765–1833). One was once given to Poussin and is now attributed to Coypel, while the other retains its traditional attribution.[130]

Reynolds's drawing is related to a dated canvas of 1648, which is a revered mature specimen of Poussin's poetic treatment of landscape. The picture has been in British collections from the third quarter of the eighteenth century, and was formerly with the Earls of Plymouth at Oakly Park, Shropshire (private collection).[131] The foreground is dominated by a sombre group of pallbearers. Poussin made the leading figure in front in this drawing turn back to take one last view of Athens in the distance; in the painting, though, he looks straight out in grim resolve. The drawing received a brief mention in the French translation of Jonathan Richardson's *Treatise on painting and sculpture* in 1728, which Reynolds undoubtedly knew.

FIG. 32

Richard Earlom
(1743–1822)
after Nicolas Poussin
Venus and Adonis
(1766)
etching, 42.5 x 53.6 cm
British Museum, London
(PD 1864,1114.457)

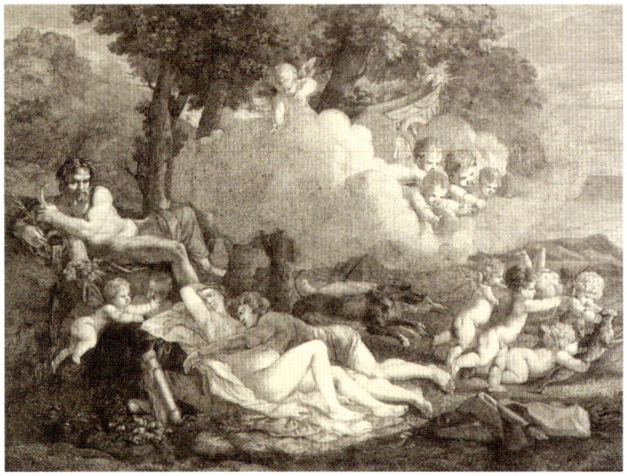

CAT. 71

Andrea Sacchi
(1599–1661)
Studies of two men running
pen and brown ink, with brown wash, over red chalk,
20.2 x 30.4 cm
Courtauld Institute Gallery (Samuel Courtald Trust), London (D.1952.RW.1232)

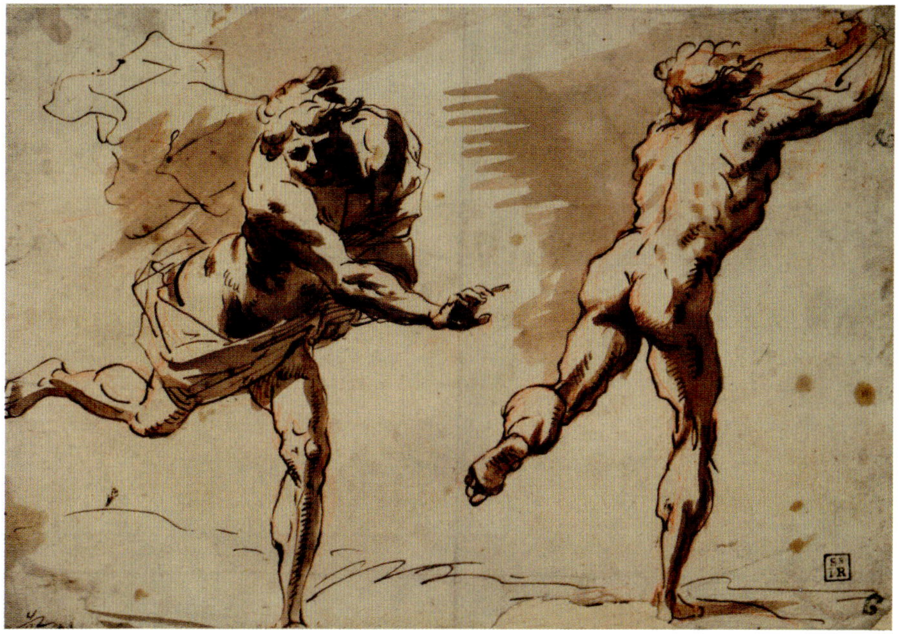

PROVENANCE: Anonymous (Lugt 474); Sir Joshua Reynolds (1723–92; Lugt 2364); Savile Gallery, London; Sir Robert Witt (1872–1952), by whom bequeathed in 1952.

EXHIBITION HISTORY: None.

LITERATURE: Anthony Blunt, *Hand-list of the drawings in the Witt Collection* (London: University of London, 1956), p.87.

THE ROMAN PAINTER SACCHI TAUGHT Maratti, whom Reynolds deeply admired and owned many of his drawings (CAT. 82, p. 156). He also collected Sacchi widely with both paintings and drawings. Reynolds owned, for example, the untraced canvas *The death of Abel*, which he allowed to be published by John Boydell (1719–1804) in an engraving by Richard Earlom in 1766. He also had a small, yet powerful, double-sided head study (after Sacchi) for *The vision of Saint Romuald* (1631; Vatican, Rome), now in the British Museum[132] and a red chalk study of a male nude, which had previously belonged to Hudson.[133] Charles Rogers included Sacchi's drawing of *Saint Anthony of Padua* in his *A collection of prints in imitation of drawings* (1778).

Sacchi was frequently mentioned in Reynolds's Discourses and the present sheet is one of Sacchi's more lively performances. It appears to be related to a group of dancing musicians, nude except for fluttering loose drapery, in *Allegory on the birth of Pope Urban VIII*, which was engraved by Charles Audran (1594–1674).[134] The drawing plays with the physical limitations of drawn representations: the figures appear to be contained by the sheet's edges.

FEW DRAWINGS BY MOLA OWNED BY Reynolds can be traced, and none as spectacular as this example. Two other drawings, formerly attributed to him, are also in the British Museum. One, a pen and ink and wash of *The Flight into Egypt*, is now thought to be the work of the French-born Italian painter Guglielmo Cortese (1628–79), and entered the Museum collection in 1799.[135] The other (now anonymous) drawing is an extremely slight sheet of figure studies, and consequently bears the Reynolds mark on the verso. Reynolds's friend Nathaniel Hone owned a red and black chalk drawing of a straining figure now in the Szépművészeti Múzeum, Budapest.[136] Reynolds bought this bearded study from the artist and collector Jan van Rymsdyk, from whom he also acquired Rembrandt drawings, such as one now in Paris (CAT. 74). Many other drawings were acquired by Reynolds from the same source, with examples found now as far apart as Oslo, Avignon, Amsterdam and New York.

Mola was a pupil of Francesco Albani (Richardson the Elder has inscribed on the mount 'a disciple of Albani'). Nicholas Turner has noted that the head resembles, in reverse, that of Nicodemus in Federico Barocci's altarpiece *The Entombment* (1579–82; Santa Croce, Senigallia), with the difference that in the present drawing he wears a wide-brimmed hat; in Barocci's painting he wears a turban. Mola may well have visited Senigallia, on the Adriatic coast, but no other evidence apart from this drawing apparently exists to substantiate it. On the other hand, he could have made his copy from one of Barocci's own drawn studies for the altarpiece. Nonetheless, Mola's strongly modelled head is a stunning example of the handling of coloured chalks.

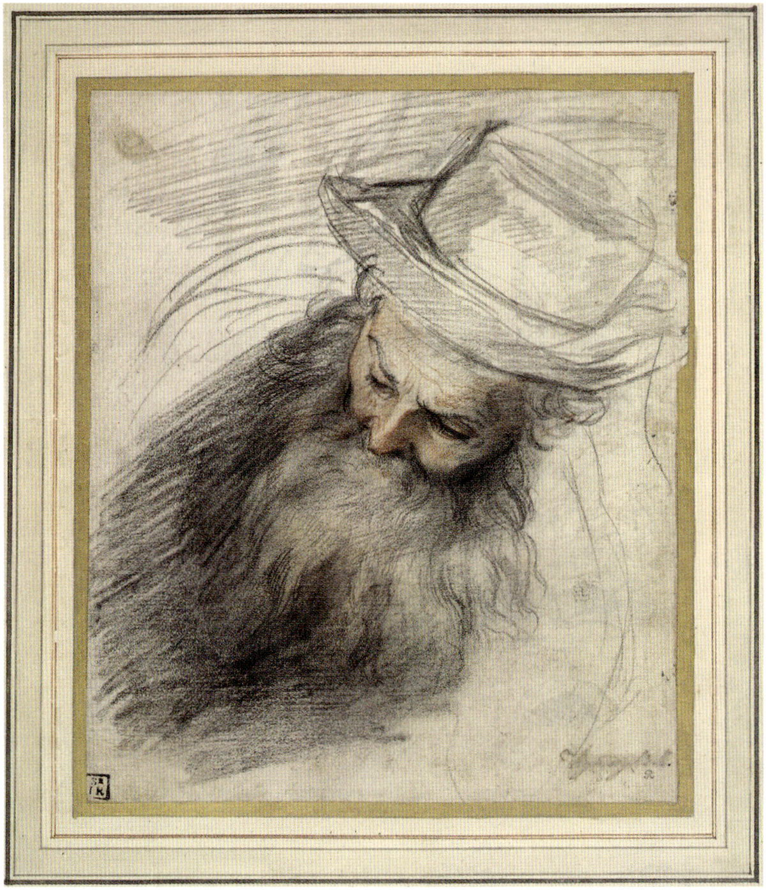

CAT. 72

Pier Francesco Mola
(1612–66)
Head of a bearded man wearing a wide-brimmed hat
black and red chalk, 25.2 x 21.6 cm
British Museum, London (PD Pp, 4.89)

PROVENANCE: Jonathan Richardson I (1665–1745; Lugt 2184 and Lugt 2984); Jan van Rymsdyk (*c.*1730–1788/9; Lugt 2167); Sir Joshua Reynolds (1723–92; Lugt 2364), Harry Phillips, London, 15 March 1798, lot 978 as '1 [drawing], F. Mola'; Richard Payne Knight (1751–1824), by whom bequeathed in 1824.

EXHIBITION HISTORY: 1978, London, British Museum, 'Gainsborough and Reynolds in the British Museum', no.258; 1982, Manchester, Whitworth Art Gallery, 'The arrogant connoisseur: Richard Payne Knight 1751–1824', no.149.

LITERATURE: Michael Clarke and Nicholas Penny (eds), *The arrogant connoisseur: Richard Payne Knight 1751–1824* (Manchester: Manchester University Press, 1982), p.167, no.149, colourplate x; Nicholas Turner, *Italian drawings in the Department of Prints and Drawings in the British Museum: Roman Baroque drawings, c.1620 to c.1700* (London: British Museum Press, 1999), pp.158–59, no.229; Jennifer Tonkovich, '"Rymsdyk's Museum": Jan van Rymsdyk as a collector of Old Master drawings', *Journal of the History of Collections*, 17 (2), Summer 2005, pp.155–71 (168).

CAT. 73

Rembrandt
(1606–69)
Jan Lutma
(1656)
etching on Japan paper,
19.5 x 15 cm
British Museum, London
(PD 1868,0822.696)

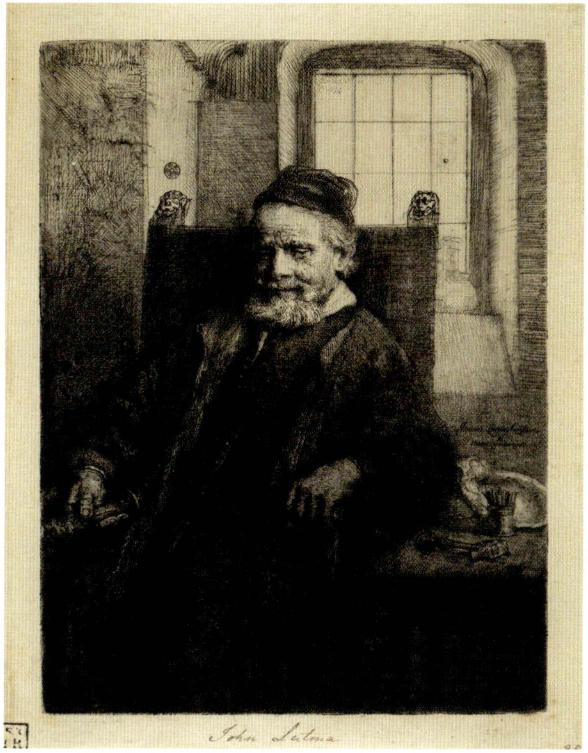

PROVENANCE: Sir Edward Astley (1729–1802; Lugt 2775), London, March-April 1760; Sir Joshua Reynolds (1723–92; Lugt 2364); Felix Slade (1790–1868), by whom bequeathed in 1868.

EXHIBITION HISTORY: 2001, London, British Museum, 'Rembrandt the printmaker', no.83; 2006–07, Hull, Ferens Art Gallery, Bath, Victoria Art Gallery, Newcastle, Laing Art Gallery, Stoke-on-Trent, Potteries Museum and Art Gallery and Blackpool, Grundy Art Gallery, 'Rembrandt as printmaker', no.53b.

LITERATURE: Adam Bartsch, *Catalogue raisonné de toutes les estampes qui forment l'oeuvre de Rembrandt, et ceux de ses principaux imitateurs* (Vienna: A Blumauer, 1797), pp.229–30, no.276; Arthur M Hind, *A catalogue of Rembrandt's etchings, chronologically arranged and completely illustrated* (London: Methuen & Co, 1923), vol.I, p.116, no.290 ii/iii; Christopher White and Karel G Boon, *Rembrandt's etchings: An illustrated critical catalogue in two volumes* (Amsterdam: London: New York: Van Gendt & Co, A Zwemmer and Abner Schram, 1969), vol.I, p.129, no.B276 ii/iii, vol.II, plate 224; Ger Luijten in Erik Hinterding *et al.*, *Rembrandt the printmaker* (London: British Museum Press, 2001), pp.332, 335–37, no.83; Martin Royalton-Kisch, *Rembrandt as printmaker* (London: Hayward Gallery Publishing, 2006), pp.81, 96, no.53b.

REMBRANDT WAS WELL REPRESENTED in Reynolds's collection. In addition to many paintings and drawings (CAT. 74), he also owned fine examples of his printmaking. He owned an impression of *The Descent from the Cross by Torchlight* (1654), one of Rembrandt's celebrated three prints from the Passion of Christ.[137] Rich in drypoint and printed with marked plate-tone, the impression is a sparkling play of light and dark areas. Nonetheless, the item was judged to be 'inferior' and Reynolds's stamp was applied to the verso, indicating its lower monetary value. Large groups of Rembrandt's graphic work were formed in eighteenth-century London; Richardson the Elder, for example, had over 120 drawings by 1745.[138] Sir Reginald Pole-Carew (1753–1835) had once owned Rembrandt's etching *Abraham Entertaining the Angels* (1656) among many others.[139] Reynolds had painted his father Reginald Pole early in his career[140] and the young collector and Reynolds knew one another well. Reynolds obtained his Lutma portrait in 1760 from the large collection formed by Sir Edward Astley.

Lutma was a silversmith but his hammer and pot of punches are difficult to make out; here he is posing not working. Reynolds's impression was a revision of the first state that omits the window with a glass bottle. Rembrandt admired fine papers and often experimented with printing on a selection of papers, including some from abroad as here.

CAT. 74

Rembrandt
(1606–69)
Study of a man, half-length, in a cloak
pen and brown ink, with later framing lines, 9.1 x 5.8 cm
Musée du Louvre, Paris (RF 4694)

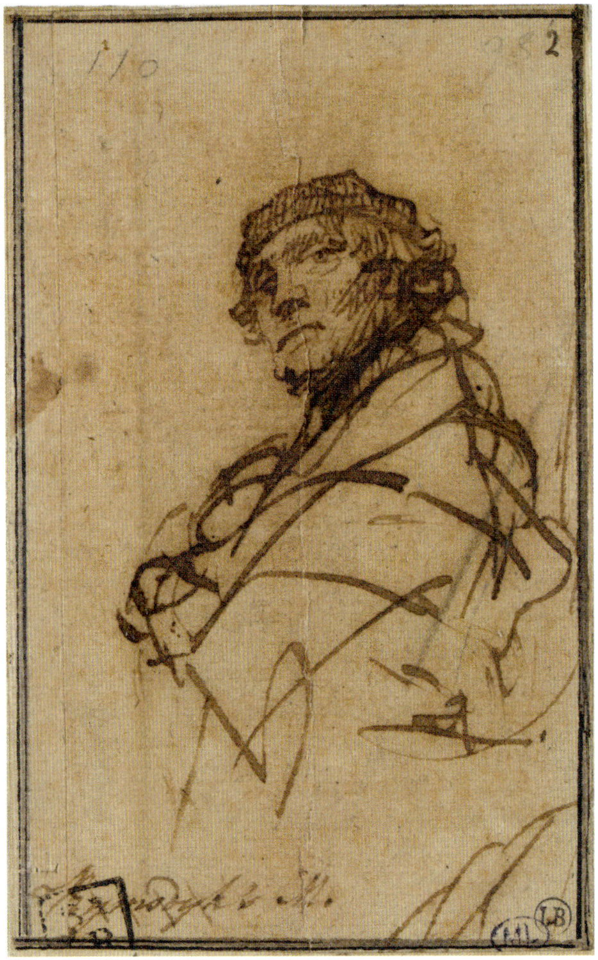

PROVENANCE: Jan van Rymsdyk (c.1730–88/89; Lugt 2167); Sir Joshua Reynolds (1723–92; Lugt 2364); Sir Thomas Lawrence (1769–1830; Lugt 2445); Léon Bonnat (1833–1922; Lugt 1714), by whom presented in 1919.

EXHIBITION HISTORY: 1988–89, Paris, Musée du Louvre, 'Rembrandt et son école', no.13.

LITERATURE: Émile Michel, *Rembrandt: Sa vie, son oeuvre et son temps* (Paris: Hachette, 1893), p.587; C Hofstede de Groot, *Die handzeichnungen Rembrandts* (Harlem: F Bohn, 1906), p.164, no.715; Frits Lugt, *Musée du Louvre: Inventaire général des dessins des écoles du nord, école Hollandaise, no.III: Rembrandt, ses élèves, ses imitateurs, ses copistes* (Paris: Musées nationaux de France, 1933), pp.22–23, no.1164, pl.xxxvii; Otto Benesch, *Rembrandt: Werk und forschung* (Vienna: Gilhofer & Ranschburg, 1935), p.22; Otto Benesch, *The drawings of Rembrandt* (London: Phaidon, 1954), vol.II, p.67, no.273, fig.299; Werner Sumowski, 'Bemerkungen zu Otto Benesch Corpus de Rembrandt-Zeichungen I', *Wissenschaftliche Zetschrift der Humboldt-Universität zu Berlin*, 6, 1956-7, p.263; R H Fuchs (ed.), Hans van de Waal, *Steps towards Rembrandt: Collected articles 1937–1972* (Amsterdam and London: North-Holland, 1974), p.74; Emmanuel Starcky in Emmanuel Starcky and Menehould de Bazelaire, *Rembrandt et son école: Dessins du Musée du Louvre, Paris* (Paris: Éditions de la Réunion des musées nationaux, 1988), p.25, no.13; Jennifer Tonkovich, '"Rymsdyk's Museum": Jan van Rymsdyk as a collector of Old Master drawings', *Journal of the History of Collections*, 17 (2), Summer 2005, pp.155–71 (169).

REYNOLDS OWNED DOZENS OF SUPERB Rembrandt drawings, many of which are found now in such distinguished collections as the Kupferstichkabinett in Berlin, the Metropolitan Museum of Art in New York and the British Museum in London. Otto Benesch's *catalogue raisonné* from 1954–57 identified 54 Rembrandt drawings that had once belonged to Reynolds.[141] Recently, more have come to light. For example, one small drawing of a male figure (undescribed by Benesch) proved so interesting to Reynolds that he copied it in a drawing in the Hershel Album (private collection).[142] Reynolds had many figurative drawings, including some portraits as well as landscapes and biblical subjects by Rembrandt. He owned paintings by him, too, and openly confessed that he 'even borrowed money for this purpose. The possessing [of] portraits by Titian, Van Dyck, Rembrandt and company, I considered as the best kind of wealth.'[143] Reynolds also had both paintings and related drawings, such as the panel painting *The Lamentation* (c.1635; National Gallery, London)[144] and drawing now in the British Museum.[145]

Hudson owned a superb model sheet by Rembrandt, now in the Maida and George Abrams Collection in the USA.[146] It is likely that the present drawing, certainly cut from a larger sheet, was from one such model sheet, with many varied poses studied from different figures. Reynolds himself owned an intact model sheet, with three male figures; it is now in the Institut Néerlandais (Fondation Custodia) in Paris.[147]

REYNOLDS OWNED BOTH PRINTS AND drawings by this painter. The most impressive was a large pen and ink wash drawing that was published by Reynolds's friend Charles Rogers in *A collection of prints in imitation of drawings: To which are annexed lives of their authors, with explanatory and critical notes* (1778). The drawing was later owned by Poggi and is now in the Szépművészeti Múzeum, Budapest.[148] Canuti was much influenced by Ludovico Carracci and Guercino, both artists collected by Reynolds (CAT. 56 and 69). Reynolds collected other artists' etchings, including examples by Rembrandt and the Italian Guido Reni (CAT. 73 and CAT. 60, p. 134).

Canuti worked principally in his native Bologna, but was in Rome for two periods in 1651–55 and 1672–77. He specialised in ceiling frescoes, and the drawing once owned by Reynolds in Budapest, *Jupiter places the newborn Bacchus under the care of Mercury*, was a study for such work. Like most painters, he made a few etchings in his lifetime, which have a different character from the work of professional printmakers. The print is not thought to relate to other work by Canuti, and depicts Mary and Christ blessing Bologna. The central figural element has been strongly bitten by acid to retain more ink, and hence print more darkly than the surrounding areas of the plate, especially the pale distant skyline of the city, which is lightly bitten. It is signed bottom left: 'DMCF[ecit]' ('D[omenico] M[aria] C[anuti] Made This').

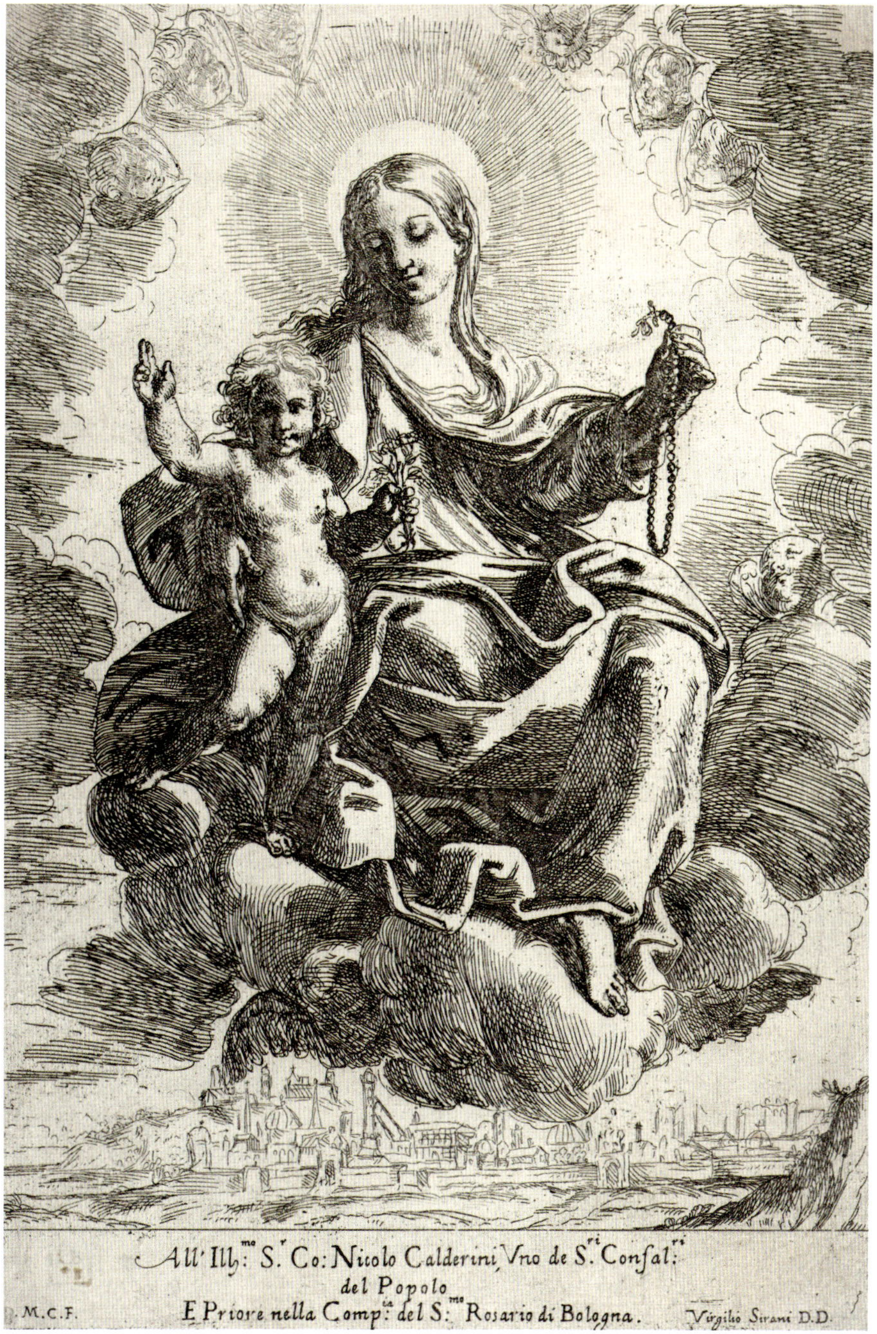

CAT. 75

Domenico Maria Canuti
(1626–84)
Madonna of the Rosary
etching, 21 x 10.5 cm
National Gallery of Scotland, Edinburgh (P2595)

PROVENANCE: Sir Joshua Reynolds (1723–92; Lugt 2364 verso); Sir Donald Pollock (1868–1962), from whose estate purchased in 1964.

EXHIBITION HISTORY: None.

LITERATURE: Adam Bartsch, *Le peintre graveur: Peintres ou dessinateurs Italiens, maîtres du dix-septième siècle, première partie* (Vienna: Pierre Mechetti, 1819), vol.XIX, p.223, no.1; Giovanna Gaeta Bertelà, *Incisori Bolognesi ed Emiliani del secolo XVII (Sezione III)* (Bologna: Associazone per le Arti 'Francesco Francia', 1973), n.p., no.137; Simonetta Stagni, *Domenico Maria Canuti, pittore (1626–1684): Catalogo generale* (Rimini: Luisè, 1988), p.219, no.80.

CAT. 76

Jan Thomas
(1617–78)
after Peter Paul Rubens
(1577–1640)
Pastoral scene with men and women merrymaking
etching, 26.5 x 35.8 cm
British Museum, London
(PD S.5576)

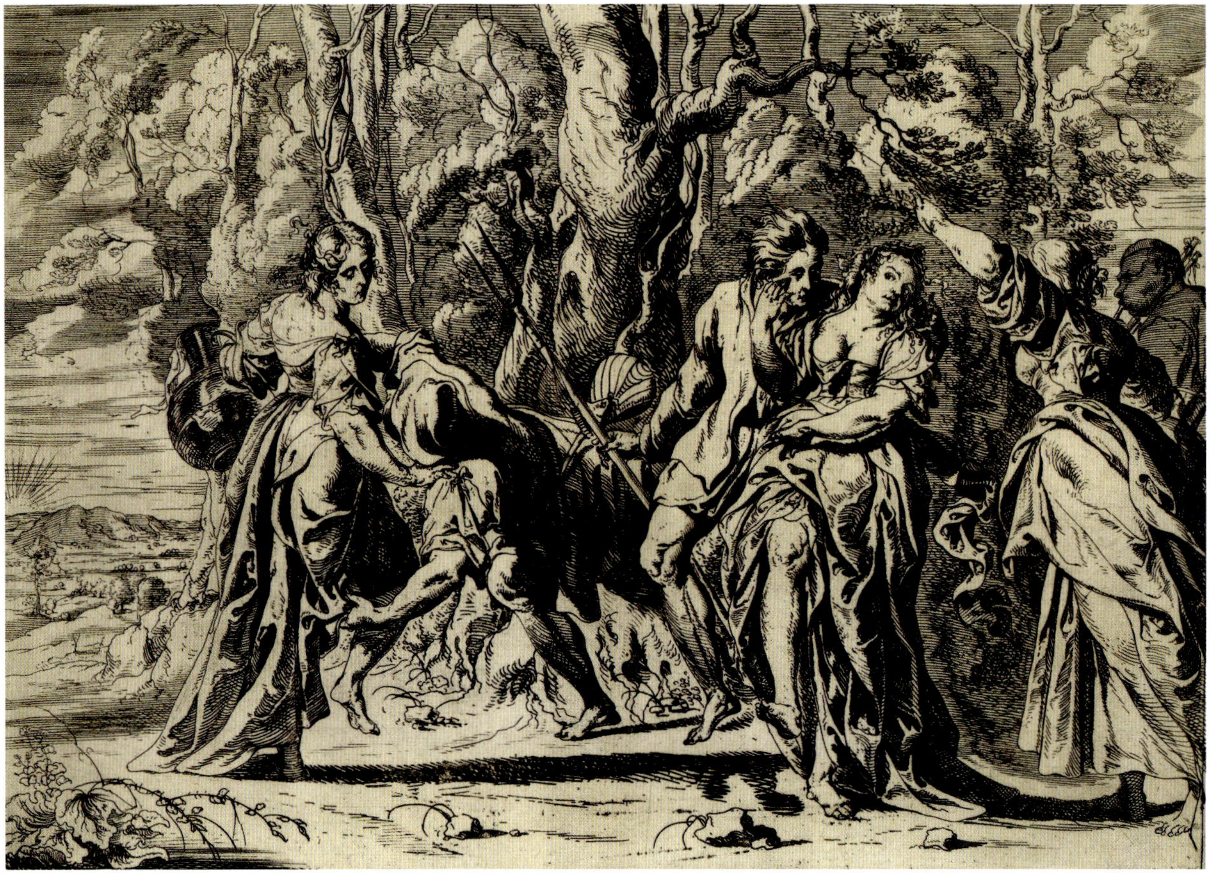

PROVENANCE: Sir Joshua Reynolds (1723–92; Lugt 2364 verso); John Sheepshanks (1787–1863), from whom purchased in 1836.

EXHIBITION HISTORY: None.

LITERATURE: C G Voorhelm Schneevoogt, *Catalogue des estampes gravées d'après P.P. Rubens, avec l'indication des collections ou se trouvent les tableaux et les gravures* (Haarlem: Les Héritiers Loosjes, 1873), p.151, no.118; Ger Luijten, *Hollstein's Dutch and Flemish etchings, engravings and woodcuts, c.1450–1700: Cornelis Anthonisz. T(h)eunissen to Johannes Den Uyl* (Amsterdam: AL Van Gendt & Co, 1986), vol.XXX, p.89, no.3 ii/ii.; Jan van Tatenhove, 'Miscellanea: 3, Jan Thomas van Yperen (1617–78)', *Delineavit et Sculpsit*, 15, May 1995, pp.39–41 (40).

REYNOLDS ADMIRED THE ART OF RUBENS and, as he did with Rembrandt, collected his work in a variety of media: paintings, prints and drawings. Besides dozens of fine drawings and some paintings, including the famous *Moonlit Landscape* now in the collection of the Courtauld Institute of Art in London, Reynolds also had many prints after Rubens' work. One of these, a religious image by Rombout Eynhoudts, Reynolds reworked in his search for a more complete understanding of Rubens's use of colour (CAT. 83). Here the interest lies in the grouping and rhythm of dancing figures in a pastoral landscape. Rubens ran a large workshop and many of his pupils' works were also collected by Reynolds, perhaps to display the notion of artistic lineage.

Thomas was a painter and printmaker who had trained under Rubens in Antwerp. The figure with the bagpipe was re-used by Thomas in one of his own paintings, now in the Musée des Beaux-Arts, Caen.[149] The print was published by Thomas's Flemish contemporary Frans van der Wyngaerde (1614–79) and appears to have been based on a drawing supplied by Rubens, in the opposite direction, which was sold in Paris in 1920 from the collection of Alfred Beurdeley (1847–1919).[150]

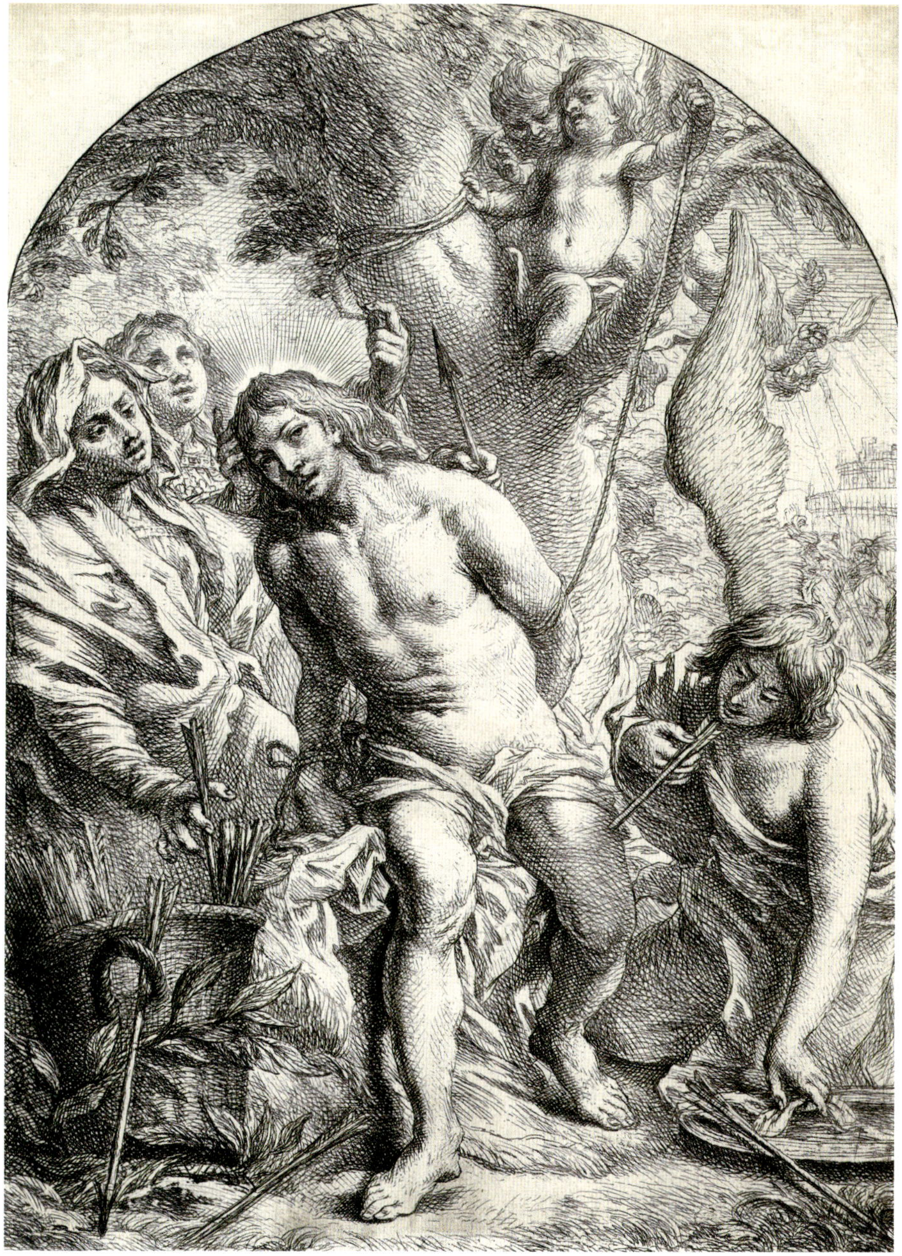

CAT. 77

Rombout Eynhoudts
(1613–80)
after Cornelis Schut
(1597–1655)
Saint Sebastian aided by Saint Irene and a companion, with angels
etching, 29.9 x 22.3 cm
Courtauld Institute Gallery (Samuel Courtauld Trust), London (G.1990.WL.2348)

SCHUT'S APPEAL FOR REYNOLDS MUST in large part have derived from the closeness of the Flemish painter's work to that of Rubens, one of his great favourites, with whom Schut trained. He owned prints after both master and pupil, as well as their drawings, and other work by Eynhoudts (CAT. 83). Reynolds also owned the elaborately worked *The Rape of Europa* in the British Museum.[151]

Eynhoudts's etching reproduces a canvas in the church Onze-Lieve-Vrouwkerk, Temse, which was commissioned in 1650. Schut's mature style remained strongly Rubensian. Indeed, the powerfully built male figure of the early Christian Roman commander shot with arrows by his own men, and the figural grouping, is partly taken from Rubens's canvas *The Martyrdom of Saint Sebastian* (c.1608; Palazzo Corsini, Rome). Here, though, *putti* replace angels aiding Sebastian's release from the cords that bound him to a tree, and in the background towards the right, lightly bitten, can be glimpsed the famous Roman Castel Sant'Angelo. The print was later reissued after Eynhoudts's death by the French publisher Jacques Philippe Le Bas (1707–83) and carries his address on the Rue de la Harpe, Paris.

PROVENANCE: Sir Joshua Reynolds (1723–92; Lugt 2364 verso); Sir Robert Witt (1872–1952), by whom presented to the Witt Library, Courtauld Institute of Art, London in 1945; transferred in 1990.

EXHIBITION HISTORY: None.

LITERATURE: F W H Hollstein, *Dutch and Flemish etchings, engravings and woodcuts, c.1450–1700: Douffet-Floris* (Amsterdam: Menno Hertzberger, 1952), vol.VI, p.206; Marie Louise Hairs, *Dans le sillage de Rubens, les peintres d'histoire anversois au XVIIe siècle* (Liège: University of Liège, 1977), p.203; Gertrude Wilmers, *Cornelis Schut (1597–1655): A Flemish painter of the High Baroque* (Turnhout: Brepols, 1996), pp.159–60, no.A92, fig.92a.

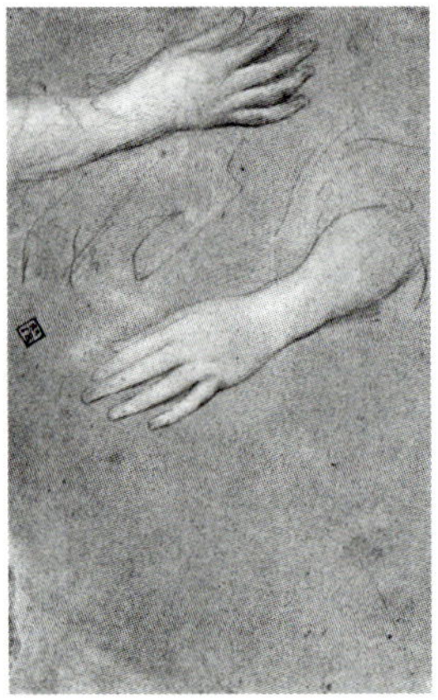

FIG. 33

Sir Peter Lely
(1618-1680)
Study of hands
coloured chalks
on brown paper,
27.9 x 17.8 cm
The Huntington Library, Art Collections, and Botanical Gardens, San Marino, California (acc.no.63.52.129)

CAT. 78

Sir Peter Lely
(1618-1680)
Head of a young girl
black and white chalk, touched with red,
on brown-grey paper, 28.2 x 19.7 cm
British Museum, London (PD 1983,0723.35)

PROVENANCE: Sir Joshua Reynolds (1723–92; Lugt 2364); Thomas Poynder, by descent to his third daughter Sarah Matilda Dickson, née Poynder; by descent to her son Sir John Poynder Dickson-Poynder, Baron Islington (1866–1936), by descent in the family, Christie's, London, 29 March 1983, lot 71 bought Martin Gruss; Thomas Agnew & Sons, London, from whom purchased in 1983.

EXHIBITION HISTORY: 1956–57, London, Royal Academy of Arts, 'British Portraits', no.550; 1978–79, London, National Portrait Gallery, 'Sir Peter Lely 1618–80', no.73; 1984, London, British Museum, 'Master drawings and watercolours', no.159; 1987, London, British Museum and New Haven, Yale Center for British Art, 'Drawing in England, from Hilliard to Hogarth', no.88.

LITERATURE: John Woodward, *Tudor and Stuart drawings* (London: Faber and Faber, 1951), p.50, no.39, plate 39; Oliver Millar, *Sir Peter Lely 1618–80* (London: National Portrait Gallery, 1984), pp.77–78, no.73; Lindsay Stainton and Christopher White, *Drawing in England, from Hilliard to Hogarth* (London: British Museum Publications, 1987), pp.123, 125, no.88.

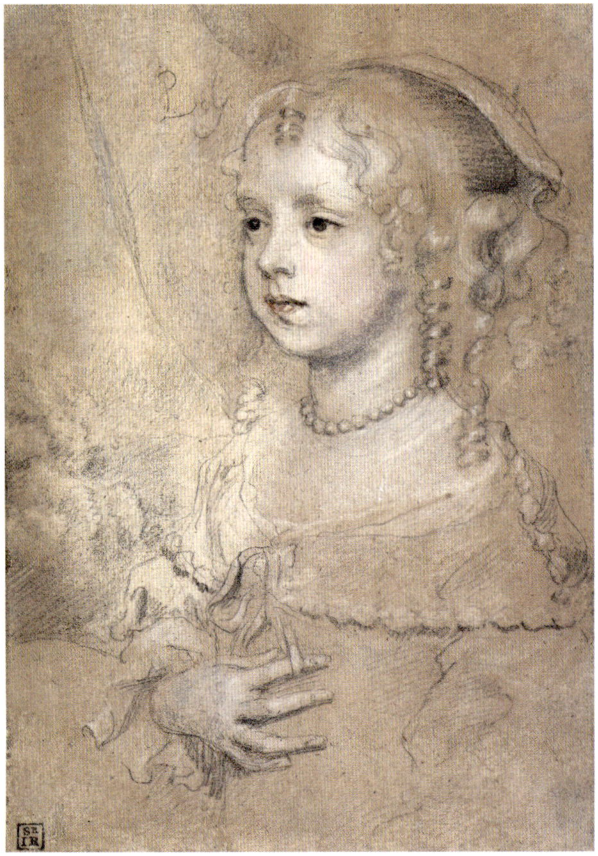

LELY PRESENTED REYNOLDS WITH A formidable reputation as both an adept portraitist (he was 'Principal Painter' to King Charles II) and an important collector of Old Master prints and drawings; his collection was three times the size of Reynolds's, numbering some 10,000 sheets. Drawings by Lely himself were avidly collected in Britain following his death, and Hudson in particular formed a decent group of them. Reynolds probably first encountered Lely's drawings while a student under Hudson. The present example is undoubtedly the finest Lely that Reynolds would come to own. The prominent signature signals the sheet as a 'finished' work of art. The portrait has been linked to Lely's painting of *Elizabeth Seymour, Countess of Ailesbury (1655–1697)* at Longleat House in Wiltshire and made when Elizabeth was a small child.

Reynolds owned many other Lely drawings, including several more now in the British Museum and a stunning study of a pair of hands, in the same medium as the present example, now in the Huntington Library, Art Collections and Botanical Gardens in San Marino, California (FIG. 33).[152] Hudson had owned a similar sheet of three hand studies, now in the Ashmolean Museum, Oxford. Both Hudson and Reynolds must have been impressed with Lely's delicate handling of coloured chalks and pastel. Rarely though did Reynolds venture to make his own, one exception being the tender pastel study of his great-niece Theophila Gwatkin (1757–1848), also drawn when the sitter was a small child, in the British Museum.[153]

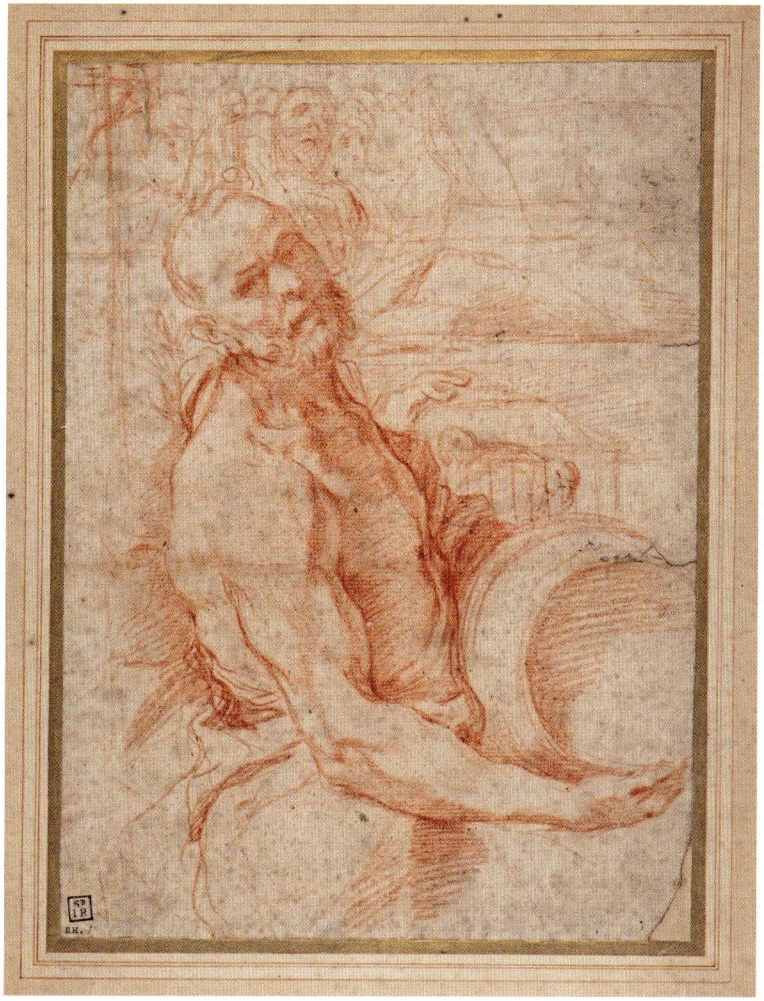

CAT. 79

Mattia Preti
(1613–99)
Man holding a barrel, study for the painting 'The Pope inspired by the Holy Ghost receives homage from the ecclesiastical orders' (San Domenico, Siena)
(c.1670)
red chalk, 31.7 x 23.4 cm
National Gallery of Scotland, Edinburgh (D2249)

REYNOLDS OWNED A FEW OTHER PRETI drawings. Two drawings in red chalk are in the Szépművészeti Múzeum in Budapest and the Ashmolean Museum, Oxford.[154] Another splendid male figure seen from below is in Copenhagen.[155] Preti's red chalk drawings recall the fine draughtsmanship of Andrea del Sarto and Correggio in the same medium, both artists collected by Reynolds. One other Preti drawing in pen and ink is in Bowdoin College Museum of Art, Brunswick, Maine.

Preti's painting was commissioned for the Piccolomini chapel in the church of San Francesco in Siena, but following the suppression of the convent and the closure of the church it was moved to the church of San Domenico at the end of the nineteenth century. The painting was engraved in the eighteenth century by Giuliano Traballesi (1727–1812), which Reynolds might have known. Though mottled, the monochrome sheet is sparkling and drawn entirely in red chalk of various intensities, with faintly outlined onlookers in the background suggesting the swelling numbers of distant figures seen in the finished painting. The model engages the viewer with his tilted head and Preti has used the whiteness of the paper to model his muscular arm that dominates the sheet. The historic mount's drawn red ink lines have been chosen to complement the drawing's medium: red chalk. The barrel has painted upon its base the papal tiara and crossed keys, perhaps symbolic of the bountiful munificence of the church. An earlier drawing for the figure, in red chalk, is in the British Museum.[156] The sheet in Edinburgh is closer to the finished painting.

PROVENANCE: Richard Houlditch (d.1736; Lugt 2214); Jonathan Richardson I (1665–1745; Lugt 2184), 1747; Sir Joshua Reynolds (1723–92; Lugt 2364); William Findlay Watson (1810–1881), by whom bequeathed in 1881.

EXHIBITION HISTORY: 1938, London, Royal Academy, 'Seventeenth-century art in Europe', no.427; 1953, London, Royal Academy, 'Drawings by Old Masters', no.154; 1962, Barnard Castle, Bowes Museum, 'Neapolitan Baroque and Rococo painting and drawing', no.23; 1966, London, Colnaghi, 'Old Master drawings: A loan exhibition from the National Gallery of Scotland', no.46; 1981, Edinburgh, 'Drawings from the bequest of W F Watson 1881–1981', no.25.

LITERATURE: Walter Vitzthum, 'Le dessin baroque à Naples', *L'Oeil*, 97, January 1963, pp.40–51, 88 (46); Keith Andrews, *Catalogue of Italian drawings in the National Gallery of Scotland* (Cambridge: Cambridge University Press, 1968), vol.I, p.99, vol.II, fig.689.

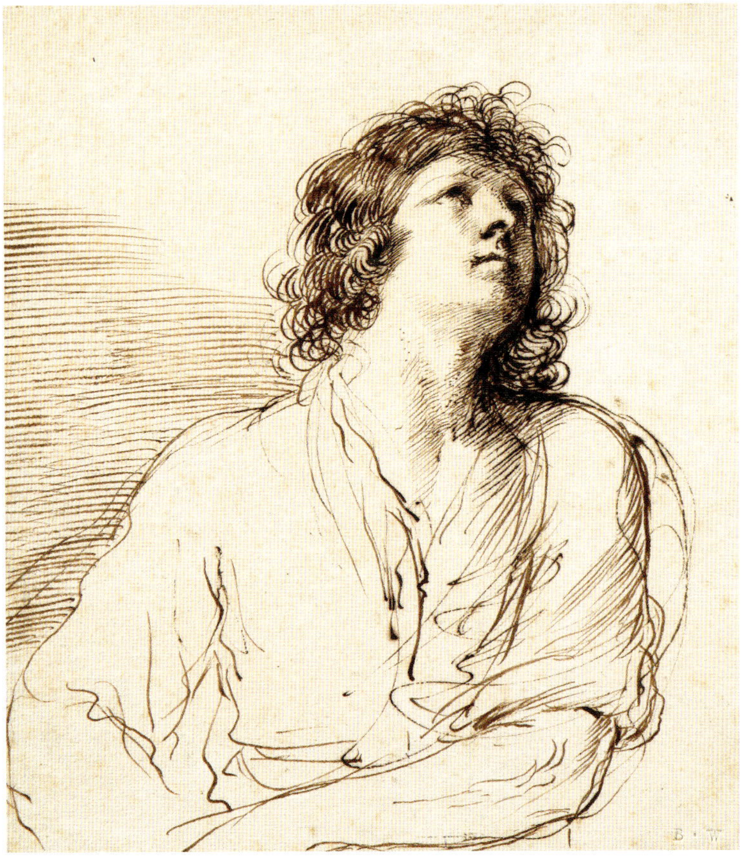

CAT. 80

Sir Joshua Reynolds
after Guercino
(1591–1666)
A young man, half-length, looking up to right
pen and brown ink, 17 x 15.5 cm
Institut Néerlandais (Fondation Custodia), Paris (inv.1043)

PROVENANCE: Benjamin West (1738–1820; Lugt 419), Christie's, London, 9–13 June 1820, part of lot 45 as 'Four heads in pen and ink, by Sir J Reynolds, after Guercino' bought Lansdowne; Henry Petty-Fitzmaurice, 3rd Marquess of Lansdowne (1780–1863); by descent to Henry William Edmund Petty-Fitzmaurice, 6th Marquess of Lansdowne (1872–1936), Sotheby's, London, 25 March 1920, part of lot 61, bought Thomas Agnew & Sons, London; from whom purchased by Frits Lugt (1884–1970; Lugt 1028), 25 March 1923 and presented in 1947.

EXHIBITION HISTORY: 1968, Bologna, Palazzo dell'Archiginnasio, 'Il Guercino (Giovanni Francesco Barbieri, 1591–1666)', no.225.

LITERATURE: Denis Mahon, *Il Guercino (Giovanni Francesco Barbieri, 1591–1666): Catalogo critico dei disegni* (Bologna: Alfa, 1969), p.225, no.225; Roseline Bacou, 'Bolognese drawings of the seventeenth century', *Apollo*, CIV (177), November 1976, pp.382–87 (385, f.39); James Byam Shaw, *The Italian drawings of the Frits Lugt collection* (Paris: Institut Néerlandais, 1983), vol.I, pp.354–55, no.355, vol.III, plate 408.

REYNOLDS WAS PUT TO WORK, WHILE under Hudson, copying drawings by Guercino. These two copies are fine examples of Reynolds' draughtsmanship that reveal his early responses to the Old Masters. Reynolds also made red chalk copies of red chalk originals by Guercino in Hudson's collection. One of these has been brought together in recent times with the Guercino original, and both are in the collection of Sir Denis Mahon (b.1910).[157] Reynolds's drawing follows the Italian drawing closely. While in this instance the Guercino did not pass into Reynolds's collection, at his death Reynolds's executors believed his copy to be an Old Master and, along with other copies, duly stamped it with his collector's mark.

Reynolds made numerous copies of Old Master works during his trip to Italy in several sketchbooks, two in the British Museum and two others in the Soane Museum in London (CAT. 99). He continued to make copies of works in his own collection, including a pen and ink after Rembrandt and a sheet in black chalk after Correggio made in about 1752 (FIG. 34).[158] Reynolds seems to have given the Correggio copy to Nathaniel Hone (another gift of Reynolds to him is in the British Museum), and it was bought back by Reynolds himself at Hone's death in 1784.

Later in life Reynolds would come to own dozens of original sheets by Guercino, including one in Truro (CAT. 69, p. 143). He also owned Guercino's charcoal drawing *St Francis kneeling*, which had previously belonged to Hudson and then to Reynolds's friend Charles Rogers, who might have presented the sheet as a gift.[159] One black chalk drawing by Guercino of *Hercules*, in the Ashmolean Museum in Oxford, resembles Reynolds's own studies of nudes.[160] Reynolds's enthusiasm for Guercino was shared by the Parker family at Saltram House, who assembled a 'fine collection of drawings, by Claude [Lorrain], Guercino, [Willem] Vendevelde, and other ancient masters'.[161]

The first owner of both of these sheets was Benjamin West, who immediately followed Reynolds as President of the Royal Academy. West, a voracious collector, must have competed with Reynolds for key works offered at auction. Perhaps Reynolds gave West these particular drawings as a gift since they bear neither Reynolds's nor Hudson's mark (who retained some other copies, such as one now in Liverpool).[162]

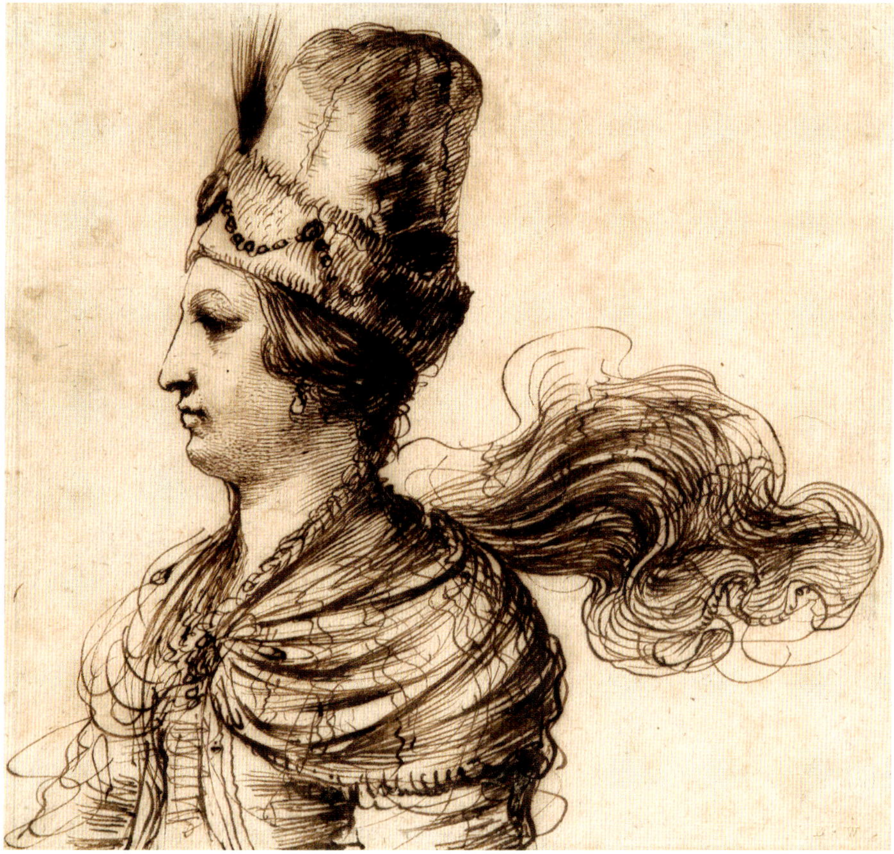

CAT. 81

Sir Joshua Reynolds
after Guercino
(1591–1666)
Woman in high plumed hat, in profile to left, with flowing hair
pen and brown ink, 18.5 x 20.3 cm
Institut Néerlandais (Fondation Custodia), Paris (inv.1981-T.30)

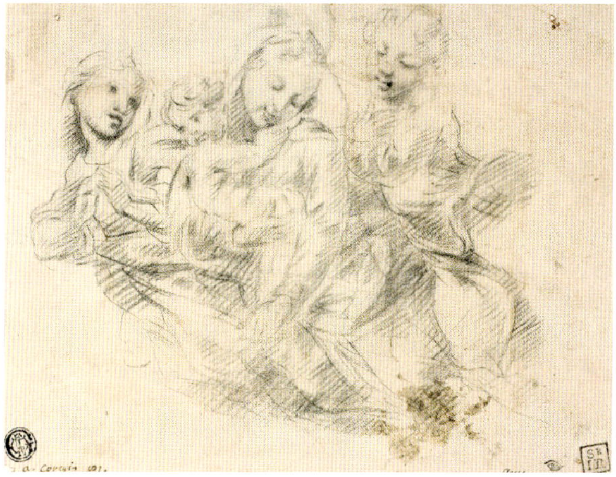

FIG. 34
Sir Joshua Reynolds
after Correggio
(c.1489–1534)
Study after Correggio's 'Madonna della Scala'
(c.1752)
black chalk, 14.5 x 18.9 cm
Art Institute of Chicago (1922.462)

PROVENANCE: Benjamin West (1738–1820; Lugt 419), Christie's, London, 9–13 June 1820, part of lot 45 as 'Four heads in pen and ink, by Sir J Reynolds, after Guercino' bought Lansdowne; Henry Petty-Fitzmaurice, 3rd Marquess of Lansdowne (1780–1863); by descent to Henry William Edmund Petty-Fitzmaurice, 6th Marquess of Lansdowne (1872–1936), Sotheby's, London, 25 March 1920, part of lot 61, bought Thomas Agnew & Sons, London; from whom purchased by Charles A Jackson, 1932; anonymous, Christie's, London, 22 November 1966, lot 15 bought Besterman; Theodore Besterman (1904-1976; mark not in Lugt), Christie's, London, 17 November 1981, lot 58 purchased by the Fondation Custodia, through Thomas Agnew & Sons, London, in 1981.

EXHIBITION HISTORY: 1969, London, Leger Galleries, 'English watercolours and drawings from the collection of Theodore Besterman', no.61.

LITERATURE: James Byam Shaw, *The Italian drawings of the Frits Lugt collection* (Paris: Institut Néerlandais, 1983), vol.I, p.356, no.357, vol.III, plate 410.

REYNOLDS OWNED LARGE NUMBERS of drawings by Maratti, a leading Roman Baroque painter. Six others are now in the British Museum and the variety of these drawings range from crude satirical portrait heads to refined chalk drawings on coloured paper. Reynolds might have been inspired by one of his superb Maratti drawings in the British Museum, which was previously owned by Hudson, for the unusual form of his portrait *Frances Isabella Keir Gordon* (1786–87; Tate, London).[163] One other of Reynolds's Maratti drawings, a study of four heads and a hand (cut from a larger sheet) entered the collection of the Dutch art historian Johan Quirijn van Regteren Altena (1899–1980) and was sold in 2006.[164] A stunning Maratti of *Religion adored by four parts of the world* formerly in Reynolds's collection is in Smith College Museum of Art, Northampton, Massachusetts.[165]

This drawing was made in connection with Maratti's incomplete scheme for the decoration of the audience chamber in the Palazzo Altieri in Rome, and relates specifically to the unexecuted part.[166] The study at the left on the recto has been gone over in brown ink, and the pose slightly altered. The spandrel's form has been clearly articulated. All three studies on the sheet of the figure of Virtue are different, the final position of the head undecided. The verso is another study for the figure of Virtue.

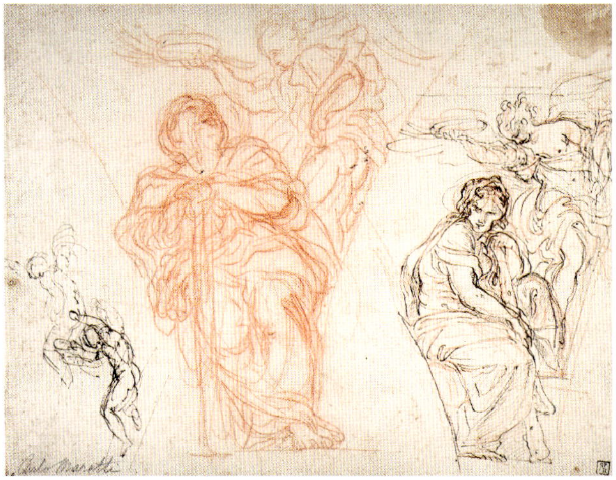

CAT. 82

Carlo Maratti
(1625–1713)
Studies of a seated female figure, crowned by another ('Virtue Crowned by Honour') and two other figure studies *(recto)*
and
Study of a seated female figure, crowned by another ('Virtue Crowned by Honour') *(verso)*
red chalk with pen and brown ink (recto) and red chalk (verso), 32.1 x 42.5 cm
National Gallery of Scotland, Edinburgh (D639)

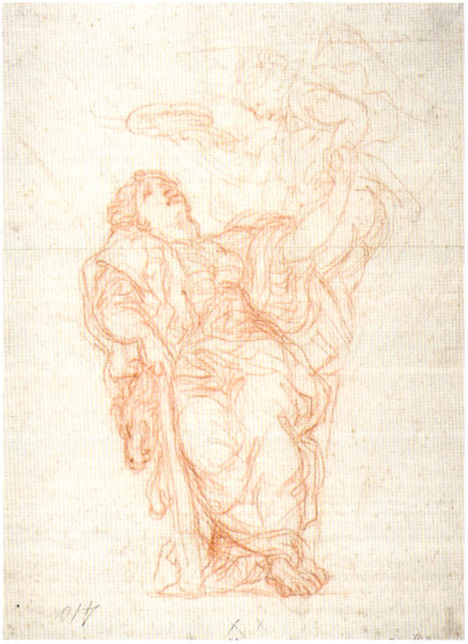

PROVENANCE: Sir Joshua Reynolds (1723–92; Lugt 2364); Sir Thomas Lawrence (1769–1830; Lugt 2445); David Laing (1793–1878) bequeathed to Royal Scottish Academy, Edinburgh in 1878; transferred in 1910.

EXHIBITION HISTORY: None.

LITERATURE: Walter Vitzthum, 'Drawings by Carlo Maratta for the Altieri Palace in Rome', *The Burlington Magazine*, CV (725), August 1963, pp.365–69 (368), fig.37 (verso), fig.39 (recto); Keith Andrews, *Catalogue of Italian drawings in the National Gallery of Scotland* (Cambridge: Cambridge University Press, 1968), vol.I, p.70, vol.II, fig.689; Jennifer Montagu, 'Bellori, Maratti and the Palazzo Altieri', *Journal of the Warburg and Courtauld Institutes*, XLI, 1978, pp.334–40 (340).

CAT. 83

Sir Joshua Reynolds
and
Rombout Eynhoudts
(1613–1680)
after Peter Paul Rubens
(1577–1640)
Sacra Conversazione with Saints Bonaventure and George
etching reworked with red chalk and brown wash,
34.7 x 25.2 cm
British Museum, London
(PD 1885,0509.1578)

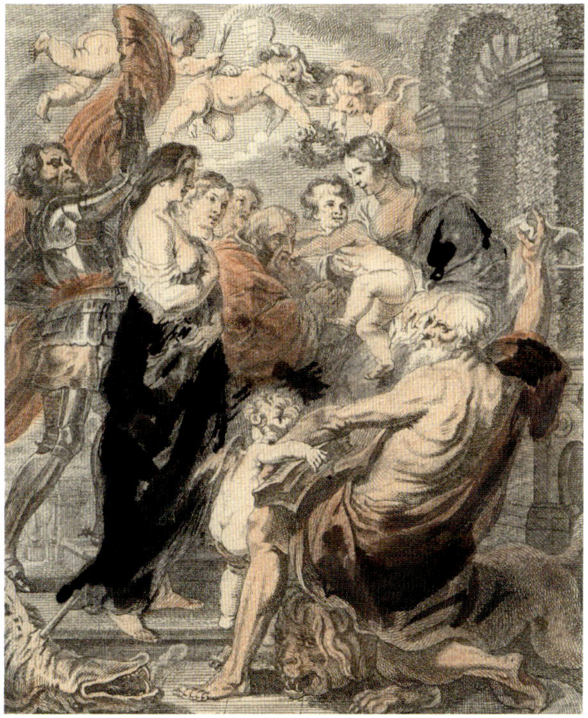

PROVENANCE: Sir Joshua Reynolds (1723–92; Lugt 2364 verso), Harry Phillips, London, 12 March 1798, part of lot 640 as '4 [prints] from Rubens, retouched by Sir Joshua Reynolds, with remarks on the margin'; Sir Lawrence Thomas (1769–1830; Lugt 2446); William Russell (1800–84), Christie's, London, 12 December 1884, lot 217, from whom purchased through Alphonse Wyatt Thibaudeau in 1884.

EXHIBITION HISTORY: None.

LITERATURE: C G Voorhelm Schneevoogt, *Catalogue des estampes gravées d'après P.P. Rubens, avec l'indication des collections où se trouvent les tableaux et les gravures* (Haarlem: Les Héritiers Loosjes, 1873), p.70, no.49; Laurence Binyon, *Catalogue of drawings by British artists… in the Department of Prints and Drawings in the British Museum* (London: Trustees of the British Museum, 1902), vol.III, p.198, no.11; F W H Hollstein, *Dutch and Flemish etchings, engravings and woodcuts, c.1450–1700: Douffet-Floris* (Amsterdam: Menno Hertzberger, 1952), vol.VI, p.206; Harry Mount (ed.), *Sir Joshua Reynolds: A journey to Flanders and Holland* (Cambridge: Cambridge University Press, 1996), p.77, plate ix; Giovanna Perini, 'Sir Joshua Reynolds and Italian art and art literature: A study of the sketchbooks in the British Museum and Sir John Soane's Museum, *Journal of the Warburg and Courtauld Institutes*, 51 (1988), pp.141–68 (162).

REYNOLDS KNEW WELL THE PAINTING that this print reproduces; it decorates the altar of Rubens' own family chapel in the St-Jacobskerk, Antwerp. He saw it in 1781 on his journey to the Low Countries. Reynolds cited two prints he knew after the Rubens panel, one by Paulus Pontius (1603–58) and this print by Eynhoudts that 'has more of the [true] effect of the picture'.[167] This suggests a wide familiarity with reproductive printmaking.

Drawings by Reynolds himself were not normally stamped with his collector's mark. Perhaps the coloured reworkings Reynolds added to this print were thought to be by an Old Master (conceivably, even Rubens himself, who is known to have corrected proofs of prints after his work). This impression, a counterproof, would have facilitated this since this would 'correct' the normal reversal of the printed image with respect to the original source, allowing a direct comparison. The areas of darkest wash correspond to the darkest areas of Rubens's work, and the red tints, such as the swirling banner, to the areas of red paint on the panel. The annotations (such as 'virgin dark blue/sky grey') might have been made *in situ* and the reworkings in wash added separately afterwards while the image of the picture, and its tonalities, were fresh in Reynolds's mind.

CAT. 84

James Basire
(1730–1802)
after William Aikman
(1682–1731)
James Thomson
(1761)
engraving with etching,
27.8 x 20.7 cm
Fitzwilliam Museum,
Cambridge (P.6485-R)

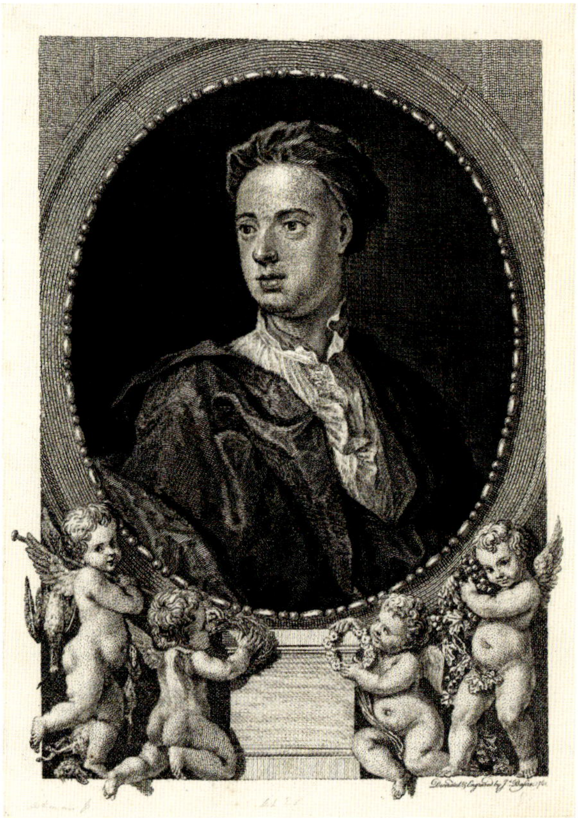

PROVENANCE: Sir Joshua Reynolds (1723–92; Lugt 2364 verso); Earls of Northwick; Colnaghi, London, purchased in 1930 by John Charrington (1856–1939; Lugt 572), by whom presented in 1933.

EXHIBITION HISTORY: None.

LITERATURE: Freeman O'Donoghue, *Catalogue of engraved British portraits preserved in the Department of Prints and Drawings in the British Museum* (London: Trustees of the British Museum, 1914), vol.IV (S–Z), p.273, no.1.

CONTEMPORARY WORK SAT ALONGSIDE much older material in Reynolds's graphic collection. Such eighteenth-century Italian painters as Donato Creti (1671–1749), Giovanni Antonio Guardi (c.1689–1760) and Giovanni Battista Marcola (1711–80) were represented by fine drawings, and some, such as Antonio Maria Zanetti the Elder (1680–1767), with both prints and drawings. Hudson, too, had modern work in his collection, such as drawings by the sculptor Michael Rysbrack (1694–1770), who was also an important collector of Old Master prints and drawings.

Reynolds owned a variety of portrait prints, from the flashy self-portrait *Baccio Bandinelli* by Niccolò della Casa (c.1544),[168] to the reserved *Jan Lutma* by Rembrandt (CAT. 73). He also owned the elaborate portrait engraving of *Louis Dauphin de Bourgogne* by Pierre Drevet (1663–1738) after Hyacinthe Rigaud (1659–1743) (1707; British Museum, London).[169] This print, after Aikman's painting, now in the Scottish National Portrait Gallery, Edinburgh, depicts the Scottish poet James Thomson (1700–48), author of *The Seasons*. Below the oval medallion, *putti* decorate Thomson's altar with floral tributes.

SIR JOSHUA REYNOLDS LEGACY

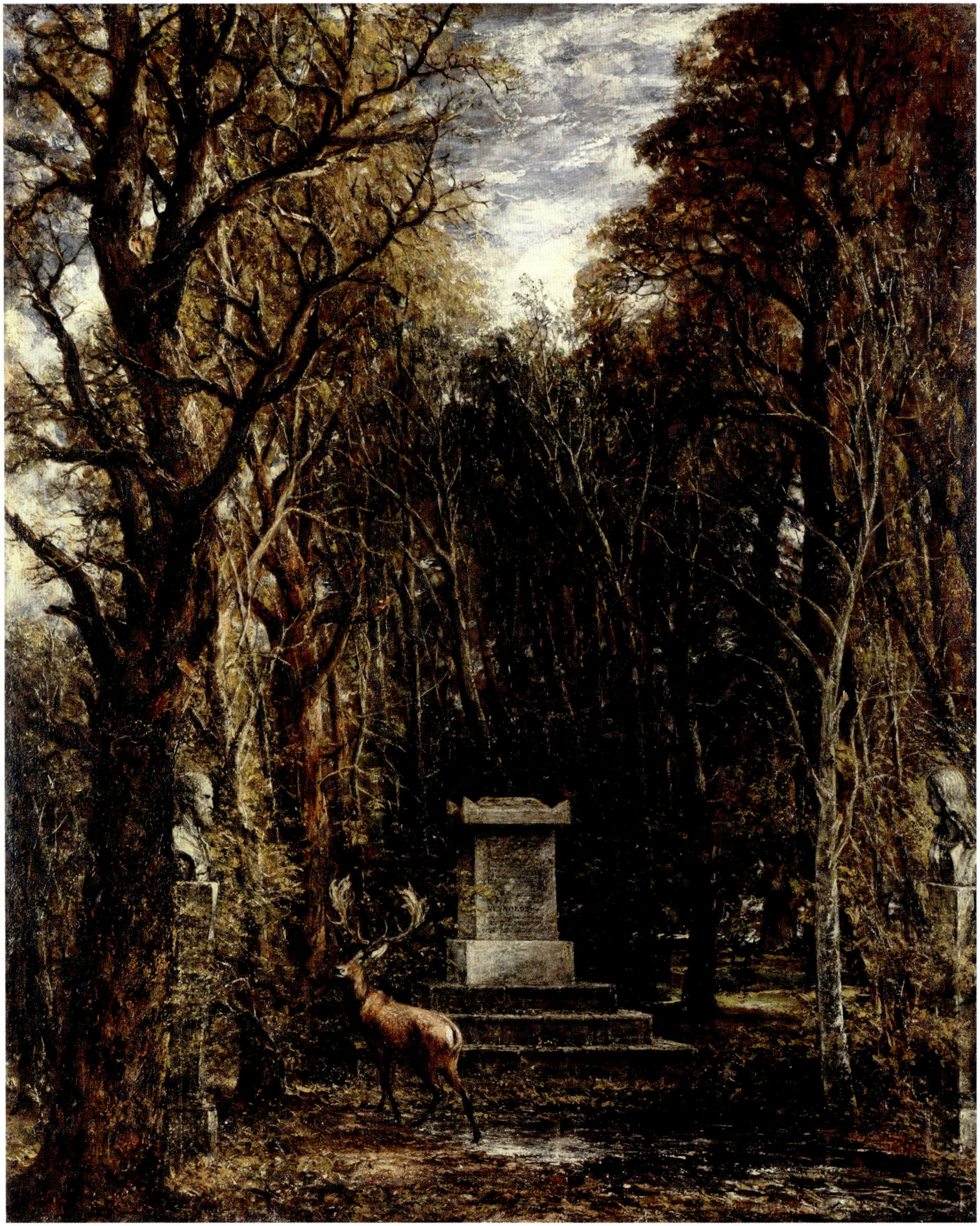

FIG. 35

John Constable
(1776–1837)
Cenotaph to the Memory of Sir Joshua Reynolds erected in the grounds of Coleorton Hall, Leicestershire, by the late Sir George Beaumont, Bt.
(1833–36)
oil on canvas,
132 x 108.5 cm

POSTHUMOUS FORTUNES

IN 1986, ON THE OCCASION OF A ROYAL Academy exhibition celebrating the career of its first President, the *Burlington Magazine* was explicit in its belief that the time was right for a Reynolds revival. At a moment when public funding for the arts was in short supply under a Conservative government, Reynolds, it was suggested, with his effortlessly simultaneous grasp of social politics, his practical craft, and all that had preceded him in the canon – 'artist'; 'connoisseur'; 'deeply clubbable' – was a talismanic figure, the protean character that 'every department and museum needs... a formidable champion of higher spending on the arts'. Indeed, the editorial continued, reflecting a particular academic preoccupation of the late twentieth century, Reynolds was the original interdisciplinary scholar, one who believed in the utmost necessity of viewing the principles of painting in the context of her literary, sister arts.[1] Thus Reynolds, in common with other cultural figures such as Shakespeare, or even Reynolds's own idol Michelangelo, has been reinvented by each subsequent generation in its own image. It is no coincidence, for example, that two decades on, another Reynolds retrospective placed his portraiture in the context of a concept of celebrity culture which is as much a part of our own consciousness as it was true of Georgian London.[2] Reynolds's own celebrity has remained a constant since his lifetime. In particular, contrary to the common misapprehension that Reynolds and the academic values for which he stood were ousted by successive nineteenth-century movements from the Romantics to Pre-Raphaelitism, the Victorian age loved Sir Joshua, the founder of the British art world which by that time prospered as never before.

FROM THE ROMANTICS TO THE VICTORIANS

From his death in 1792 to the mid-nineteenth century, Reynolds's reputation rested chiefly upon his presidency of the Royal Academy and his authorship of the *Discourses*. Through his role in life as a public figure, in death he was adopted as the figurehead for the improved social status of art during the crucial period of its transition from a gentrified luxury to a nationalist imperative. The first painter to be buried in St Paul's Cathedral, it was Reynolds's public office that earned him an ostentatious funeral, paid for by the Academy and its members, and a tomb in the company of other national heroes from British naval, military and literary history. Unlike Hogarth, Gainsborough or Romney, whose funerary monuments in the churchyards of their local parishes were paid for by family and friends, Reynolds's memorial statue in St Paul's was funded by the fruits of his intellect, by the sale of the copyright to Malone's *Life and Works of Sir Joshua Reynolds*.[3] And again, unlike the modest symbols of private affection erected in honour of his contemporaries, Reynolds's memorial traded on the future market value of a major public figure.

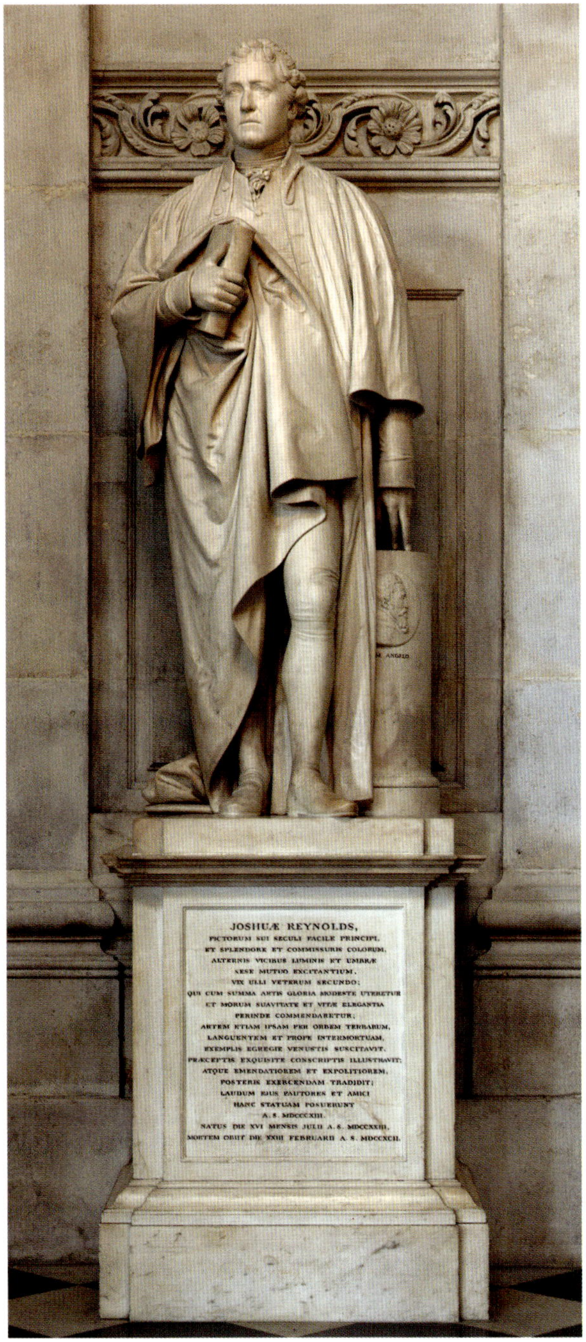

FIG. 36

John Flaxman
(1755–1826)
Memorial statue of Sir Joshua Reynolds
(1813)

The monument, executed by Flaxman (FIG. 36), celebrates this presidential image of Reynolds, the *Discourses* clasped prominently to his breast, his doctoral robes suggesting, as they do in his self-portraits (CAT. 33, p. 98), Reynolds's place in an intellectual tradition. Indeed, the full realisation of Reynolds's status as it was projected by his memorial statue came only posthumously. In 1813, the year Flaxman's sculpture was completed, Reynolds officially became an Old Master in the first of the British Institution's annual exhibitions of past art. 142 of his paintings went on public display, following an inaugural dinner at which the Prince Regent was seated below Flaxman's statue.[4] An important patron of Reynolds during his lifetime, the future George IV conferred royal status upon the artist after his death that was never forthcoming under George III, who famously preferred Benjamin West. Twenty of the twenty-three works by Reynolds now in the Royal Collection were bought by George IV, who also had the miniaturist Henry Bone make copies after his Reynolds collection.[5]

Broadly speaking, it was this establishment view of Reynolds which attracted his hostile critics during the nineteenth century, most famously Blake, Hazlitt and the Pre-Raphaelites. To be sure, Blake's marginalia in his copy of Malone's *Life and Works* in 1808 – 'Villainy! A Lie!' – disparaged the maxim of the Ideal which runs through the *Discourses* ('to Generalize is to be an Idiot'), but it was primarily the urbane luxury of Reynolds's life as a society portraitist that was out of step with the Romantic vision of creativity. Elsewhere, a letter to Thomas Butts has Blake agreeing with Reynolds's views on line and colour ('So Says Sir Joshua, and So say I').[6] Likewise, the youthful antipathy of the Pre-Raphaelites towards the Academy's first President – 'Sir Sloshua' (CAT. 90 and 91, p. 172) – was as much a rejection of academic convention under the sign of Reynolds, as it had to do with his loose style of painting alone. Later, some of the Pre-Raphaelites and their circle would call explicitly on Reynolds's influence, such as Julia Margaret Cameron's composition of her photographs around the organizing principles of the *Discourses*, or Millais's adoption of a Reynoldsian style in his bid to succeed him as the definitive British portrait painter.[7] And for

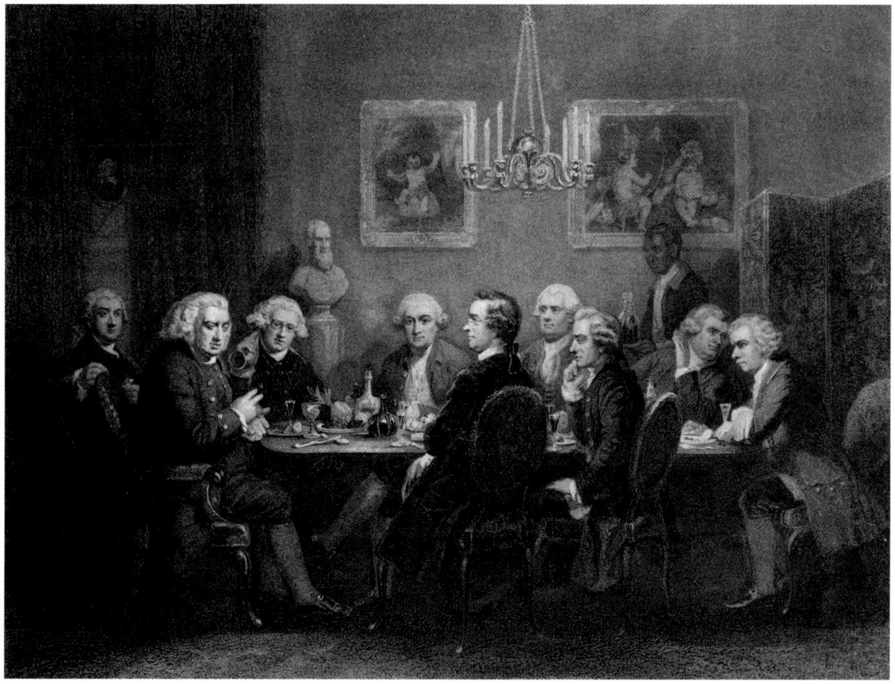

FIG. 37

William Walker
(1791–1867)
after James Doyle
A Literary Party at Sir Joshua Reynolds's
(c.1848)

all Hazlitt's denigrations of Reynolds's principle of the Ideal, pro-Reynoldsian opinion would pour forth from even the most progressive of literary organs, such as the *Athenaeum*, which in 1838 directed Hazlitt – rhetorically, of course, since he had been dead eight years – to the public baths or whipping-posts if his desire to see Nature was that urgent.[8]

Thus Reynolds can't easily be bracketed off from broad movements like Romanticism or Pre-Raphaelitism; he was the constant around which everything else was negotiated. The poetic lines that adorn the cenotaph to Reynolds at the country estate of the connoisseur Sir George Beaumont, erected in 1812, for example, were penned by Wordsworth, while Byron and Constable were in attendance at the inaugural banquet for Reynolds's posthumous exhibition at the British Institution in 1813.[9] Later, Constable's haunting image of Reynolds's cenotaph (FIG. 35) showed something of those mixed contexts. The autumnal, wooded scene, into which a stag has wandered, simultaneously suggests the Romantic turn to nature, a more gentrified view of British landscape, and the arcadian echoes of the Old Masters favoured by Reynolds and his generation, Poussin or Claude, or Raphael and Michelangelo, whose busts flank Reynolds's memorial. In the same period, the career of the young artist George Richmond reminds us, too, that membership of the Ancients, the circle of Blake and Palmer, or an apprenticeship with Fuseli, was not incompatible with an homage to Reynolds, as Richmond's youthful self-portrait with shaded eyes demonstrates (CAT. 89, p. 171).

By the mid-Victorian period, new attention was being paid to Reynolds's paintings, at the Manchester Art Treasures exhibition of 1857, for example, which included 52 of his works as part of its rubric to show off the British school in the company of the Old Masters loaned from aristocratic collections. British art was now presented as a mature tradition, with Reynolds as its grand patriarch. In 1861, when a memorial bust of Reynolds (CAT. 95, p. 177) was unveiled in Plymouth, the gathering included not only the descendants of his South West patrons, such as the Molesworths of Pencarrow, but John Ruskin and the art critic of *The Times,* Tom Taylor, who, as Reynolds's biographer, addressed the crowd.[10]

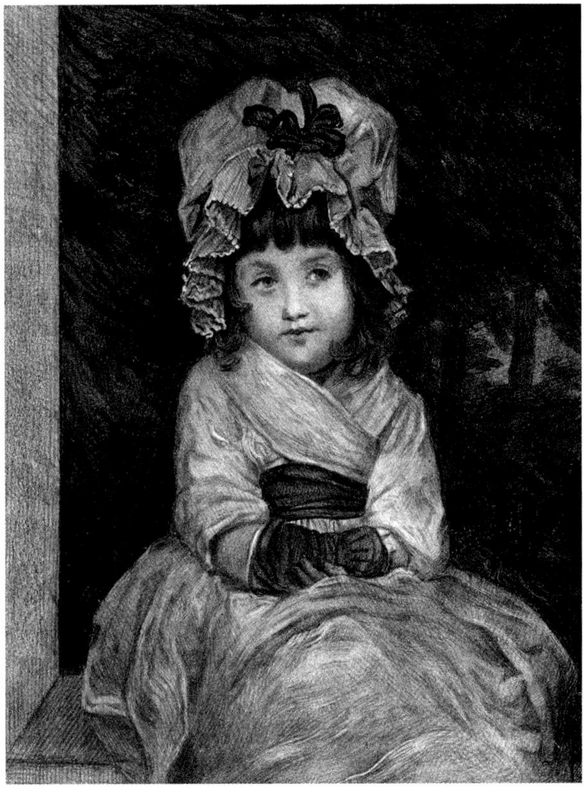

FIG. 38

Penelope Boothby by Sir Joshua Reynolds
from *The Portfolio* (1873)

Courtesy of the Victoria andAlbert Museum, London
© V&A Images

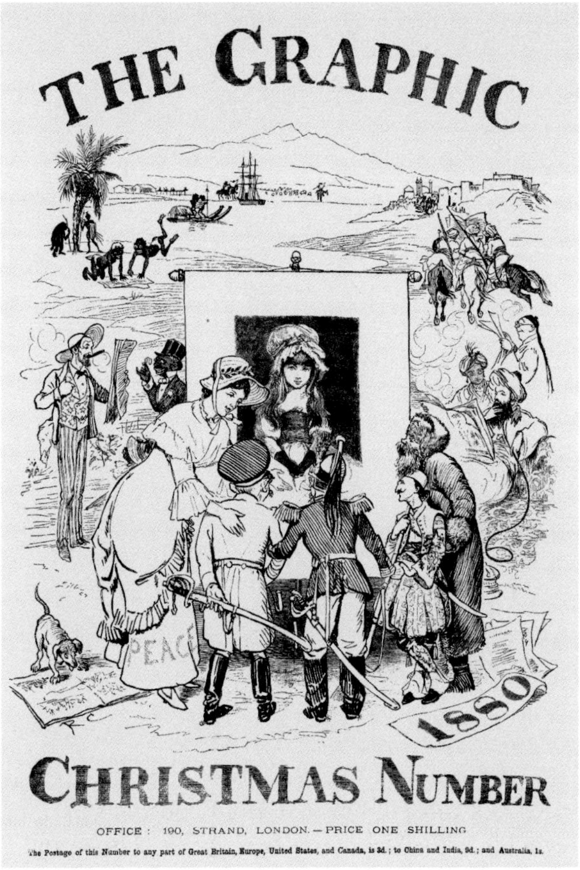

FIG. 39

Randolph Caldecott
(1846–86)
Cover design with Millais's 'Cherry Ripe'
from *The Graphic's Christmas Number* (1880)

Courtesy of the Victoria andAlbert Museum, London
© V&A Images

By 1883, Reynolds's cult of celebrity was such that a major retrospective exhibition of his works at the Grovesnor Gallery boasted a glass case of Sir Joshua's personal relics, including examples of his celebrated spectacles.[11]

THE VICTORIAN CULT OF THE CHILD

The reassessment of Reynolds as an artist during the middle decades of the nineteenth century rested particularly on his child portraits. Even during the 1820s, Reynolds's detractor William Hazlitt had praised the natural quality of Reynolds's children, in keeping with the broader Romantic interest in childhood as a state of innocence. Indeed, Reynolds's *The Age of Innocence* now at Tate Britain, of which several versions exist (CAT. 85, p. 168), was sold in 1844 for £1,596 at a time when the average adult portrait rarely fetched more than £100.[12] A decade later, the Marquis of Hertford paid £2,205 for *The Strawberry Girl*, or, as it was reported by the *Illustrated London News*, forty-two times its original price.[13] All three of Lord Hertford's portraits by Reynolds – *The Strawberry Girl*, *Nellie O'Brien* and *Miss Bowles Caressing Her Dog* – were the toast of the Manchester Art Treasures exhibition the following year.[14] This new image of Reynolds as the painter of children also found its way into the genre scenes of his life that were an essential part of the revival of an Old Master in the nineteenth century. John James Chalon's *Sir Joshua Reynolds Painting a Fancy Portrait of a Child* (CAT. 88), for example, takes the Royal Collection's late self-portrait (CAT. 34, p. 100) as its model for the bespectacled Reynolds – a softer, more human image of the artist – as does another genre picture from the same period, James Doyle's *A Literary Party at Sir Joshua Reynolds's* (FIG. 37). Here, the fashionable connection between Reynolds and his child portraits is made by the inclusion of two particularly celebrated examples – *Puck* and *The Infant Academy* – which hang on the wall behind the artist and his fellow members of The Club.

The appeal of Reynolds's children lay in their evocation of a rosy, Edenic England before the Industrial Revolution, an idealised world in which children, whether genteel or countrified, were content in the simplicity of the social order. When *The Graphic* reproduced Reynolds's *The Infant Academy* in 1871, for example, it extended that rhetoric to the Royal Academy itself, contrasting its modern politics with Reynolds's idyllic scene in which there was 'no Hanging Committee', the only membership requirement being:

> *you should be about three feet high, and about three years old, you should have delightfully plump legs and arms, and you should be accustomed to mix in society in a very undress condition...*[15]

The shift in Reynolds's image from public official to a more sensitive, emotionally intelligent artist, in touch with nature through his special relationship with children, was not only played out in the sale-rooms or the popular press. In 1867, F.G. Stephens – the unlikeliest of critics to turn to Reynolds, perhaps, once a founding member of the Pre-Raphaelite brotherhood – published an art historical account of Reynolds's child portraits in the context of the Old Masters. If Fra Angelico's children were too angelic, Raphael's too childish and Murillo's too coarse, only Reynolds surpassed the examples of Velázquez and Rubens as the painter of 'childhood proper'. Reynolds's historical portraits in the grand style, however, are given short shrift on account of their allegiance to the seventeenth-century Baroque, to Domenichino, Guido Reni and Guercino, an epoch of art history that by Stephens's day was seen as mannered and overblown. Thus Mrs Siddons's 'Tragic Muse' is only a 'boarding-school girl's notion of the character'; or like 'a lady-housewife, who, having quarrelled with her servants, is too well bred to be loud in her rage'. Only Reynolds's children, thinks Stephens, invoking the by-then familiar tropes, have the natural touch, suggestive of all that he portrayed best: the 'poetry of home, of gentleness, refinement, education', in short, of 'civilisation'.[16]

THE FIN-DE-SIÈCLE

By the last decades of the nineteenth century, that utopian image of the eighteenth century as a Golden

Age of British life had blossomed into a full-scale revival of all things Georgian with Reynolds as its leading example. Sheridan's *The School for Scandal* was revived at the Prince of Wales Theatre, Ellen Terry took the lead role in a new adaptation of Goldsmith's *The Vicar of Wakefield*, and Reynolds's portraits of well-heeled young ladies, in particular, offered a reassuring picture of British prosperity at a time of economic slowdown during the agricultural depression that took root around 1873. Kate Greenaway and John Everett Millais dressed the young protagonists of their book illustrations in mob-caps, while Millais's portrait, *Cherry Ripe*, of 1879, consciously revived Reynolds's *Miss Penelope Boothby*, which had enjoyed widespread popularity after its appearance at the Royal Academy's exhibition of Old Masters in 1871 and its reproduction in *The Portfolio* in 1873 (FIG. 38, p. 164). By appropriating Reynolds, Millais promoted the strength of the British Empire, protector of its female subjects – appropriately sentimentalised – and thus its future, but also the strength of the British art tradition to which he now aspired (FIG. 39).[17]

Indeed, Reynolds offered a useful model for artists' ambitions regarding the canon's living embodiment, the Royal Academy, of which Millais was finally elected President in 1896 during the last months of his life, having followed in Reynolds's footsteps to become Britain's leading society portraitist. During the same period, John Singer Sargent also made his name as an overtly Reynoldsian portrait painter who famously remade contemporary generations of aristocratic families, such as the Marlboroughs of Blenheim, in the image of their forebears as they were painted by Reynolds. Sargent brought a new edge to the nostalgic image of the eighteenth-century child that proved especially marketable, endowing his young girls with a savvy appropriate to the era of the New Woman. Not all critics appreciated the shift, however, D.S. MacColl bridling at the frank authority of one seven-year-old sitter, Victoria Stanley, with her bright red coat and riding crop. 'Imagine,' he wrote, 'a portrait of Little Red Riding Hood by the Wolf.'[18] By the end of his life, Sargent executed the ultimate career manoeuvre by being the only living artist to have his work enter the National Gallery on the back of his Reynolds period. 'Well done,' intones a chorus of Old Masters in a contemporary *Punch* cartoon (FIG. 40), including Reynolds and Velázquez, who gather to greet Sargent as he mounts the Gallery's steps. 'You're the first… to break the rule and get in here alive.'[19]

Beyond the individual elements of Reynolds's achievement, then, the *Discourses*, his portraits, the ease with which he negotiated eighteenth-century society in all its aspects, his lasting legacy seems to have been the model he provided for a British artistic tradition, one which could at last envisage itself, even as it was in the making, as a canon in perpetuity. This aspect of Reynolds's *fortuna* is nowhere better demonstrated than by the fin-de-siècle's obsession with Reynoldsiana, with objects that bore the double aura of having once belonged to him but also to his successors as these mascots were passed down from one Academy President to another. Thus the fin-de-siècle not only saw the maturing of the Reynolds revival, with the appearance of an unprecedented number of biographies or new editions of the *Discourses* with contemporary commentaries, such as Roger Fry's edition of 1906, but also a new level of memorialisation in the context of the Royal Academy's own maturation. When Frederic Leighton presented the sitter's chair from Reynolds's studio to the Academy in 1879, for example, its value was redoubled by its provenance, since Reynolds's day, as the successive property of five further Presidents of the Royal Academy.[20] Reynolds's chair was later joined on 10 December 1898, the 130th anniversary of the Academy's founding date, by his silver tea caddy. Inside the lid of this reliquary-like object was placed an engraved plate on which an illustrious register of Royal Academicians, including Poynter, Thornycroft and Sargent, paid homage to Reynolds's legacy. These were no longer simply relics of Reynolds the man, but of the British art world he had set in motion.

FIG. 40

The Young Master
from *Punch, or the London Charivari*
(17 January 1923)

Courtesy of The Bodleian Library, University of Oxford (N.2706 d.10)

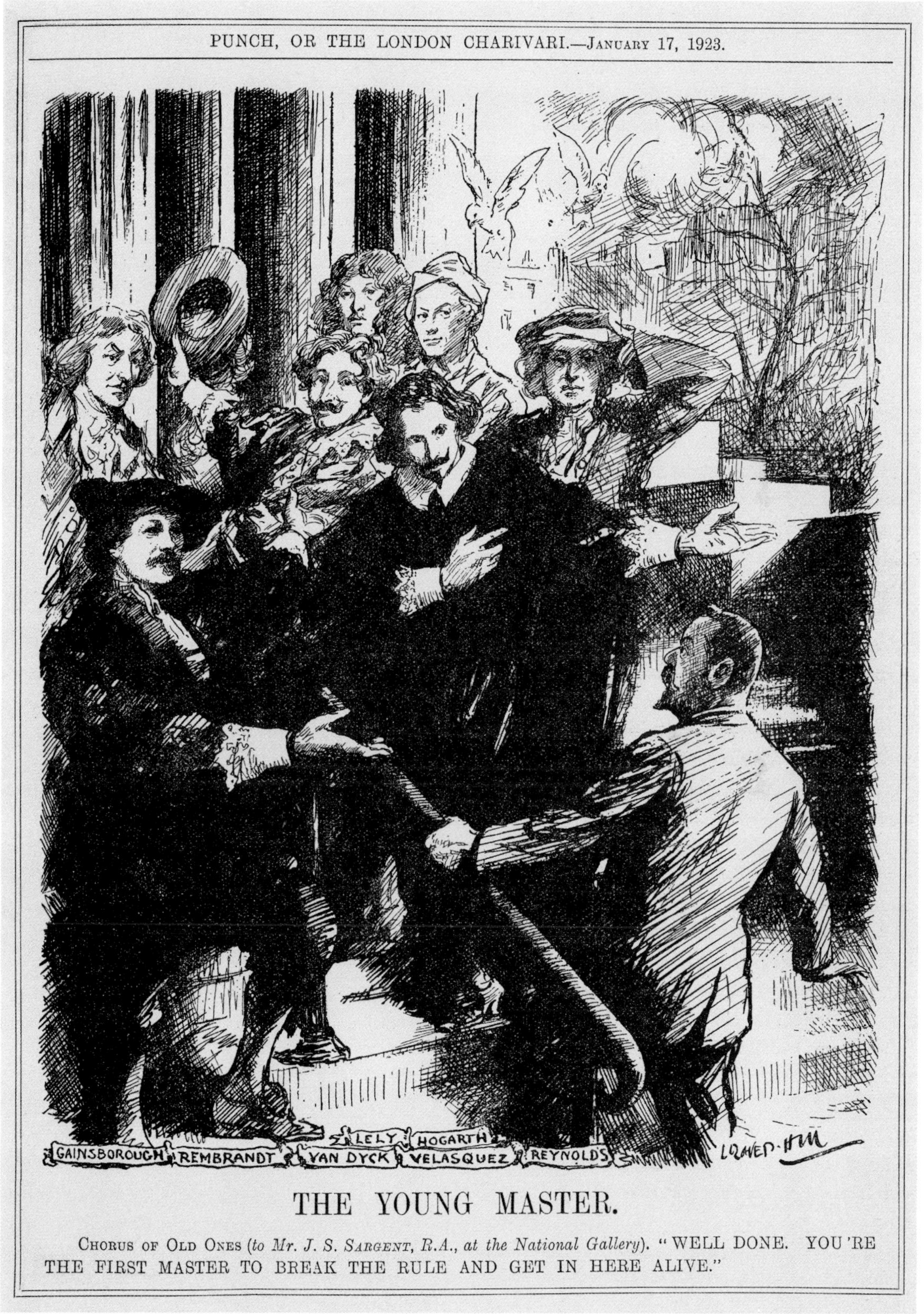

ARTISTIC RESPONSES AND REYNOLDSANIA

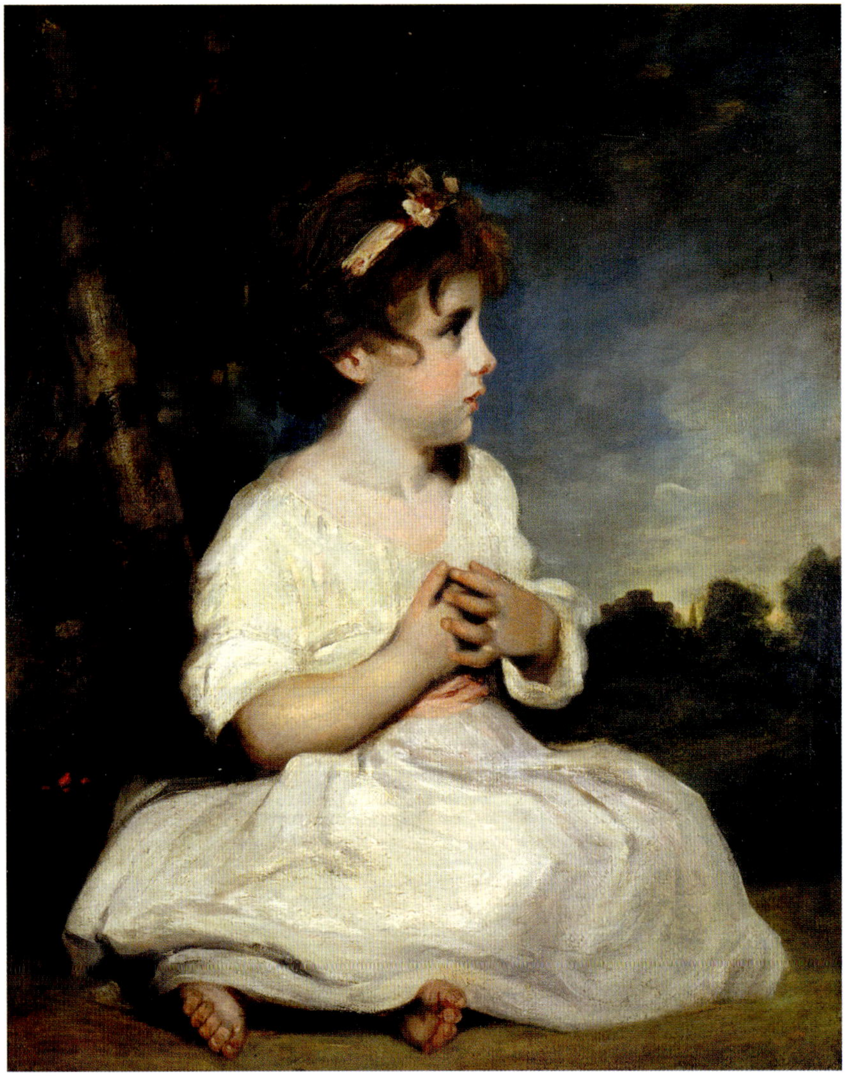

CAT. 85

The Age of Innocence
(c.1785–88)
oil on canvas, 75.5 x 63 cm
Plymouth City Museum and Art Gallery: Plympton St Maurice Guildhall

PROVENANCE: Charles Long, 1st Baron Farnborough (1760–1838), Paymaster-General and connoisseur, by c.1788; by descent to Colonel S Long; Christie's, 11 May 1882 (156), bought in by his daughter, the Hon. Mrs R M W Dawson; by descent to her daughter, Norah Phoebe Dawson; Christie's, 1 March 1946 (68), bought in; bequeathed by Miss Calmady Hamlyn to Plymouth Corporation to hang in the Old Town Hall; transferred to Plymouth City Museum and Art Gallery, 1984.

EXHIBITION HISTORY: Paris, 1985 (64); Royal Academy, 1986 (145); Bath, 1989 (45).

LITERATURE: Graves and Cronin, vol.3, p.1130; p.1480; Hudson, 1958, p.125; exh. cat. RA, 1986, p.317–18; Mannings, 1986, p.762; Mannings, 2000, p.508.

THE PRECISE DATE OF THIS PAINTING IS not known nor the identity of the sitter, who seems to be five or six years old. The child has often been assumed to be Reynolds's great-niece Theophila 'Offy' Gwatkin (1782–1844). This would give an approximate date of 1788 for the picture.

No painting entitled *The Age of Innocence* was exhibited by Reynolds; the present title derives from the reproduction of this subject as an engraving in 1794, two years after his death. It has been suggested that a picture with the title *A Little Girl* exhibited by Reynolds at the Royal Academy in 1785 may represent the same composition. If so, Offy being

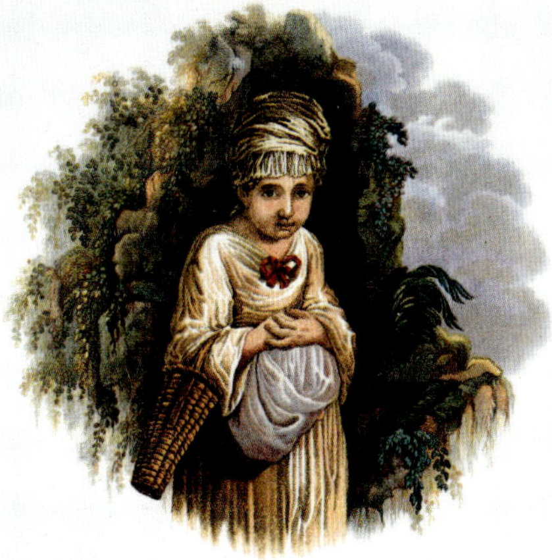

CAT. 86

after Sir Joshua Reynolds
The Strawberry Girl
(mid-nineteenth century)
earthenware tile, 15.3 x 15.3 x 0.8 cm
Fitzwilliam Museum, Cambridge (GPL.180–1928)

only three, another child must have sat to the artist. This picture became one of Reynolds's best known works when one version of it – in rather poor condition – was presented to the National Gallery in 1847 (transferred to Tate in 1951). The painting shown here is probably the version closest to Reynolds's intentions. It was exchanged by Reynolds himself with the collector Charles Long for a *Triumph of Venus* by one of Reynolds's favourite Old Masters, Giulio Romano, which Long had bought in Bologna.

During the nineteenth century, *The Age of Innocence* enjoyed particular fame alongside *The Strawberry Girl* as one of the best-known of Reynolds's child portraits. According to the National Gallery's Annual Reports for the period 1856–93, not only were Reynolds's children the most popular of his subject pictures among copyists at the Gallery, but *The Age of Innocence* was its most copied British picture in the period, with 323 entries to 253 for Turner's *The Fighting Temeraire*, or only 46 for Constable's *The Haywain* (Mannings, p.505).

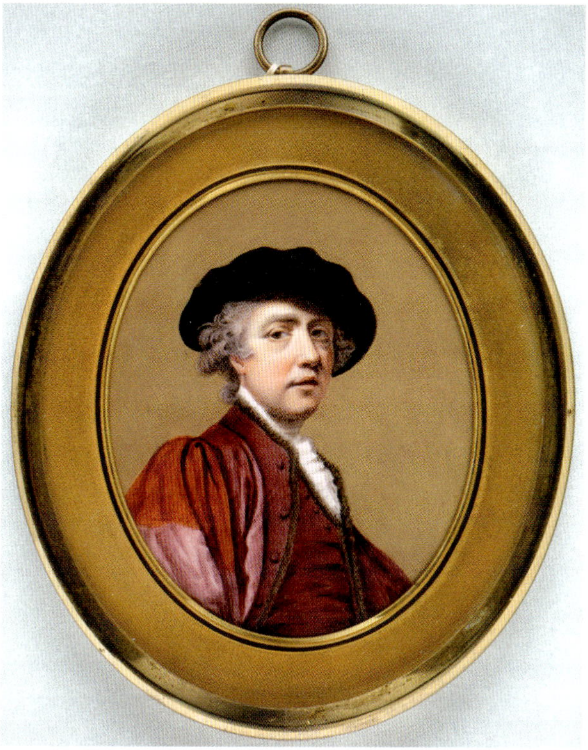

CAT. 87

Sarah, Countess of Essex
(c.1766–1838)
after Henry Bone
(1755–1834)
after Joshua Reynolds
Portrait of Joshua Reynolds (Self-Portrait)
(1806)
enamel, 9 x 7 cm
Musée du Louvre, Paris (RF 30884)

KNOWLEDGE OF REYNOLDS'S PAINTINGS was not only spread during successive generations by the many engravings after his work but by enamel reproductions and miniatures. Reynolds's contemporary Henry Bone, also a West Country artist, specialised in this genre, producing many copies after Reynolds for the Prince Regent and others after the artist's death. The present example, modelled directly on Bone's miniature of Reynolds's famous Royal Academy self-portrait, demonstrates that Reynolds's image as President of the Royal Academy was already iconic by 1806.

CHALON'S GENRE SCENE WAS PROBABLY painted for the Sketching Society which met in the evenings to draw specially selected historical or literary subjects. By the Victorian age, Reynolds's status as the definitive Old Master of the British school is underlined by the number of genre scenes after his life which were made in this period, including Angelica Kauffman visiting Reynolds's studio or Reynolds at Gainsborough's deathbed. Chalon represents Reynolds in his best-loved role at this time, however, as the painter of children, his sympathetic appearance based on the late self-portrait in the Royal Collection (CAT. 34, p. 100).

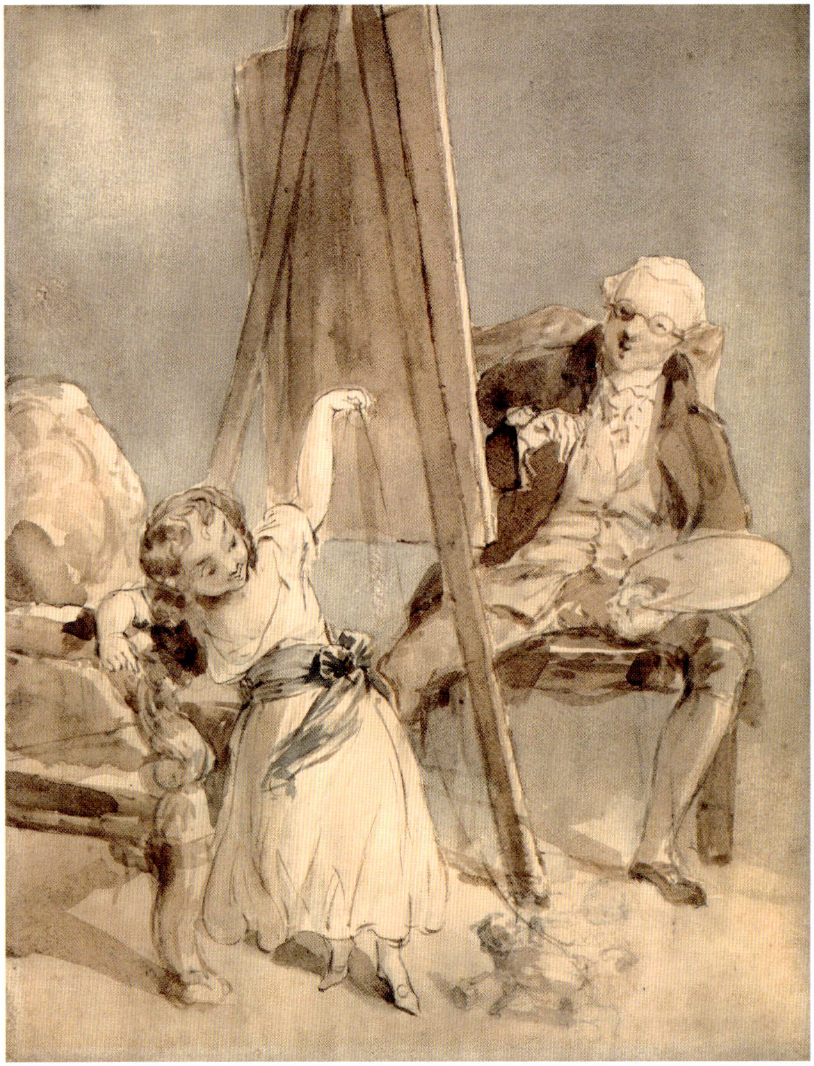

CAT. 88

John James Chalon
(1778–1854)
Sir Joshua Reynolds painting a fancy picture
(undated)
brush in grey, brown, black and blue wash over graphite sketch, 45.5 x 35.5 cm
British Museum, London

PROVENANCE: Christopher Pouncey; Henry Moore-Gwyn, from whom purchased in 2007 with funds from the Friends of Prints and Drawings.

EXHIBITION HISTORY: British Museum, 2007, 'Prints and Drawings: Recent Acquisitions'.

LITERATURE: None.

RICHMOND WAS A BRITISH PAINTER who trained at the Royal Academy Schools where he first met Samuel Palmer, with whom he formed 'The Ancients', specialising in works after Blake's visionary manner. Richmond's homage to Reynolds comes at the beginning of his later career as one of the leading portraitists of the Victorian period, a role in which he would naturally turn to Reynolds as a worthy exemplar (compare CAT. 32, p. 96).

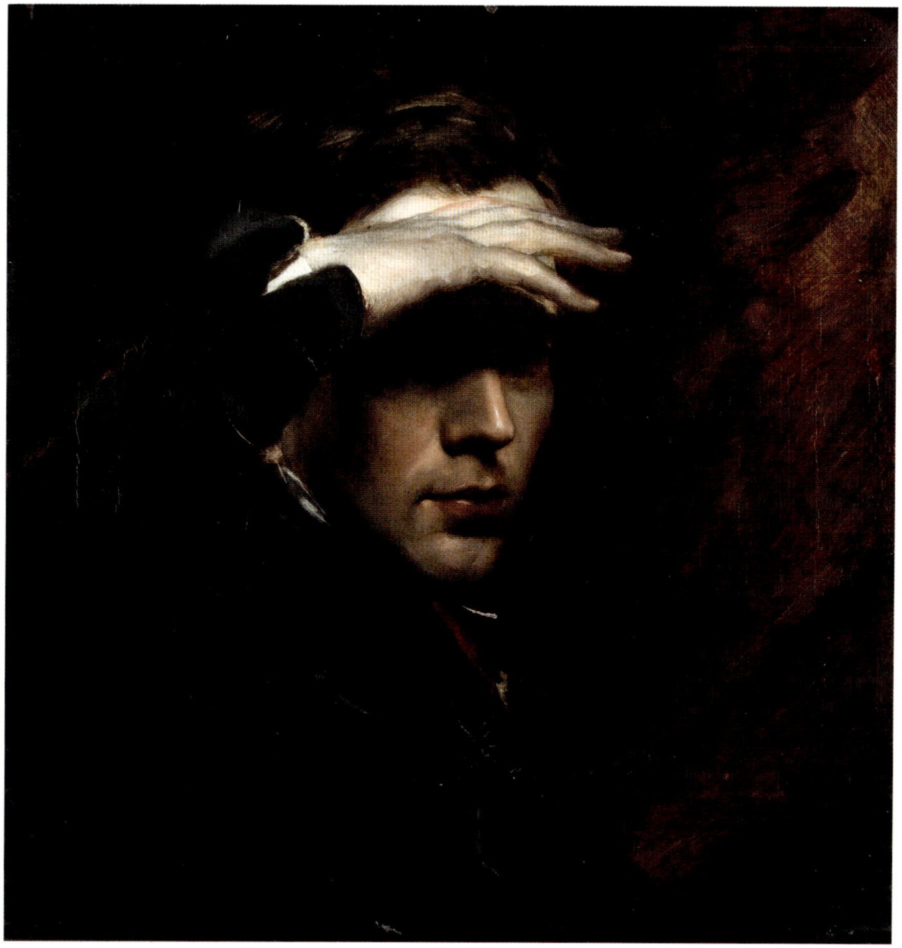

CAT. 89

George Richmond
(1809–96)
Self-Portrait
(1840)
oil on canvas, 40.9 x 40.6 cm
Fitzwilliam Museum, Cambridge (PD.179–1975)

PROVENANCE: The artist's daughter-in-law, Jane Richmond; sold to Kerrison Preston (1884–1974); sale, Sotheby's, 20 March 1974 (30), withdrawn. Allocated under terms of settlement of death duties on the estate of Kerrison Preston, 1974.

EXHIBITION HISTORY: 1962, London, Arts Council, 'British Self-portraits' (79).

LITERATURE: J W Goodison, *Catalogue of Paintings in the Fitzwilliam Museum, Cambridge*, vol.3 (Cambridge: Cambridge University Press, 1977), p.208.

THE PRE-RAPHAELITES ARE NOTORIOUS for their youthful dismissal of Reynolds as 'Sir Sloshua' on account of his loose brushwork and the dark, discoloured state into which some of his works had fallen by the mid-nineteenth century. During his early career, Rossetti particularly followed Blake as a proponent of anti-academicism, acquiring one of Blake's notebooks in 1847 (now in the British Library) which abounds with humorous doodles and jibes at conventional artistic values. Rossetti's sketches are in the same satirical vein, Hunt agreeing wholeheartedly with Millais's rejection of some unworthy example as 'Slosh', a term which Rossetti also extended to Rubens, and much of the Louvre collection when he saw it in 1849.

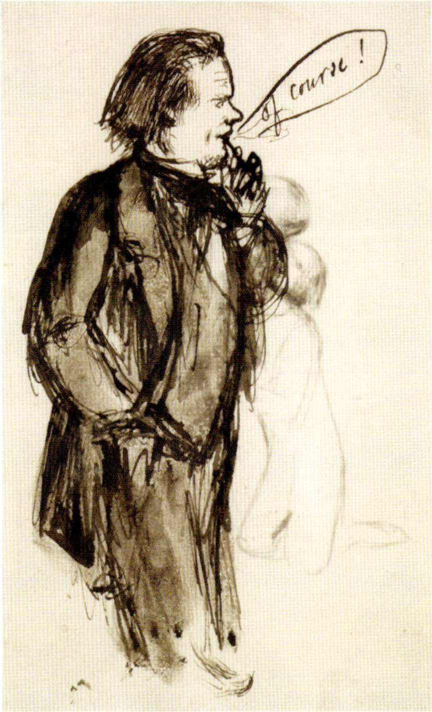

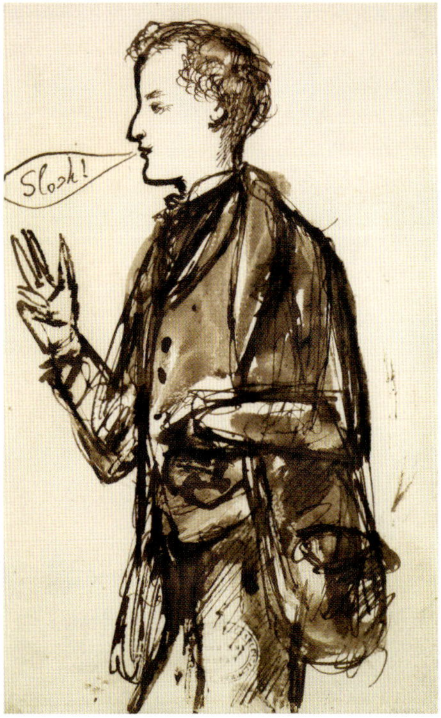

CAT. 90 and 91

Dante Gabriel Rossetti
(1828–82)
William Holman Hunt exclaiming 'Of course!'
(c.1851–53)
John Everett Millais exclaiming 'Slosh!'
(c.1851–53)
pen and brown ink with brown wash, 18 x 11.1 cm and 17.9 x 11.1 cm
Birmingham Museums and Art Gallery (1904P436 and 1904P437)

PROVENANCE: John Pollard Seddon (1827–1906), from whom purchased by Charles Fairfax Murray (1849–1919); from whom purchased in 1904.

EXHIBITION HISTORY: Birmingham Museum and Art Gallery 1947, no.203 (c); no.203 (b).

LITERATURE: Virginia Surtees, *The Paintings and Drawings of Dante Gabriel Rossetti (1828–1882): A Catalogue Raisonné*, 2 vols (Oxford: Clarendon Press, 1971), vol.I, pp.208–9, nos.591 and 592, vol.II, plate 434; Michaela Giebelhausen, *Painting the Bible: Representation and Belief in Mid-Victorian Britain* (Aldershot: Ashgate, 2006), pp.75–77.

APPENDIX

OTHER EXHIBITS

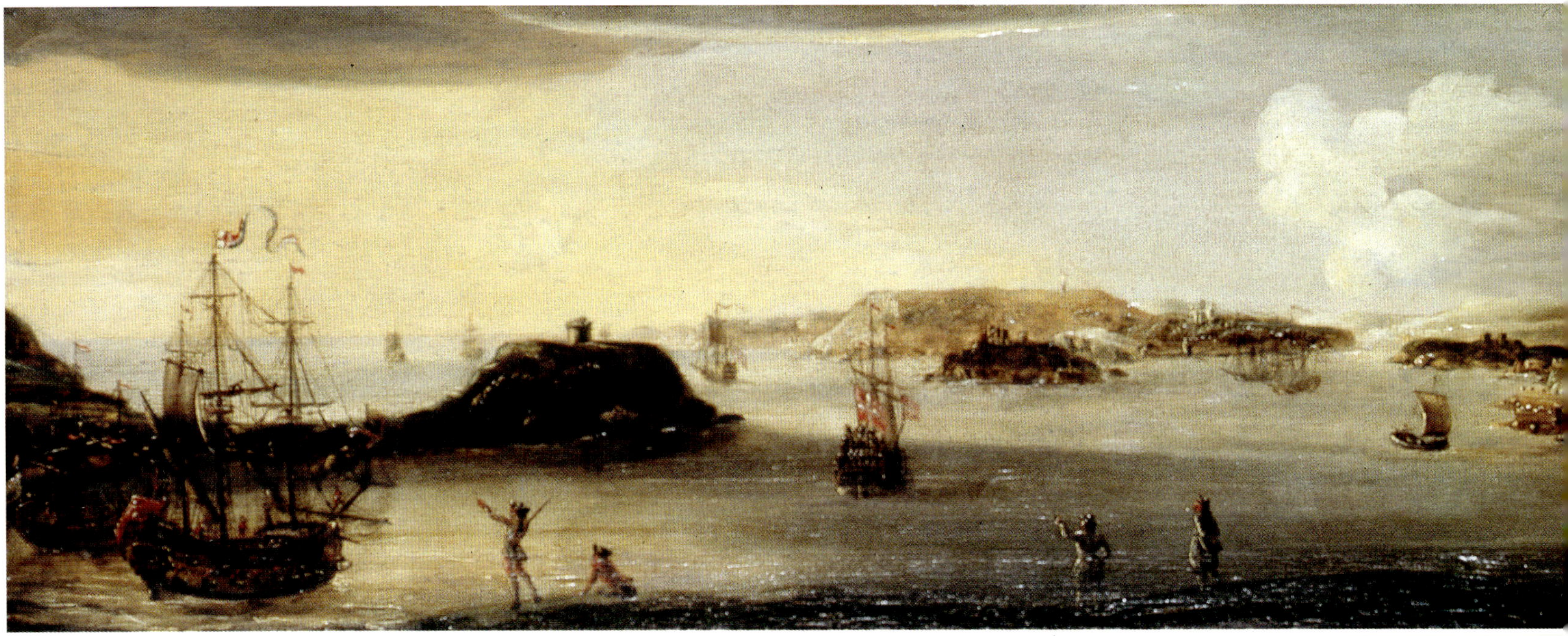

CAT. 92

A View of Plymouth Sound
(c.1748)
oil on panel, 26.6 x 137.2 cm
The Trustees of the Port Eliot Estate

PROVENANCE: By descent.

EXHIBITION HISTORY: 1873 Exeter, no.6.

LITERATURE: Cotton 1856, p.64; Leslie and Taylor, vol.1, p.34; F G Stephens, 1867, p.20; Graves and Cronin, vol.3, p.1235; *Country Life*, 5 November 1948; Hilles 1952, p.21.

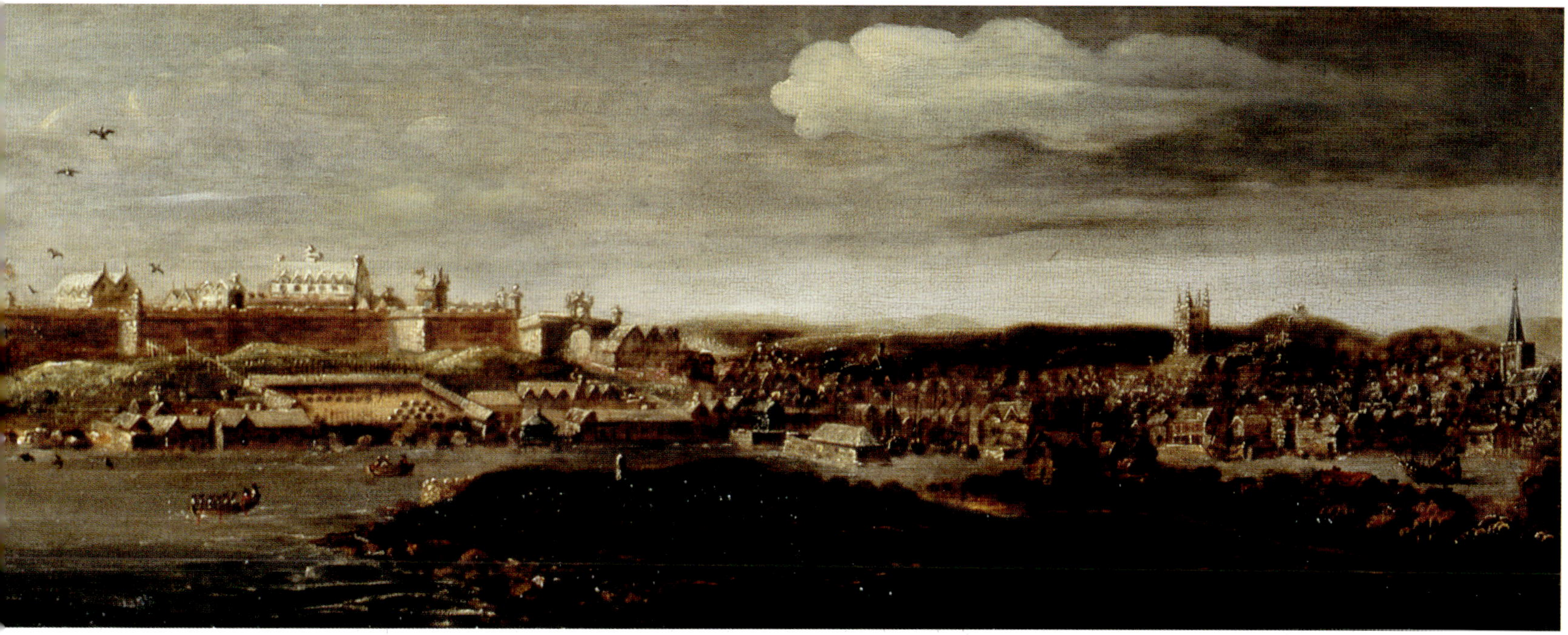

A VIEW OF PLYMOUTH SOUND HAS A LONG tradition of attribution to the young Reynolds before he left Devon for Italy in 1749. Of particular interest to successive generations of the Eliot family, since it shows a local and still identifiable panorama of the Plymouth estuary from Cattedown, the landscape is recorded at Port Eliot as a Reynolds in several nineteenth-century volumes including Charles Leslie and Tom Taylor's biography of the artist. Exhibited at the British Institution in 1823, it was later questioned by F G Stephens, for example, who thought it 'rather dry and poor in painting'.

IN HIS *LIFE OF SIR JOSHUA REYNOLDS* James Northcote, Reynolds's pupil, records that Reynolds, early in his career, benefitted from examining William Gandy's paintings in Devon collections, admiring particularly his treatment of the head. Reynolds seems to have been acquainted with some of Gandy's ideas, too, approving of his remarks about the need for a rich, creamy texture in the application of colour.[1] Reynolds was only six years old when Gandy died so must have been introduced to his works and observations by an intermediary, perhaps his master Thomas Hudson, who might conceivably have received some instruction from Gandy in his teens before leaving Devon for London.[2]

Gandy's father, James Gandy (1619–89) was a portrait painter who had studied with Van Dyck and William Gandy in his 'Notes on Painting' (c.1673–99) included observations on the technique of that artist, Peter Lely, Godfrey Kneller and others.[3] Having worked in Ireland and then in London, Gandy moved to Devon in about 1699 and painted local worthies in Exeter and Plymouth. Yet for all his abilities he failed to prosper. As an appendix to his biography of Reynolds, Northcote includes a moralising 'Memoir of William Gandy' relating how his abilities were squandered in Devon through a combination of fecklessness and vanity, the very opposite of Reynolds's industriousness and professionalism.

John Patch (1691–1746) is shown undertaking a dissection of the arm. He had trained in Paris, introduced the lithotomy procedure to the West of England and would later become one of the original surgeons of the Devon and Exeter Hospital which opened in 1743. The painting once carried a Latin inscription by the Exeter scholar William Musgrave in praise of both surgeon and artist as 'givers of life.' One of Patch's sons, Thomas Patch, although originally intended for a career in medicine, elected to become an artist instead, basing himself first in Rome and then in Florence (CAT. 96).

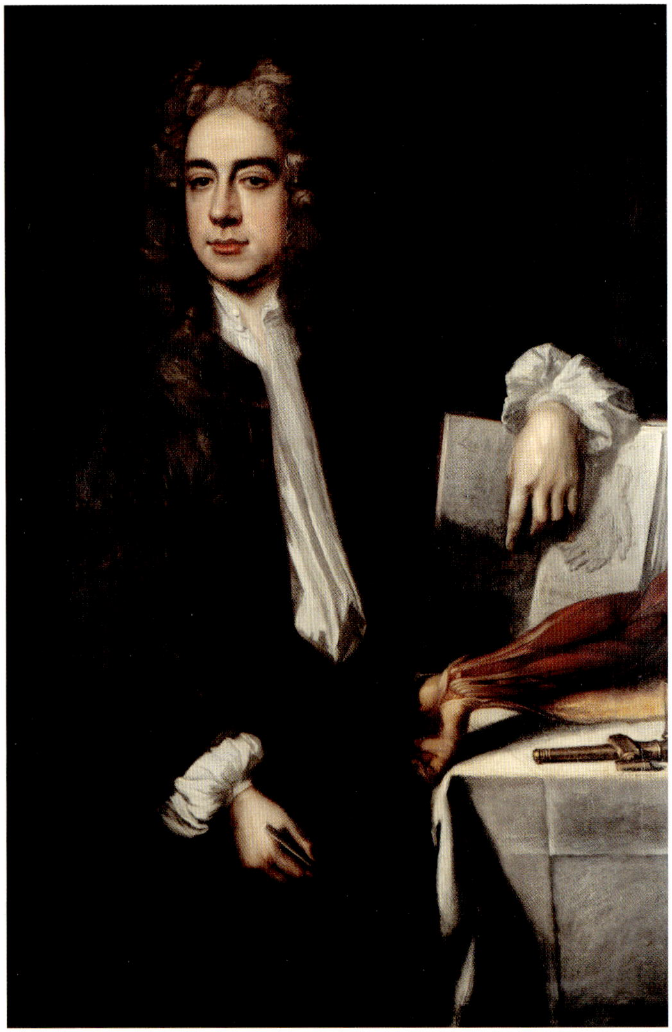

CAT. 93

William Gandy
(c.1655–1729)
John Patch
(1717)
oil on canvas, 120 x 81.3 cm
Royal Devon and Exeter NHS Foundation Trust

PROVENANCE: By descent; Presented to the Devon and Exeter hospital by John Patch jnr. in 1783.

EXHIBITION HISTORY: Royal Albert Memorial Museum, Exeter: 'Municipal Loan Exhibition of Portraits and Pictures', 1902 (22), 'Works by Early Devon Painters born before the year 1800', 1932 (218), 'English Painting 1560–1860 from the Museum's permanent and loan collections', 1968 (ex. catalogue).

LITERATURE: J. Delpratt Harris *The Royal Devon and Exeter Hospital, Exeter,* 1922, p.26; P.M.G. Russell *A History of the Exeter Hospitals 1170–1948*, Exeter 1976, p.40.

CAT. 94

Thomas Hudson
(1701–79)
The Admiral John Byng
(1749)
76.2 x 63.5 cm
National Maritime Museum, Greenwich, London

PROVENANCE: By descent to Edmund Henry Byng, sixth Earl of Strafford; presented by him in 1941 to the National Maritime Museum.

EXHIBITION HISTORY: None.

LITERATURE: Ellen Gross Miles 'Thomas Hudson (1701–79): Portraitist to the British Establishment' (PhD thesis, Yale University, 1976), no.29.

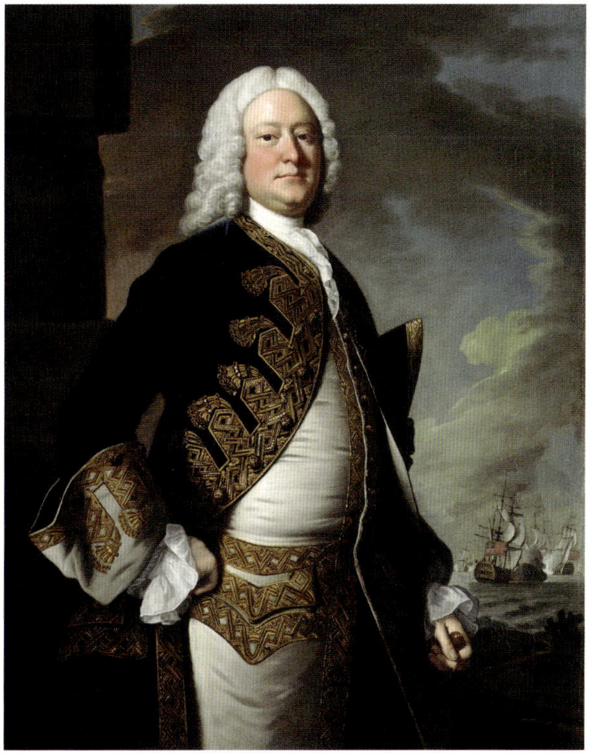

THOMAS HUDSON, WHO WAS REYNOLDS'S master, had himself studied under Jonathan Richardson the Elder. He was the leading portrait painter of the previous generation to Reynolds and *The Honourable John Byng* is a good example of his style, the model Reynolds would have looked to in his early portraits.

The Honourable John Byng (1704–57), the fifth son of Admiral Viscount Torrington, had risen to the rank of Admiral largely through his connections rather than demonstrating any ability to command in battle. In 1756 he was ordered to relieve Menorca, which was under French blockade, but failed to break the siege. Recalled to England, he was court-martialled for neglecting his duty and executed by firing squad on the quarterdeck of his flagship.

CAT. 95

William Behnes
(1794–1864)
after Giuseppe Ceracchi
(1751–1801)
Bust of Sir Joshua Reynolds PRA
(1860)
marble, on a base of scagliola, height 68.5 cm
Plymouth City Museum and Art Gallery: Cottonian Collection

PROVENANCE: Commissioned by William Cotton and presented to the Plymouth and Cottonian Library on 22 July 1861.

EXHIBITION HISTORY: Plymouth 1992 (31a).

LITERATURE: Mannings, 2000, p.591.

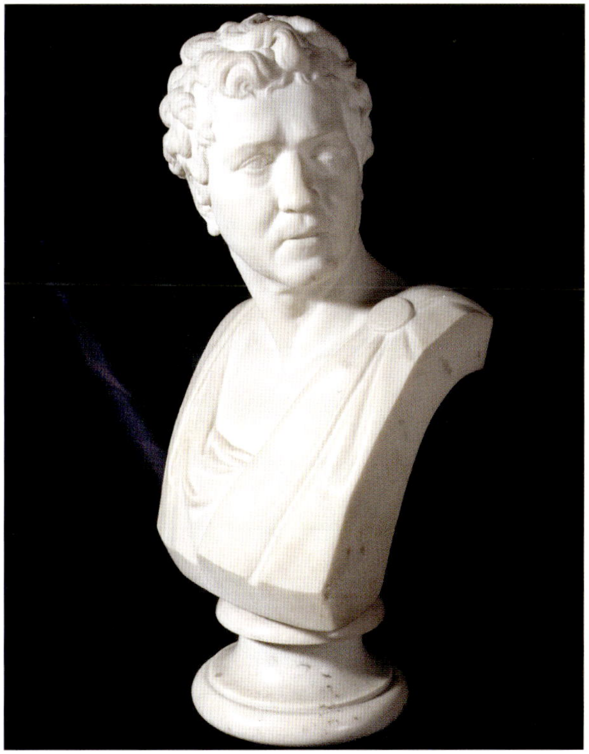

THIS BUST COMMISSIONED BY WILLIAM Cotton (1795–1863), a great admirer of Reynolds, was placed on view along with the rest of his collection of Reynolds-related material in the Proprietary Library in Cornwall Street, Plymouth. It is derived from the bust of Reynolds made by Giuseppe Ceracchi (c.1778–79).

CAT. 96

Thomas Patch
(1725–82)
A Caricature Group in Florence
(c.1760)
oil on canvas,
83.6 x 118.7 cm
Royal Albert Memorial Museum, Exeter

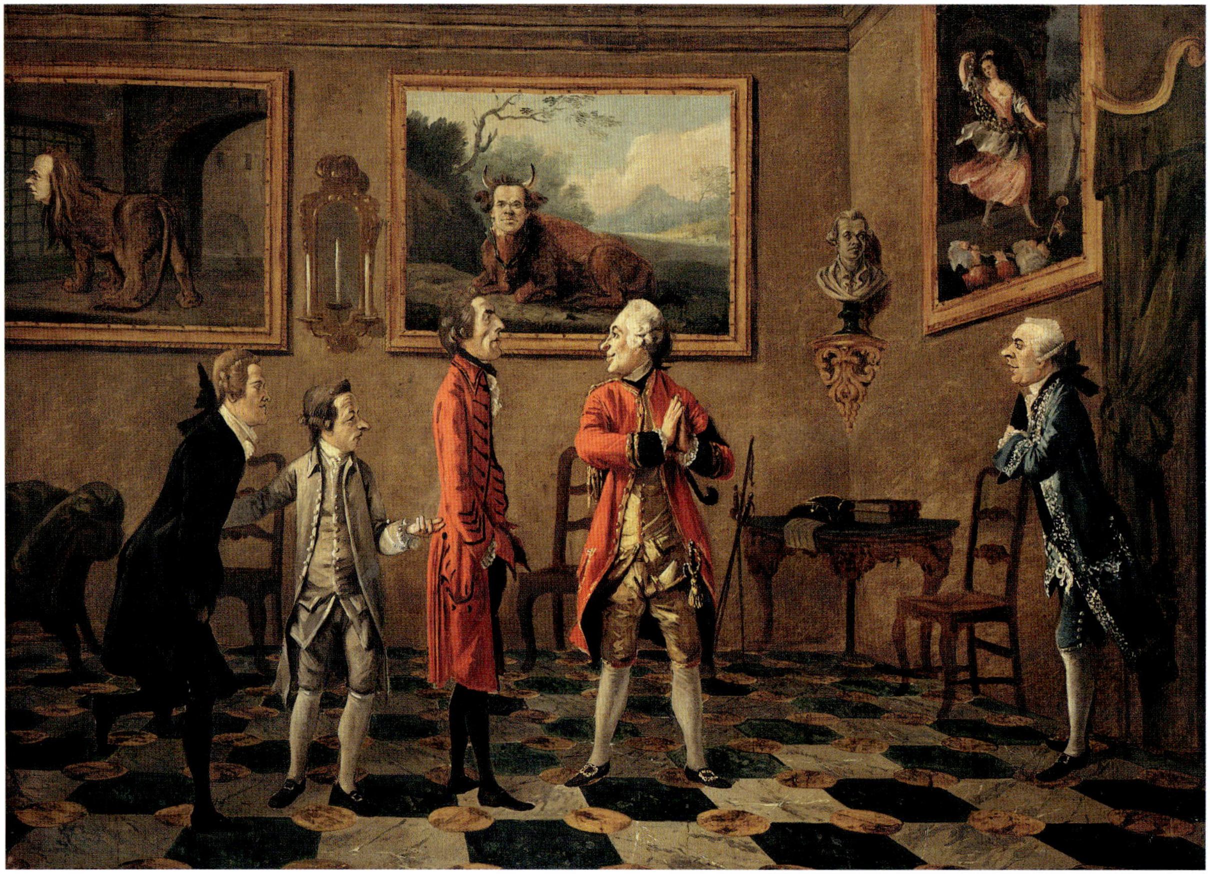

PROVENANCE: By 1864 in collection of Sir Peyton Estoteville Skipwith, Bt (1857–91); by descent to Sir S E Skipwith, Bt; Charles Ricketts, RA; M. Knoedler & Co 1932; Presented to the Royal Albert Memorial Museum & Art Gallery, Exeter (RAMM) by the National Art Collections Fund 1935.

EXHIBITION HISTORY: Agnew's London, 1929 (7); RAMM, 'Works by Early Devon Painters born before the year 1800', 1932 (236); RA, 'Winter Exhibition', 1960 (266), 1964 (454); Walker Art Gallery, Liverpool, 'Gifts to the Galleries – works acquired with the aid of the NACF for galleries outside London', 1968 (67); RAMM, 'Centenary Exhibition: Treasures of the Exeter Museums', 1969 (79); Holburne Museum of Art, Bath, 'Every Look Speaks: Portraits of David Garrick', 2003.

LITERATURE: Gerald K S Edwards 'Thomas Patch', *Apollo*, vol.xxvi, 1937, pp.220–21; F J B Watson, 'Thomas Patch (1725–1782): Notes on his Life Together with a Catalogue of His Known Works', *Walpole Society*, 1940, pp.35–36; Desmond Shawe-Taylor *Every Look Speaks: Portraits of David Garrick*, Holburne Museum of Art, Bath, 2003.

THOMAS PATCH WAS BORN IN EXETER but spent most of his life in Italy, principally in Florence where he was befriended by the British Envoy there, Sir Horace Mann. Patch made his living as a connoisseur, offering advice to English collectors, painting landscapes and also painting and later etching caricature groups of tourists. In Rome, Reynolds, too, produced a few canvases like these. He stayed with Patch in the same locanda and included him in his parody *Travesty of the School of Athens* (1751). In the 1770s Patch undertook a ground-breaking series of engravings after early Italian artists whose works he studied in Florence. On receiving his copy of Patch's work on the frescoes of the Church of the Carmine, Horace Walpole (CAT. 28, p. 93) recommended Reynolds to examine it.

The painting *A Caricature Group in Florence* has been supposed to show Horace Mann, at the right, greeting David Garrick (with hands together) in the company of other visitors; Garrick's wife, the dancer Eva Maria Veigel, being shown in the portrait displayed on the right. However, while possible, there is no documentary evidence that confirms these figures' identities. (Reynolds's contemporary portrait of Garrick; CAT. 26, p. 90.)

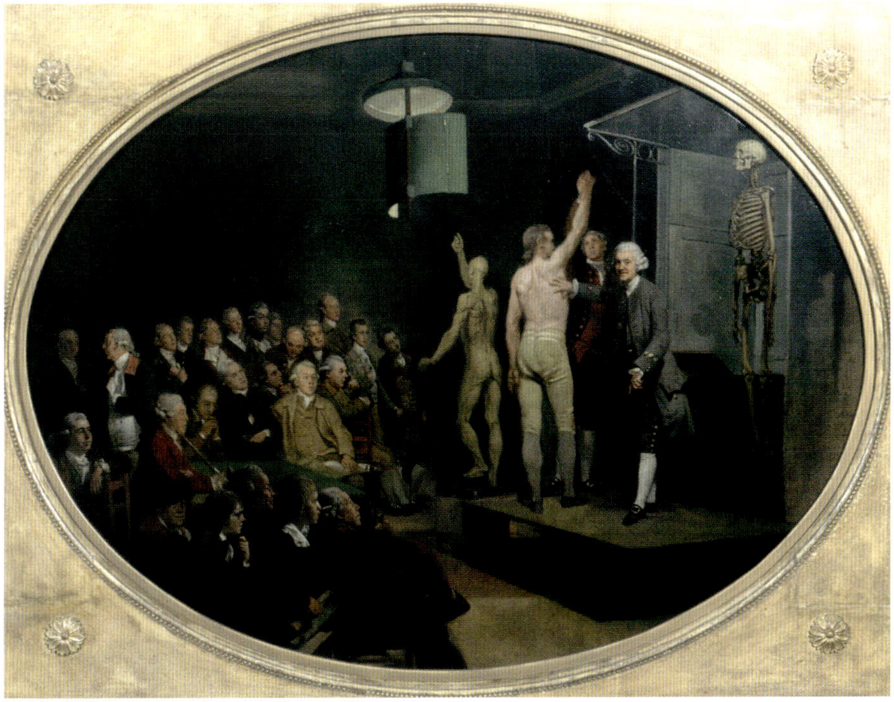

ONE OF THE PURPOSES OF THE ROYAL Academy was to offer English artists a more rigorous training, with lectures on the history of art and courses of instruction in perspective, anatomy and other disciplines. William Hunter (1718–83) was the first teacher of anatomy appointed. He was a distinguished obstetrician and anatomist and personal physician to Queen Charlotte. In Johan Zoffany's *Dr William Hunter teaching anatomy at the Royal Academy* Hunter uses the life model to explain the movement of the muscles of the back, also demonstrated by the écorché anatomical model on a pedestal.[4] Reynolds can be seen in the audience holding his ear trumpet.

CAT. 97

Johan Zoffany
(1733–1810)
Dr William Hunter teaching anatomy at the Royal Academy
(c.1775)
oil on canvas,
77.4 x 103.5 cm

PROVENANCE: William Hunter, about 1775(?); Matthew Baillie, Hunter's nephew and heir, about 1783(?); Presented in 1823 by Mrs. Baillie.

EXHIBITION HISTORY: International Exhibition, London, 1862 (36); National Portrait Exhibition, London, 1867 (506); Royal Academy (Winter Exhibition),1871, (265); Whitechapel Gallery, 1906, (23); 'The Eye of Thomas Jefferson', National Gallery of Art, Washington, DC, 1976, (111), 'Zoffany: Painter of the Georgian Scene', National Portrait Gallery, London, 1977, (75); 'Georgian Canada: Conflict and Culture 1745–1820', Royal Ontario Museum, Toronto, 1984, (181); 'Glasgow's Glasgow: People within a City', 1990; 'The Artist's Model: Its Role in British Art from Lely to Etty', Nottingham University Art Gallery & The Iveagh Bequest, Kenwood, London, 1991, (75); 'The Anatomy Lesson: Art and Medicine', National Gallery of Ireland, 1992; 'L'âme au corps: arts et sciences 1793–1993', Galeries nationales du Grand Palais, Paris, 1993–94, (73); 'Die Kunst hat nie ein Mensch allein besessen', Akademie der Künste, Berlin, 1996 (1.4/5); 'The Healing Touch', Scottish National Portrait Gallery, Edinburgh, 2005; 'Highest Pleasures'. Hunterian Art Gallery, Glasgow, 2007.

LITERATURE: *Annals of the Royal College of Physicians of London*, 22 December 1823, pp.219–20; *A List of Portraits &c. in the Royal College of Physicians of London*, London, 1864, cat.no.27, p.12; *The Roll of the Royal College of Physicians of London*, London, 1878, vol.3, p.397; *A List of Portraits &c. in the Royal College of Physicians of London*, London, 1900, p.5; Hingston Fox, R, *William Hunter*, London, 1901, p.65, no.7; Manners, V & Williamson, G C, *John Zoffany*, London, 1920, p.226, ill.; *A Descriptive Catalogue of the Portraits, Busts, Silver and other Objects of Interest in the Royal College of Physicians of London*, p.25, London, 1926; Wolstenholme, G (ed.), *Portraits*, London, 1964, p.230, p.232, ill. p.233.

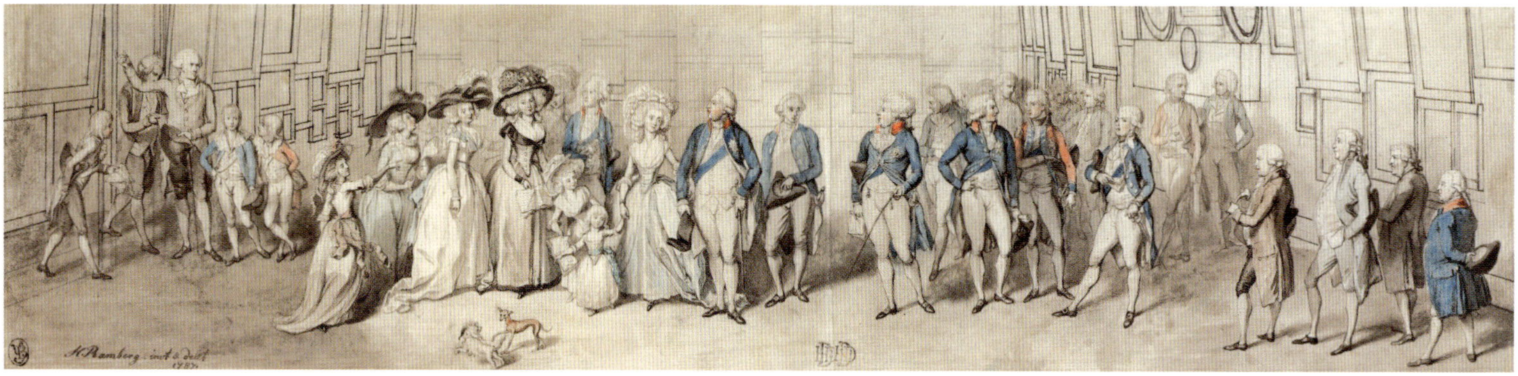

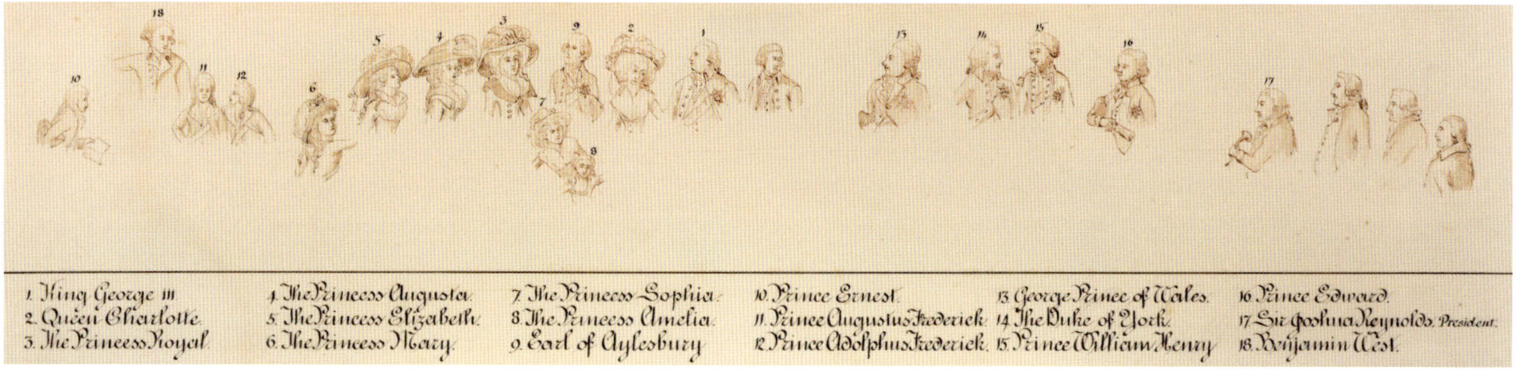

CAT. 98

Johann Heinrich Ramberg
(1763–1840)
The Royal Family at the Royal Academy in 1788
(1787)
pen and ink, with watercolour over graphite
(two sheets joined together), 12 x 48 cm (x2)

The Courtauld Institute Gallery (The Samuel Courtauld Trust), London (D.1995.XX.2)

PROVENANCE: Pierre Defer (1798–1870); by descent to his son-in-law Henri Dumesnil (1823–98; Lugt 739), Hôtel Drouot [Féral & Danlos], Paris, 10–12 May 1900, lot 207 bought Beurdeley; Alfred Beurdeley (1847–1919), Galerie Georges Petit [Féral], Paris, 13–15 March 1905, lot 309 bought Henry Lascelles, 6th Earl of Harewood (1882–1947); by descent to his eldest son George Lascelles, 7th Earl of Harewood (b.1923), Christie's London, 9 July 1985, lot 50; Spink & Son Ltd, from whom purchased from the Sherlock Fund with contributions from The Art Fund and the Victoria & Albert Museum Purchase Grant Fund (Museums and Galleries Commission) in October 1994.

EXHIBITION HISTORY: 2005, Bath, Holburne Museum of Art and Kendal, Abbot Hall Art Gallery, 'Pictures of innocence: Children in portraits from Hogarth to Lawrence', no.50.

LITERATURE: Tancred Borenius, *Catalogue of the pictures and drawings at Harewood House and elsewhere in the collection of the Earl of Harewood, K.G., G.C.V.O, D.S.O.* (privately published, 1936), pp.163–64, no.403; John Murdoch, 'Architecture and experience: The visitor and the spaces of Somerset House, 1780–1869', in David Solkin (ed.), *Art on the line: Royal Academy exhibitions at Somerset House 1780–1836* (New Haven and London: Yale University Press, 2001), pp.9–22 (20–21), fig.16; Amina Wright *et al.*, *Pictures of innocence: Children in portraits from Hogarth to Lawrence* (Bath: Holburne Museum of Art, 2005), pp.4,83, no.50.

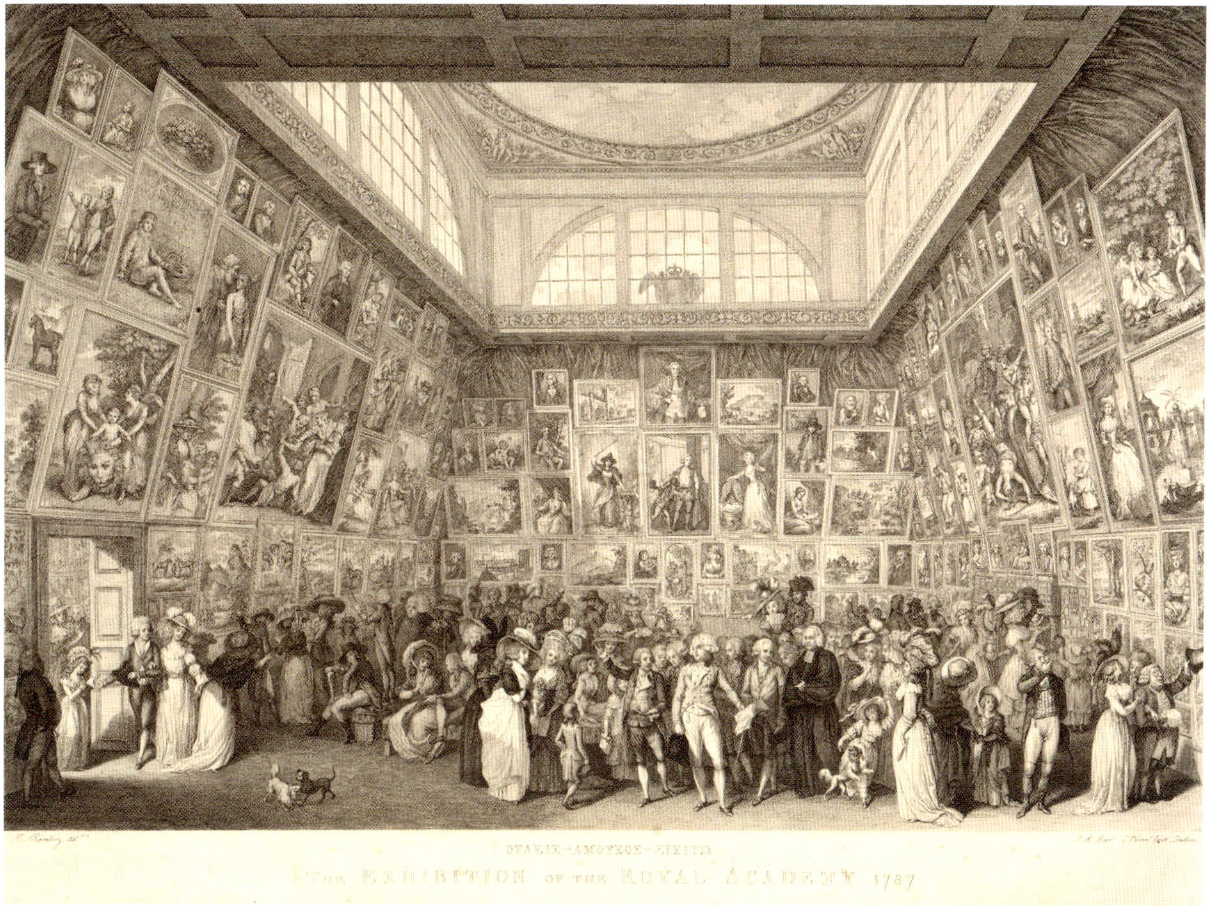

FIG. 41

Pierre-Antoine Martini
(1739–1800)
after Johann Heinrich Ramberg
The exhibition of the Royal Academy 1787
(1787)
etching with engraved lettering, 36.6 x 51.2 cm
British Museum, London
(PD Aa,1.24)

THE ROYAL ACADEMY'S ANNUAL exhibitions quickly established themselves as social occasions, attracting the elite in society. In Johann Heinrich Ramberg's drawing for a print (CAT. 98), the large royal entourage takes centre stage, with Reynolds at the right carrying his ear trumpet and Benjamin West, his successor as President of the Royal Academy, on the left. Ramberg shows the tight hanging of the pictures as they were displayed at the Royal Academy's exhibitions, the most prominent position being 'on the line' with the frame touching the ledge that ran around the room at a height of eight feet from the floor.[5]

Ramberg was born in Hanover, and during the 1780s was in London under the patronage of King George III, and became a pupil of Benjamin West. The figural grouping seen in this particular drawing seems closest to a print by Pierre-Antoine Martini (1739–1800), and published under the title *Portraits of their Majesty's* [sic] *and the Royal Family viewing the exhibition of the Royal Academy, 1788.*[6] A closely related print by Martini, *The exhibition of the Royal Academy 1787* (CAT. 99), was published in July 1787 by Cesare Antonio Poggi, a close friend of Reynolds.

REYNOLDS FILLED A NUMBER OF SKETCH-books during his years spent travelling throughout Italy. This example principally records his studies in Bologna and Naples. In July 1752 he was in Bologna, and was deeply struck by the art he found there. Perini has identified copies by the young Reynolds in the Soane sketch-book after (among others) Guido Reni, Guercino, Annibale and Ludovico Carracci. Later in life Reynolds would come to own original works by all these painters (CAT. 61, 69, 55 and 56). Reynolds, in Discourse XI, advised the students of the Royal Academy to seek out the works of Italian Old Masters critically:

> *Whoever should travel to Italy and spend his whole time there only in copying pictures… would return with little improvement… he must consider their works as the means of teaching him the true art of seeing nature… the great business of study is to acquire a mind…*

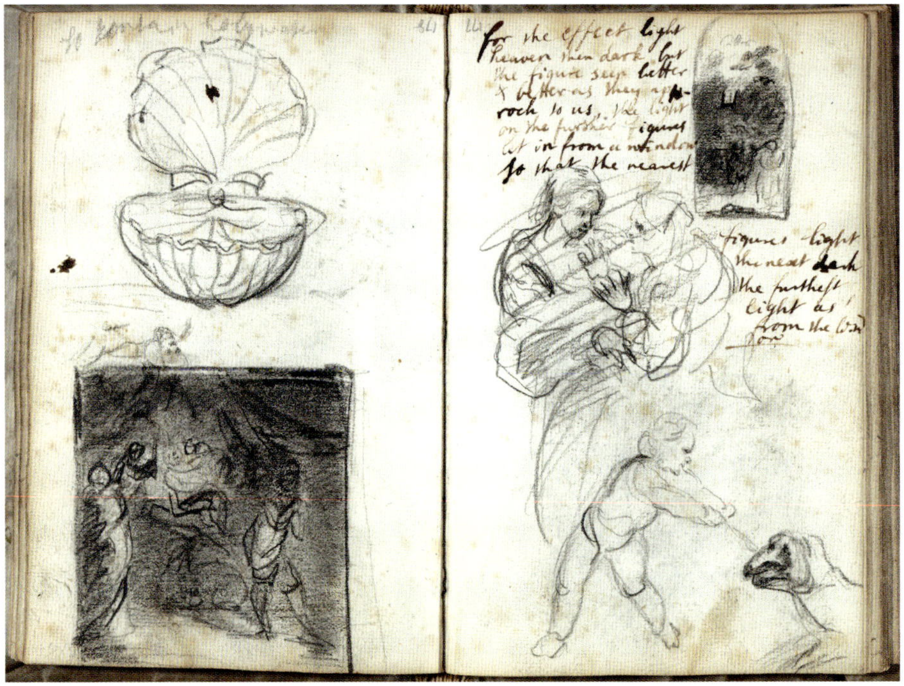

CAT. 99

Studies of unidentified pictures
'Italian sketchbook' (folio 177 and 178)
(1751–52)
black chalk, 22 x 17 cm each folio
Sir John Soane Museum, London (vol.32)

PROVENANCE: By descent from the artist to his niece Mary, Marchioness of Thomond, née Palmer (1750–1820), Christie's, London, 26 May 1821, lot 63 bought Soane; Sir John Soane (1753–1837), by whom bequeathed in 1837.

EXHIBITION HISTORY: None.

LITERATURE: Giovanna Perini, 'Sir Joshua Reynolds and Italian art and art literature: A study of the sketchbooks in the British Museum and in Sir John Soane's Museum', *Journal of the Warburg and Courtauld Institutes*, 51 (1988), pp.141–168; Giovanna Perini, 'Sir Joshua Reynolds a Bologna (1752): Considerazioni preliminari ad un'edizione critica dei taccuini di viaggio basate sul taccino conservato al Sir John Soane's Museum di Londra', *Storia dell'arte*, 73, (September–December 1991), pp.361–412.

ALSO ON DISPLAY, COURTESY OF THE Royal Academy of Arts, London: Reynolds' tea caddy (20 x 31 x 17 cm), palette case (55.5 x 37.4 x 4.5 cm); palette within case (44 x 25 x 0.3 cm), gold-rimmed spectacles (4.4 x 13.2 x 10 cm) and silver-rimmed spectacles (5.4 x 13.5 x 1.1 cm).

ENDNOTES

INTRODUCTION

1 Comment on Discourse VI, in Robert R. Wark (ed.) *Sir Joshua Reynolds. Discourses on Art*, New Haven and London: Yale University Press, 1975, p.309; See also pp.310–13. Not all the artists we now associate with the Romantic movement were so hostile. J.M.W. Turner, for example, in the lectures he gave as the Royal Academy's Professor of Perspective, paraphrased Reynolds's belief that genius could be reconciled with rules.
2 Royal Academy of Arts Archive MS REY/3/4.
3 Royal Academy of Arts Archive MS REY/3/7.
4 Wark, *Discourses*, p.97.
5 Ibid., pp.112–13.
6 Ibid., p.27.
7 Ibid., p.100.
8 Ibid., p.33
9 James Northcote, *The Life of Sir Joshua Reynolds*, second edition, London: Henry Colburn, 1819, vol. ii, p.243. See also, vol. i, pp.3, 227.
10 Wark, *Discourses*, p.113.
11 Ibid., p.201.
12 Ibid., p.72.
13 Ibid., p.200.
14 Ibid., p.73.
15 Northcote, *Life*, ii, p.78.
16 On this debate see John Barrell *The Political Theory of Painting from Reynolds to Hazlitt: 'The Body of the Public'*, New Haven and London: Yale University Press, 1995.
17 Wark, *Discourses*, p.169.

CITY AND COUNTRY

1 Reynolds in conversation with James Boswell, 20 December 1791, quoted John Edgcumbe, 'Reynolds's Earliest Drawings', *Burlington Magazine*, vol.129, no.1016 (November 1987), pp.724–26. For Reynolds's childhood reading, see *Literary Career*, ch.1.
2 Samuel Reynolds, Plympton, to Charles Cutcliffe, 17 March 1740, transcribed Leslie and Taylor, vol.1, pp.15–17.
3 For Samuel Reynolds's correspondence with Cutcliffe see Leslie and Taylor, vol.1, ch.1; a letter from Samuel Reynolds to Bulteel, dated 16 May 1738, was published in *The Times*, 21 July 1738, when reference was made to others, since lost. In old age Cranch wrote his will, dated 9 September 1766, and on 9 November went to visit Reynolds in London, accompanied by Lord Edgcumbe who presumably made the reintroduction. Reynolds painted Cranch's portrait (Mannings 441) and intended to make a gift of a silver cup, but Cranch died before he was able to present it. Leslie and Taylor, vol.1, pp.15, 23.
4 Samuel Reynolds, 17 March 1740, transcribed Leslie and Taylor, vol.1, pp.15–17.
5 *South Carolina Gazette*, 21 January 1766; Warwell also advertised 'A COLLECTION OF ANCIENT DRAWINGS to be sold.' Described by Samuel Reynolds as 'both a painter and a player' (letter 17 March 1740), Warwell is presumably the actor named in London newspapers from 1732 to 1734, latterly as a member of His Majesty's Company of Comedians. Thereafter Warwell moved widely in the West Country: his children were baptised at Melcombe Regis (1735), Modbury (1737), Totnes (1741; a son, Michael Angelo), and Tiverton (1743; perhaps also Truro, 1756). In 1765 he emigrated to South Carolina, to join Michael Angelo. Warwell advertised his painting services in America and died there, 'a noted limner', in 1767, on which his widow Maria announced her intention to return to England. See Anna Wells Rutledge, 'Artists in the Life of Charleston', *Transactions of the American Philosophical Society*, vol.39 part 2 (1949), pp.118, 147, 223.
6 Samuel Reynolds, 17 March 1740, transcribed Leslie and Taylor, vol.1, pp.15–17.
7 For Hudson, it made sense to employ additional assistance, at a time when he was expanding his London studio to fill the gap in the market left by the retirement of the capital's most prominent portraitist, Jonathan Richardson (1667–1745) in late 1740. Ellen Gross Miles, *Thomas Hudson (1701–1779) Portraitist to the British Establishment*, 1976 (Yale, unpublished PhD thesis), vol.1, p38.
8 Letters from Samuel Reynolds, 1 January 1741 and 20 April 1742, transcribed Leslie and Taylor, vol.1, pp.22–23.
9 Mannings 1029–32, 1061. Nineteenth-century biographers also identified among Reynolds's early clients a Councillor Bury and his wife, and John Facey, Mayor of Plymouth 1749–50. For Plympton Corporation's commission see the entry on George Edgcumbe.
10 Mannings 605, 733, 913, 1017, 1240–41, 1382, 1458, 1515, 1519 and 1932.
11 Mannings 1972, 1975 and 354, the last being 'Captain Chaundy', ostensibly a portrait of Bartholomew Chaundy (1727–77) of Ascot-under-Wychwood, Oxfordshire. *Report and Transactions of the Devonshire Association*, July 1887, vol.xix, p.203, stated also that Reynolds painted Philip Worth RN, an old school friend, 'half length, dressed in uniform, wearing the scarlet waistcoat of the period, and having his hat under his left arm. On the back of the canvas is written "Philip Worth, 1744. J.Reynolds, painter". Mr B Curgenven, who has recently given these particulars, says the portrait has never been out of the possession of the family.' A further, unrecorded, portrait c.1747–48, was on sale at Philip Mould, London in 2009.
12 Mannings 1295, 1772; see the entry for the Eliot family.
13 Mannings 1332, 1402, 1625–26, 1785. Martha Neate married the 'eminent West-India Merchant' of Bristol and London, Narris Neate (d.1742), whose two children Thomas (1740-1825) and Martha (1742) are shown with their tutor in Mannings 1332. In 1744 Martha married another Quaker merchant, Samuel Vandewall (d 1761) of Lincoln's Inn Fields and Greenwich; their baby Joseph Moore Vandewall (26 July 1745–28 February 1747/8) is the sitter in Mannings 1785. *Daily Advertiser*, 23 November 1744.
14 Rennell was a pupil at Exeter Grammar School under Reynolds's uncle. His painting of Huxham, engraved in 1756, is Royal Society P/0075. A portrait of Mary Amyatt (1727–88) of Totnes, sold Bonham's, Bath, 15 October 2007, lot 330, is here attributed to Rennell. eds Paul Williamson and Amal Asfour, 'William Jackson: A Short Sketch of my own Life', *Gainsborough's House Review 1996/97*, Sudbury 1997, p.61; Northcote 1819, vol.1, p.4; British Library Add Mss 47792, f.15v.
15 William Schupbach, 'The Fame and Notoriety of Dr. John Huxham', *Medical History*, vol.25 (1981), pp.415–21.

16 Malone dates this to 'about the year 1743 or 1744. Soon afterwards he painted… Captain Hamilton'. Clearly '1743 or 1744' is wrong, as Reynolds only arrived in Plymouth in 1743; but elsewhere Malone dated the Hamilton portrait to 1746, which would make sense of Reynolds's account. Sir James Prior, *Life of Edmund Malone*, 1860, pp.404–05, quoted DNB.

17 'In the first squadron that went to the Mediterranean', according to Walpole, in Lewis Walpole Library, Yale, *Horace Walpole's Book of Materials*, vol.1, f.5.

18 R Campbell, *The London Tradesman*, London 1747, p.97.

19 Malone, quoted ed. Martin Postle, *Joshua Reynolds The Creation of Celebrity*, London 2005, p.92.

20 James Boswell, 20 April 1791, in the dedication to Reynolds of *The life of Samuel Johnson*, Dublin 1792, vol.1, pp.iii–iv.

21 Mannings 34–41; 103–5, 131–36, 557–8, 663, 665, 667, 920, 1075, 1262–66, 1379, 1394–1401, 1708–10, 1796–99, 1849.

22 Mannings 1308–10; John Lloyd (1726–1806) and John Foote (c.1718–68) were also Plymouth sitters of the 1750s and 1760s. Mannings 654, 1136.

23 John Brewer, *Pleasures of the Imagination*, London 1997, chapter 16; Raymond Williams, *The Country and the City*, St Albans 1975; Keith Thomas, *Man and the Natural World*, London 1984, pp.243–54.

24 Dror Wahrman, 'National Society, Communal Culture', *Social History*, vol.17 no.1 (January 1992), pp.43–72.

25 For metropolitan cultural influence over provincial centres, see Peter Borsay, 'The London Connection: Cultural Diffusion and the Eighteenth-Century Provincial Town', *The London Journal*, vol.19 no.1 (1994), pp.21–36; and Brewer 1997, ch.16.

26 Wahrman 1992, pp.58–61.

27 John Ireland, *Hogarth Illustrated*, London 1791, vol.1, pp.iii–iv.

28 Edmund Malone, *The Works of Sir Joshua Reynolds*, London 1798, vol.1, p.x.

29 Farington, 1819 (5th edition of *Literary Works*), vol.1, p.cxli. Northcote was much nearer to Malone, in believing that Reynolds's comment 'arose most probably from a regret that he had not sooner established himself in London, which he always considered as the proper field for the display of talents.' Northcote, 1817 (Philadelphia edition), p.18.

30 James Northcote, *The Life of Sir Joshua Reynolds*, London 1819, vol.1, p.24; see also Edmond Malone, *The Works of Sir Joshua Reynolds*, London 1797, vol.1, p.v; *The Biographical Magazine*, London 1794, p.109; and William Seward, *Anecdotes of some distinguished persons*, London 1795–96, p.351.

31 The uncle in the Temple with whom Reynolds lodged was first identified as Rev John Reynolds by the painter's very elderly niece, Theophilia Gwatkin, in the mid-nineteenth century, in RA Library REY 3/95i. As John Reynolds has no known link with London, probably a more likely candidate is Thomas Potter, baptised 9 April 1690 at Lostwithiel in Cornwall, who was the brother of Joshua Reynolds's mother. He died 19 October 1769 and his will, dated 4 February 1768, describes him as 'late of London but now of the City of Exeter.' He made pecuniary bequests of £1,150, and a property in Woolfardisworthy, near Bideford. Reynolds's sister Jane (d.1766) lived with him in Exeter, probably as housekeeper. Samuel Reynolds mentioned 'my brother Potter's case, who did not serve but a few years in London' in his 7 October 1740 letter to Cutcliffe. Reynolds again lodged with 'an uncle who resided in the Temple' when he left Hudson, according to Joseph Farington, *Memoirs of the Life of Sir Joshua Reynolds*, 1819, pp.16-18; Frederic Thomas Colby, *Pedigrees of Five Devon Families*, Exeter 1884, p.12; Leslie and Taylor, 1865, vol.1, p18.

32 Farington gave the schoolmaster's income as '£200 a year or more' in 1809. ed. Kathryn Cave, *The Diary of Joseph Farington*, Yale 1982, vol.10, pp.3574. Eighteenth-century commentators describe Devon's reputation for cheap living, with costs roughly 50% lower than in London.

33 Samuel Reynolds, Plympton, to Charles Cutcliffe, 26 October 1740, transcribed Leslie and Taylor, 1865, vol.1, p.19. George Treby (1685–1742) of Plympton House, MP for Plympton Erle 1708–27 and for Dartmouth 1727 to 1742. Master of the Household 1730–40 and a Lord of Treasury 1740–42. Treby's two sons were probably both pupils of Samuel Reynolds. eds Eveline Cruickshans, Stuart Handley and D W Hayton, *The House of Commons 1690–1715*, vol.5, p.661.

34 Samuel Reynolds, Plympton, to Charles Cutcliffe, 26 October 1740, transcribed Leslie and Taylor, 1865, vol.1, pp.19–20.

35 On clientele, see Richard Wendorf, *Sir Joshua Reynolds*, Harvard, 1996, ch.5.

36 John Millan, *Millan's universal register of court and city-offices*, London 1760, p.22; *The court and city kalendar… for the year 1759*, London 1759, p.182.

37 *The Plymouth-Dock Guide*, Plymouth 1796 [first published 1792], p.5.

38 Stebbing Shaw, *A Tour to the West of England in 1788*, London 1789, p.355.

39 *The Plymouth-Dock Guide*, Plymouth 1796, pp.14, 24.

40 James Boswell, *The Life of Samuel Johnson*, London 1799, vol.1, pp.438–39.

41 James Boswell, *The Life of Samuel Johnson*, London 1799, vol.1, p.439.

42 RA Library HU/2/90, 2 November 1779: W. Hawker, Poundisford Lodge, to Ozias Humphry.

43 Leeds VR6015 no.14470, 8 December 1769.

44 For example Anon, *The Tricks of London Laid Open*, London c.1785 (6th edition); Anon, *Squire Randal's Excursion round London*, London 1776.

45 British Library (BL) Add Mss 48218 f.121: Therese to Grantham, Saltram, 20 October 1772.

46 British Library, Add Mss 48218, f.192: Therese to Fritz, Sackville Street, 3 May 1773.

47 Todd Gray and Margery Rowe, *Travels in Georgian Devon*, Tiverton 1998, vol.2, pp.9–11.

48 Richard Polwhele, *The History of Devonshire*, Exeter 1806, vol.3, p.452

49 John Trusler, *The Way to be Rich and Respectable*, London 1776 (2nd edition), pp.6–10. Trusler's text was in its seventh edition by 1796 and appeared again in 1800, revised by William Green for his *Plans of Economy*.

50 *Universal Magazine*, August 1792, p.81.

51 George Lipscomb, *A Journey into Cornwall*, London 1799, pp.284–88.

52 Holger Hooch, *The King's Artists*, Oxford 2003, p.114; Dian Kriz, *Genius as Alibi*, Yale 1997.

53 Rosemary Sweet, 'Topographies of Politeness', in *Transactions of the Royal Historical Society*, 6th series, vol.12 (2002), p.370.

54 RA Library NOR/9, 8 April 1772.

55 ed. Katharine C. Balderston, *Thraliana The Diary of Mrs. Hester Lynch Thrale (Late Mrs Piozzi) 1776–1809*, Oxford 1951, vol.1 (1776–84), p.330.

56 ed. Kenneth Garlick and Angus Macintyre, *The Diary ofJoseph Farington*, vol.6 (Yale 1979), p.2232: entry for Saturday 4 February 1804.

57 *Letters*, 91.
58 Wendorf 1998, p.68, Leslie and Taylor vol.1, p.461.
59 RA Library NOR/3, 10 August 1771.
60 Howard J Bell, 'The Deserted Village and Goldsmith's Social Doctrines', *PMLA*, vol.59 no.3 (September 1944), pp.747–72.
61 Sir Joshua Reynolds, 'A Discourse, delivered at the Opening of the Royal Academy, January 2, 1769, by the President', in Sir Joshua Reynolds, *Seven Discourses delivered in the Royal Academy by the President*, London 1778, pp.5–8.
62 Oliver Goldsmith, *The Deserted Village*, London 1770, Dedication page.
63 Samuel Northcote, Plymouth, to James Northcote, 9 September 1772, transcribed Stephen Gwynn, *Memorials of an Eighteenth Century Painter (James Northcote)*, London 1898, pp.73–74. Reynolds was to serve as Mayor of Plympton in 1773; his pocket book states was 'to be sworn Mayor' on Monday 4 September 1773; Cotton 1856, p.122.
64 Rev Christopher Wyville quoted E.C.Clark, *The Association – British Extra-parliamentary Political Organisation 1769–1793*, Harvard 1963, p.33.
65 Thus, in 1776 Reynolds began to adjust his theory of civic humanism, expounded annually in the lecture he gave to Royal Academy students, to remedy the idea that an individual's constitutional rights were privileged over the authority of established custom. John Barrell, *The Political Theory of Painting from Reynolds to Hazlitt*, Yale 1986, pp.71–72, 136–141.
66 *The Times*, 16 February 1795.
67 Bedfordshire and Luton Archives and Record Service, Bedford (BLARS) L 30/14/333/66, 23 September 1770.
68 Farington 1819, pp.9–10, 21.
69 ed. Katharine C. Balderston, *Thraliana The Diary of Mrs. Hester Lynch Thrale (Late Mrs Piozzi) 1776–1809*, Oxford 1951, vol.1, pp.79–80.
70 Hon John West to Simon, 1st Earl Harcourt, then Viscount Nuneham, 26 June 1759. HMC Harcourt Papers vol.8, p.30, quoted Martin Postle, ' 'The Modern Apelles': Joshua Reynolds and the Creation of Celebrity', in ed. Martin Postle, *Joshua Reynolds The Creation of Celebrity*, Tate 2005, pp.26–27.
71 Allan Cunningham, *The Life of Sir David Wilkie*, London 1843, vol.1, pp.239–41.

THE REYNOLDS FAMILY

1 Mannings 1017, 1382, 1515 and 1519.
2 Martin Postle ed., *Joshua Reynolds: The Creation of Celebrity*, London 2005, p.19; see also Penny 1986, p.166.
3 for Frances Reynolds and her relationship with her brother, see Wendorf 1998, pp.65–81; ed. Kenneth Garlick and Angus Macintyre, *The Diary of Joseph Farington*, Yale 1979, vol.6, p.2232.

THE EDGECUMBE FAMILY

1 W S Lewis, Warren Hunting Smith & George L Lam (eds), *Horace Walpole's Correspondence with Sir Horace Mann and Sir Horace Mann the Younger*, Yale 1971, vol.25, p.518.
2 Farington 1819, pp.16–18; Northcote 1819, p.26. Malone, writing about the period of Samuel Reynolds's death, states that Reynolds 'became acquainted with George, the third Lord Edgcumbe' only 'after spending a few more years in the practice of painting, partly in London and partly in Devonshire.' Malone, 1819 (5th edition), vol.1, pp.xi–xii.
3 Farington 1819, pp.20–21.
4 Northcote 1819, vol.1, p.26.
5 Farington 1819, p.30.
6 Northcote, *The Life of Sir Joshua Reynolds*, 1818, vol.1, pp.52–53.
7 W Mason 'Anecdotes of Sir Joshua Reynolds, chiefly relative to his manner of colouring' in William Cotton ed. *Sir Joshua Reynolds' Notes and Observations on Pictures*, London 1859, p.50.
8 Martin Postle, 'An Early Unpublished Letter by Sir Joshua Reynolds', *Apollo*, vol.cxli, no.400 (June 1995), pp.13–15.
9 Mannings 559. *The Edinburgh Magazine*, vol.1 (February 1785), p.99; also Samuel Felton, *Testimonies to the genius and memory of Sir Joshua Reynolds*, London 1792, pp.9–10.
10 Britton and Brayley 1803, p.187–88.
11 Lady Ernestine Edgcumbe, 'Mount Edgcumbe,' *Cornish Magazine*, 1899, vol.2, p.36. The article reproduces a photo of the saloon showing the three busts.
12 In 1750 Reynolds was looking around Rome for a suitable painting to copy for Lord Edgcumbe, 'the larger the better'. *Letters* 6.
13 *The new foundling hospital for wit. Being a collection of fugitive pieces…, new edition*, London 1786, vol.6, pp.106–10. Edgcumbe himself alludes to his difficult paternal relationship in BL Add Mss 51403, f.174, 15 August 1749.
14 James Northcote: T*he Life of Sir Joshua Reynolds*, 1818, vol.1, p.59.
15 In a hyper-critical review of William Cotton, *Sir Joshua Reynolds and his Works*, London 1856, in Sylvanus Urban ed., *The Gentleman's Magazine*, vol.202 (vol.2 new series), London 1857 (February 1857), p.208. The anecdote is repeated in Leslie and Taylor, vol.1, p.14.
16 Leslie and Taylor, vol.1, pp.16–17. A letter dated 20 June 1740 mentions 'a specimen of Joshua's performances in painting, which I think is his first in colours.' All other contemporary references to Reynolds's early artistic output are to drawings, as are the surviving works themselves.
17 Mannings 1632. Lewis Walpole Library, Yale, Horace Walpole's Book of Materials I, f.153.
18 Francis Bickley ed., *The Diaries of Sylvester Douglas (Lord Glenbervie)*, London 1928, vol.1, pp.134-5: entry for 31 March 1797.
19 Lewis Walpole Library Yale, Walpole's note on Liotard, photostat of the original ms at Harvard; Marcel Roethlisberger & Renee Loche, *Liotard*, Netherlands 2008, vol.1 no.375: 'Homme inconnu', Rijksmuseum (inv SK-A-1196); Northcote 1818, vol.1, pp.59–61.
20 Lewis Walpole Library, Yale, Hanbury Williams Correspondence vol.48, ff.93–94, 4 August 1744; also ff.85–86, 7 July 1744. On his return he became a founding member of the Divan Club, for English visitors to Turkey. Sir Francis Dashwood, *The Dashwoods of West Wycombe,* London 1987, pp.22–24. The club operated from 1744 to 1746.
21 BL Add Mss 51403, f.139, 7 August 1747; BL Add Mss 51403, f.194, 13 November 1750; BL Add Mss 51403, f.208, 18 September 1753.
22 Quoted Eveline Cruickshanks, *The History of Parliament* [electronic database]: 1715–54, vol.II: Members E–Y. For example in 1756 Dick 'tumbled above six Thousand within this fortnight.' Lewis Walpole Library, Yale, Hanbury Williams Correspondence, vol.64, ff.136–39, 10 April 1756.
23 Horace Walpole, *A description of the villa of Horace Walpole*, Twickenham 1774, p.4.
24 Mannings 561–62.
25 W S Lewis and Ralph S Brown eds, *Horace Walpole's Correspondence with George Montagu*, Yale 1970, vol.9, p.417.
26 Ibid., p.186. Edgcumbe's original painting is now untraced.
27 Will of Richard Edgcumbe, PROB 11/865, dated 19 February 1761;

Lewis Walpole Library, Yale, Hanbury Williams Correspondence, vol.52, ff.55–58, 25 September / 6 October 1750; BL Add Mss 51403, f.188, 17 September 1750.

28 The complete list is transcribed in Mannings vol.1, pp.175–76.

29 Mannings 553–57, 564.

29 Penny 1986, pp.173–74, 256–57; Cotton 1859, p.93.

30 George Wightwick, *Nettleton's Guide to Plymouth*, Plymouth 1836, p.116.

31 *Jacobite's Journal*, 5 March 1748; *General Advertiser*, 7 March 1748; *Whitehall Evening Post or London Intelligencer*, 10 March 1748.

32 Kathryn Cave ed., *The Diary of Joseph Farington*, vol.10 (Yale 1982), pp.3577–78.

33 Northcote 1817, pp.150–51.

34 Cotton 1859, p.92.

35 J Brooking Rowe, *The History of Plympton*, Exeter 1906, p.410.

THE ELIOT FAMILY

1 *London Recorder*, 4 March 1792.

2 Catherine Eliot 'is unmarried' in Sir Egerton Brydges, *Collins's Peerage of England*, London 1812, vol.8, p.6; but ed. William Courthope, *Debrett's Complete Peerage*, London 1836 (21st edition), p.154, states that Catherine, Augusta and Hesther all died infants.

3 *London Recorder*, 4 March 1792; *Letters*, 114, 116. In 1785 Eliot married Harriot Pitt (1758–86), the Prime Minister's sister.

4 *Letters*, 114. Reynolds's 1773 pocket book gives an appointment at Port Eliot on Wednesday 29 September. The 1780 pocket book lists a dinner appointment on Monday 3 September, and another visit on Sunday 15 September.

5 BL Add Mss 48218, f.115, 26 June 1772: Therese Parker wrote that Reynolds was 'rather active in promoting a scheme of Mr. Eliots & Footes which I fear will take place, Mr. Footes proposes having a sort of Jubilee at Truro in Cornwall the place of his Birth, which he is to make out as well as he can for a week, by different amusements.' *Letters*, 114: 'My love to Mr. Gwatkin and if he will not come to see me next year I will come to see him in Cornwall.'

6 George Lipscomb, *A Journey into Cornwall*, London 1799, pp.288–89.

7 CRO EL/B/2/2/2, 14 June 1748: Sir Charles Williams to Lord Chesterfield, quoted in Chesterfield's letter to Edward Eliot's father.

8 BLARS L30/14/333/98, 27 May 1778.

9 Samuel Reynolds, 3 January 1743/4, quoted Leslie and Taylor, vol.1, p.27. Philip Vanbrugh was brother of architect Sir John Vanbrugh (1664–1726) and of the Plymouth MP Charles Vanbrugh (1680–1740). Matteo Giunti, *Leghorn Merchant Networks*, at www.geneanet.org.

10 Edward Wedlake Britton and John Brayley, *The Beauties of England and Wales*, London 1809, vol.2, p.381, describe a portrait of Edward Eliot dated 1783, perhaps Mannings 570 or 571.

11 CRO EL/B/2/1/10, 10 April 1750. 'Jack Trevanion' cannot refer to William Trevanion's father, John, who died in 1740, leaving William, 'about fifteen years old, Heir to 4000 l. per Ann'. Trevanion's 'good place' refers to his appointment as a Groom of the Bed-Chamber to Frederick, Prince of Wales, in April 1749. *Universal Spectator*, 30 August 1740; *London Evening Post*, 6 April 1749.

12 CRO EL/B/3/2/1, 19 August 1746.

13 Sotheby's 13 November 1994, lot 52. Hudson omits baby Pollexfen, who died in July 1742, and shows William (born c.1741) at about one year old.

14 Quoted John Ingamells, *A Dictionary of British and Irish Travellers to Italy*, Yale 1997, p.406; ed. Mary Eyre Matcham, *A Forgotten John Russell*, London 1905, p.210, which contains many references to Burrington Goldsworthy and Philip Vanbrugh.

15 CRO EL/B/1/4/1/2, 10 August 1746; CRO EL/B/3/2/1, 19 August 1746.

16 George Lipscomb, *A Journey into Cornwall*, London 1799, p.287.

17 Britton and Brayley, vol.2, p.382.

18 George Lipscomb, *A Journey into Cornwall*, London 1799, p.287.

19 DRO 346M/F234, 3 January 1753. The correspondent, N Drake, adds that 'Mr. Reynolds ye. Painter is gone to Town, He has / Drawn Several pictures at Plymth, – I think very well' and alluding to a commision that Sir Francis Drake had recently given Reynolds to make 'a Copy of your Ansestor.'

20 Centre for Kentish Studies, Maidstone, U42/C1, 1 May 1786.

JAMES BULLER

1 For the history of King's Nympton see www.parksandgardens.ac.uk, and N Pevsner and B Cherry, *The Buildings of England: Devon*, London 1989, p.522.

2 Beard and Gilbert eds, *Dictionary of English Furniture Makers 1660–1840*, 1986, pp.166, 350, 540. In addition to the published notes of Buller's purchases from Chippendale are the following payments: 5 February 1763, £16 12s (CRO BU/311-312); 10 March 1766, £28 10s 3d (CRO BC/28/56).

3 CRO BU/337/3, 29 January 1757.

4 CRO BU/739, 29 July 1741.

5 CRO BU/337/12, 17 March 1759.

6 Mannings 272. In addition to the portraits of James Buller and Reginald Pole, also at Antony are portraits by Reynolds of Thomas, 8th Earl of Westmorland and John, the 9th Earl (Mannings 594, 596), which were bought on the London art market c.1903; and the *Piping Shepherd Boy* (Mannings 2156), bought at Christie's in 1919.

7 Mannings 1842.

8 Mannings 273–74.

9 Mannings 275.

10 CRO BC/28/62. Robert Nugent (1709–88; Viscount Clare from 1767), MP for St Mawes, was married in to Anne Craggs (c.1697–56), sister of Harriot Craggs of Port Eliot. CRO BC/28/66 records the 1775 annuity payment, and also a payment to Reynolds 'for Mrs B: Picture £73.10.0'. A note (CRO BU/356, 12 June 1784) refers to the arrangement: 'Mr John Radcliffe presents his Complimts to Mr Buller and acquaints him, that ye Bond for [?] ye [?] to Sir Joshua Reynolds is dated the 4th day of May 1772, And that on ye 22d May 1778 Mr Buller executed to Sir Joshua a Bond for ye Principal Sum of 365£:7s – which Mr Radcliffe apprehends was in full of ye Annuity to that time – Mr Radcliffe hath left with Mr Wildman ye Drat of ye Reassignment of ye Words &c in [?].'

11 Buller's appointments at 10am on 31 January and 1pm on 10 February were cancelled (Mrs Buller kept the 10 February meeting).

12 In addition Reynolds wrote, for the week of 14 February, 'Send Mrs Bullers [illegible, perhaps 'cloth']. She wears a dark grey shawl over a ruched crimson sacque.'

13 *Letters*, 256 (the payment had been addressed in error to 'John Reynolds'). Buller's instruction to his bank, to pay Reynolds, also survives; the bank also noted the payment in its statement of account. CRO BU/311–12.

THE MOLESWORTH FAMILY

1 Christopher Hussey, 'Pencarrow, Cornwall', *Country Life*, vol.cxvi (1965), pp.118–21.

2 Mannings 1262–66, 1708.
3 Mannings 1262–64.
4 An oil sketch attributed to Reynolds (Fitzwilliam Museum, Cambridge) may be a preparatory study for this painting, but Mannings lists it as a copy (Mannings 1263b).
5 Mannings 1479.

THE POLE FAMILY

1 Henry F Waters, 'Genealogical Gleanings in England,' *The New England Historical and Genealogical Register*, vol.48 (1894), p.493.
2 Pole subscribed to Henry Fielding, *Miscellanies*, London 1743; the chambers are mentioned in his will, PROB 11/955, dated 26 September 1767.
3 Henry F Waters, 'Genealogical Gleanings in England', *The New England Historical and Genealogical Register*, vol.48 (1894), p.493.
4 *London Evening Post*, 4 July 1751; *Whitehall Evening Post*, 29 April 1758; *London Gazette*, 10 April 1762.
5 *Lloyd's Evening Post*, 30 January 1765.
6 Antony Muniments PC/Lib.9/3, Lord Edgcumbe 24 December 1745.
7 And portraits of his grandfather Sir John Pole and aunt Lady Urith Trevelyan, which Carolus Pole had inherited from his mother, Lady Ann Pole (d.1713). PROB 11/955, dated 26 September 1767.

THE PARKER FAMILY

1 Samuel Reynolds, Sarah Bound and John Cranch witnessed George Parker's will, dated 13 November 1742. PROB 11/727.
2 Leslie and Taylor, vol.1, p.9.
3 For the pre-eighteenth-century history of Saltram, and a summary of its later history and contents, see Johnson 1998, pp.40–41.
4 John Parker married Frances Hort on 17 January 1764. His date of birth is unknown, but an 1864 plan of the family vault in Plympton church states that he died on 27 April 1788, aged 55. John and Lady Katharine Parker also had a daughter, Henrietta (d.1808). *The Exeter Mercury*, 20 January 1764; Plymouth and West Devon Record Office, Plymouth (PWDRO) Acc 3102.
5 Frances Parker died at Naples on 28 August 1764, aged 30. A local newspaper incorrectly reported her place of death as Lisbon. *The Exeter Mercury*, 12 October 1764; PWDRO Acc 3102.
6 Northcote 1819, vol.1, p.24, in which the painting is described in the context of the events of 1746. In a letter to his brother dated 18 April 1776 (RA Library, NOR/21), Northcote implies a slightly earlier date, writing that 'Sir Joshua has a head of her done by him more than thirty years at Saltram before he went to Italy.'
7 BL Add Mss 48244, ff.31–35.
8 Lady Catherine Parker died in Conduit Street on 11 August 1758. Hudson's portrait of her is reproduced in Johnson 1998, p.4; *London Chronicle*, 12 August 1758. I am grateful to Alastair Laing for his suggestion that this is, in fact, a portrait of Frances Hort.
9 George Parker had also been MP for Plymouth from 1695 to 1698.
10 *London Evening Post*, 16 October 1759. Edward Augustus, Duke of York and Albany (1739–67), heir presumptive following his brother's accession as George III in October 1760.
11 Mannings 786. In his commentary on John Parker [I] and [II], Mannings characterises the Guise portrait as a gift to John Parker [I], but in the entry on the portrait itself he suggests that Guise failed to pay for it and Parker bought it for 10gns in 1763. The pertinent evidence is Reynolds's note, dated 1 March 1763, against a payment of 10gns 'Mr Parker – exchange of a Picture due & / a frame for General Guise / a frame for General Guise / 3G[uineas].' Guise's portrait was at Saltram by 1785 when the Portugese Ambassador mistook it for Lord Bathurst's. BLARS L30/15/39/33, 3 September 1785; Mannings vol.1, p.365.
12 Hoare vol.46, f.313v.
13 *Catalogue of the Pictures, Casts, and Busts, belonging to the Earl of Morley, at Saltram*, Plymouth 1819, now known in a unique copy at the National Art Library, London. This is the 'catalogue of the pictures… printed at the expense of their noble owner, for the use of strangers, who are at all times allowed to have access to them' mentioned in an 1824 travel book. Probably the catalogue was the initiative of Frances, Countess of Morley. F W L Stockdale, *Excursions in the County of Cornwall*, London 1824, p.34.
14 The Campidoglio was sold before Saltram was acquired by the National Trust. Broun 1987, vol.2, p.264.
15 Hoare, vol.52, f.420v.
16 Louise Lippincott, *Selling Art in Georgian London*, Yale 1983, pp.28, 83, 115.
17 Waterhouse 1985, p.270. This doubt was encouraged by the revised edition of the 1819 catalogue, published in 1844, in which the statement about Reynolds's purchases in Rome was altered, so that it is unclear whether his client was John Parker [I] or [II].
18 Monke was Parker [III]'s mistress. Thomas H Williams, *Devonshire Scenery*, Exeter 1827; PWDRO 1259/2/339, 23 September 1797; PWDRO 1259/2/341, 1 October 1797.
19 Mannings vol.1, p.364. Waterhouse, having rejected the idea that Reynolds helped John Parker I, links these appointments with John Parker II. Waterhouse 1985, p.271. Johnson 1998, p.42, identifies Mannings 1399 speculatively as a portrait of John Parker [I].
20 Mannings 1506. Radcliffe was a friend of both Parker and Reynolds. *Letters*, pp.23–24, 247 Acc Bk 1770–78.
21 Mannings 849, in which Harrison is identified as one of three potential sitters. The death of 'Commodore Thomas Harrison, of the navy' was reported in February 1768; his will is dated 7 October 1767. One of his daughters, Charlotte Ann Harrison, married John McBride who was later a vice-admiral. *London Magazine*, 1768 p.166; PROB 11/941; National Archives ADM 106/1142/15, 29 January 1765.
22 Radcliffe paid for his portrait between 1761 and 1763, but Harrison died before making any payment. Mannings states the portrait of Harrison was owned by Lord Morley 'by 1899' but both are listed in Saltram 1819, p.27. Walter Radcliffe may have been acquired from Warleigh at the same time as the painting of Radcliffe's girlfriend, Miss Fordyce. Mannings states that Reynolds made a note to call on Mrs Radcliffe on 22 August 1782 but as neither Walter Radcliffe or his brother and heir John (d.1805) ever married, she was presumably no relation. Mannings vol.1, pp.244, 388–89, nos.849, 1506.
23 Painted for Sir Charles Bingham, Bt. It was sold from Saltram in 1876. John Parker [III]'s godfather, Lord Poulett, was one of two noblemen to have considered marrying Fisher. DNB.
24 Mannings 612, 661. *Miss Fordyce* was sold from Saltram in the 1880s.
25 The argument, advanced in Mannings that Reynolds's strict adherence to social forms requires 'Mr Parker' to signify Parker [I] (Parker [II] would presumably have been 'Mr J Parker'), is unconvincing. As Northcote noted, Reynolds was no stickler for proper usage. Even allowing this, the notebooks were a private and informal aide memoire; names and titles were abbreviated with no concern for social propriety. If Reynolds knew whom he meant by 'Mr Parker,' then no further details were necessary. Richard Wendorf, *Sir Joshua Reynolds*, Harvard 1996, pp.164–65.

26 *The Exeter Mercury*, 12 October 1764 and 9 November 1764; John Ingamells ed., *A Dictionary of British and Irish Travellers in Italy 1701–1800*, Yale 1997, p.738.

27 Photocopies of Reynolds's Sitter Books, Mellon Centre Library, London, and transcribed in Mannings vol.1, pp.364–65, who locates the 'Mr Parker's Copy' in the 1768 book.

28 BL Add Mss 48244, f.5.

29 The large family archive is primarily the correspondence of Therese's family, spread across four record offices: Plymouth and West Devon Record Office, Plymouth (PWDRO); Bedfordshire and Luton Archives and Record Service, Bedford (BLARS); West Yorkshire Archive Service, Leeds (WYAS); and the British Library, London (BL). Parker's own papers were probably destroyed, with his consent, by Nanny Robinson.

30 Mannings vol.1, pp.364–65.

31 Acc Bk 1770–78; Mannings vol.1, p.364.

32 Acc Bk, 1778–88; Mannings vol.1, p.365.

33 In Mannings vol.1, p.365; BLARS L30/14/333/186. Also: dinner with Mr Parker and Frederick Robinson at Sackville Street, 31 January 1779 (pocket book: '4 Mr Parker'; BLARS L30/14/333/176); dinner at Sackville Street with John Parker, Mr Pelham, Mr Lee and Frederick Robinson, 4 February 1779 (pocket book: '4 Mr Parker'; BLARS L30/14/333/176); dinner at Sackville Street with John Parker, Sir John Key, Mr Chichester, Lord Sheldham, Mr Lee, Mr Masters, Frederick Robinson, 27 March 1779 (pocket book: '5 Mr Parker' BLARS L30/14/333/192); dinner at Sackville Street with John Parker II, Ann and Frederick Robinson, Lady Coghill, two Miss Cramers, the two Miss Palmers, Lord Shuldham, and 'the two Bastards', 1 May 1779 (pocket book: '5 Mr Parker'; L30/14/333/204); dinner at Sackville Street with John Parker II, Sir Thomas Acland, Frederick Robinson and 'Mr Hugh', 21 May 1779 (pocket book 'Mr Parker Richmond'; BLARS L30/14/333/211); dinner at Reynolds's house at Richmond with John Parker II, Mr Lloyd of Plymouth, Mr Dunning, Frederick Robinson, the two Miss Palmers, Miss Elliot and Mr Elliot, Mr Lee, 30 May 1779 (pocket book: 'Mr Dunning'; BLARS L30/14/333/213); dinner at Reynolds's house on 4 December 1779, with Lord Grantham, Mr Parker and Lord Chatham (pocket book: '5 Mr Parker'; BLARS L30/17/4/262, 26 November 1779).

34 BL Add Mss 48218, f.159, 5 May 1775. Also: dinner with Waddilove and the Parkers at Sackville Street, 2 February 1774 (BL Add Mss 48218, f.141); tea at Sackville Street, 10 June 1774 (BL Add Mss 48218, f.149); dinner at Sackville Street with the Parkers and Fritz Robinson, who had recently returned from Spain, 24 April 1778 (BLARS L30/14/333/88, 24 April 1778); Fritz Robinson met Reynolds 'who is not at all chang'd, is as deaf & makes more money then ever', 30 April 1778 (BLARS L30/14/333/90); dinner at Mr Dunning's, Putney, with John Parker II and III, Ann and Frederick Robinson, Thomas Pelham, Mr Bastard and 'some lawyers', 17 May 1778 (BLARS L30/14/333/96); dinner at Reynolds's house in Richmond with John Parker II and III, Ann and Frederick Robinson, Thomas Pelham, Mr Lee, 'the three Mr Bastards' and 'Mr Elliot & his son', 24 May 1778 (BLARS L30/14/333/98); dinner at Prince's with John Parker, Frederick Robinson, Mr Skipwith, Mr Lee and Mr Pigott, 29 November 1778 (BLARS L30/14/333/148); dinner with Frederick Robinson and John Parker, 4 December 1778 (BLARS L30/17/2/201); at Sackville Street with John Parker, Frederick Robinson, Mr Chichester and Sir Charles Davies 10 February 1779 (BLARS L30/14/333/178); John Parker II and III, Anne and Frederick Robinson, Mr Lee made 'a tour of Painters' which ended up at Reynolds's house, 20 February 1779 (BLARS L30/14/333/181); dinner at Lord Ossory's with Lord and Lady Ossory, Mr Gibbon, Frederick Robinson, 'Richard', '& the ubiqu[it]ous George Barker', 24 March 1779 (BLARS L30/14/333/191); dinner at Sackville Street with John Parker II, Lord Milsington, Frederick Robinson and Mr Walpole, 14 May 1779 (BLARS L30/14/333/207); a morning visit by Frederick Robinson to Reynolds at Leicester Square, 18 June 1779 (PWDRO 430/2/52); Frederick Robinson called on Reynolds at Leicester Square, 26 October 1780 (BLARS L30/14/333/231); a morning visit by Lord Grantham to Reynolds at Leicester Square – 'he sets out tomorrow for ye West', 5 September 1783 (BLARS L30/15/54/201); dinner at Leicester Square, guests included John Parker II and Ann Robinson, 21 September 1784 (BL Add Mss 48218, f.63); visit of Lord and Lady Grantham to Reynolds at Leicester Square, 21 January 1785 (BLARS L30/15/54/253); visit of John Parker III, Sir Robert Palk and Lawrence Palk to Reynolds at Leicester Square, 16 October 1786 (BL Add Mss 48218, f.75); John Parker III and Mr Ley at Frederick Robinson's house in Park Street, London, circa 22 March 1787 (BLARS L30/15/50/105).

35 Neatby provided an ostensibly complete list of 15 payments to Reynolds, but there are actually 32 entries that refer to him. All the payments come from two mss volumes of accounts at PWDRO Acc 3102 Box 3, covering Parker's expenditure from May 1770 to August 1778 and from September 1778 to Parker's death in April 1788. Neatby 1977, p.24.

36 The 19 July 1777 mortgage document is in very poor condition. Parker met Reynolds at 9am on 20 July 1777, and paid him £345 15s – perhaps a clearing up of outstanding debts prior to the payment of the loan. Parker repaid £1,000 on 6 April 1780; and made interest payments of £100 on 26 June 1781, 25 June 1782 and 17 June 1784, and (perhaps) of £200 on 2 June 1787; PWDRO Acc 3102 Box 3, John Parker's Account Books 1770–78 and 1778–88, PWDRO ref 69 (Morley of Saltram), uncatalogued deeds.

37 Mannings notes that Reynolds and Parker had a 5pm meeting on 10 March 1780. Mannings vol.1, p.365.

38 Also 21 May 1779, 'To Sir Joshua lost,' £8 8s; 23 March 1780, 'To Sir Joshua Reynolds Lost at Cards,' £36 15s (Mannings notes a 5pm meeting between Reynolds and Parker on 23 March 1780). The following payments to Reynolds are also probably gambling debts: 19 July 1777, £10 10s; 12 June 1778, £5 5s; 31 May 1781, £5 5s; 24 January 1783, £16 16s; 23 November 1784, £4 4s. These receipts from Reynolds presumably also resulted from nights out: 11 May 1775, £26 5s; 13 February 1779, £11 0s 6d; 24 January 1783 £50. Reynolds also made records of gambling debts. In the 29 June 1775 ledger he wrote: 'Mr Parker left about the 26 of June – 40 G[uineas] / Mr Parker – Cards, just before he left town – 12 ½ G.' On 29 June 1775 he seems to have won 7.5gn from Therese Parker. Mannings vol.1, pp.364–65.

39 Mannings notes a cancelled appointment with Parker in Reynolds's pocket book for 5 February 1780. Mannings vol.1, p.365.

40 Both 2 June 1787: 'To Ditto [ie Sir Joshua Reynolds] Little Girls Picture' £52 10s; and 'To Do [ie Sir Joshua Reynolds] for a picture of a Grapes [sic]' £10.

41 22 May 1771, £38; 2 February 1778, £21.

42 ed A R Waller, *The Collected Works of William Hazlit – Table Talk and Conversations of James Northcote, Esq. R.A.*, London 1903, p.349.

43 Rev Hill Wickham ed., *Journals and Correspondence of Thomas Sedgewick Whalley, DD, of Mendip Lodge, Somerset*, London, 1863, vol.2, p.130. The letter is undated but appears between others of 25 October and 8 December 1799, and Lord Boringdon is described as 24 years old (he was born 1772).

44 BLARS L30/15/54/81, 23 September 1778.

45 PWDRO 430/1/88, 17 June 1779.

46 BLARS L30/14/333/181, 23 February 1779.

47 Mannings allowed that his 'identification not entirely certain'. The sittings are listed on p.364 but not linked to any painting. Johnson 1998, p.42, identifies no.1399 as a portrait of John Parker [I]. Apart from the late eighteenth or early nineteenth century inscription on no.1399 which names the sitter as John Parker [II] (an identification endorsed by the authors of the 1819 catalogue who were closely related to the sitter), the sitter closely resembles John Parker [II] as painted by Angelica Kauffmann, ed. Wendy Wassying Roworth, *Angelica Kauffmann*, London 1992, p.18 fig.2. Finally, no.1399 is clearly a painting of the 1760s and the sitter is middle-aged; for it to be John Parker [I] the painting must either date from the 1740s, which it clearly does not, or Parker (born 1703) had retained an extremely youthful appearance in the months before his death, which is unlikely.

48 The sittings are listed under Mannings 1399.

49 Mannings 40 is a version of no.39, datable to 1766–67, and still at Killerton, Acland's Devon seat. Parker's portrait, sent to Killerton but now untraced, is Mannings 1400, wrongly identified as a portrait of Montagu Parker. Apart from the inherent weakness of that identification, the occasion for swapping portraits provided by Parker [II]'s inheritance of Saltram in 1768 and Parker [II]'s very close and well documented friendship with Acland both argue that the note refers to John Parker and not his brother. For Parker's friendship with Acland, see WYAS VR6015 no.14475, 10 August 1769; WYAS VR6015 no.14466, 3 September 1769; BLARS L30/14/333/49, 20 October 1769; BL Add Mss 48218, f.121, 20 October 1772.

50 Mannings 356. Nanny Robinson called Acland and Chichester Parker's 'two Oldest Friends'. BLARS L30/15/50/57, 20 December 1784.

51 Mannings 1441. The gift was between September 1767 and January 1773, but probably near the earlier date as Shelburne gave a similar portrait of himself to his disciple Isaac Barre (1726–1802) at that time (Mannings 1440). Shelburne was created Marquess of Lansdowne in 1786. In 1785 the Portugese Ambassador saw both this and a portrait of Barre at Saltram, raising the intriguing possibility that Parker, who knew Barre, also received his portrait by Reynolds (Mannings 114–15, 1766) as a gift; however no such portrait is described in the 1819 catalogue. BLARS L30/15/39/33, 3 September 1785.

52 Hoare vol.D, f.411v. It seems very likely that Parker had this £32,233 in mind when, in his will dated 21 September 1762, he bequeathed £25,000 for the use of John Parker [II]'s trustee, Ann Poulett, to purchase lands on Parker [II]'s behalf. PROB 11/940. BL Add Mss 48218, f.20.

53 Reynolds was at Dover, on his way to France, on 10 September 1768. Mannings vol.I, p.364. Hoare vol.D, f.412v.

54 For Saltram in the late 1760s and 1770s, see Eileen Harris, *The Genius of Robert Adam*, Yale, p.233–41.

55 BLARS, Lucas no.14542, Group 4A uncatalogued typescript, 1 September 1769; BL Add Mss 33099, f.39, 1 September 1769; WYAS VR6015 no.14476, 17 September 1769.

56 BLARS L30/14/333/61, 11 September 1770. A 1803 guidebook mentions that 'In the upper apartments is a fine collection of Drawings, by Claude, Guercino, Vendervelde, and other ancient masters.' Britton and Brayley 1803, vol.4, p.143. The fate of these drawings is unknown.

57 Mannings ref for Mrs Parker. BL Add Mss 48218, f.24, 3 March 1772. For the portraits of Mrs Parker and Sir Thomas Parker, see Kate Retford, 'Reynolds's portrait of Mrs Theresa Parker', *British Art Journal*, vol.iv, no.3 (autumn 2003), pp.80–86.

58 Therese reported on sales in Paris and London in 1772 and 1773. BL Add Mss 48218, f.178, 9 April 1772; BL Add Mss 48218, f.128, 5 March 1773.

59 Presumably the *Three Huntresses* still in the Saloon, ascribed to Rubens's studio and Frans Snyders in Neatby 1977, pp.36–37, no.67T.

60 It was bought at an unknown date, but before the sales of Reynolds's own collection (as it is not mentioned there), and surely during John Parker [II]'s life. It was identified as Reynolds's property in an etching by John Hamilton Mortimer, published by John Boydell in 1766. The painting is a copy of the Guercino in the National Gallery of Scotland. Reynolds 'may have acquired' the picture in Italy; Neatby 1977, p.21, no.12.

61 As suggested in Alastair Laing, *In Trust for the Nation*, London 1995, p.30.

62 Lot 27 'attribué par les uns à Titiano Vecelli, & par les autres à André Schiavone', M. de Merval's sale, Paris, 9 May 1768 (Lugt 1681).

63 The two Claudes are now at the Timken Art Gallery (The Putnam Foundation), San Diego, California, and the Metropolitan Museum of Art, New York. The collection of M de Merval, of rue Bourg l'Abbe, Paris, took place from 9 to 17 May 1768 (Lugt 1681). Evidently he was a dealer, as he advertised a 'COLLECTION of the very best and finest original Pictures, by the best and greatest Masters of Italy, France and Flanders' in the *Gazetteer and London Daily Advertiser*, 19 July 1763. BL Add Mss 48218, f.111, 2 April 1772; BL Add Mss 48218, f.180,1 September 1772; Broun 1987, vol.2, pp.192–98.

64 Therese asked her brother to look out for paintings, and he responded, from Spain, with a list of potential purchases. BL Add Mss 48218, f.111, 2 April 1772; BL Add Mss 48218, f.119, 10[16?] August 1772.

65 BL Add Mss 48218, f.192, 3 May 1773.

66 As Parker already knew her in 1764, it cannot have been true that 'Reynolds was responsible for introducing the Parkers to Angelica Kauffmann'; Trevor Lummis and Jan Marsh, *The Woman's Domain*, London 1990, p.72. Waterhouse suggested that Parker himself had introduced Kauffmann to Reynolds. Waterhouse 1985, p.271.

67 Quoted Waterhouse 1985, p.271. As further evidence of their friendship, in about 1774 Parker made a gift of cider to Kauffmann, for which he paid 4gns to 'Ashford' on 23 May 1774. Acc Bk 1770–78.

68 At any rate it was at Saltram by 1803, when it was in the 'Green Breakfast Room'. Perhaps Kauffmann's own *Self Portrait playing a Guitar*, also at Saltram, was acquired with the same agenda; Britton and Brayley 1803, vol.4, p.143. Kauffmann's portrait of Parker is reproduced in ed. Wendy Wassying Roworth, *Angelica Kauffmann*, London 1992, p.18 fig.2.

69 BLARS L30/14/333/190, 23 March 1779; BLARS L30/15/54/133 11 April 1779; BLARS L30/14/333/88, 24 April 1778; BLARS L30/17/4/195, 30 April 1778.

70 BLARS L30/14/333/144, 10 November 1778; BL Add Mss 48218, f.53, 18 November 1778; Johnson 1998, p.49.

71 The prime version of Davers's portrait is at Ickworth (Mannings 482). Davers is presumably the 'Sir Charles Davies' who dined with Reynolds and the Parkers in February and March 1779. Acc Bk 1770–78; BLARS L30/14/333/178, 12 February 1779; BLARS L30/14/333/186, 12 March 1779.

72 As well as 2gns on 27 May 1778. Hoare vol.D, f.412v; PWDRO Acc 3102, Acc Bk 1770-1778,, 1778–88, February 1781 outgoings; Broun 1987, vol.2, p.245; Ozias Humphry and Joseph Meyer, *A Memoir of George Stubbs*, London 2005, p.57.

73 PWDRO Acc 3102, John Parker's Account Book 1778–88, June 1787 outgoings. On the same day a payment of 1gn was made to 'Ralph', presumably Reynolds's longstanding servant Ralph Kirkley who delivered the picture to Sackville Street.
74 For details of Stuart's work at Saltram, see Neatby pp.10, 58–60.
75 *Letters*, 53.
76 On 2 March 1778 Parker paid £20 to 'Tomkin for cleaning pictures at Saltram'; on 15 June 1779 he gave Tomkin £31 10s 'to pay Zuchi. Acc Bks 1770–78, 1778–88.
77 BLARS L30/15/50/147, 21 June 1788.
78 '1795, II, 9: bought in £1.18.0. 1807, 15; by Marlow (*Landscape,* but V&A catalogue annotated *View of Plympton*) £2.' Broun 1987, vol.2, p.246.
79 BLARS L30/15/50/67, 18 October 1785.
80 BLARS L30/15/39/70, 16 March 1788; PWDRO 1259/2/51, 4 April 1788; PWDRO 1259/2/53, 3 September 1788; PWDRO 1259/2/59, 13 November 1788.
81 James Boswell, *Life of Samuel Johnson*, London 1799, vol.1, pp.436–39. Northcote first saw Reynolds on his 1762 visit. Stephen Gwynn, *Memorials of an Eighteenth Century Painter James Northcote,* London 1898, pp.34–35.
82 In 1762 Reynolds revisited the orchard adjoining his childhood home in Plympton; ed. Kathryn Cave: *The Diary of Joseph Farington*, vol.10 (Yale 1982), p.3577, entry for 10 October 1809
83 The pocket book entries were published in Cotton 1856, pp.107–9.
84 BLARS L30/14/333/61, 11 September 1770.
85 BLARS L30/14/333/62, 14 September 1770.
86 Cotton 1856, p.107. The note was written by Reynolds on a blank leaf of the pocket book.
87 BLARS L30/14/333/63, 16 September 1770.
88 In 1740 Reynolds's sister Mary or 'Molly' (1716–94) married John Palmer (1708–70), an attorney from Great Torrington, who died on 14 September 1770. Leslie and Taylor, vol.1 p.369; Mannings vol.1, p.361 no.1381. BLARS L30/14/333/64, 18 September 1770.
89 BLARS L30/14/333/66, 23 September 1770.
90 BLARS L30/14/333/67, 25 September 1770.
91 BLARS L30/14/333/68, 28 September 1770. John Lloyd (1726–1806) of Pound, north of Plympton, who worked for the Admiralty at Plymouth. Reynolds met him again in London on Sunday 28 October 1770. Mannings vol.1, p.309 no.1136.
92 Acc Bk 1770–78. After Saltram Reynolds returned to Torrington, where he dined at Mr Palmer's (8 October) and Mr Young's (9 October). He travelled to Exeter on 10 October and stayed the night at Whiteway, Montagu Parker's house near Chudleigh. The following day he dined at Mamhead with Lord Lisburn. On 12 October he was again at Whiteway, and dined in Exeter with his brother Robert (1714–87), an iromonger, before setting off back to London, which he reached on 14 October.
93 BLARS Lucas Group 4A uncatalogued typescript no.14560, 13 September 1770.
94 Kauffmann's portrait of Reynolds was the subject of some verse in the *Advertiser* newspaper, quoted Leslie and Taylor, vol.1, p.326
95 WYAS VR6013 no.14563, 20 September 1770. Fritz trained as a lawyer, hence references to Sir Edward Coke (1552-1634) and Sir William Blackstone (1723–80); 'Miss— mourning her Bird' presumably refers to Reynolds's portrait of Miss Gwynn (Mannings 394) or, more probably, the print after it; Henry Stockman was the local builder responsible for much of the work at Saltram commissioned by Therese Parker; Lord Grantham played the cello. Anthony Poggi painted Stockman's portrait for John Parker (10 March 1776, £20 'for two Pictures'), which was 'engraved by a son of Tomkins the Landscape painter'. Acc Bk 1770–78; BLARS L30/14/333/125, 25 August 1778.
96 BL Add Mss 48218, f.115, 26 June 1772. In July 1772 Northcote stated that Reynolds was to go to Plympton with his niece to become an alderman; but in September Reynolds himself confirmed that 'it was not in my power to pay my respects to you this year and return my thanks in person however next year I hope to do myself that honour.' RA Library NOR/11, 27 July 1772; *Letters*, p.40, no.32.
97 Mannings vol.1, p.364.
98 BLARS L30/17/2/67, 4 October 1773.
99 The only appointment noted for the Torrington week was 'Mr Morrison' on 8 October, but Reynolds also noted in the pocket book page for this week: 'Send Mr Young account / …Sister Palmer / Mr Storer[?] / Mr Morrisons print / of Hope / Mr Mudges money[?] / Mr Storer[?]…'
100 As well as perhaps 'Edysfield [?]' at the end of week commencing 20 September. The pocket book entries for Reynolds's 1773 trip were published in Cotton 1856, pp.121-22.
101 BL Add Mss 48218, f.58, 12 September 1780.
102 BLARS L30/15/54/201, 5 September 1783.
103 BLARS L30/15/50/42, 14 September 1783.
104 Reynolds was back in London by 18 October, when he wrote to Sir William Forbes. *Letters*, 114, 115.
105 *Letters*, 114.
106 The sketch, mounted and measuring 5¾ x 4½ inches, was reported missing not long after it was photographed in 1963.
107 For the portrait and its meanings see Kate Retford, 'Reynolds's portrait of Mrs Theresa Parker', *British Art Journal*, vol.iv, no.3 (autumn 2003), pp.80–86
108 BL Add Mss 48218, f.121: Therese to Grantham, Saltram 20 October 1772.
109 Letters, 30; BLARS L30/14/326/1.
110 BL Add Mss 48218, f.176, 12 March 1772.
111 BL Add Mss 48218, f.133, 15 June 1773.
112 BL Add Mss 48218, f.121, 20 October 1772; BL Add Mss 48218, f.123, 10 November 1772.
113 BL Add Mss 48218, f.27, 23 June 1772.
114 BL Add Mss 48218, f.159, 5 May 1775.
115 BL Add Mss 48218, f.128, 5 March 1773.
116 BL Add Mss 48218, f.111, 2 April 1772.
117 BL Add Mss 48218, f.128, 5 March 1773.
118 BL Add Mss 48218, f.159, 5 May 1775.
119 Mannings vol.1, p.366.
120 BLARS L30/17/4/52, 17 May 1773; BLARS L30/17/4/53, 31 May 1773.
121 Watson was paid £47 5s on 19 May 1775. BL Add Mss 48218, f.212, 24 August 1775; Acc Bk 1770–78.
122 BLARS L30/17/4/59, 23 August 1773; BLARS L30/17/4/57, 26 July 1773; BLARS L30/17/4/60, 6 September 1773.
123 BLARS L30/17/4/66, 6 December 1773.
124 BL, Add Mss 48218 f.139, 10 January 1774.
125 *The Public Advertiser*, 29 December 1775. A slightly altered version appeared in The London Magazine, vol.xlv, 1776, p.111. AMS copy, allegedly in Reynolds's hand, is BL Add Mss 48252, f.15.
126 BL Add Mss 33126, ff.245, 247, 30 December 1775.
127 BL Add Mss 48244, ff.7-10.
128 *Literary Career*, pp.86–87; also Kate Retford, 'Reynolds's portrait of Mrs Theresa Parker', *British Art Journal*, vol.iv, no.3 (autumn 2003), pp.84–85.
129 BLARS L30/14/315/14, 15 January 1776.
130 *Literary Career*, p.87.

131 BL Add Mss 33126, f.273, 23 January 1776, and transcribed by W T Whitley, and Kate Retford.
132 Hilles states that in his published account Northcote 'confesses ignorance' as to the altered word, but Reynolds's intended wording appears in Northcote's Mss autobiography. *Literary Career*, p.88; BL Add Mss 47792.
133 James Northcote, *The Life of Sir Joshua Reynolds*, 1818, vol.2, p.15–17; RA Library NOR/15, 3 January 1776; RA Library NOR/20, 4 April 1776.
134 BLARS L30/14/333/176, 5 February 1779.
135 BLARS L30/14/333/178, 12 February 1779.
136 BLARS L30/14/333/180, 19 February 1779; BLARS L30/14/333/181, 23 February 1779.
137 BLARS L30/14/333/185, 9 March 1779.
138 BLARS L30/14/333/186, 12 March 1779; BLARS L30/14/333/187, 16 March 1779.
139 BL Add Mss 48218, f.55, 26 March 1779, quoted Mannings vol.1, p.366.
140 BLARS L30/15/54/121, 25 February 1779; BLARS L30/17/4/241, 25 February 1779; BLARS L30/15/54/122, 27 February 1779; BLARS L30/15/54/123, 5 March 1779; BLARS L30/17/4/243, 11 March 1779; BLARS L30/14/333/187, 16 March 1779; BLARS L30/15/54/128, 30 March 1779; BLARS L30/14/333/192, 30 March 1779.
141 BLARS L30/14/333/199, 20 April 1779.
142 PWDRO: portion of Nanny letter mounted on card and stuck onto back of Reynolds's portrait of the Parker children, removed in 1976, quoted Mannings vol.1, p.366 when dated 14 April 1779.
143 BLARS L30/14/333/206, 7 May 1779. Mannings records the 7 May sitting as an appointment with John Parker [II].
144 BLARS L30/14/333/208, 14 May 1779.
145 PWDRO 430/2/52, 18 June 1779.
146 BLARS L30/17/2/215, 7 July 1779.
147 PWDRO, 1259/1/26, 27 July 1779; PWDRO, 1259/1/27, 8 August 1779.
148 BLARS L30/14/333/181, 23 February 1779.
149 BLARS L30/14/333/132, 15[13?] September 1778.
150 BLARS L30/14/333/190, 23 March 1779; Saltram 1819, p.40, no.187.
151 BLARS L30/14/333/89, 28 April 1778; BLARS L30/14/333/92, 8 May 1778.
152 BLARS L30/14/333/181, 23 February 1779.
153 BLARS L30/14/333/190, 23 March 1779.
154 BLARS L30/14/333/182, 26 February 1779.
155 BLARS L30/14/333/99, 2 June 1778; BLARS L30/15/54/53, 26 June 1778. Fritz suggested Pohl as the artist, and a price of £25 per picture, but as Pohl was unavailable the copies were painted by Agustin Esteve.
156 For the progress of the Murillo copies, see BLARS L30/14/333/153, 20 December 1778; BLARS L30/15/54/112, 10 January 1779; BLARS L30/15/54/113, 13 January 1779; BLARS L30/15/54/115, 24 January 1779; BLARS L30/17/4/237, 28 January 1779; BLARS L30/15/54/116, 29 January 1779; BLARS L30/17/14/4/238, 4 February 1779; PWDRO 430/1/78, 18 February 1779; BLARS L30/15/54/120, 21 February 1779; BLARS L30/14/333/184, 5 March 1779; BLARS L30/14/333/187, 16 March 1779; BLARS L30/17/2/244, 18 March 1779; BLARS L30/17/4/245, 25 March 1779; BLARS L30/15/54/128, 30 March 1779; BLARS L30/15/54/138, 9 May 1779; PWDRO 430/1/88, 17 June 1779; BLARS L30/17/4/266, 27 December 1779; BLARS L30/15/50/1, 7 January 1780.
157 BLARS L30/17/4/247, 14 April 1779.
158 Reynolds may have known the Murillo compositions through miniature copies owned by his acquaintance Robert Waddilove. The Reni etching is BM U.3.143.
159 Amal Asfour and Paul Williamson, *Gainsborough's Vision*, Liverpool 1999, pp.269–71.
160 BLARS L30/14/333/91, 4 May 1778; BLARS L30/14/333/102, 12 June 1778; PWDRO 1259/1/9, 6 July 1778.
161 BLARS L30/14/333/194, 6 April 1779; PWDRO 1259/1/21, 25 June 1779.
162 BLARS L30/14/315/6: Porteus to Grantham, Peterborough, 26 August 1775.
163 Waterhouse considered Mannings 1541 the prime version and 1542 a studio copy. However, in a letter written from Stanmer just after his return to England, Grantham's reference to 1542 may imply the reverse: 'You must know I have been found thinner than I was, & at first actually younger, tho' having shivered as I told you for a day or two, I do not think I look so well. Sr Joshua says I never was so like the picture of me, which is here.' BLARS L30/17/4/257, 8 August 1779.
164 Nigel Glendinning, Enriqueta Harris and Francis Russell, 'Lord Grantham and the Taste for Velazquez', in *Burlington Magazine*, vol.141, no.1159 (October 1999), pp.598–605.
165 BLARS L30/15/54/136, 23 April 1779; BLARS L30/14/333/198, 27 April 1779; BLARS L30/14/333/203, 30 April 1779; BLARS L30/14/333/211, 25 May 1779; BLARS L30/15/54/201, 5 September 1783; BLARS L30/15/54/164, 20 January 1780.
166 BLARS L30/15/54/253, 21 January 1785; BLARS L30/9/81/100, 10 October 1785; BLARS L30/14/333/337, 21 December 1785.
167 Mannings 1543. BLARS L30/15/50/130, 22 December 1787; BLARS L30/15/39/65, 30 December 1787; BLARS L30/16/16/16, 24 January 1788; BLARS L30/16/16/17, 2 February 1788; BLARS L30/15/50/134, 23 February 1788; BLARS L30/15/50/135, 8 March 1788.
168 For references to the *Discourses*, see BL Add Mss 48218, f.111, 2 April 1772; BLARS L30/17/4/54, 14 June 1773; BLARS L30/17/4/46a, 8 March 1773; BLARS L30/14/109/125, 18 February 1777; BLARS L30/14/333/199, 20 April 1779; BLARS L30/15/54/125, 19 March 1779; BLARS L30/14/333/182, 26 February 1779.
169 At Grantham's behest, in 1777 Reynolds sent 'the prints from Claude Lorrains designs to Mengs at Rome'; a few months later Mengs was still 'very anxious about his Prints Sr Joshua Reynolds wrote him word that he has sent them to Leghorn but we has nothings of them yet, & wishes you would be so good as to write to Sr. Joshua about them.' PWDRO 430/2/46, 14 July 1777; BLARS L30/15/42/13, 2 September 1777; BLARS L30/15/54/68, 10 August 1778; BLARS L30/14/333/183, 2 March 1779.
170 Jeremy Black and Nicholas Penny, 'Letters from Reynolds to Lord Grantham', in *Burlington Magazine*, vol.129 no.1016 (November 1987) pp.730-734; also *Letters*, 30, 35, 40, 65. Reynolds's letters are mentioned in BL Add Mss 48218, f.111, 2 April 1772; and BL Add Mss 48218, f.33, 27 April 1773. None of Grantham's letters to Reynolds survive but Therese wrote that 'Sr. Joshua is much pleased with your Letter.' BL Add Mss 48218, f.115, 26 June 1772.
171 BLARS L30/17/4/45, 8 February 1773.
172 Bedford L30/17/4/173, 26 October 1777.
173 BL Add Mss 48218, f.161, 2 June 1775.
174 BL Add Mss 48218, f.166, 18 July 1775.
175 BL Add Mss 48218, f.107, 23 August 1771; BLARS L30/17/1/7, 21 October 1771; BL Add Mss 48218, f.111, 2 April 1772; BL Add Mss 48218, f.119, 10[16?]August 1772.
176 BLARS L30/14/315/6, 26 August 1775.
177 WYAS VR6013 no.14561, 16 September 1770.
178 BLARS Lucas Group 4A uncatalogued typescript no.14542, 1 September 1769; BLARS L30/14/333/49, 20 October 1769; WYAS VR6013 no.14559, 11 September 1770; BL Add Mss 48218, f.107,

23 August 1771; BL Add Mss 48218, f.172, 13 September 1771; BL Add Mss 48218, f.174, 29 November 1771; BL Add Mss 48218, f.31, 25 October 1772.

179 For instance PWDRO 1259/1/46, 4 January 1790.

180 PWDRO 1259/1/132, 16 February 1790; PWDRO 1259/1/162, 10 November 1790.

181 PWDRO 1259/1/194, 16 October 1791; BL Add Mss 48218, f.75, 16 October 1786; BLARS L30/15/50/105, 22 March 1787.

182 Bought at Dr Newton's sale at Christie's on 30 April 1790, lot 99 for 40gns to Grozer, Reynolds's agent; it was sold from Saltram at Sotheby's in 1964 for £18. Broun 1987, vol.2, p.276. Britton and Brayley 1803, vol.4, p.143.

183 Mannings 29, Britton and Brayley 1803, p.143; Saltram 1819, p.28.

184 Nicholas Penny ed., *Reynolds*, London 1986, p.257.

185 Mannings vol.1, p.77, no.126. 'This picture was painted in 1771, for the collection of Mr.Thrale, of Streatham Park; a note in the handwriting of Northcote at the back of the frame, identifies it.' Saltram 1844, p.31.

186 The Mannings provenance, identical to Penny's in 1985, differs slightly from that given by Albert, 3rd Earl of Morley (1843–1905) in a 1902 MSS catalogue in the collection of the National Trust at Queen Anne's Gate, London. In 1902 the painting, then at 31 Prince's Gardens, London, was said to have been purchased in 1854 from the Treby family, and remained at Whiteway until 1897.

187 Parker redecorated several rooms, moved some of the pictures and had many restored. PWDRO 1259/2/262, 8 October 1795; PWDRO Acc 3102, box 4, 29 November 1795.

188 Kathryn Cave ed., *The Diary of Joseph Farington*, Yale 1982, vol.10, p.3578 (entry for 10 October 1809).

189 Quoted Johnson 1998, p.51.

190 Saltram 1819, pp.27–29. In his memoir, begun 23 November 1809, John Parker [III] noted of one Reynolds portrait that it was 'afterwards removed with all the other Sir Joshua's to the Library.' BL Add Mss 48244, f.18.

191 John Britton and Edward Wedlake Brayley, *Devonshire Illustrated*, London 1829, p.53.

THE ROAD TO THE ROYAL ACADEMY

1 Joseph Farington, *Memoirs of the Life of Sir Joshua Reynolds; with some observations on his talents and character*, London, 1819, p.39. Reynolds is recorded as arriving in London on 16 October, the date presumably being calculated on the new calendar adopted the previous month, when 3 September was changed to 14 September, with the 'loss' of eleven days.

2 J.T. Smith stated that 104 St Martin's Lane was for many years kept by Williams, a Button-Maker, and that Thornhill and, after him, the sculptor Van Nost lived in a large house behind. 'In this house,' Smith wrote, 'after Van Nost's time, Francis Hayman once lived; and also Sir Joshua Reynolds, before his knighthood, and before he went to live in the house, now No.5, on the north side of Great Newport-Street, whence he went to Leicester Fields, where he died'. See J.T. Smith, *Nollekens and his Times*, 2 vols, London, 1828, vol.2, pp.228–31. Also Derek Hudson, *Sir Joshua Reynolds. A Personal Study*, London, 1958, p.50. However, Hugh Phillips, *Mid-Georgian London*, London 1964, p.112 disputes that Thornhill and Van Nost ever lived at 104 St Martin's Lane.

3 Farington, op.cit., p.40.

4 James Northcote, *The Life of Sir Joshua Reynolds*, 2 vols, London 1818, vol.1, p. 54. The story of Hudson's reaction to the painting was told by Marchi to Farington.

5 See Northcote, op.cit., vol.1, p.52.

6 William Mason in William Cotton, *Sir Joshua Reynolds's Notes and Observations on Pictures*, London, 1859, p.50.

7 John Ingamells and John Edgcumbe, *The Letters of Sir Joshua Reynolds*, New Haven and London 2000, pp.14–15.

8 Edmond Malone, *The Literary Works of Sir Joshua Reynolds*, 3 vols, London 1798, vol.1, p.xxiii.

9 See Martin Postle, 'An early unpublished letter by Sir Joshua Reynolds', *Apollo*, vol.CXLI, 1995, pp.11–18.

10 'I asked Marchi "When Toms the drapery painter, first began to paint Draperies for Sir J. Reynolds." He said, "When Sir Joshua lived in Newport Street." Toms had fifteen guineas for painting the Drapery to a *whole length* figure. Sir Joshua, Marchi sd. "Was never pleased with anything that was done for Him".' See Kenneth Garlick, Angus Macintyre and Kathryn Cave, eds, *The Diary of Joseph Farington*, 16 vols., New Haven and London 1978–84, vol.9, p.3238.

11 See David Mannings and Martin Postle, *Sir Joshua Reynolds. A Complete Catalogue of his Paintings The subject pictures catalogued by Martin Postle*, 2 vols, New Haven and London 2000, vol.1, pp.1–6.

12 For Reynolds's practice in the 1750s see Ellis K. Waterhouse, 'Sir Joshua Reynolds's Sitter-Book of 1755, *Walpole Society*, 1966–68, vol.XLI, pp.112–64.

13 See David Mannings, 'Notes on some eighteenth-century portrait prices in Britain', *British Journal for Eighteenth Century Studies*, vol.6, 1983, pp. 185–96.; also Mannings, op. cit., vol.1, pp.21–22.

14 See Hudson, op.cit., p.50. As Hudson notes, the house in which Reynolds lived (number 5) was demolished in 1766–67. The site is presently occupied by numbers 10 and 11 Great Newport Street (not the present number 5 which bears an unofficial, and misinformed, plaque).

15 The Honourable John West to Simon, 1st Earl Harcourt, then Viscount Nuneham, 26 June 1759. See E.W. Harcourt, ed., *The Harcourt Papers*, 14 vols, printed privately, Oxford, 1880–1905, vol.8, p.30.

16 William Hazlitt, *Conversations of James Northcote, Esq., R.A.*, London 1830, p.289.

17 Cornelia Knight, *Autobiography*, ed. J.W. Kaye, London, 1861, vol.1, p.9.

18 Horace Walpole to Sir David Dalrymple, 25 February 1759, in W S Lewis, ed., *Horace Walpole's Correspondence*, 48 vols, New Haven and London.

19 Reynolds noted 'Mr Ramsay' in his sitter-book opposite the week beginning 17 October 1757. For their subsequent social engagements see Alastair Smart, *Allan Ramsay: Painter, Essayist and Man of the Enlightenment*, New Haven and London 1992, pp.258–59.

20 Alastair Smart, *Allan Ramsay. A Complete Catalogue of his Paintings*, ed. John Ingamells, New Haven and London 1999, p.85.

21 J T Smith, *Nollekens and his Times*, 2 vols, London 1828, vol.2, p.296. It was suggested by Sir Ellis Waterhouse that Smith had meant to refer to Reynolds's portrait of the Earl of Lauderdale, which is compositionally close to Ramsay's portrait of Lord Rockingham. (See Ellis Waterhouse, *Painting in Britain 1530–1790*, Harmondsworth 1953, p.157.) However, Smith was quite specific, noting that he was referring to the portrait of Rockingham engraved by Edward Fisher (whereas *Lauderdale* was not engraved). A close reading of Smith's text reveals that, unlike Ramsay's *Bute*, Reynolds had 'not given a strut to the left leg': in other words, I would suggest that in this instance, he wanted his portrait to be distinguished from Ramsay's, not to emulate it.

22 See Mannings, op.cit., vol.1, cat. 715, p.214. See also *Gainsborough and Reynolds. Contrasts in Royal Patronage*, exhibition catalogue,

The Queen's Gallery, Buckingham Palace, London 1994, cat.7, p.32.

23 Joseph Farington noted on 9 August 1807: 'Lady Thomond I met at two o'Clock at Sir Joshua Reynolds's late House in Leicester Square, a Sale of the goods remaining there being to be sold by auction on Tuesday next. The lease of the House will expire in September next'. *The Diary of Joseph Farington*, vol.8, p.3103. See also vol.8, p.3106.

24 It was probably as a direct result of Reynolds's rebuilding work that the rateable value of his house rose to £100 per annum. For the history of Reynolds's house, its rateable value and Reynolds's redecoration of the property see Hudson, op.cit., pp.72–74 and F H W Shepherd (ed), *Survey of London vol.xxxiv The Parish of St Anne Soho*, London 1966, pp.508–12.

25 Northcote, op.cit., vol.1, pp.102–3.

26 William Mason reported to Lord Harcourt: 'I went also to Sir Joshua's, but the picture was still at Gaskell's for a second copy, & Sir Joshua desired me to tell his Lordship so & apologise for not writing himself. But Charles who had more *empressement* went (as he tells me) to Gaskell's, & likes my lady better than either My lord or the Colonel'. Harcourt, ed., op. cit., vol.7, p. 61. Reynolds's copyists also included at that time several miniaturists, notably Christopher Barber (c.1736–1810) and John Smart (1741–1811). For Smart and Barber see Reynolds's Memorandum Book at note 25 below (PMC neg. 1526/13A and 1526/29A).

27 Private collection. There is a photographic copy of the Memorandum Book in the Paul Mellon Centre for Studies in British Art, London (PMC neg. 75 1525/25-1527/9).

28 Reynolds's sitter book for 1769 contains, folded in a piece of paper marked 'Lady Carlisle', a lock of brown hair, which was presumably an *aide-mémoire* for the portrait now at Castle Howard. See Mannings, op.cit., vol.1, cat. 995, pp.2678; vol.2, fig.998.

29 See Mannings, op. cit., vol.1, p. 387.

30 For further information see Martin Postle, 'Peter Toms', *Oxford Dictionary of National Biography* at www.oxforddnb.com. For Hudson's probable use of Toms see Ellen G. Miles and Jacob Simon, *Thomas Hudson, 1701–1779. Portrait painter and collector. A bicentenary exhibition*, exhibition catalogue, The Iveagh Bequest, Kenwood (unpaginated).

31 See Mannings, op.cit., vol.1, cat. 611, p.188; also Nicholas Penny, ed., *Reynolds*, exhibition catalogue, Royal Academy of Arts, London 1986, cat. 31, p.193.

32 On tour in Italy, later in the century, Dr Parkinson encountered Trevisani's painting *Cleopatra dissolving the Diamond*, and noted: 'Sir Joshua Reynolds has taken her for his Kitty Fisher'. See Dr J. Parkinson, ms. journal of his tour of France and Italy, 1784, 4 vols, quoted from material in the Brinsley Ford Archive, Paul Mellon Centre for Studies in British Art, London. See also Penny, ed., op.cit., cat.34, pp.195–96 and Edgar Wind, *Hume and the Heroic Portrait. Studies in Eighteenth-Century Imagery*, Jaynie Anderson, ed., Oxford, 1986, pp.42, 70, 84, 123, figs.80–81.

33 See Robin Simon, 'Reynolds and the double-entendre: The Society of Dilettanti portraits', *The British Art Journal*, vol.3. no.1 (2002), pp.69–77; also Bruce Redford, *The Antic and the Antique in eighteenth-century England*, Los Angeles 2008, pp.106–7.

34 See H. Bleackley, *Casanova in England*, London, 1932, p.144, and Penny, ed., op.cit., p.195.

35 *Viscountess Folkestone* was exhibited (without a catalogue number) perhaps as an afterthought. Penny, ed., op.cit., cat.40, pp. 203–4. Reynolds's note in his Memorandum Book, 'Write to Mr Stern & General Kingsly [*sic*]', suggests that he wrote to both sitters to request permission to exhibit their portraits (see Memorandum Book, PMC neg. 75 1525/32).

36 See Penny ed., op.cit., cat. 37, pp.199–200.

37 Desmond Shawe-Taylor, *Genial Company. The Theme of Genius in Eighteenth-Century British Portraiture*, exhibition catalogue, Nottingham University and the Scottish National Portrait Gallery, 1987, p.48.

38 See Mungo Campbell, '*Lord Cardross* and the *Boy with a squirrel*; Sir Joshua Reynolds's first encounter with the Earl of Buchan and John Singleton Copley' *The Burlington Magazine*, vol.CXXIX (1016), 1987, pp.728–30 (729). The quotation is taken from autobiographical notes made by Lord Buchan in 1794, Glasgow University Library, Murray 502/66. As Campbell notes, the portrait of William Feilding, 1st Earl of Denbigh (National Gallery) was already acknowledged as being by Van Dyck rather than Rubens.

39 Campbell (loc.cit.) suggests that Reynolds copied Van Dyck's etching of the painting rather than the original. However, given the original painting's presence in the studio and Reynolds's known use of mirrors it would seem more likely that he painted it from a reflection.

40 Ozias Humphry to his brother, the Rev. William Humphry, 19 September 1764, G B Hill, ed., *Johnsonian Miscellanies*, 2 vols, Oxford, 1897, vol.2, pp.401–2.

41 Edmond Malone stated that Reynolds's first idea of forming the Club was 'started to Dr. Johnson at his own fireside'. See Sir James Prior, *Life of Edmond Malone, editor of Shakespeare with selections from his Manuscript Anecdotes*, London 1860, p.434.

42 Thomas Percy to James Boswell, 28 February 1788. See *Samuel Johnson 1709–84. A Bicentenary Exhibition*, exhibition catalogue, National Portrait Gallery, London, cat.65, p.100.

43 See Mannings, op.cit., vol.1, pp.219–20. Here the portrait is dated c.1770, the year it was exhibited by Reynolds at the Royal Academy. It could, however, have been painted earlier, since Goldsmith's name had appeared in Reynolds's sitter books since the summer of 1766 (although a number of these engagements would social rather than appointments for portrait sittings).

44 Northcote, op.cit., vol.1, p.326.

45 See Mannings, op.cit., vol.1, cat. 1863, p.468; Penny, ed., op.cit., cat.70, pp.236–38.

46 See Oliver Millar, *Van Dyck in England*, exhibition catalogue, National Portrait Gallery, 1982, cat. 57, pp. 96–97, figs. 44–45, and colour plate XI; see also Penny, ed., p.237.

47 'Large sketch for the portraits of the Marquis of Rockingham, and Mr Burke, and ditto of Euphrosyne / £11 0s 6d', Marchioness of Thomond sale, Christie's, London, 26 May 1821, lot 14.

48 John Hayes, *The Letters of Thomas Gainsborough*, New Haven and London 2001, p.38.

49 Although Cotes employed Toms, his portrait prices remained lower than Reynolds. In 1768 Cotes charged 25 guineas for a head, 40 guineas for a half-length, and 80 guineas for a full-length. Reynolds's fees were then respectively 30 guineas, 70 guineas, and 150 guineas. See Edward Mead Johnson, *Francis Cotes. Complete edition with a critical essay and a catalogue*, Oxford 1976, p.16.

50 Johnson, op.cit., p.41.

51 Kauffman's letter, to her father, is dated 10 October, 1766. See Lady Victoria Manners and Dr G C Williamson, *Angelica Kauffmann, R.A. Her Life and Her Works*, London 1924, p. 20. It is not certain whether Reynolds painted Kauffman's portrait at this time. An unfinished portrait of Kauffman by Reynolds, formerly in the collection of Earl Spencer, is considered to have been painted around 1777–78. See Mannings and Postle, op.cit., vol.1, cat.1026, pp.284–85.

52 See Reynolds's sitter book, 17 October 1766. See also the following associated entries on 30 June, 'Miss Angelica', and 1 October,

'Miss Angelica / Fiori'.

53 See Wendy Wassing Roworth, ed., *Angelica Kauffman. A Continental Artist in Georgian England*, London, 1992, pp.42–57.

54 See Penny, ed., op. cit., cat.169, pp.339–40; Desmond Shawe-Taylor, *Genial Company: the Theme of Genius in eighteenth-century British Portraiture*, exhibition catalogue, Nottingham University Art Gallery and Scottish National Portrait Gallery, Edinburgh 1987, pp.28–31; Roworth, ed., op. cit., pp.38–42.

55 Roworth, ed., op.cit., p.41.

56 Shawe-Taylor, op.cit., p.29.

57 John Pye, *Patronage of British Art*, London 1845, pp. 121–23. For a detailed account of the machinations within the Society of Artists, leading up to the formation of the Royal Academy, see Matthew Hargraves, *'Candidates for Fame'. The Society of Artists of Great Britain 1760–1791*, New Haven and London 2005, pp.43–88.

58 See William Thompson, *The Conduct of the Royal Academicians while members of the Incorporated Society of Artists of Great Britain, viz. from the year 1760, to their expulsion in the year 1769. With some part of their transactions since*, London 1771, p. 42. f; Robert Strange, *An Inquiry into the Rise and Establishment of the Royal Academy of Arts*, London, 1775, pp.74–75. Also Charles Robert Leslie and Tom Taylor, *Life and Times of Sir Joshua Reynolds*, 2 vols, London 1865, vol.I, pp. 316–17.

59 See Thompson, op.cit., pp. 45–46. Also Leslie and Taylor, op.cit., vol.I, p.280.

60 Edward Fryer, ed., *The Works of James Barry*, 2 vols, London 1809, vol.I, p.92.

61 See Timothy Clifford, Antony Griffiths, and Martin Royalton-Kisch, *Gainsborough and Reynolds in the British Museum*, exhibition catalogue, British Museum, London 1978, p.47.

62 See Peter Leach, *James Paine*, London, 1988, p. 193; William T Whitley, *Artists and their Friends in England, 1700–1799*, 2 vols, London 1928, vol.I, p.213.

63 See Leach, op.cit., p.34.

64 See Pye, op.cit., pp.127–29.

65 Strange, op.cit., p.98; Thompson, op.cit., p.44.

66 'Mr Paine', Reynolds's sitter book, 4 pm, 20 November 1768.

67 See Minutes of the Society of Artists, Royal Academy of Arts, ms. SA\34\4. For Reynolds's intention to write to Gainsborough see his sitter book, 21 November 1768.

68 *The Diary of Joseph Farington*, 12 December 1804, vol.6, p.2469. See also John Galt, *The Life, Studies and Works of Benjamin West*, London, 1820, Part 2, p.42; Leslie and Taylor, op.cit., vol.I, p.296.

69 Northcote, op.cit., vol.I, pp.166–67. See also Leslie and Taylor, op.cit., vol.I, pp.295–96.

70 See Sidney C. Hutchison, *The History of the Royal Academy 1768-1968*, London 1968, pp.209–13. See also Royal Academy of Arts archive, RAA/FI.

71 Reynolds does not mention the General Assembly on 14 December 1768 in his sitter book, even though his signature appears among the Minutes. See General Assembly Minutes of the Royal Academy, vol.I, pp.1–4. The first reference to the Academy appears in the sitter book at 6 pm on 17 December, when several Professors were appointed. The following morning Reynolds noted an appointment with William Chambers at 9.30 am.

72 Leslie and Taylor, op.cit., vol.I, p.294.

73 *The Diary of Joseph Farington*, 12 December 1804, vol.6, p.2469.

74 For Johnson's politics see B H Bronson, *Johnson Agonistes and Other Essays*, Cambridge, 1946; Donald J Greene, *The Politics of Samuel Johnson*, New Haven, 1960.

75 Leslie and Taylor, op.cit., vol.I, p.380, note I.

76 The sittings for George III and Queen Charlotte took place in 1779. See Mannings, op. cit., vol.I, pp.214–16.

77 Reynolds, sitter book, 21 April 1769: 'Knighted at St James'. See also *Baldwin's London Weekly Journal*, 29 April, 1769: 'SATURDAY, April 22. Yesterday his Majesty was pleased to confer the Honour of Knighthood on Joshua Reynolds, Esq. President of the Royal Academy of Painting, &c.'.

SELF-PORTRAITS

1 Reynolds's Papers, as cited in Charles Robert Leslie and Tom Taylor, *Life and Times of Sir Joshua Reynolds with Notices of Some of His Contemporaries*, vol.II, London: John Murray, 1865, p.611.

2 Despite the acuity of vision suggested by this self-portrait, Reynolds's sight gave him caused for concern in his later years; his eyes had been affected by a 'violent inflammation' in Januray 1783 and from the summer of 1789 the onset of the eye disease gutta serena would deprive him of all his vision in his left eye. See John Ingamells and John Edgumbe eds *The Letters of Sir Joshua Reynolds*, New Haven and London: Yale University Press, 2000, pp.114, 198, 206, 222, 225, 228n.

3 James Northcote, *The Life of Sir Joshua Reynolds*, vol.II, London: Henry Colburn, 1818, vol.II, p.322.

4 Edmund Burke, Obituary notice, as cited in Leslie and Taylor, *Life and Times*, vol.II, p.629.

'CARE, TASTE AND JUDGEMENT'

The title of this essay is taken from the declaration of Reynolds's executors, Edmund Malone and Philip Metcalfe, printed in the opening text of the sale catalogue of Reynolds's collection (Henry Phillips, London, 5 March 1798).

1 Frits Lugt, *Les marques de collections de dessins et d'estampes* (Amsterdam: Vereenigde, 1921), pp.441–42, no.2364.

2 In Reynolds's picture sale at Christie's London on 14 March 1795, lot 9 was an untraced work by Charles Tomkins (1757–1823) described as 'A View of Plympton, Devonshire'. See Robert R Wark, *Early British drawings in the Huntington collection, 1600–1750* (San Marino, CA: The Huntington Library, 1969), p.24 for a view of Pymouth.

3 Hamburg (inv.no.21044). See David Klemm, *Von Leonardo bis Piranesi: Italienische zeichnungen von 1450 bis 1800 aus dem Kupferstichkabinett der Hamburger Kunsthalle* (Hamburg: Hamburger Kunsthalle and Hachmann-edition, 2008), pp.32–33, 219, no.10.

4 It was later owned by the French painter and lithographer Jean François Gigoux (1806–94), and is now in Besançon. See Catherine Loisel in Diederik Bakhuÿs *et al.*, *Le génie de Bologne des Carracci aux Gandolfi* (Montreuil: Gourcuff Gradenigo, 2006), pp.100–1, no.42.

5 Fitzwilliam Museum, Cambridge (inv.2581).

6 This copy was later owned by the Devonian painter Benjamin Robert Haydon (1786–1846), who idolised Reynolds, and was proud both to have shared the birthplace of his illustrious predecessor, and to have been educated at the same school.

7 Martin Sonnabend, *Michelangelo: Zeichnungen und zuschreibungen/ Drawings and attributions* (Frankfurt: Städel Museum, 2009), pp.33–40, no.2.

8 James Northcote, *The Life of Sir Joshua Reynolds* (London: Henry Colburn, 1819), vol.I, p.19.

9 Probably that now in the British Museum (PDT, 14.6).

10 Carol Gibson-Wood, *Jonathan Richardson: Art theorist of the English Enlightenment* (New Haven and London: Yale University Press, 2000), p.96.

11 For Reynolds's collection of paintings, see Francis Broun, *Sir Joshua Reynolds' collection of paintings*, unpublished Ph.D., University of Princeton, 1987.

12 Martin Royalton-Kisch, *Drawings by Rembrandt and his circle in the British Museum* (London: British Museum Press, 1992), pp.53–55, no.12.

13 Broun, op.cit., vol.II, pp.283–84, no.1 (Guercino). The prime version is in the National Gallery of Scotland, Edinburgh (NGS 40).

14 *Italian seventeenth-century drawings from British collections: Edinburgh Festival 1972* (Edinburgh: Edinburgh Festival Society Ltd, 1972), p.26, no.67.

15 British Museum (PD Pp, 4.43).

16 Northcote, op.cit., vol.I, p.18. Some of these 'Guercinos' by Reynolds are now in the collection of the Italian Baroque scholar and collector Sir Denis Mahon (b.1910).

17 One is now in the Metropolitan Museum of Art, New York (29.100.935): Benesch 324; the other was sold in Hôtel Drouot, Paris, 22 March 1983, lot 16: undescribed by Benesch.

18 Nicholas Turner, 'John Bouverie as a collector of drawings', *The Burlington Magazine*, 136 (1091), February 1994, pp.90–99 (91).

19 National Gallery of Art, Washington (1972.5.1).

20 Two are now in the British Museum: A E Popham, *Italian drawings in the Department of Prints and Drawings in the British Museum: Artists working in Parma in the sixteenth century* (London: Trustees of the British Museum, 1967), vol.I, p.4, no.6, vol.II, plate 4 (recto) and plate 5 (verso) and p.12, no.18.

21 Northcote, op.cit., vol.I, p.119.

22 Courtauld Institute Gallery (Princess Gate Collection), London.

23 Edgar Wind believed the sheet to be one in the École des Beaux-Arts in Paris. See Edgar Wind, 'The Maenad under the Cross: Comments on an observation by Reynolds', *Journal of the Warburg and Courtauld Institutes*, 1, 1937–38, pp.70–71, plate 9d.

24 Martin Royalton-Kisch, 'Reynolds as a collector', pp.61–75 (62) in Timothy Clifford, Antony Griffiths and Martin Royalton-Kisch, *Gainsborough and Reynolds in the British Museum* (London: British Museum Publications, 1978).

25 David McTavish in Katharine Lochnan (ed.), *Drawing attention: Selected works on paper from the Renaissance to Modernism, Art Gallery of Ontario* (London and New York: Toronto: Merrell and Art Gallery of Ontario, 2008), pp.30–31, no.2.

26 David Franklin in David Franklin (ed.), *Leonardo da Vinci, Michelangelo and the Renaissance in Florence* (Ottawa: New Haven and London: National Gallery of Canada and Yale University Press, 2005), pp.274–75, 353, no.98.

27 The Ottawa sheet retained the hallowed attribution for two centuries until first published by David Franklin in 2005 as a work by Pontormo, a younger Florentine closely influenced by Michelangelo, and of whose work Reynolds owned other examples. Ibid., pp.217–19, 347, no.73.

28 Most recently, a drawing by Simone Cantarini (1612-1648) from the collection of the American Joseph McCrindle (1923-2008), Christie's South Kensington, 2 December 2008, lot 303.

29 Stephen Lloyd, *Richard and Maria Cosway: Regency artists of taste and fashion* (Edinburgh: National Galleries of Scotland, 1995) and Julius Bryant, *Thomas Banks (1735–1805): Britain's first modern sculptor* (London: Sir John Soane's Museum, 2005).

30 Kristin Lohse Belkin, Gregory Martin and Fiona Healy, *A house of art: Rubens as collector* (Antwerp: Rubenshuis & Rubenianum, 2004).

PRINTS AND DRAWINGS ACQUIRED BY REYNOLDS

References to 'Lugt' indicate the two standard catalogues of collectors' marks and inscriptions. See Frits Lugt *Les marques de collections de dessins et d'estampes* (Amsterdam: Vereenigde, 1921) and the supplementary work *Les marques de collections de dessins et d'estampes: supplément* (The Hague: Martinus Nijhoff, 1956).

1 Mantegna *St. James Led to Execution* (British Museum, London; PD 1976,0616.1), *Studies of St John the Baptist and a Suppliant* (private collection), *Virgin and Child* (Institut Néerlandais, Lugt Collection, Paris; inv.4983), *Bird on a branch with fruit* (National Gallery of Art, Washington; 1976.33.1), *Bird on a branch catching a fly* (British Museum, London; PD 1946,0713.7).

2 Albertina, Vienna; inv.3061.

3 Formerly attributed to Raphael. See Suzanne Folds McCullagh and Laura M Giles, *Italian drawings before 1600 in the Art Institute of Chicago* (Chicago: Art Institute of Chicago, 1997), pp.362–63, no.577.

4 Xanthe Brooke, *Mantegna to Rubens: The Weld-Blundell drawings collection* (London: Merrell Holberton, 1998), pp.72–73, 150 no.30.

5 Portrait of a boy with a cap (British Museum; PD 1910, 0212.30), *Madonna and Child Enthroned* (Fitzwilliam Museum; no.2932).

6 Institut Néerlandais (Fondation Custodia) inv.no.2903. James Byam Shaw, *The Italian drawings of the Frits Lugt collection* (Paris: Institut Néerlandais, 1983), vol.I, pp.7–8, no.4, vol.III, plate 5.

7 Paul Joannides, *The drawings of Raphael, with a complete catalogue* (Oxford: Phaidon, 1983), p.204, no.285 and Loránd Zentai in Teréz Gerszi (ed.), *Leonardo to Van Gogh, master drawings from Budapest* (Chicago and Washington: Art Institute of Chicago and National Gallery of Art, 1985), pp.30–31, no.7.

8 The same inscription in the same hand is found on a genuine drawing by Fra Bartolommeo (once owned by Reynolds) in the British Museum (PD Pp, 1.56). See Charles S. Ellis, 'Two drawings by Fra Bartolommeo', *Paragone*, 19–20 (479–81), January–March 1990, pp.3–19 (12), plate 11a.

9 Victoria and Albert Museum (Dyce 177), and British Museum (PD Pp, 1.52 and Pp, 1.56).

10 Phillips London, 20-21 March 1798, lots 1311 and 1416. Nicholas Penny (ed.), *Reynolds* (London: Royal Academy of Arts and Weidenfeld and Nicolson, 1986), p.236.

11 Marco Dente da Ravenna *Vulcan* and Eneo Vico *Bacchanal*, Fine Arts Museums of San Francisco (PD 1963.30.3144 and PD 1963.30.3249); Agostino Veneziano *Apollo*, British Museum (PD H, 2.70*).

12 Mannings 41.

13 Art Institute of Chicago; Mannings 278. See John Heneage Jesse, *George Selwyn and his contemporaries; with memoirs and notes* (London: Richard Bentley, 1843–44), vol.II, p.292 quoted in Francis Russell, 'Guercino and England' in Michael Helston *et al.*, *Guercino in Britain: Paintings from British collections* (London: National Gallery Publications and Burlington Magazine Publications, 1991), pp.4–10 (5).

14 One large and complex drawing is in the Staatliche Graphische Sammlung, Munich (inv.2514).

15 Mannings 2089.

16 Sylvie Béguin *et al.*, *Disegni della donazione Marcel Puech al museo Calvet di Avignone* (Naples: Paparo Edizioni, 1998), vol.II (Inventario), p.82, no.409.

17 Sotheby's, London, 5 December 1972, lots 6, 7, 9, 14, 15, 26, 32, 34, 55, 66 and 75.

18 National Gallery of Art, Washington (1973.29.1). Christine Begley in Janet Cox-Rearick (ed.), *Giulio Romano, master designer: An exhibition of drawings in celebration of the five hundredth anniversary of his birth* (New York: Bertha and Karl Leubsdorf Art Gallery,

Hunter College of the City University of New York, 1999), pp.82–83, no.19.

19 *Allegory of the Virtues of Federico Gonzaga*, (British Museum; PD 1895, 0915.642); Reynolds's drawing for Camera dei Giganti, Getty Museum (94.GA.32). See Valerie Taylor in Cox-Rearick (ed.), op.cit., pp.108–9, no.30.

20 Margaret Schwartz in Cox-Rearick (ed.), op.cit., pp.66-7, no.13 and pp.68–69, no.14.

21 Achim Gnann, *Parmigianino: Die zeichnungen* (Petersberg: Michael Imhof Verlag, 2007) nos. 8, 29, 53, 100, 123, 230, 234, 243, 247, 286, 302, 350, 356, 357, 380, 408, 471, 484, 486, 519, 542, 577, 586, 648, 675, 680, 843, 916, 925, 930, 937, 957, 989, 1011 and 1012. This expanded in turn the work of Sylvie Béguin, Mario Di Giampaolo and Mary Vaccaro, *Parmigianino: The drawings* (Turin and London: Umberto Allemandi & Co, 2000).

22 Bruce Davis, *Master drawings in the Los Angeles County Museum of Art* (Los Angeles: Los Angeles County Museum of Art, 1997), pp.16–17, no.2 [Popham (1971), no.750].

23 Adam Bartsch, *Le peintre graveur: Les clair-obscurs des maîtres Italiens* (Vienna: J V Degen, 1811), vol.XII, pp.79–80, no.28. I am grateful to Christopher Mendez for this information.

24 A E Popham, *Italian drawings in the Department of Prints and Drawings in the British Museum: Artists working in Parma in the sixteenth century* (London: Trustees of the British Museum, 1967), p.21, no.29, plate 25 B (as Gatti).

25 Sotheby's, New York, 23 January 2001, lot 184.

26 Adam Bartsch, *Le peintre graveur: Les graveurs de l'école de Marc-Antoine Raimondi* (Vienna: J V Degen, 1813), vol.XV, p.297, no.31.

27 Karen Jacobson (ed.), *The French Renaissance in prints from the Bibliothèque Nationale de France* (Los Angeles: University of California at Los Angeles (Grunwald Center for the Graphic Arts), 1994), pp.470–71.

28 Respectively British Museum, PD 1946, 0713.524; and Metropolitan Museum of Art, 52.124.2.

29 The drawing was described as 'attitudine michelangiolesca' by Barocchi, op.cit., p.227.

30 Mannings 2045. See Martin Postle in Mannings, *loc.cit.*, p.518, no.2045.

31 Victoria and Albert Museum, Dyce 355.

32 British Museum, PD Pp, 2.125 and PD 1946,0713.42. For latter see Dominique Cordellier in Dominique Cordellier (ed.), op.cit., pp.183–84, no.67.

33 Vittoria Romani in Dominique Cordellier (ed.), ibid., pp.299–300, no.138.

34 D2893. See Aidan Weston-Lewis in Peter Humfrey *et al.*, *The age of Titian: Venetian Renaissance art from Scottish collections* (Edinburgh: National Galleries of Scotland, 2004), pp.238–39, no.99.

35 Walker Art Gallery, WAG 1995.249; and the Szépművészeti Múzeum, inv.no 1869 and 1953. Xanthe Brooke, *Mantegna to Rubens: The Weld-Blundell drawings collection* (London: Merrell Holberton, 1998), pp.69–70, 149, no.28.

36 Kupferstichkabinett, KdZ 19. See Elfried Bock, *Staatliche Museen zu Berlin: Die Deutschen meister* (Berlin: Julius Bard, 1921), vol.I, p.28, vol.II, plate 38.

37 Saint Louis Art Museum, 66:1951.

38 Christie's, London, 4 December 2007, lot 1.

39 British Museum, PD 1895,0915.979.

40 Ursula Mielke, *The New Hollstein, German engravings, etchings and woodcuts 1400–1700: Albrecht and Erhard Altdorfer* (Rotterdam: Sound & Vision Interactive, 1997), p.88, 92, no.E119.

41 The drawing was on sale in 1875 as 'Donatello'; *Original drawings and sketches by the Old Masters… formed by the late Mr William Mayor, of Bayswater Hill, London* (London, 1875), p.2, no.5.

42 British Museum (PD 1860,0616.31). This drawing passed to Richard Cosway and then Sir Thomas Lawrence. See Roger Ward, *Baccio Bandinelli, 1493–1560: Drawings from British collections* (Cambridge: Fitzwilliam Museum, 1988), pp.45–46,106, no.22.

43 Courtauld Institute, D.1952.RW.2726. See Ward, op.cit., pp.78–79, 130, no.45.

44 Gere and Pouncey, op.cit., vol.I, p.205, no.328, vol.II, plate 312 and vol.I, pp.209–10, no.334, vol.II, plate 321.

45 *Frederick Howard, 5th Earl of Carlisle*, Mannings 946; *Peregrine Bertie, 3rd Duke of Ancaster*, Mannings 169.

46 Harold E Wethey, *Titian and his drawings, with reference to Giorgione and some close contemporaries* (Princeton, NJ: Princeton University Press, 1987), p.143, no.18, fig.39.

47 Metropolitan Museum of Art, New York (11.66.13), see Wethey, ibid., p.225, no.X-8, fig.225.

48 Agnes Mongan and Paul J Sachs, *Drawings in the Fogg Museum of Art* (Cambridge, MA: Harvard University Press, 1940), vol.I, pp.100–1, no.190.

49 Michael Bury in Peter Humfrey *et al.*, *The age of Titian: Venetian Renaissance art from Scottish collections* (Edinburgh: National Galleries of Scotland, 2004), p.298, no.140.

50 Mary Newcome Schleier, *Genoese drawings (Italian drawings in the Department of Prints and Drawings, Statens Museum for Kunst)* (Copenhagen: Statens Museum for Kunst, 2004), pp.41–42, no.5.

51 For the Texas drawings see Bertina Suida Manning and Robert Manning, *The Genosese Renaissance, grace and geometry: Paintings and drawings by Luca Cambiaso from the Suida-Manning collection* (Houston: Museum of Fine Arts, 1974), pp.30, 60, no.35 and pp.33, 75, no.50.

52 Cleveland Museum of Art, 1959.200. See Nancy Ward Neilson, *Italian drawings selected from Mid-Western collections* (Saint Louis, MI: Saint Louis Art Museum, 1972), n.p., no.10.

53 Mannings 2010.

54 D725. Andrews, op.cit., vol.I, p.12 and vol.II, fig.110.

55 Inv.24359. Walter Koschatzky *et al.*, *Dessins italiens de l'Albertina de Vienne* (Paris: Éditions des musées nationaux, 1975), pp.94–95, no.39.

56 British Museum, PD Pp, 3.199.

57 On copper. Sold at Christie's, London on 31 March 1795, lot 78, to Lord Hawkesbury. I am grateful to Dawson Carr for this information. The work is now attributed to Ludovico Carracci (1555–1619). See Broun, op.cit., vol.II, pp.269–70.

58 PD 1946,0713.26.

59 Éric Pagliano in Olivier Le Bihan and Patrick Ramade (eds), *Splendeur de Venise 1500–1600: Peintures et dessins des collections publiques françaises* (Paris: Somogy, 2005), pp.120–21, no.46.

60 Robert Randolf Coleman in Edward Olszewski (ed), *A corpus of drawings in Midwestern collections: Sixteenth-century Italian drawings* (Turnhout: Harvey Miller, 2008), vol.I, p.191, no.155.

61 Karl T Parker, *Catalogue of the collection of drawings in the Ashmolean Museum: Volume II (Italian Schools)* (Oxford: Oxford University Press, 1956), p.107, no.223.

62 Mario Di Giampaolo in Catherine Monbeig Goguel *et al.*, *The Katalan collection of Italian drawings* (Poughkeepsie, NY: Vassar College, 1995), pp.80–81, no.33.

63 *Old Master drawings* (London: Colnaghi, 1985), n.p., no.21.

64 Sonja Brink, *Italienische zeichnungen des 16. bis 18. Jahrhunderts: Eine auswahl aus den Beständen der Kunsthalle Bremen* (Bremen: Kunsthalle Bremen, 1994), pp.150–51, no.69.

65 PD 1901,0417.29.
66 Catherine Loisel Legrand, 'The fate of Annibale's drawings', pp.24–33 (28, 32) in Daniele Benati *et al.*, *The drawings of Annibale Carracci* (Washington: National Gallery of Art, 1999).
67 Richard Beresford and Peter Raissis, *The James Fairfax collection of Old Master paintings, drawings and prints* (Sydney: Art Gallery of New South Wales, 2003), pp.82–83, no.21.
68 PD 1938,1104.1.
69 Clare Robertson and Catherine Whistler, *Drawings by the Carracci from British collections* (London and Oxford: Hazlitt, Gooden & Fox and Ashmolean Museum, 1996), p.43, no.4 and p.51, no.11. Bohn, op.cit., p.409, no.260 and pp.146–47, no.39.
70 Richard J Campbell and Jane Immler Satkowski (eds), *Master drawings from the collection of Alfred Moir* (Minneapolis, MN: Minneapolis Institute of Arts, 2000), pp.34–35, no.15. Bohn, op.cit., p.99, no.4.
71 Christie's, London, 10 July 2001, lot 51. Bohn, op.cit., p.370, no.221.
72 Christie's, London, 11 April 1978, lot 10. See Jeremy Wood, 'Padre Resta as a collector of Carracci drawings', *Master Drawings*, (34), 1996, pp.3–71 (53), fig.35. However, Bohn rejects the attribution, op.cit., p.612, no.R94.
73 Felton Gibbons, *Catalogue of Italian drawings in the Art Museum, Princeton University* (Princeton, NJ: Princeton Univeristy Press, 1977), vol.I, p.8, no.19.
74 Mannings 1268.
75 Timothy Clifford, 'Polidoro and English Design', *Connoisseur*, August 1976, 192 (774), pp.282–91 (287).
76 Blanton Museum of Art, University of Texas at Austin. This may bear Reynolds's own inscription '[R]afael d'Urbino' on the front of the sheet (Suida-Manning Collection; 334.1999).
77 D.1952.RW.1772.
78 One of these is a study for the altarpiece *The Assumption of the Virgin with St Francis and St Clare* in the church of San Francesco in San Genesio (Macerata) of around 1605 (PD 2002,0928.1). See Julian Brooks, 'Boscoli in the Marches: A drawing and a document for a lost commission', *Apollo*, CLVII, March 2003, pp.3–5 (5), fn.7.
79 Fitzwilliam Museum, PD.28-1956; and University of Leiden; PK 6949. I am grateful to Julian Brooks for this information.
80 Marco Chiarini and Catalina Macovei, *I disegni italiani della biblioteca dell'Accademia di Romania a Bucarest: Catalogo generale* (Florence: Cento Di, 2004), p.101, no.LIV.
81 Julian Brooks, 'Andrea Boscoli's "Loves of *Gerusalemme Liberata*"', *Master Drawings*, XXXVIII (4), 2000, pp.448–59 (449); Julian Brooks and Catherine Whistler, *Graceful and True: Drawing in Florence c.1600* (Oxford: Ashmolean Museum, 2003), pp.68–71, nos.19–22. Sotheby's, London, 8 July 2009, lot 2.
82 Inv.6629. See James Byam Shaw, *The Italian drawings of the Frits Lugt collection* (Paris: Institut Néerlandais, 1983), vol.I, pp.41–42, no.34, vol.III, plate 43.
83 PD 1910,1013.2. Purchased directly from Arthur Melville Champernowne (1871–1946), who perhaps in a spirit of local fidelity (he was born and lived in Totnes) acquired dozens of examples that had once belonged to Reynolds, including many now in Chicago. Champernowne also owned many of Reynolds's Old Master prints, including the etching by Marco Agnolo del Moro (c.1537–after 1586) of the *Lamentation at the Cross* (1572; private collection, London). Hudson had painted his predecessor, Jane Champernowne (private collection). Ellen G Miles, *Thomas Hudson 1701–1779: Portrait painter and collector, a bicentenary exhibition* (London: Greater London Council, 1979), n.p., no.29.
84 Ann H Sievers *et al.*, *Master drawings from the Smith College Museum of Art* (New York: Hudson Hills Press, 2000), pp.52–56, no.9.
85 Suzanne Folds McCullagh and Laura M Giles, *Italian drawings before 1600 in the Art Institute of Chicago* (Chicago: Art Institute of Chicago, 1997), pp.91–92, no.116.
86 Mannings 172.
87 Circle of Girolamo Genga or Battista Franco, see Suzanne Folds McCullagh and Laura M Giles, *Italian drawings before 1600 in the Art Institute of Chicago* (Chicago: Art Institute of Chicago, 1997), pp.115–16, no.147.
88 Andrea Czére, *Seventeenth-century Italian drawings in the Budapest Museum of Fine Arts: A complete catalogue* (Budapest: Szépművészeti Múzeum, 2004), pp.252–54, no.263.
89 Christies, London 14 March 1795, lot 68. See Broun, op.cit., vol.II, p.310.
90 Yale University Art Gallery, New Haven; 1937.333. See Walter Vitzthum, *A selection of Italian drawings from North American collections* (Regina: Norman Mackenzie Art Gallery, 1970), pp.46–48, 140, no.36.
91 D Stephen Pepper, op.cit., pp.242–43, no.79, plate 106. Engraved by Pierre Louis Surugue (1716–72) and Bernardino Curti (1611–79) in 1650.
92 Metropolitan Museum, 1990.196. The work was later sold at Christie's, London, 26–27 March 1790, lot 87 bought William Petty, 1st Marquess of Lansdowne (1737–1805). See Broun, op.cit., vol.II, pp.136–38.
93 Mannings 2046.
94 Mannings 2047.
95 KDZ 5685. Anne-Marie Logan and Michiel C Plomp, *Peter Paul Rubens: The drawings* (New York: New Haven and London: Metropolitan Museum of Art and Yale Univeristy Press, 2005), pp.138–39, no.33.
96 See, for example, Rubens's study of a young woman, possibly his second wife Hélène Fourment (1614-1673). Sotheby's, London, 9 July 2008, lot 21.
97 Michiel C Plomp in Anne-Marie Logan and Michiel C Plomp, op.cit., p.43.
98 Ibid., p.39.
99 Inv.no.1518.
100 John Smith, *A catalogue raisonné of the works of the most eminent Dutch, Flemish, and French painters*, vol.III (Van Dyck and David Teniers) (London: Smith & Son, 1831), p.221, no.785 and Ignatz von Szwykowski, *Anton van Dyck's bildnisse bekannter personen: Iconographie, ou le cabinet des portraits d'Antoine van Dyck* (Leipzig: Rudolph Weigel, 1859), p.198.
101 Felice Stampfle, *Netherlandish drawings of the fifteenth and sixteenth centuries and Flemish drawings of the seventeenth and eighteenth centuries in the Pierpont Morgan Library* (New York and Princeton, NJ; Pierpont Morgan Library and Princeton University Press, 1991), p.123.
102 D.1952.RW.849, 851 and 949.
103 Michael Jaffé (1923–97) first attributed the drawing to Van Dyck. However, Otto Benesch considered it a work by Annibale Carracci, while Horst Vey and Jan Gerrit van Gelder also rejected Van Dyck. Jaffé thought the attribution to Van Dyck entirely fine (Departmental Register, Fitzwilliam Museum, Cambridge).
104 Felton Gibbons, *Catalogue of Italian drawings in the Art Museum, Princeton University* (Princeton, NJ: Princeton University Press, 1977), vol.I, p.147, no.464.
105 Suzanne Folds McCullagh and Laura M Giles, *Italian drawings before 1600 in the Art Institute of Chicago* (Chicago: Art Institute of Chicago, 1997), pp.157–58, no.204 and p.159, no.206.

106 PD 1946,0713.395.
107 PD 1859,0806.616.
108 Mannings 1271.
109 BL Add.MS. 22,950, folio 15 quoted in Oliver Millar, *Sir Peter Lely 1618–80* (London: National Portrait Gallery,1978), p.74.
110 The Morgan Library drawing is similar in composition and in the same medium as this sheet and retains its historic mount. See Felice Stampfle, *Netherlandish drawings of the fifteenth and sixteenth centuries and Flemish drawings of the seventeenth and eighteenth centuries in the Pierpont Morgan Library* (New York and Princeton, NJ; Pierpont Morgan Library and Princeton University Press, 1991), p.123, no.271.
111 NG 49. Susan Barnes in Susan Barnes, Nora De Poorter, Oliver Millar and Horst Vey, *Van Dyck: A complete catalogue of the paintings* (New Haven and London: Yale University Press, 2004), pp.186–88, no.II.43. Bought from Reynolds's sale (as of Rubens) by Angerstein, who had sat to Reynolds.
112 Oliver Millar in Barnes *et al.*, op.cit., pp.532–33, no.IV.132.
113 Horst Vey in Barnes *et al.*, op.cit., p.267, no.III.28.
114 Mannings 1729.
115 Though it had once belonged to King Charles I, throughout the eighteenth century the portrait was in Paris. Horst Vey in Barnes *et al.*, op.cit., pp.329–30, no.III.102.
116 PD 1917,1208.1994 and 2136.
117 Catherine Loisel Legrand, 'The fate of Annibale's drawings', pp.24–33 (28) in Daniele Benati *et al.*, *The drawings of Annibale Carracci* (Washington: National Gallery of Art, 1999).
118 James Byam Shaw, *The Italian drawings of the Frits Lugt collection* (Paris: Institut Néerlandais, 1983), vol.I, pp.163–64, no.160, vol.III, plate 183.
119 Jacob Bean, *17th-century Italian drawings in the Metropolitan Museum of Art* (New York: Metropolitan Museum of Art, 1979), pp.104–5, no.136.
120 David Franklin, *Italian drawings from the National Gallery of Canada* (Ottawa: National Gallery of Canada, 2003), pp.84–85, 167–68, no.32.
121 Per Bjurström and Börje Magnusson, *Italian drawings: Umbria, Rome, Naples: Drawings in Swedish public collections 6* (Stockholm: Nationalmuseum, 1998), n.p., no.677.
122 I am grateful to Martin Olin for this information (email 8 October 2008).
123 D.1952.RW.2.
124 PD 1946, 0713.81. See Nicholas Turner, *Italian drawings in the Department of Prints and Drawings in the British Museum: Roman Baroque drawings, c.1620 to c.1700* (London: British Museum Press, 1999), vol.I, pp.65–66, no.100.
125 Catherine Loisel in Diederik Bakhuÿs *et al.*, *Le génie de Bologne des Carracci aux Gandolfi: Dessins des XVIIe et XVIIIe siècles* (Montreuil: Gourcuff Gradenigo, 2006), pp.100–1, no.42.
126 David M Stone, *Guercino: Master draughtsman, works from North American collections* (Cambridge, MA: Harvard University Art Museums, 1991), pp.188–89, no.82.
127 RL 2413. See Denis Mahon and Nicholas Turner, *The drawings of Guercino in the collection of Her Majesty the Queen at Windsor Castle* (Cambridge: Cambridge University Press, 1989), p.100, no.232, plate 216.
128 Mannings 2045.
129 NG 6277. See Broun, op.cit., vol.II, pp.208–9.
130 Szépművészeti Múzeum, Budapest, inv.2847 and 2886.
131 Anthony Blunt, *The paintings of Poussin: A critical catalogue* (London: Phaidon, 1966), p.124, no.173 and Christopher Wright, *Poussin paintings: A catalogue raisonné* (London: Harlequin, 1985), p.208, no.152. The picture was engraved by Étienne Baudet (1638–1711) in 1684 and Simon Vallée (1680–after 1730).
132 PD Pp, 4.65.
133 Tentatively attributed to Sacchi. Sotheby's, New York, 5 June 1979, lot 37.
134 Ann Sutherland Harris, *Andrea Sacchi* (Oxford: Phaidon, 1977), pp.101–2, no.84, plate 167. Darmstadt has another drawing, in red chalk, which is possibly related to the same group. Gisela Bergsträsser and Roseline Bacou, *Dessins du Musée de Darmstadt (Hessisches Landesmuseum)* (Paris: Réunion des Musées Nationaux, 1971), pp.22–23, no.17, plate VIII.
135 PD Ff, 3.211.
136 Andrea Czére, *Seventeenth-century Italian drawings in the Budapest Museum of Fine Arts: A complete catalogue* (Budapest: Szépművészeti Múzeum, 2004), pp.239–40, no.253.
137 Acquired by the Saint Louis Art Museum in 1992 (29: 1992). Francesca Herndon-Consagra and Paul Crenshaw, *Rembrandt: Master etchings from St. Louis collections* (Saint Louis: Saint Louis Art Museum, 2006), pp.44–48, 155–56, fig.29.
138 Carol Gibson-Wood, *Jonathan Richardson: Art theorist of the English Enlightenment* (New Haven and London: Yale University Press, 2000), p.96.
139 Saint Louis Art Museum (104:1994); Herndon-Consagra and Crenshaw, op.cit., pp.68–71, 151, fig.48.
140 Mannings 1458.
141 Otto Benesch, *The drawings of Rembrandt: First complete edition in six volumes* (London: Phaidon Press, 1954-57), nos. 24, 61, 78, 87, 95, 154, 171, 201,206, 223, 240, 273, 291, 305, 324, 387, 452, C9, C26, A12, A13, 477, 585, 609, 633, 642, 671, 672, 687, 698a, 717, 718, 748, 757, A44, 908, 921, 956, 965, 1010, 1078, 1134, 1138, 1223, 1307, 1309, 1345, 1372, 1382, A65, A67, A68, A88 and Addenda 16. This list does not take into account post-Benesch re-attributions. I am grateful to Martin Royalton-Kisch for confirming the attribution of the present sheet.
142 Hôtel Drouot, Paris, 22 March 1983, lot 16.
143 Edmund Malone (ed.), *The works of Sir Joshua Reynolds* (London: Cadell & Davies, 1797), vol.I, p.xxix. I am grateful to Richard Stephens for this reference.
144 NG 43.
145 PD 00,9.103; Benesch 154.
146 William W Robinson, *Bruegel to Rembrandt: Dutch and Flemish drawings from the Maida and George Abrams collection* (Cambridge and New Haven and London: Harvard University Art Museums and Yale University Press, 2002), pp.118–19, no.46.
147 Benesch 87.
148 Andrea Czére, *Seventeenth-century Italian drawings in the Budapest Museum of Fine Arts: A complete catalogue* (Budapest: Szépművészeti Múzeum, 2004), pp.64–66, no.51. The drawing was engraved by Ryland in 1764 and given to Ludovico Carracci.
149 Inv.720.
150 Galerie Georges Petit [Jules Féral et Paulme], Paris 8–10 June, 1920, lot 287. See Luijten, op.cit., p.89.
151 PD 1943,1113.67.
152 Robert R Wark, *Early British drawings in the Huntington collection, 1600–1750* (San Marino, CA: Huntington Library, 1969), p.36, no.B (Lely).
153 PD 1902,0212.1.
154 Hugh Macandrew, *Catalogue of the collection of drawings in the Ashmolean Museum: Volume III (Italian Schools: Supplement)* (Oxford: Oxford University Press, 1980), pp.135, 137, no.928A, plate LXX.

155 Chris Fisher and Joachim Meyer, *Neapolitan drawings (Italian drawings in the Department of Prints and Drawings, Statens Museum for Kunst)* (Copenhagen: Statens Museum for Kunst, 2006), pp.78–79, no.28.
156 PD 1874,0808.45. See Nicholas Turner, *British Museum prints and drawings series: Italian Baroque drawings* (London: British Museum Publications, 1980), pp.144–45, no.63.
157 Ellen G Miles, *Thomas Hudson 1701–1779: Portrait painter and collector* (London: Greater London Council, 1979), n.p., nos 69 and 70.
158 Suzanne Folds McCullagh and Laura M. Giles, *Italian drawings before 1600 in the Art Institute of Chicago* (Chicago: Art Institute of Chicago, 1997), pp.330, 332, no.474.
159 Denis Mahon in Gabriele Finaldi, Michael Kitson *et al.*, *Discovering the Italian Baroque: The Denis Mahon collection* (London: National Gallery Publications, 1997), p.169, no.81.
160 David Ekserdjian and Helen Davies in Massimo Pulini *et al.*, *Nel segno di Guercino: Disegni dalle collezioni Mahon, Oxford e Cento/Guercino as master draughtsman: Drawings from the Mahon collection, the Ashmolean Museum at Oxford, and the City of Cento* (Cento and London: Pinacoteca Civica and Dulwich Picture Gallery, 2005), pp.176–77, no.62.
161 Britton and Brayley, op.cit., (1803), vol.IV, p.143. I am grateful to Richard Stephens for this reference.
162 Xanthe Brooke, *Mantegna to Rubens: The Weld-Blundell drawings collection* (London: Merrell Holberton, 1998), pp.76–78, 150, no.33.
163 Mannings 742. See Martin Postle in Martin Postle (ed.) *Joshua Reynolds: The creation of celebrity* (London: Tate Publishing, 2005), pp.212–13 (212), no.64.
164 Sotheby's, London, 5 July 2006, lot 34.
165 Ann H Sievers *et al.*, *Master drawings from the Smith College Museum of Art* (New York: Hudson Hills Press, 2000), pp.73–76, no.15.
166 Other drawings for the same spandrel are in the Albertina, Vienna (inv.1078 and 1079), Metropolitan Museum of Art, New York (61.169 and 64.295.1) and one other in the Academia de San Fernando, Madrid (no.1730).
167 Harry Mount, op.cit., p.77.
168 National Gallery of Canada, Ottawa; inv.41343.
169 PD 1946,0327.1.

POSTHUMOUS FORTUNES

1 *Burlington Magazine*, 128 (March 1986), Neil MacGregor, 'The Right Moment for Reynolds', editorial p.183.
2 Martin Postle (ed.), *Joshua Reynolds: The Creation of Celebrity* (Tate, 2005), esp. pp.17, 37.
3 Cherry Elizabeth Sandover, '"The Dome of his Mausoleum": Commemorating the 18th Century Artist', *Transactions of the Romney Society*, 5 (2000), 18–25, esp. pp.21–23.
4 Lord Ronald Sutherland Gower, *Sir Joshua Reynolds* (George Bell and Sons, 1902), p.134.
5 Martin Postle, 'A Taste for History: Reynolds, West, George III, and George IV', *Apollo*, 138 (September 1993), pp.186–91, p.118; p.122.
6 Alexander Gilchrist, *Life of William Blake*, 2 vols, London: MacMillan & Co., 1863, vol.2, P.187.
7 Sara Selwood, 'Photography as High Art: Julia Margaret Cameron', *The Antique Collector*, 55 (April 1984), 68–73; Lauren Bradley, 'From Eden to Empire: John Everett Millais's *Cherry Ripe*', *Victorian Studies*, 34 (winter 1991), 179–203, esp. pp.182–83.
8 *Athenaeum*, 561 (28 July 1838), p.527.
9 For Constable, see Richard Wendorf, *After Sir Joshua: Essays on British Art and Cultural History* (Yale University Press, 2005) p.18; for Lord Byron, see Gower, p.134.
10 *Illustrated London News* (17 August 1861), p.171.
11 F G Stephens, *Exhibition of the Works of Sir Joshua Reynolds, P.R.A. With Historical Notes* (Chiswick Press, 1883), p.50.
12 Bradley, p.184.
13 *Illustrated London News* (9 August 1856), p.143.
14 Bradley, p.200.
15 *The Graphic* (29 April 1871), p.396.
16 F G Stephens, *English Children as Painted by Sir Joshua Reynolds* (Seeley, Jackson and Halliday, 1867), esp. p.v; pp.2–4; and p.26.
17 Bradley, p.187–92.
18 Barbara Dayer Gallati, *Great Expectations: John Singer Sargent Painting Children* (Bulfinch, 2004), p.168; also pp.174–75.
19 Gallati, p.169.
20 F G Stephens, *Exhibition of the Works of Sir Joshua Reynolds*, pp.84–85.

OTHER EXHIBITS

1 James Northcote, *The Life of Sir Joshua Reynolds*, London: Henry Colburn, vol.i, pp.21–22.
2 This has been proposed by Ellen Gross Miles, 'Thomas Hudson (1701–79): Portraitist to the British establishment', PhD thesis, Yale University, 1976, p.11.
3 The 'Notes on Painting' are transcribed in Ozias Humphrey's memorandum book, dated 1777–95 (BL Add. Mss. 22, 950). They are attributed to Gandy by Mansfield Kirby Talley *Portrait Painting in England: Studies in the Technical Literature before 1700*, London: published privately by the Paul Mellon Centre, 1981, pp.308–15.
4 Zoffany painted a similar group portrait, *The Academicians of the Royal Academy* (1771–72) (Royal Collection), showing the life room with the model being posed, with the academicians and Hunter in attendance.
5 See David Solkin, *Art on the Line: The Royal Academy Exhibitions at Somerset House 1780–1836*, Yale University Press, 2001.
6 The British Museum has another related monochrome watercolour, of the same format, and also dated 1787 (PD 1936, 0918.1).

COLLECTIONS

Public collections holding examples of the former graphic collection (prints and drawings) of Reynolds:

AUSTRALIA
Art Gallery of South Australia, Adelaide; National Gallery of Victoria, Melbourne; University of Melbourne (Baillieu Library), Melbourne; Art Gallery of New South Wales, Sydney

AUSTRIA
Albertina, Vienna

CANADA
National Gallery of Canada, Ottawa; Art Gallery of Ontario, Toronto

DENMARK
Statens Museum fur Kunst, Copenhagen; J F Willumsen Museum, Frederikssund

FRANCE
Musée des Beaux-Arts, Angers; Musée Calvet, Avignon; Musée Bonnat, Bayonne; Musée des Beaux-Arts et d'archéologie, Besançon; Musée Condé, Chantilly; Musée des Beaux-Arts, Dijon; Palais des Beaux-Arts, Lille; Musée des tissues et d'arts décoratifs, Lyon; Musée des Beaux-Arts, Orléans; Bibliothèque Nationale, Paris; Musée du Louvre, Paris; Institut Néerlandais (Fondation Custodia), Paris; École des Beaux-Arts, Paris; Musée Saint-Croix, Poitiers; Musée des Beaux-Arts, Rouen; Bibliotheque Municipale, Rouen; Musée des Beaux-Arts, Rennes; Musée Paul-Dupuy, Toulouse

GERMANY
Kupferstichkabinett, Berlin; Kunsthalle, Bremen; Kupferstichkabinett, Dresden; Städelsches Kunstinstitut, Frankfurt; Kunsthalle, Hamburg; Staatliche Graphische Sammlung, Munich; Staatsgalerie, Stuttgart

GREECE
Pinacoteca, Athens

HUNGARY
Szépművészeti Múzeum, Budapest

ITALY
Fondazione Horne, Florence; Biblioteca Ambrosiana, Milan; Biblioteca Reale, Turin; Biblioteca Apostolica, Vatican City; Galleria dell' Accademia, Venice; Museo Correr, Venice

THE NETHERLANDS
Rijksmuseum, Amsterdam; Rembrandthuis, Amsterdam; Museum voor Stad en Lande, Groningen; Rijksuniversitat (Prentenkabinet), Leiden; Museum Boymans-van Beuningen, Rotterdam

NORWAY
Nasjonalmuseet for kunst, arkitektur og design, Oslo

ROMANIA
Academia Română, Bucharest

RUSSIA
University of Moscow, Moscow

SWEDEN
Nationalmuseum, Stockholm; University of Uppsala (Library), Uppsala

UNITED KINGDOM
University of Birmingham (Barber Institute of Fine Arts), Birmingham; Fitzwilliam Museum, Cambridge; National Gallery of Scotland, Edinburgh; Hunterian Museum and Art Gallery, University of Glasgow, Glasgow; Walker Art Gallery, Liverpool; British Museum, London; Courtauld Institute Gallery (Samuel Courtauld Trust), London; Victoria and Albert Museum, London; Manchester Art Gallery, Manchester; Ashmolean Museum, Oxford; Lady Lever Art Gallery, Port Sunlight; Rugby School, Rugby, Warwickshire; Royal Cornwall Museum, Truro; Royal Collection (Royal Library), Windsor

UNITED STATES OF AMERICA
University of Michigan Museum of Art, Ann Arbor, Michigan; Blanton Museum of Art, University of Texas, Austin, Texas; Museum of Fine Arts, Boston, Massachusetts; Isabella Stewart Gardner Museum, Boston, Massachusetts; Museum of Art, Bowdoin College, Brunswick, Maine; Fogg Art Museum, Harvard University Art Museums, Cambridge, Massachusetts; Art Institute of Chicago, Chicago, Illinois; Cincinnati Art Museum, Cincinnati, Ohio; Cleveland Museum of Art, Cleveland, Ohio; Detroit Institute of Arts, Detroit, Michigan; Wadsworth Athenaeum, Hartford, Connecticut; Indianapolis Museum of Art, Indianapolis, Indiana; Spencer Museum of Art, University of Kansas, Lawrence, Kansas; Getty Museum, Los Angeles, California; Los Angeles County Museum of Art, Los Angeles, California; Chazen Museum of Art, University of Wisconsin, Madison, Wisconsin; Minneapolis Institute of Arts, Minneapolis, Minnesota; Chrysler Museum of Art, Norfolk, Virginia; Metropolitan Museum of Art, New York; Morgan Library and Museum, New York; Smith College Museum of Art, Northampton, Massachusetts; Snite Museum of Art, University of Notre Dame, Notre Dame, Indiana; Allen Memorial Museum of Art, Oberlin, Ohio; Philadelphia Museum of Art, Philadelphia, Pennsylvania; Princeton Museum of Art, University of Princeton, Princeton, New Jersey; Memorial Art Gallery, University of Rochester, Rochester New York; Saint Louis Art Museum, Saint Louis, Missouri; Fine Arts Museums of San Francisco, San Francisco, California; Huntington Library, Art Collections and Botanical Gardens, San Marino, California; National Gallery of Art, Washington DC